EX LIBRIS

MOUNT MARY COLLEGE

Henry David Thoreau
'When we now look back at the solitude of his erect and spotless person, we
lament that he did not live long enough for all men to know him'
From a daguerreotype taken in 1856 by B. E. Maxham

THOREAU

BY HENRY SEIDEL CANBY

WITH ILLUSTRATIONS

BOSTON

HOUGHTON MIFFLIN COMPANY

The Riverside Press Cambridge

The Riverside Press
CAMBRIDGE · MASSACHUSETTS
PRINTED IN THE U.S.A.

ACKNOWLEDGMENTS

So MANY STUDENTS, collectors, and friends of mine and of Thoreau, have helped me with advice, information, and material in the preparation of this biography, that a listing of names would indicate only the breadth, and not the depth, of my indebtedness. I must begin by acknowledging my dependence for facts of Thoreau's life which would otherwise have been irrecoverable, upon the biographies written by his two friends, William Ellery Channing and Franklin B. Sanborn. My indebtedness to Sanborn, particularly, for factual material is too extensive to be always indicated in my notes. I owe especial thanks to the custodians of five great storehouses of Thoreau books and manuscripts: the Huntington Library of California, the Harvard Library, the Julian Willis Abernethy Library of American Literature at Middlebury College, the Morgan Library of New York, and the Thoreau library of Mr. W. T. H. Howe, at Freelands, Mentor, Kentucky. I am in debt to Mr. Warren H. Colson of Boston for the privilege of consulting unpublished manuscripts; to Miss Estelle Ward of Evanston, Illinois, for permitting me to use copies of the letters of the Ward family in the possession of her family; and to Mrs. Louise Osgood Koopman of Cambridge, daughter of Ellen Sewall, for access to her family papers, and permission to use a daguerreotype of her mother. Mr. Edward W. Forbes, grandson of Emerson, has allowed a search to be made in the papers of his family now in the Ralph Waldo Emerson Memorial Association collection, and has given me access to the unpublished portions of his grandfather's journal. He has also allowed me to reproduce here Rowse's crayon portrait of his grandmother, Lidian Emerson. Mr. Van Wyck Brooks and Mrs. Adams Tolman of Concord have allowed me to use letters and other manuscript material relevant to Thoreau, and Mrs. Tolman has let me reproduce from her copy of *The Concord Freeman* a picture of the Walden hut, and a photograph in her possession of Concord Main Street about the time of Thoreau's death. To Miss Sarah R. Bartlett of the Concord Library I owe thanks, not only for a photograph of the Parkman house, but also for many helpful suggestions. Professor Raymond Adams, for so many years an authority on Thoreau's life, has made all students of Thoreau his debtors. The librarians of the Aldis Collection of American literature at Yale have been most helpful in giving me access to rare volumes not easily obtained elsewhere.

I wish to note here thanks to many owners of the Manuscript Edition of Thoreau, who have given me copies of or access direct to the fugitive leaves of Thoreau manuscript included in the six hundred sets of that edition issued in 1906.

I wish to thank particularly a fellow worker in the fields of Concord, Professor Odell Shepard of Trinity College, who has been most generous, not only with ideas, but also with discoveries of his own making. And I acknowledge with thankfulness the help of those who have read this book, and have given me the benefit of their criticisms: Mr. Francis H. Allen, editor and scholar, Professors Townsend Scudder and Robert E. Spiller of Swarthmore College, and my wife, Marion G. Canby. In the difficult area of Transcendental thinking and Oriental influences, Professor Christy of Columbia has been most helpful, and generous in the loan of photostats. Nor do I forget the co-operation of my publishers, Houghton Mifflin Company, hereditary publishers of Thoreau.

Without the assistance in verification and supplementary research of Miss Nathalia Wright, this book would have been long delayed. Her aid in the notes has been a full collaboration, and the bibliography and index have been prepared by her. My debt to her is great.

KILLINGWORTH, CONNECTICUT
May 1, 1939

CONTENTS

CONTENTS

BOOK TWO
Naturalist and Nature Writer

ILLUSTRATIONS

PREVIEW

In the Morgan library is a leather-covered notebook which once belonged to William Ellery Channing, the unwavering friend of Henry David Thoreau. It was Channing who pushed through the shrub oak a step or two behind the stumpy figure in a homespun suit of the poet-naturalist, bound cross lots for Walden or Conantum; or sat with him under an upland elm, exchanging quotations from Herbert or Virgil or Homer. It was Channing who breathed the same intellectual air as Thoreau, loved the same Concord fields and rivers, and who was, if possible, more eccentric, more independent, and more incalculable to the common man than Thoreau himself. Lowell put them both into 'A Fable for Critics' as imitators of Emerson, and no one knows certainly yet which ' —— ' was meant for Channing and which for Thoreau, for both were below middle height:

> There comes ——, for instance; to see him's rare sport,
> Tread in Emerson's tracks with legs painfully short;...
> Fie, for shame, brother bard; with good fruit of your own,
> Can't you let Neighbor Emerson's orchards alone?
> Besides, 'tis no use, you'll not find e'en a core, ——
> —— has picked up all the windfalls before.

And yet Channing, who knew him best, and who wrote,

in defense of his friend, the first biography, was more puzzled by Thoreau's baffling mixture of sweetness, perversity, wilfulness, and genius than he admitted in his book. It was not easy to understand this Concord individualist, who sat in company 'with a certain iron-pokerish-ness,' this ugly man with puckered, expressive lips and 'terrible eyes' of gleaming gray-blue, this friend of woodchucks and enemy of the state. Even Channing, who much preferred an hour of Thoreau's time or Emerson's to the company of his beautiful wife, was often baffled.

Channing's notebook in the Morgan library contains a selection of passages from Thoreau's then unpublished Journal, and a memorandum in pencil recording that it was lent to Emerson to help him write an account of H. D. T.[1] The most interesting item is a preface, presumably written for Emerson, of which, characteristically, the first page and the top of the second have been cut out, for Channing was always cutting up his books and manuscripts. What he left uncut begins: 'Nothing bothered him so much as the friendships. Those and his moral sensitiveness,' a true and shrewd remark; and continues: 'I have never been able to understand what he meant by his life. . . . Why was he so disappointed with everybody else &c. Why was he so much interested in the river and the woods and the sky &c. Something peculiar I judge.'

Peculiar is the right word, though you would never guess from Channing's 'Thoreau, The Poet-Naturalist,' already in manuscript form, that the meaning of his friend's life had ever puzzled him. Nevertheless, Channing's insistent 'why' still echoes. Those who feel that among American writers Thoreau is one of the three or four who have surely contributed to world literature, and is the one who today seems most challenging to the contemporary imagination, will wonder if there is an answer in his story. I believe that there is, for he has been much misunderstood, even by his friends.

2

The story of Henry David Thoreau (born July 12, 1817; died May 6, 1862) has been many times told, both at length and briefly, so that some excuse is necessary for retelling it in these pages. No biography of Thoreau has been written since 'The Life of Henry David Thoreau' by the Englishman, H. S. Salt, in 1890, the most coherent and the least interesting account of Thoreau, and Léon Bazalgette's dramatization of Thoreau's books and earlier biographies, called 'Henry Thoreau, Sauvage.' Paris, 1914. This in itself would be a reason for another biography, even if there were no new material available, since each significant figure of history needs to be reinterpreted for every generation that has use for him. But for Thoreau's life there is much new material; and some phases of his work and thought which seemed of little importance have come to life in our own day. The poet-naturalist Thoreau has been amply recorded by his first biographers, Channing and F. B. Sanborn, whose books are indispensable for our knowledge of his career; but the would-be lover, the home-bred philosopher, the dynamic individualist, escape from this too narrow classification. Thoreau will be remembered as a geographer rather than as a naturalist, as a maker of magnificent prose but scarcely as a poet, and as a protagonist of man against the state as often as a historian of the environment of the *genus homo* in Concord.

The life of Thoreau not only needs retelling, but is worth retelling. That great journalist, H. G. Wells, who is sometimes shrewder than professional historians, once remarked that the most interesting history of the nineteenth century was the growth of the United States. If history is essentially human nature reacting to environment, then surely the most interesting years of this American experiment were Thoreau's own, from the 1830's to the outbreak of the Civil War, for it was in those years that the United States cut the umbilical cord with the old countries, though still dependent upon European culture. In that era began an incredible expansion toward material prosperity, paralleled by an outburst of spiritual and intellectual fervor. The crust of Puritanism broke, and from its fiery core came new idealisms and strange fantastic religions. Eccentrics walked the land, reformers sprang up like brush in the cut-over woodlands. A part of the nation became humanitarian, and with a tender conscience turned the moral energy of the Puritan or Quaker heritage toward the perfectibility of man. Another part dropped all its old disciplines in a chase for the dollars which began to roll everywhere. Still another, aware that the country had become a continent, began that concentrated accumulation of economic power which still goes on.

It was an age of violent contrasts. Outwardly stable in the long-settled East and South, inwardly it was bubbling with change. It was an age of conflicts, between idealism and materialism, between Abolitionism and slavery, between zeal and common sense, between the capitalist East and the adventurous West, between religion and the gospel of success. The same man in the same country could hear Emerson lecturing on the Over-Soul and be hunting buffalo with the Sioux a week later. He could study the classics in Cambridge, while across the river in Boston was an economics of power that had forgotten philosophy. He could see, at the cost of a little travel, wage slavery beginning in the North and involuntary servitude approaching its tragic climax in the South. He could find pre-Marxian communism and sheer feudalism side by side in the same state. It was the true youth of the American people, and indeed, like our own era, emphatically a time for youth. It was for youth that Emerson wrote, Parker preached, and Greeley edited. But this American youth inherited the experience of two hundred years of growing, and, particularly

in New England and Virginia and South Carolina, seemed more
like a maturing civilization than before or since.

The thirties, the forties, and the fifties were the years of
maturity of Henry Thoreau. In spite of his eccentricity, he was
one of the typical Americans of this age, although first of all a
New Englander. His eccentricity was to keep out of the greeds,
the brawls, the current enthusiasms, and the blind strenuosities
of his time, and his very obstinacy, helped by his genius, made
him one of the best historians of the American mind in conflict.
Living near the shrine of the Olympian Emerson, he made an
American town — some streets, some lakes, many farms, and
stretches of swamps, hardwood scrub, and pine groves — into
his Delphi, where sometimes perversely, but often humorously
and with eloquence, an oracle spoke.

It is this eccentricity of Thoreau, which even Emerson regarded as perverse ('Instead of engineering for all America, he
was the captain of a huckleberry-party') that makes it difficult
to write his biography. The man had a dual nature, one half
positive, and passionate to yearning, one half negative, satirical,
and really perverse. Or rather, let us say that the thwarting of
his natural desires back-fired into his genius. His importance
lies entirely in what he wrote, not in what he did, and yet he
could never have written his best work if he had not lived a life
of such contradiction to all current modes that most of his
neighbors counted it no life at all. His seed has borne flower and
fruit in many alien soils. What was there in Concord fields and
rivers and his life therein which explains such seminal power?
And what portion of the virile, vigorous life of these decades did
this so-called hermit make his own?

3

The truth is that there are a half-dozen possible biographies of Thoreau, depending upon the view the biographer takes of his subject. This is true of all complex characters, but seems to be particularly the case with this reserved researcher into the values of living. The choice of approach is not dependent upon Thoreau's contacts with the wide world. Here is no Cooper or Irving acquainted with both America and Europe, or Poe fighting his way through the swamps of journalism. Here is no scene of importance but Concord, no striking events that did not strike hardest in the mind of the man. Nine-tenths of his biography is written, sometimes plainly, sometimes obscurely, in his Journal.

My contention will be that the Concord 'skulker,' as Stevenson called him before he recanted, was in some respects so typically American that his life can be used to illustrate typical American problems of living. And yet in other respects so cosmic, as Brooks Atkinson has called him, and so eccentric to convention, as to become equally typical of problems in which all enlightened human nature has been and always will be involved. But before beginning a narrative which, contrary to common opinion, is not a futility but a success story, the history, not of an ascetic hermit but of a man of letters of deep and troubling emotions, let me list some of the ways in which the biography could be told, all of which are true.

First there is the life of Thoreau as an arch Yankee. A Yankee, as everyone knows, is a shrewd realist, active in pursuit of his ends. But an arch Yankee, such as Thoreau, while retaining the energy and the common sense of the New England type that made the name, sees around his own qualities and is skeptical of his own success as a practical man. He is committed by temperament to the active life — his genius, as was

said in Thoreau's textbook, the 'Bhagavad-Gita,' is active —
but his faith is in contemplation. To him, therefore, both doing
and thinking are vital, and usually in conflict. We have had
many such New Englanders, but Thoreau is their perfect
example, and the conflict was for him a life history.

Next, Thoreau was perhaps the best of many American
examples of the creative artist and thinker in search of a career
in a country and an era dominantly materialistic in its estimate
of success and its offer of a livelihood. Here is a problem that
has obsessed thousands of the best of American youth, and still
obsesses them in spite of our more mature esthetics and the
growth of our universities which shelter, if they do not always
free, the creative intellect. Thoreau's whole life was a search
for a career, and to its dilemmas he presented in 'Walden' one
of the classic answers. That he was Yankee enough to have no
use for poets who starve in garrets,[2] makes his case history all
the more interesting.

In still another aspect he was, as Channing called him, a
Yankee Pan in the woods of New England. But Thoreau was
Pan in a sense more deeply classical than Channing can be
supposed to have meant. He was Pan moralized, intellectual-
ized, and nearly smothered by Harvard, spiritualized by
Hindu philosophy, who, nevertheless, kept unimpaired a gusto
for living, an essential passion for emotional experience, rare
in New England of the Puritans, and especially in Concord.
The town of Concord, as will be seen later, was a concourse of
stiff farmers and merchants and stiffer lawyers, through whom,
as Emerson said, moved lonely souls, a town where only young
Louisa Alcott and the ne'er-do-wells on the river and in the
bar-rooms ever let go. Until the 1850's and his early forties,
Thoreau was actually a burning heart seeking for relief in a
community whose emotional temperature seldom rose far
above Walden ice, unless intellectual passions burned over a

philosopher's feast of apples.[3] Hence, inevitably, he was, or he became, a neurotic who sublimated his passions first in a ruthless analysis of his friends and neighbors, and then more successfully (perhaps the first real sublimation) in a loving study of nature. She was more responsive than his friends. But his yearning for emotional nearness to others was never quenched; indeed, he made from it a passion in which love and friendship were curiously blended as in the Platonic eras. He remained to the end the man most alive in Concord.

And there is also the difficult success story of a poor Concord boy, familiar only with a respectably intellectual household and a meagre academicism, his father a bankrupt storekeeper become pencil maker. This youth was suddenly introduced to what may be called, without exaggeration, world society, in the persons of Emerson, Margaret Fuller, Channing, Hawthorne, Alcott, men and women of varying social experiences but all at home wherever minds moved freely. With no means to support his opportunities (here began his scorn of manners and dress), he devised for himself the home-town job which none of the celebrities, not even Alcott, would tackle, and made Concord his metropolis in defiance of Hawthorne's colonial aristocrats, Margaret Fuller's literary lions, and Emerson's internationalism. Too rustic to feel at ease in the world, he thumbed his nose, if a Transcendentalist could use so undignified a gesture, at the worldly, and resolved to be famous for staying at home.

There is still another story, of a Transcendentalist in lifelong conflict with a science just coming to its own. Much has been said about this struggle, which became later for a while, and in a slightly different phase, a national controversy. But there is more to be said now that Thoreau's defects as a naturalist are better known, and particularly since science itself begins to view its boundaries and turn back toward the intuitiveness which was Thoreau's great gift.

Much also has been written, recently, upon that aspect of Thoreau's life in which he seems most modern. He was an individualist, independent to excess, in conflict with a society which, if not yet in any sense autocratic, was deferential to majority will, and confident of the success of the industrial revolution. He encountered in early youth the forces of the economic state disguised as the public opinion of his townsmen in Concord, and in later life the political state stretching its weak hands over the institution of slavery. That it was the loose and little powerful government of nineteenth-century America did not prevent him from understanding, as perhaps no other man of his time did, all the implications. If he did not foresee fascism (communism he knew at first hand), at least he prepared the American answer. Thoreau's individualism was his life, and his life is significant as a vital type of individualism.

Last, and least written of by his biographers although much dealt with elsewhere, Thoreau was a life-long apprentice to the art of good writing, next to Poe perhaps the most truly professional of great American writers. His literary biography, what might be called his rhetorical history, is of extraordinary interest to anyone who wishes to know how a man of letters is made — and marred. Thoreau belongs with the Shakespeares in that he wrote by line and passage, leaving his wholes often incomplete. But he belongs with the Popes and the Drydens and the Poes in that he was intensely self-conscious of his methods and constant in self-criticism. Like many writers who are also critics, like Coleridge, for example, he was afflicted by that uncertainty of aim which comes from too much listening to the inner voice and too many attempts to shape words to fit it. As a result his writing life was the most laborious with which I am familiar.

All of these biographies of Thoreau must enter into any

biography that aims to give the whole man. I hope to do justice to them and to other aspects of a career that is like a confusion of trails in a forest which all lead, nevertheless, in the same direction. My feeling is, however, that a life of Thoreau must chiefly emphasize the creative thinker with weighted wings, and the ascetic with a passion for living. These two aspects of Thoreau will explain much which is obscure, and may even seem absurd, in this stiff-backed, prickly, power-charged New Englander.

I

Adventurer in Life

1. CONCORD

In Concord, town of quiet name
And quiet fame as well, . . .

H. D. T.

Among the Concord celebrities, Henry David Thoreau (pronounced in Concord of that day 'Thórow' or 'Thorough' [1]) was the only one born in Concord. The others were all drawn to the community by its peace, its beauty, its good society, its easy proximity to Boston, or its low cost of living. Emerson became a Concord man, and spoke and was felt to speak for Concord, but the silent Hawthorne, the voluble Alcott, and the versatile Ellery Channing were only domiciled in Concord.

Thoreau and his family were also, in a subtle way which only the natives of an old town can understand, half alien to Concord. The Thoreaus in 1817, when Henry was born, were a two-generation family in America, a one-generation family, so far as effective residence went, in Concord. The first American Thoreau had been an Isle of Jersey man, French-speaking. Henry Thoreau himself observed so critically the mental habits of his neighbors, and so lovingly the fields, rivers, and woods in which they lived, that he may be said to have owned more of Concord than any proprietor of real estate. Indeed he said so himself, more than once. Nevertheless, the

Thoreaus had no ancestry and no history in Concord. They were Scotch, French, Tory in a community English to the core and the cradle of the Revolution. Ellery Channing says that Henry always spoke with a burr — which he thought French, but was more probably Scotch. His friends said, too, that his French blood came out in his writing — which is nonsense. No writer ever stuck closer to the English tradition than Thoreau. What they may have meant was that this youth wished to become a professional man of letters, which was not in the Concord blood. He was, indeed, just enough detached from Concord to be thoroughly conscious of it as a land and as a community. He wrote of it with an awareness which no farmer bound to his acres, no townsman with relatives on every street, and no professional man whose career was limited to Concord, could possibly have achieved. And yet this critical attitude was blended with an almost pugnacious patriotism. When his time came to write his personal sketch in the Class Book of his year at Harvard, he flaunted his Concord origin: 'I shall ever pride myself on the place of my birth. . . . If I forget thee, O Concord, let my right hand forget her cunning. . . . To whatever quarter of the world I may wander, I shall deem it good fortune that I hail from Concord North Bridge.' [2] Hence a view of Concord is an indispensable preliminary to a life of Thoreau.

Few men, indeed, have been more fortunate in their birthplace. Thoreau did not exaggerate when he said:

June 20, 1850. And then for my afternoon walks I have a garden, larger than any artificial garden that I have read of and far more attractive to me, — mile after mile of embowered walks, such as no nobleman's grounds can boast, with animals running free and wild therein as from the first, — varied with land and water prospect, and, above all, so retired that it is extremely rare that I meet a single wanderer in its mazes. No gardener is seen therein, no gates nor [*sic*]. You may wander away to solitary bowers and brooks and hills.

Concord gave him everything he needed, except a market for his writing. It offered him everything except a career.

2

There were, of course, two Concords, the village (a small town in itself) and the town. A town in New England, as everyone ought to know, is the equivalent of a township elsewhere in the United States, or of an English parish. It is an area of ten or twenty square miles, of which the 'center' may be, and usually is, a city, town, or village. Concord village, which contained most of the two thousand-odd inhabitants of Concord in Thoreau's day, was originally a mill dam and center of converging roads from which settlements spread out into the town. The village, when Thoreau was young, consisted of several long streets, tree-shaded and lined with ample if austere houses which, since the Greek revival, had been painted white, if painted at all. These streets led to or met in a green little square beyond rows of shops on what had once been a mill dam built on the brook which flowed from Emerson's meadow. So the town had its focus, the shopping and gossiping place of Concord, its rialto. Town merged into country on one side and lawns stretched to the river and the marshes on the other. Below the mill dam on the Concord River, was the old manse, and Doctor Ripley, who still wore knee breeches in 1822, and the bridge where was fired the shot heard round the world. It was a pleasant village by any standards, simpler, more rustic, quieter than today, but not unrecognizable. Thoreau did not like its architecture, but he felt that the place was beautiful.

Country Concord was an ideal land for a naturalist and geographer, a poet and a solitary. Except for his two years at Walden, Thoreau always lived on a street, but he could be and was out of village bounds in a few minutes at any hour of day or night. Cross lots and over fences was his way, and so, even in the suburbs of the village, he found the wild. But there was another path to untouched nature more convenient and quicker than the fields. Thoreau is always described as a man of the woods, while, actually, he was as much, perhaps more, a river-man. His Concord scenes are many of them waterscapes and descriptions of river banks.

The heart of the town of Concord is a river valley, through which meander slow sluggish streams. Musketaquid, or Grass-ground River, the Indians called their settlement. Indeed, it was the Great Meadows along the Concord, promising abundant hay, easily harvested, which drew the colonists there so early. And it was the long stretches of dead water, abounding in mussels, muskrats, fish, turtles, and wild fowl, that made these rivers Indian streets, and the sands of Concord 'arrow-headiferous' with their weapons of flint.

The Sudbury, a marsh and meadow stream, flower-bordered for half the year, curves sluggishly between hills and under many bridges to join the somewhat more rapid Assabet just beside Concord village. These rivers make the Concord, which barely flows through the great meadows toward the Merrimack. Not even motor roads and summer residences have changed the essential wildness of this water country, with its fluvial miles of navigable and skateable channels. On these waters, Thoreau progressed from hunter and fisher to poet, from poet to natural-ist, and to consulting expert on their flow and depths and bridges. Above the village, the Sudbury broadens into a grassy lake with the cliffs of Fair Haven above it. Here is the Baker Farm which Thoreau once tried to buy, but was content to fish in the stream of time flowing over it; and, on the other slope, that pleasant land, still secluded from main roads, which Chan-ning or Thoreau named Conantum from Conant, its owner.

Concord village, Fair Haven, and Walden are the three corners of Thoreau's most active life.

But, since the region of Concord was heavily glaciated, there stretches on either side of the rivers, but especially toward Cambridge, a region of hills and lakes and swamps among which the farms are only upland intervals. This country was, and is, heavily forested, with pine and hard wood, and the swamps thick with maple and spruce. It is wilder now than in Thoreau's youth, although the big trees are gone, and will always be wild. In between the pines, the swamps, and the fields, it is a shrub oak and huckleberry country, tough to get through, with prickly juniper also and cedar. No one can follow its fox trails in clothes presentable in Concord parlors.

In Thoreau's time, the outflowing tide of population toward the cities and the West had left Walden and White Pond, and the woods and the pastures, to the woodchoppers, the hunters and fishers, the barberry and huckleberry pickers, and foraging cattle. Here a man could have solitude and the forest within two miles of the Mill Dam and home. Here, also, on these up-lands, the aquatic flora and fauna of the marshes, with their hints of the sea, gave way to the American woods, not primeval by any means, yet still a fair sample of the forest cover which stretched north and east to the Maine wilderness. Woodchuck took the place of muskrat, chickadee of sheldrake, fern of water lily.

And also from these rough low hills and from such isolated knolls as Ponkawtasset or Fair Haven, one could see the first mountain of the noble Appalachian chain — Wachusett near Worcester —

> Wachusett, who like me
> Standest alone without society —

a friend from Thoreau's youth; and Monadnock, whose name has become a geological term for isolated peaks — and so on into the west and north.

Hence the nature lover in Concord could escape at will by boat or foot from the small-town talk of the Mill Dam or the fog of philosophies in Emerson's parlor or the boarding-house which was home, to woods or river. He could time the blooming of the flowers, write up notes for his Journal under an oak tree, listen to Melvin's reminiscences of famous pickerel, walk to George Minott's, who heard the earliest bluebird and saw the first geese fly over, or stand by the plodding, taciturn farmers while they turned over the sandy Concord soil.

Even the climate of Concord was full of contrasts, 'washing days,' as Thoreau called them, with a wind from the west, or fogs blown in from the sea, intense summer heats, and great colds and great snows. Shore birds and forest birds, every native animal except the greater quadrupeds, flowers and trees of mountain, upland, coast, and swamp were to be found there. Only in geology and mineralogy was Concord relatively uninteresting. It was just as well, for there was too much to learn as it was, and if there was a tragedy in Thoreau's life it was that he was too much engrossed in the learning.

3

The intellectual and spiritual climate of Concord was even more various, more distinctive, and in some respects more distinguished. When the Thoreau family came to Concord it was still one of those New England theocracies, with a single church, from which Doctor Ripley, a scholar, a gentleman, and a character, directed the morals of the town. He had seen and recorded the battle of Concord, and in a later day strongly objected to any version of the famous fight that differed from his own. He represented Harvard in Concord, and intellectually Concord was an outlying province of the university. When the reaction toward Trinitarianism began, families divided their allegiance, among them the Thoreaus, and some 'signed off' the church and its taxes altogether, Henry Thoreau among them, and were ready for the new gospel of Transcendentalism, which was cradled in Concord. Hence it was a community in which the religious deadness of the 1800's had already given way to controversy, and the strong ethical strain of New England had been reinforced by earnest thinking.

In ethics, indeed, the town had never wavered in its Puritanism. Concord was full of reformers. The Thoreau family were all, except Henry, Abolitionists, and he supported them later; they were prohibitionists, and Henry almost a vegetarian. If the wilder zealots who came from outside, Joseph Palmer with his cult of beards, Edward Palmer who did not believe in money, and Alcott with his themes of nature created by men, were not popular with the town-born, it was because the Yankee common sense of the community found support in the two poles of its religious life; Doctor Ripley, who spoke for tradition, and Emerson, who preached newness, were both wise and learned and tolerant men. But concern over man's duty and privilege in aspects of eternity was not confined to the townsmen. The farmers were deeply, if not fervently, religious also, although only a phrase quoted now and then from their tight lips indicates the prevailing seriousness of Concord. Only the wastrels on the river, such as Melvin and one-eyed Goodwin, Ellery Channing the intellectual dilettante, and Thoreau in his Panic moods, escaped the grave sense of responsibility which seems to have been the tone of Concord.

And yet it was not a sour and cheerless community. On a summer evening, as Thoreau describes it, neighbors and farmers, come a-shopping after their day's haying, chatted in the streets, and from the houses came the sound of many musical instruments and of singing. An hour or two at least in the evening was devoted to such poetry as the villagers could appreciate.

Concord village had character. Its lawyers and preachers were Harvard graduates. It was proud of its Revolutionary history, and its reputation for independence. Its notables were men of real character. Samuel Hoar (who could not understand why anyone should want to publish the records of Thoreau's wasted time) was a man of granite, strong, able, and of inflexible integrity. When he was mobbed in Charleston on his mission to protect free Negro sailors, righteousness was added to the cause of the North. He was Concord's leading citizen throughout Thoreau's lifetime. Doctor Bartlett, a temperance man, had, with his father, covered a century of practice in Massachusetts. Doctor Ripley knew everyone's grandfather and talked to the backsliders in terms of their family pride. Of this there was much, for Concord was intensely conscious of its past. Even the cosmic Thoreau collected Concord stories. It was a town that had always stood on its own feet, made its own heroes — a place of beginnings, not followings. It was what Emerson said and did in Concord that made his reputation in the village. Thoreau got the respect of his home town but was never famous there. The world was said to applaud his books — but why? When he died, Concord had not yet made up its mind.

It came as near as might be to a pure democracy, but it was definitely a democracy of leadership. There was neither much poverty nor much wealth, yet means commanded respect, and so did brains, character, and respectability. The Social Circle, which met on Tuesday evenings from the first of October till the last of March, and celebrated biographically the death of every member, was perhaps indicative of such social discriminations as existed in the upper register. Emerson was a member, but not Alcott or Thoreau. There was a social difference between 'farmers' and 'townsmen' which was occupational. The farmers dressed and lived and thought differently. Thoreau,

Concord Main Street about 1862
'Concord Village had character'

of course, was a townsman in spite of his woodcraft. He liked farmers, but did not altogether approve of them, because their brains were conditioned by the oxen they worked in the fields. In town, there was an underworld of riff-raff, who were imitators, and some of them descendants, of the Indians that had hunted the river banks. Drunkenness, arson, adultery, theft, when they occurred, and the first was common, were their privilege. They had never submitted to Puritanism. Those of them who lived in the woods or on the river as he did had a curious fascination for Thoreau, and he mentions Melvin in his Journal a dozen times for Emerson once. The Irish immigrants were also a society apart, substituting for the Negroes further south. Humorous, ignorant, shiftless, they, too, fascinated Thoreau by their perversion of his own theory of leisure. He never liked them, but after his trip to Catholic Canada seems to have understood them better.

Above these two depressed groups and below the leaders, it is difficult to discover social shades in Concord. If you came of good stock you could be eccentric as you pleased, like Emerson's marvellous Aunt Mary Emerson, who borrowed a horse, and rode sidewise on a man's saddle to the Manse, wearing a scarlet shawl over the flannel shroud she had made for her funeral. If a son of a shopkeeper went to Harvard, he had the entrée anywhere. And yet there is more than a suggestion that Mrs. Thoreau's fondness for displaying her ancestral china, and Thoreau's own stiff refusals to dress up for company, betrayed a consciousness that the one kept a boarding-house, and the other was the son of a bankrupt shopkeeper, and made pencils (when he had to) for a living.[3]

Let us add, finally, that ever since a dozen families had driven their livestock through swamps and forests to settle by the meadows in 1637, Concord had always been moderately prosperous. It was commercially well situated, for the raw products of upper Massachusetts and New Hampshire came down the trade routes through the town, which was just far enough from Boston to be an assembling center. The river, too, originally provided transport, and later the Fitchburg Railroad made it a first main stop on the road to the west. A man could live in Concord and yet be in touch with Boston, and many did.

I emphasize these strictly local characteristics because the intellectual renaissance of Concord, which was the making of the artist and the philosopher in Thoreau, never broke the stiff ties of his inheritance from an earlier Concord. Without the powerful stimulus of Emerson's circle, he might still have been a Gilbert White, but would never have written 'Walden.' Without his Concord mind, he would have written neither 'Walden' nor 'Civil Disobedience' nor 'Wild Apples.'

4

The effect of Emerson and his circle upon Concord life can only be compared to the birth of an academy in a village, but an academy in a Greek rather than in a modern sense. In Emerson's household, some intellectual, some cleric, some reformer was nearly always to be encountered. His circle of friends and acquaintances was a center of power and influence, a receiving station for whatever thought, spiritual, philosophical, critical, religious, was abroad in Germany, England, France, or whatever emanated from the brains and libraries of Boston and Cambridge. It is not too much to say that there was more vital awareness in Emerson's Concord of the best that was being said and thought in the contemporary civilized world than in any university town in America today. I make an exception only for economics and research science, but even here there were Transcendental reactions to whatever was being done in these fields elsewhere. Concord was also a home of learned women — Elizabeth Hoar, Mrs. Sarah Ripley, and others — and a tutoring ground for Harvard students. Dante, Virgil, and Homer were better read than contemporary fiction. The arts, however, were weak. Music was much written about, but its practice was elementary; the interest in painting was mild, in sculpture negligible. Yet Concord talk ranged widely, even in esthetics.

And if all this was not native, it was accepted by Concord, and strongly colored by the Concord environment. The town was small enough to rub elbows daily, and did assimilate its aliens and half-aliens, even finally Alcott and Thoreau, and was proud of them. The townsmen admired when they did not understand, and chuckled if their sages were too Transcendental. When Alcott designed a rustic summer house for Emerson so full of curves that Thoreau, who helped build it, fell from the roof and nearly broke a bone, the town was amused. It was more deeply stirred by the forest fire that Thoreau lit by accident than by 'Walden,' and Emerson's philosophy had no perceptible effect on its mores; yet to the proud consciousness of having begun the Revolution was added the sense of present (if eccentric) greatness. It was Emerson who in Civil War days rose up in meeting, and with his calm dignity and just one question, 'Is this Concord?' saved a Copperhead from mobbing. If the Concord celebrities failed to make a Florence of Concord they themselves (Hawthorne excepted) made union with Concord earth and their thoughts were colored by it.

2. THE THOREAUS

T<small>HE</small> T<small>HOREAUS</small> were French of the Channel Islands. They were French-speaking, although Peter, nephew of the emigrant, wrote letters in English to Thoreau's Aunt Elizabeth from 1801 to 1806, and some of the Jersey family married and lived in England, one becoming a British officer. They still have descendants there. According to tradition, they came originally from Tours. The family was much in Henry Thoreau's mind, and in his Harvard Class Book, already mentioned, he writes that they had taken refuge in Jersey after the Revocation of the Edict of Nantes. He could be as ridiculous as Alcott over genealogy, and liked to play with the idea that the name might have come from the hero of the Scandinavian north, 'Thorer the Dog-footed.' [1] His grandfather, he said, arrived in America 'sans souci, sans sous.' In a college notebook,[2] he copied a certificate in French stating that this grandfather John took the sacrament at St. Helier on May 3 of 1773, presumably just before he emigrated, and was affirmed by the Protestant rector and principals of the parish church to be a good Christian.

The Thoreaus were merchants, Philippe, the emigrant's father, a wine merchant — and some of them seafarers. John,

THE THOREAUS not—

the emigrant, was born in 1754, sought his fortune in Boston in 1773, and when the Revolution halted trade went privateering. But it must have been the merchandizing and outfitting business he entered afterward, and a good marriage, which enabled him to lay by a fortune of some twenty-five thousand dollars before his early death, since he commenced business on Long Wharf in Boston with a single hogshead of sugar.[3] He was a powerful man and very religious, the owner, when he died in 1801 of consumption, of two good houses, one in Boston, one in Concord, where he had retired for his health. There are no records of intellectual interests of any kind in the Thoreau family before Henry's generation.

His son John, who was Henry's father, learned storekeeping in Salem and Concord and, on fifteen hundred dollars borrowed from his stepmother against the Prince Street house in Boston, went into business for himself. He lost this money in a series of adversities, and in 1817 was forced to deed over the house to his sisters.[4] Much of the family estate had been already used in bringing up the family, so that the John Thoreaus by the time of Henry's birth in 1817 were poor and hard-pressed. There was still the Concord house, but this seems to have belonged to the aunts, and, except for brief periods, to have been rented.

After farming for his mother-in-law, school-keeping in Boston, selling to the Indians near Bangor, and shopkeeping, Henry's father, by this time regarded, it would seem, as a failure, settled in Concord in 1823, and by good fortune (the Thoreaus were quick with their hands) went into the business of making lead pencils, which had been introduced into Concord by his neighbor, William Monroe, some time before. This suited his quiet and studious nature, was a fitting pursuit for his inventive mind, and profited by his integrity. The Thoreau pencils became the first real rivals of the European product, and when a market developed for the finely ground graphite of which the pencils

were made, the family were slowly lifted out of their depression.
But this was not until Henry had reached his thirties.

So much for the paternal ancestry of the Thoreaus, a quite
unremarkable bourgeois family, whose chief traits seem to have
been honesty and perseverance. Sanborn remarks with Yankee
satisfaction that when Aunt Maria died, the last descendant of
John the Jerseyman in America, the family estate had again
risen to twenty-five thousand dollars, at which level John the
first had left it.

2

Thoreau's maternal ancestry of Dunbars and Joneses is more
interesting. Of the Thoreau children, Sophia and Henry were
said, in Concord tradition, to be 'clear Dunbar.' [5] It is curious,
therefore, that even Emerson should have spoken of Thoreau's
French traits. He certainly inherited the eccentric temperament of the Scottish Dunbars, and had another dose of Scotch
from his grandmother, Jane Burns Thoreau. Her father, who
was a sailorman, had to 'doff his rich apparel of gems and
ruffles' (Aunt Maria's story) before the bride's Quaker parents
would allow the marriage. This yarn must have pleased
Thoreau, who did not like Quakers, but disliked fine raiment
still more.

His mother's father was Asa Dunbar, a Harvard graduate of
some distinction and minister of a Congregational church at
Salem. He led a successful student rebellion against bad food
and severity while at Harvard, and, at the time of the Revolution, succeeded in defending his reputation for patriotism
against the feeling aroused by the known sympathies of his Tory
in-laws. Leaving the church, he became a lawyer in Keene,
New Hampshire, where Henry's mother, the dark-eyed, vivacious Cynthia, was born. He could write well.

Her mother, and Henry's grandmother, in whose house he was born, was Mary Jones, the only daughter in a family of fifteen children of Colonel Elisha Jones of Weston, near Concord, owner of some eight thousand acres, two slaves, and a fine house. Colonel Jones was an ardent Tory, who took refuge and office behind the British lines. Both he and his sons were recklessly tenacious in their loyalties. Eight were banished from the United States and their property confiscated. One guided Earl Percy to the Lexington battle; another served in the war in the South; two, who were imprisoned in Concord jail, escaped by means of files hidden in food brought to them by their mother. The Colonel, his wife, at least one or two of the sons, and Asa Dunbar seem to have been personalities with vigor, principle, and intelligence. It is perhaps significant that eight out of the twelve of the Jones great-uncles of the man who was to preach disobedience to the state should have defied what they regarded as the mob rule of the local patriotic organizations, and risked both their lives and property for a cause. Surely the Dunbar-Jones versatility, aggressiveness, and independence, of which Cynthia Thoreau and her brother, Uncle Charles, had their share, are more significant in Thoreau's inheritance of traits than the bourgeois virtues and the taciturnity under good and bad fortune of his father Thoreau. Cynthia talked and Henry Thoreau wrote under the slightest of provocations. Both reacted violently to circumstance. His meticulous integrity in business and his accuracy in money matters, we may guess were derived from the example of his father.

One last importance in this family strain is also a surmise, but legitimate. The Joneses were on the aristocratic side, the Dunbars clerical. Cynthia was proud of her old china, and ran her table with an air. She always dipped spoon in hot water when serving sugar to preserve its fine flavor.[6] And Henry was keenly aware that he came from established families. Note the pleasure he takes in recording the visit of his grandmother Dunbar to the wild lands in New Hampshire belonging to her second husband, Captain Minott; how her chaise, the first seen in the region, sent livestock flying in a panic, and the equal sensation of her fine city clothes. Though a poor scholar, living by handicrafts, it never occurred to him that he was not the social equal of Emersons and Hoars. But we may suspect from numerous references in his Journal to clothes, manners, and inherited wealth, as well as to the facts of his own genealogy, that he was not always sure that Hoars and Emersons shared his conviction.

The Dunbars were as prolific as the Joneses, Henry's grandfather of that name being one of fourteen children. His father's generation on both sides was smaller, there being four Dunbars and eight Thoreaus; nevertheless, Henry had an abundance of uncles and aunts, though not so many cousins, for New England sterility had already begun. Thus the life of this so-called solitary was indeed a family life to an extent not common in modern New England. The Dunbar-Thoreau circle was closely knit, sociable, and affectionate. No Hawthorne recluses in this group, all of whom, except John, Henry's father, and perhaps his Aunt Jane, who was very deaf, seem to have been voluble. Although Henry's youth was spent in many homes as his father followed his uncertain fortunes, in and around these homes the family circle remained unbroken.

3

Cynthia, Thoreau's mother, was manager of the home. Her husband's quiet yielding to the casualties of trade had not subdued her Dunbar energy and Jones aggressiveness. Neither Sanborn nor Ellery Channing, Thoreau's two biographers, liked her. Sanborn says, in so many words, that she was a busybody and sharp of tongue. Ellery, who was often incredible, begged Thoreau to get her out of the house when he wished to visit there; and when he did come and found her at home, turned his back on her and she on him.⁷ Actually, the record is clear and of no little importance in Thoreau's history. It is generally agreed that she was the greatest talker in Concord — and a very kind woman, though saying what she liked about her neighbors, and contentious toward all anti-reformers. When she interrupted Henry at table he would bow gravely and wait till she had finished before going on. There is a hint in an unpublished letter from Prudence Ward, her boarder, to Aunt Maria Thoreau, that she was sometimes difficult to deal with, but Isaac Hecker, the young Brook Farmer, who had a room and light from her for seventy-five cents a week, found her a second mother, inclined to coddle him, and called her '*a woman.*' ⁸ A woman she was, bustling, intelligent, watching Henry's colds, visiting about the town, where her yellow bonnet ribbons made Aunt Mary Emerson shut her eyes in disapproval because they were so 'unsuitable for a child of God and a person of your years.' And when not talking, reading. The ambition, the tireless energy even in ill health, of Henry Thoreau came from her surely. Like him, she never took 'a *second grade* of anything willingly'; it was she who led her boys barefoot to a girl's school that they might have more education after the regular school was closed. Thoreau's habit of lecturing his friends in monologues came probably from her also. He did not like these traits, especially ambition, when he saw them exercised for trivial ends, but he had them. She was emotional as a robin is emotional, cheeping or flapping over its nestlings or the cat. Her tongue dominated the home, and certainly helped drive Henry Thoreau to his Walden hermitage.

It is impossible to discover whether it was Mrs. or Mr. Thoreau who was the nature lover. Both went on nature walks in the woods and along the banks of the rivers and took the family with them. Probably she led and quiet John followed, for gossip reported that, thanks to an ill-timed excursion, one of her children was nearly born on Lee's Hill. And it was Cynthia who used to sit on the doorstep at midnight and hear nothing in the world but the ticking of the clock. She died in old age, 'bursting out with a song,' after reciting Cato's soliloquy from Addison.[9]

Henry's letters to her from his only residence away from Concord, on Staten Island, are of an affectionate, teasing nature, without a hint of the explosions in his Journal, where he compares hell to a boarding-house. There was, indeed, a lack of comprehension in her affection for him, and it was not until after his father's death that she discovered his innate tenderness.[10] She moved on a plane of excited worldliness where Henry's meticulous scholarship and his passionate Transcendentalism would be quite unheard. He who disdained clothes writes to her of shirts and the health of relatives!

Only toward the end of both their lives did Henry penetrate even a little way into the mind of his close-lipped father. Half a foot shorter than his wife, slightly deaf (or pretending to be so in the racket of talk), an inconspicuous but likable man, John Thoreau caught his son's imagination as Cynthia never did. But he must also have totally failed to understand his son, though there is reason to believe that he appreciated his rare qualities, and accepted without protest his half-hearted assistance in pencil-making. His only recorded criticism is noted by Henry in the Journal on March 21, 1856: 'Had a dispute with Father about the *use* of my making this [maple] sugar when I … might have bought sugar cheaper at Holden's. He said it took me from my studies. I said I made it my study; I felt as if I had been to a university.' It is hard to get a better instance of the family's pride in their scholar — or of the scholar's fondness for exaggeration. But he could not have told his father why he was studying the mechanics of sap. He hardly knew himself.

This quiet man, who is described as possessing an 'inward happiness,' belonged to the absorptive type of humanity, which is the beginning of scholarship. The newspaper filled most of his leisure and he seems to have read it from beginning to end. When not the newspaper it was the Mill Dam, where, in good New England fashion, he seems to have just sat and listened. Perhaps it was his years of shopkeeping that made him a listener, not a talker. In any case, there is a parallel between his absorbed reading of newspapers (his son said when he died that he knew more than anyone else of old Concord) and Henry Thoreau's own curious and sometimes distressing absorptions. Students of Henry's unassorted manuscripts, his commonplace books, and Journal must often have been struck with the immense labor of copying and digesting out of all proportion to any use made, or likely to be made, of the material. I do not refer here to his detailed nature studies or his notes for a proposed history of the Indians, since here there is a possible explanation, but to his vast bibliographies of dramatic literature which he never read, and transcripts from poetry and travel and history and geography, as if the man, in spite of his proximity to Harvard, was determined to make a library of his own. He hoarded the thought and expression of the world as his father hoarded news and anecdote. Perhaps it was some covert sympathy that made Thoreau so sympathetic with the old man. But I think that, even more, his father was to him a rock of silence in a flowing world of talk, Cynthia's, Emerson's, Channing's, Alcott's. The two spent hours and days together over the pencils, and probably said little. It is not derogatory to say that Thoreau had the same affection for his father as for the inscrutable woodchuck which let him stroke its head.

Living with the Thoreaus probably from 1830, when grandmother Minott died, was Aunt Louisa Dunbar, quite a dear
one judges, very ugly in her picture, but with a face that was
evidently accustomed to smile. Her Dunbar heavy mouth is
repeated in Sophia, and refined in Henry's strong face and
puckered lips. It was she who had been led to join the church
by Daniel Webster, who took her chaise-riding when she was
young and said to be pretty; and she was the religious member
of the family, always 'flitting away to some good meeting, to save
the credit of you all,' said Henry. Like Aunt Maria and Sophia,
she probably found 'Walden' shocking.

In and out of this household, but seldom far away, and sometimes boarding the family in the old Thoreau house on the
square, moved the two Thoreau aunts, Maria and Jane. Nothing is recorded of Jane but a sweet face. Aunt Maria, however, was a person, and her long correspondence with the Ward
family circle shows her to have been sprightly, intelligent, and
intensely curious. She was a reformer and an Abolitionist, a
flirt in her youth — indeed a very type of New England maiden
lady of the genteel kind, though far from vinegarish. It was she
with Aunt Jane who reverted to Trinitarianism, which must
have kept Cynthia and Louisa talking; and while affectionate
and admiring, she approved neither of Henry's unconventional
religion nor of his unsettled life. 'I wish he could find something
better to do than walking off every now and then.' [11]

Drifting in and out less frequently, and a resident when
Thoreau was a child at his grandmother's house, was Uncle
Charles Dunbar, an extraordinary man. He was a mixture of
comedian, professional strong man, and local character. He
could 'bust' anyone at wrestling, swallow his nose (as Henry
could also), and do tricks. He had Henry's humor without his
refinement. Thoreau mentions him often in his Journal, and
always with affection, as for example:

After talking with Uncle Charles the other night about the worthies of this country, Webster and the rest, as usual, considering who were geniuses and who not, I showed him up to bed, and when I had got into bed myself, I heard his chamber door opened, after eleven o'clock, and he called out, in an earnest, stentorian voice, loud enough to wake the whole house, 'Henry! Was John Quincy Adams a genius?' 'No, I think not,' was my reply. 'Well, I didn't think he was,' answered he.[12]

The unusual vitality of all these Dunbars is significant.

Living with the Thoreaus in the period of Henry's youth were the Wards, quite important in this history because of the part they play in it and the comments to be found in their correspondence. Mrs. Ward, widow of Colonel Joseph Ward of Revolutionary fame, and her daughter Prudence were close friends of Aunt Maria, whom they had known in Boston. Both were Abolitionists and Prudence an amateur botanist and flower painter — one of those maiden ladies who live chiefly in the experiences of their friends. It was she who introduced botany into the Thoreau family, and was responsible for Henry's first love affair.

The Wards, as Prudence's correspondence indicates, were paying guests. Later, however, Mrs. Thoreau's house was opened to any respectable person visiting Concord. One could get there either food or rooms or both. It was a guest house for cousins and aunts, and a boarding-house for those recommended, such as the preceptor of the Academy who was there with the Wards. The influence of boarders and a boarding-house upon Henry Thoreau's life and philosophy has been unaccountably neglected. The Wards brought Ellen Sewall for him to fall in love with; it was Mrs. Lucy Jackson Brown, a boarder, who made the contact with her brother-in-law Emerson which was to shape his future. And there is a striking series of indirect, but not the less poignant, comments in his Journal, beginning on October 22, 1837, when he was just out of Harvard, with 'I seek a garret,' which indicate only too clearly the effect of a family circle too much enlarged upon a scholar and lover of solitude.

4

It was, however, an affectionate and harmonious circle in which the four young Thoreaus grew up; but dominated by women, most of them spinsters. John senior was the only man in residence, and he was shadowed by his wife. The regular boarders recorded in the earlier years are all women. On Sunday, March 4, 1838, Thoreau's Journal states: 'Here at my elbow sit five notable, or at least noteworthy, representatives of this nineteenth century — of the gender feminine.' So it must have been through most of his life, when he was not in his garret, in the woods, or on the river. Even at Emerson's, his associates were usually feminine. Uncle Charles must have been a relief, even if he did go to sleep while shaving — but he was seldom seen. Mrs. Dunbar, often in residence, was a widow. So was Mrs. Ward, senior. The aunts Jane and Maria Thoreau, Aunt Louisa Dunbar, Miss Prudence Ward were all spinsters, and by the forties his sisters Sophia and Helen could be placed in the same category. Mrs. Lucy Brown's husband had been long resident abroad. No one of the Thoreau children married, although two made half-hearted attempts. When at home, Henry Thoreau lived in a predominantly woman's world, with suggestions all about him of both physical and emotional sterility.

And yet it was an agreeable household, with winds of doctrine stirring in it, strong contrasts between affectionate relatives, and free and vigorous speech. If the tone was intensely moral, and among the women genteel, it was also high and humorous.

It was an intellectual household, too. One could say anything, no matter how abstract, and wit was appreciated. The girls were musical, as their mother had been. But the art of music and the art of literature, as these women knew them, were pedagogical. Most of them had been school teachers or were to be, like the two sons. Helen, who died in 1849, comparatively young, had real intellectuality, though, to judge from her letters, it was arid. Henry writes to her in scholar's language; and it is noteworthy that it is only to her that he speaks of Mrs. Emerson, with all the implications that name had for him of a new and larger world. The rest of the family was absorbed in the interests of Concord, which, though a remarkable community, was also a small town.

There is no evidence that Henry's famous friends, when he made them, and his own family circle ever coalesced. His home life and his life as a man of letters are never identical. At home, he seems to have been the cherished child, who repaid the affections spent upon him with a lifetime of quiet services and consideration. Outside the family he was contumaciously his own. In his 'Ralph Waldo Emerson,' Oliver Wendell Holmes says, with witty shrewdness, that Henry Thoreau 'insisted on nibbling his asparagus at the wrong end.' [13] Yes, at Emerson's and Longfellow's and at the meetings of the Transcendental group, but not at home. The great importance of this affectionate home life for a truculent, aggressive spirit like his, and a thwarted temperament, is obvious. Unlike Diogenes, with whom his contemporaries liked to compare him, he was often homesick when out of his barrel. And, indeed, the best picture of this family circle is to be found in a letter in which he *says* he is not homesick, written from Staten Island when he was for the first and only time long absent from the neighborhood of Concord:

Staten Island, August 6, 1843.

Dear Mother, — ... I think of you all very often, and
wonder if you are still separated from me only by so many
miles of earth, or so many miles of memory. This life we live
is a strange dream, and I don't believe at all any account men
give of it. Methinks I should be content to sit at the back door
in Concord, under the poplar tree, henceforth forever. . . .

I fancy that this Sunday evening you are pouring over some
select book, almost transcendental perchance, or else 'Burgh's
Dignity,' or Massillon, or the *Christian Examiner*. Father has
just taken one more look at the garden, and is now absorbed in
Chaptelle, or reading the newspaper quite abstractedly, only
looking up occasionally over his spectacles to see how the rest
are engaged, and not to miss any newer news that may not be in
the paper. Helen has slipped in for the fourth time to learn the
very latest item. Sophia, I suppose, is at Bangor; but Aunt
Louisa, without doubt, is just flitting away to some good meeting, to save the credit of you all.

Much can be deduced from this letter. James Burgh's 'The
Dignity of Human Nature,' which had been several times reprinted in America, is a rather shrewd, though formal and
moralistic analysis of an eighteenth-century idea of how to dignify life. Alcott also read this book, and, according to Odell
Shepard in his 'Pedlar's Progress,' suffered in his own writing
from its 'consummate and ineffable gentility.' Perhaps Professor Shepard was thinking of Burgh's 'The Art of Speaking,'
for Burgh's 'Dignity' is better than the style current at Harvard
in Thoreau's day. At all events, it is not improbable that
Henry's reference has a sly dig in it. I suspect that Mrs. Thoreau
had been reading to him an apt passage on the danger of being
too independent when you were young and poor and thought
yourself a genius, as, for example, on 'Prudence':

It is not prudent to be singular in matters of inferior consequence. That a genius... should not be able to keep a coat
to his back [!].... Let a man have what sublime abilities he

will, if he is above applying his understanding... it is... little
to be expected, that he should acquire... fortune.... Nor is the
man of learning or genius, who is void of common prudence, to
be considered in any other character, than that of a wrong-
headed pedant, or of a man of narrow and defective abilities.[14]

This is the way Mrs. Thoreau must have talked to her son,
who at twenty-six had not determined any scheme of life for
himself, and was dependent upon the utmost in 'simplifying' in
order to get along at all, and very pugnacious about it.

Massillon was a French preacher, whose reputation in the
eighteenth century was equal to Bossuet's. Massillon, Ohio,
was named for him in 1826. His 'Sermons' are listed in Thoreau's library. *The Christian Examiner* was Sunday magazine
reading. These books were what Mrs. Thoreau browsed upon
while her son was hot after Coleridge, Wordsworth, De Quincey,
Carlyle, and the new thought generally. As for Chaptelle,[15] he
was the author of many books on the technical applications of
chemistry. John Thoreau was working at his graphite processes, even on Sunday.

5

The four young Thoreaus were all 'gifted,' as they would have
said in Concord. When they were at home together, which
seldom happened after Henry's boyhood, the Thoreau house
must have been a pleasant place to live in — and so, indeed,
the Wards found it. All were intelligent, all ambitious. This
nest of school teachers was one of the innumerable centers of
restless, pedagogic energy which made New England the
teacher of the nation.

Helen, the oldest, tubercular from girlhood, was the only
pedantic Thoreau. It was to her that Henry later wrote his
playful letters in Latin, and his letters of advice on how and

what to teach. It was Helen who reproved him for singularity
and got a prickly reply.[16] Yet Helen, like Henry, was a born
intellectual. And as it was Helen who was later instrumental in
his introduction to the Emerson circle, so it was presumably
Helen who was a factor, and probably a decisive one, in sending
him to Harvard, since with the aunts she contributed to his
expenses, and from her own earnings. All we know of earlier
plans for his career was that there was talk of apprenticing him
to a carpenter. Like all the Thoreaus, her face was strong but
homely. She looks, and probably was, a predestinate spinster,
sublimating her emotions in family affection and the teaching
of youth. Helen was an ardent Abolitionist.

John, the next to the oldest child, was different. Of his
abilities as a teacher and schoolmaster there is abundant
record. He had charm — something no other Thoreau possessed — and was genial and easily a friend. He was born
just too early to profit by the better fortunes of the family,
which began shortly after 1828; indeed, his first suit of clothes
which was not home-made was ordered for him so he could go
into a shop. Later he was 'selling' in Boston, presumably
pencils, as Henry did afterward, while peddling pencils with
his father in New York. It was too late for Harvard for him,
and so, in the successful school which Henry and he set up in
1838, he was the executive, Henry the teacher of advanced
courses. His few letters, the records of his friends, and Henry's
own testimony in 'A Week on the Concord and Merrimack
Rivers' show a simple, uncomplicated nature, free from uncertainties, and capable of easy happiness. Henry adored him,
and John's early death was a decisive factor in his career.

John was the family naturalist — very amateur, of course.
His list of Concord birds was Henry's first ornithological textbook. John was social, was deeply religious, but not bothered
about it; he had the sense of humor which Helen and Sophia

and Cynthia conspicuously lacked. Less scholarly than Henry, he was well read, and their conversation, as reported in 'A Week' and in letters, was kept on a plane of intellectual banter more like the tone of 'Walden' than the almost morbidly intellectual entries of Henry's early Journal. John had also that harmony of inner and outer life which Henry longed to attain. Horace R. Hosmer, his close friend, said that he was the 'Architect'; Henry was his 'Paul.' [17] But this is nonsense. There is no evidence that his life continued would have developed into more than that of a talented and original teacher. Like all the male Thoreaus, he was interested in inventions. Emerson, years afterward, recorded his gratitude for the daguerreotype of young Waldo which John had arranged to have made of the boy, just before his death.

Sophia, the youngest, was the homebody, homely, awkward if her picture tells truth, but vivacious. She was feebly artistic (her portrait of John now in the Concord Antiquarian Society is atrocious, and she left one of Henry which she, perhaps wisely, wanted no one to see); also she was a passionate lover of flowers, with which she filled the Thoreau houses. Her journal and letters indicate no intellectual resemblances to her older brother, but she was his lifelong and devoted admirer, and fought Ellery Channing over his literary remains. She was the most genteel of the Thoreaus, so genteel that she and her friends regarded Henry's emotional life as too sacred to talk about.

This was the family which sent Henry Thoreau off to Harvard on August 9, 1833, and welcomed him home when he walked out from Cambridge alone, or with his friends, once making the last two weary miles in stocking feet.

And this was the Thoreau circle — bourgeois in their virtues, yet with minds set upon dignifying human nature, devoted but not demonstrative, educated, cultivated, yet still living in a stiff little New England world of moralities and respectabilities. This was the circle from which Thoreau escaped to his books and his Journal in the garret, and later to his hut at Walden — but came back constantly, and indeed in his last illness had his bed brought down to the sitting-room of the family, so that he should end his days in their society.

3. DAVID HENRY THOREAU

It was with this name that Doctor Ripley christened him three months after his birth on July 12, 1817. He was born in the easternmost of the upper chambers of the house on the Virginia Road which was owned by his grandmother, who had become the widow Minott. The house was moved later, but the road still winds a mile or so out of Concord from Emerson's end of the village to the site of the house above the Bedford levels, a plain of meadows and peat marsh, with the Walden woods in sight, and the Concord River not far away. Here his father was 'carrying on' for that year, farming the widow's 'thirds' which were her share of the estate, in an interlude between shop and shop, failure and failure. The family were living in genteel poverty, with another family in one end of the house, which was of gray, unpainted boards, with a grassy, unfenced dooryard and a brook in front. Thoreau was named for his uncle David Thoreau, who died when he was six weeks old; the provenance of 'Henry' is unknown. After Harvard, the boy changed the order of his names, perhaps because 'Henry David' is easier to say, and by then he hoped to be famous.

With a characteristic sense of the importance of geography, and with the assistance of his mother, Thoreau in 1855 wrote down one of the most concise autobiographies on record. It is chiefly an account of houses, for he lived in many, and of towns, for until 1823, when he was six, the family was migratory. From this, and the assembled reminiscences in Channing and Sanborn, it is necessary to select only a few significant items of his early years. Thoreau's youth, until his mind suddenly flowered when halfway through Harvard, was the youth of thousands of New England boys brought up between the country and the village street.

His father had moved to the nearby village of Chelmsford in 1818, opening a shop where Cynthia waited on purchasers, while he painted signs as a side business, and dealt out hard liquor as a bonus to good customers, his moral fitness for the liquor trade having been attested by Doctor Ripley. There the child stayed until 1821, and, if failure had not caught up with his father again, might have gone to school to Emerson, who taught in Chelmsford about 1822 or 1823. Instead, his education began in Boston, where his father is listed in the Directory of 1822 as a schoolmaster. Boston city, then, and later, made no impression on Thoreau's imagination. He preferred through all his life the wharves, which he must have seen in childhood and where his grandfather had amassed a fortune, and the railroad station with its train ready to take him home to Concord. Indeed, the one childhood memory he kept green from the time before the family's return to Concord in 1823 was of a drive to Walden Pond with his grandmother Minott. There is a reference in 'Walden,' but the full account is in the Journal of August, 1845, written in his Walden hut:

> Twenty-three years since, when I was five years old, I was
> brought from Boston to this pond, away in the country, —
> which was then but another name for the extended world for

Drawing of Thoreau's birthplace
'He was born in the easternmost of the upper chambers'
From a contemporary sketch

me, — one of the most ancient scenes stamped on the tablets of my memory.... That woodland vision for a long time made the drapery of my dreams. That sweet solitude my spirit seemed so early to require that I might have room to entertain my thronging guests, and that speaking silence that my ears might distinguish the significant sounds. Somehow or other it at once gave the preference to this recess among the pines, where almost sunshine and shadow were the only inhabitants that varied the scene, over that tumultuous and varied city, as if it had found its proper nursery.

Cynthia is reported to have been at her marriage a 'city girl' who did not know how to milk a cow properly. There is this much truth in Thoreau's romantic memory of Walden Pond, that, though no country child, he was early dedicated to the woods, lakes, and the companionship of nature. He was a town boy converted to the wild.

He was a dreamy child, who 'hated games, street parades and shows' and 'company in the house'; liked rather to sit on Sundays in the 'Gothic' window of the Shattuck house in Concord watching the hawks circle in the sky.[1] He was nicknamed 'the Judge' by Samuel Hoar because of his gravity, and the boys listened to him while he sat on the fence and talked. The Lyceum movement, of which more later, reached Concord by 1829, and he was a member at or soon after the permissible age of twelve, hearing the debates there on alternate weeks. He may have heard Emerson lecture there in 1835, for ten years later one of his own boy students, Edmund Sewall, was taken to hear the philosopher and reported in a letter home: 'It was on literature. I was not at all interested.'

An academy, where Latin, Greek, and French could be studied, had been opened in Concord about 1820, and there he fitted for Harvard. Music and dancing were also both taught in this Puritan town. Probably his brother John, or his sister Helen, who gave music lessons, helped him with his first pipes on the flute, which afterward he loved so much; but dancing he was regularly taught; and dance he did in later life, but without a partner and as an outlet for exuberant emotion. A friend of Sophia's visiting saw him dance about the sitting-room and jump over the table.² If he went to parties in early youth he must have been unhappy, for he hated them afterward. He could see the point of looking at a pretty girl, as he once remarked in his Journal, but not of talking to one just because she was pretty.

2

There is nothing here to indicate any singularity in this youth-time of an eccentric genius, unless that it was spent in the moralized, self-confident atmosphere of Concord, where nevertheless boys and girls skated, frolicked, and were frivolous. The young Thoreau shows no originality, no distinction, and no perversity. Only his dreams were unusual, as that recurrent dream of Rough and Smooth in which all existence was satisfaction or dissatisfaction, and which symbolized, as he says very truly, all his later waking life.³

Nor does his first recorded essay, 'The Seasons,' written when he was ten, prove anything except that here was another New England boy with an orderly mind, a vocabulary, a liking for nature, and a willingness to write. Indeed, it is only what might be called the extra-curricular that is interesting in Thoreau's boyhood. His Journal is full of nostalgic reference to his happiness in the woods and fields and along the river: 'I think that no experience which I have to-day comes up to, or is comparable with, the experiences of my boyhood. . . . My life was ecstasy.' ⁴ The canal boat memories of 'A Week' give part of the picture:

> The news spread like wildfire among us youths, when formerly, once in a year or two, one of these boats came up the

Concord River, and was seen stealing mysteriously through the meadows and past the village.... We admired unweariedly how their vessel would float, like a huge chip, sustaining so many casks of lime... and that, when we stepped on it, it did not yield to the pressure of our feet. It gave us confidence in the prevalence of the law of buoyancy, and we imagined to what infinite uses it might be put. The men appeared to lead a kind of life on it, and it was whispered that they slept aboard. Some affirmed that it carried sail, and that such winds blew here as filled the sails of vessels on the ocean; which again others much doubted. They had been seen to sail across our Fair Haven Bay by lucky fishers who were out, but unfortunately others were not there to see.[5]

Such a childhood discovery of commerce might have happened on the Norfolk Broads or the Marne. What Concord with its still wild woods, and its wide, unpeopled stretches of water meadows and swamps had especially to offer to the village boy was the hunting life of the Indian who preceded him. At ten or twelve Thoreau shouldered a gun and was off with his older brother John; and a fishing pole must have been in his hands much earlier. There were muskrats and duck on the river, shore birds in the meadows, rabbits, hares, partridges, and 'tantivies' of wild pigeons in the woods. The boy had no realized nature worship in these early years, but only the hearty, primitive pleasure of the chase, his senses half-consciously registering beauty.

The family were amateur naturalists, but not Henry, yet. Sophia was the family botanist. It was John, as has been said, who kept the elaborate classification of birds in the notebook now in the possession of Mr. W. T. H. Howe. The 'former lord' of birds, Henry called him in a poem written after his death. Later, this notebook came into Henry's possession, but his entries are few. Before he became a naturalist, he had to pass through the Transcendental passion, half spiritual, half

romantic, which he caught from Emerson's 'Nature.' As a boy
he was a hunter who later called a gun the perfect tool:

> There are few tools to be compared with a gun for efficiency
> and compactness.... I have seen the time when I could carry
> a gun all day on a journey, and not feel it to be heavy though I
> did not use it once. In the country a boy's love is likely to be
> divided between a gun and a watch; but the more active and
> manly choose the gun.[6]

And also a fisherman whose object was to catch fish, not to
study them:

> I remember that once some 15 years ago, when I was a
> spearer myself — I was out with my brother with a home-
> made spear of boar tusks, & a crate made of an old tin pan with
> a hole punched in the bottom to hold our fire. It was a dark
> still night very fit for our purposes — and we had just fairly
> commenced operations & speared a few fish, when suddenly
> the imperfect fastenings of the crate was burnt away & down
> it plunged with all its fiery contents & a loud sizzling sound to
> the bottom of the meadow where I discovered its rusty outlines
> the next summer, leaving us astonished in total darkness. But
> we improved the opportunity to play a trick on some other
> spearers whose light oarsmen stole up the stream with muffled
> paddles till we lay directly opposite to them only 4 or 5 rods
> distant — and watched all their motions and the expressions
> of their faces as revealed by their fire, while they were intently
> engaged in spearing. They were familiar acquaintances &
> neighbors of whom we thus had advantage — did not dream
> of the neighborhood of other mortals — .[7]

Henry became a naturalist who went far beyond them all,
giving up rod and gun for notebook and spy glass. But this
was not until his first youth was past and even then he left
with reluctance the hunter's and the fisher's joys. He learned
to hate killing, and to distrust the eating of meat; yet in a preliminary manuscript of his defense of vegetarianism, in 'Walden,'
he wrote a faint postscript: 'But practically I am only half-

converted by my own arguments for I still fish.[8] The legend
of the boy naturalist must be dismissed. It is doubtful whether
he knew the names of any but the commonest flowers and birds
before his early thirties. His mind was busy elsewhere.

This vigorous, happy life of the hunter was Thoreau's life
as a youth. And it was this that he remembered with pleasure
and escaped to often, while he was breaking himself to scholarship at Harvard. 'The sough of the wind in the woods of
Concord' echoed in his mind when he should have been studying calculus.[9] And when he wrote to John of what had been
happening in Concord in 1837, it was in a poor imitation of
the language of Cooper's Indians: 'Tahatawan, Sachimaussan,
to his brother sachem.' This impulse to go wild, to hunt and
eat savage food, to take readily to the Indian way of life, was
so common among American youth who lived near free woods
and waters that we overlook its distinguishing traits in the
conditioning of the American temperament. For Thoreau, with
his extraordinarily sensitive imagination, the familiar experience
of village boys in their little wildernesses near at hand was so
intense as to mark him for life. He was a boy Indian, not a boy
naturalist in his youth. The Indian he sought in Maine and
later in the West was himself in his vagrant and uncomplicated
childhood and adolescence. And to this self he often reverted,
as in the half humorous passage in 'Walden':

> As I came home through the woods with my string of fish,
> trailing my pole, it being now quite dark, I caught a glimpse of
> a woodchuck stealing across my path, and felt a strange thrill
> of savage delight, and was strongly tempted to seize and devour
> him raw; not that I was hungry then, except for that wildness
> which he represented. Once or twice, however, while I lived at
> the pond, I found myself ranging the woods, like a half-starved
> hound, with a strange abandonment, seeking some kind of
> venison which I might devour, and no morsel could have been
> too savage for me.... I love the wild not less than the good....

> Perhaps I have owed to this employment [fishing] and to
> hunting, when quite young, my closest acquaintance with
> Nature.[10]

I am at some pains to give this picture of a healthy, outdoor
boyhood, normal in all its reactions, because so much of the
later history of Thoreau will have to do with curiously conflicting emotions in a personality not always free from morbidity.
He will prove a neurotic in love, a rebel in social contacts, and
a thwarted genius. But something kept him sane, as sane as
and more realistic than Emerson; something kept alive in him
the capacity for happiness; something made possible the humor
of 'Walden' and the loving enthusiasm of the 'Excursions.' I
believe that the influence and the memories of the green fields
of his youth, and the simple affections of his family circle, are
not to be neglected here. Happiness — especially if it comes
early enough to be uncomplicated by too much thinking — has
a durable and recurrent quality.

And these happy experiences contributed to the gusto for
living which is so characteristic of his maturity. On August
28, 1841, he wrote in his Journal:

> My life hath been the poem I would have writ,
> But I could not both live and live to utter it.

This cryptic saying he explains in 'A Week on the Concord and
Merrimack Rivers,' in which it was later inserted:

> There is always a poem not printed on paper... stereotyped
> in the poet's life. It is *what he has become through his work*. Not
> how is the idea expressed... is the question, but how far it
> has obtained form and expression in the life of the artist.[11]

Thoreau was determined to *live*. If he could utter it, well and
good, but his life must be *the* poem. Something held him back
from following the literary fashions of his time, kept him original,
made him delay his utterance until he had touched bottom in

experience. I believe the wood, field, and river happiness of his youth, already discussed, was of the utmost importance here. There was something in his nostalgic memories which kept him busy with his life, a life absorbed, as we shall see, in learning every shade and classification of his boyhood environment. Through the complexities of the never-to-be-reconciled conflict between idealism and science he sought a harmony in which he believed because he had known it in simple essence. Every careful reader of the fourteen volumes of his Journal knows that Thoreau's youth was ever present in his imagination. There was good reason, for the conditioning processes of his boyhood are closely related both to his failures and to his success. As a satirist, as a prophet of values in living, as a rebel, this boy matured early; as a creative artist who proposed to make Concord the microcosm of truth in nature, including man, it may fairly be said that he never grew up.

4. HARVARD

Dᴀᴠɪᴅ Hᴇɴʀʏ Tʜᴏʀᴇᴀᴜ, as he was known then, wished it to be thought that he just squeezed into Harvard. 'I was fitted,' he wrote in 1847 for his class records, 'or rather made unfit for college at Concord Academy and elsewhere, mainly by myself, with the countenance of Phineas Allen, Preceptor. "One branch more," to use Mr. Quincy's words [Quincy was the Harvard president], "and you had been turned by entirely. You have barely got in." ' Could it have been of this remark that he was thinking later, when he spoke up from the corner of Emerson's study? Emerson was saying to a young admirer that they taught all branches of learning at Harvard. 'Yes, indeed,' said Thoreau, 'all the branches and none of the roots.' [1] He was conditioned, but as only six out of the eighty candidates passed all the branches when Edward Everett Hale came up for examination two years later, the hazard was probably not great. Once in, says Hale, three to four hours a day were all that a well-prepared boy could spend in preparation for the dead routine of classroom tests.[2] The 'roots' gave little concern in the Harvard of 1833–1837.

And so he was entered on September 1 of 1833, rooming

in Hollis,[3] eating at a commons table with four or five others for $1.35 a week, and going to chapel in a green homespun coat when black was required, not from perversity, like the dandy Charles Sumner, who had recently been disciplined for exceeding the required black and white, but because he had no other.[4]

Two biographical myths have been passed from book to book about his university career, first that Thoreau did not do well at Harvard, and second that he owed little or nothing to his Alma Mater. They should be dispelled, once for all.

It was so easy for an able boy to do well at Harvard that failure to take the highest rank was more likely to be an indication of broad interests than of remissness. Henry Thoreau, except after his illness in 1836, was always in what today would be called the honor group of the class, once, at least, in the first eight who were asked to take part in the 'exhibitions,' and at his graduation among the first twenty-four or so, who were required to speak. He was ill in the spring of his junior year, and home for a long while recovering from what was presumably the first spot on the lung of this member of a tubercular family. The mark book for his class, now in the Harvard Library, records as of May 28, 1836, that he had 'left college,' and when he did return in the autumn states that he was 'on probation.' In this senior year, President Quincy complained in a letter to Emerson that he had 'imbibed some notions concerning emulation and college rank, which had a natural tendency to diminish his zeal, if not his exertions.' He may have been talking; or perhaps it was the essay he wrote in '37 for Professor Channing on 'Barbarism and Civilization.' 'Education ... is far safer in the hands of Nature than of Art. ... Our Indian is more of a man than the inhabitant of a city. ... Learning is Art's creature, but it is not essential to the perfect man;

it cannot educate.' This was heresy in a college, especially in a college as lifeless as was the Harvard of 1837.

For Harvard was then in a somnolent period. If he had gone to Yale he might not have done so well by the classics, since his teachers, Professor Felton, 'a loud-laughing, gentle-minded' person who had 'mastered the whole classical literature of Greece,' [5] and Jones Very, the occasionally mad poet of Transcendentalism, were remarkable Grecians, but he would have earlier felt the stimulus of modern science which Agassiz was later to bring to Harvard. There were no great men at Harvard in Thoreau's day, although Edward Tyrrell Channing was a first-rate teacher of rhetoric, who made or marred more important writers than any other American professor, and Benjamin Pierce, the mathematician, was at least a distin-guished astronomer. Two less conspicuous members of Tho-reau's faculty were later to become celebrities, Professor Webster, the chemist, Harvard's most celebrated murderer, and Henry Wadsworth Longfellow. More of them later.

The curriculum, however, though a routine, was neither as narrow nor as rigid as might be supposed. To the inattentive student it offered only a discipline in mathematics, rhetoric, Latin, and Greek. The rest he could and did take lightly. But for the hard worker with an interested mind — and it is fair to assume that Thoreau was often so described — there was a great deal more. There were approaches toward science in lectures for the whole class (sometimes with experiments) in natural philosophy, chemistry, anatomy, mineralogy, and geology; and a textbook to be studied on natural history. Botany was op-tional. Under Professor Pierce, mathematics was carried into elementary physics and astronomy.[6] Thoreau did not take Professor Webster's chemistry as a regular course, although a letter from his classmate Peabody [7] suggests that he may have belonged to the Davy Club, where stinks and explosions were enthusiastically perpetrated. If he had known Webster well, we should have heard of it later, for Thoreau was always interested in rascals.

The evidence of his Journal, as well as the mark book of the class, shows that his education was chiefly linguistic, literary, and mathematical. His science, except for the stimulus of lectures, he got later from the Harvard library. Greek and Latin he mastered and read and translated afterward for pleasure, and perhaps for the profit of others, since his translation of 'Seven Against Thebes,' made on Staten Island, is said to have been used as a 'trot' in Greek courses. He knew French thoroughly, and some Spanish, Italian, and German. The Spanish must have been a smattering, but Italian and German really seem to have been studied, the latter carried on enthusiastically with Mrs. Sarah Ripley later in Concord, as well as with Orestes A. Brownson, to whom it served as a card of introduction.

In the spring of his senior year, he took the informal round table course in German, in which the young dandy, Longfellow, just back from Europe, translated ballads and talked of German literature.[8] It was Longfellow's first actual course, and may have proved too informal for the serious young man of Concord to whom German as the tongue of the philosophers already meant so much. At all events, he dropped it after a few meetings. He surely listened with the rest of the class to Longfellow's first lectures, two of which were devoted to the Anglo-Saxon and 'Northern' literatures, for one of his later commonplace books is stuffed with copies of Anglo-Saxon in translation. He may also have heard Longfellow discuss the Dante he mentions in the Journal, and unquestionably disapproved of his light kid gloves and wine-colored waistcoats. Here were two luminaries of the next period, though one waited long to shine, who were at the poles of American temperament; one genial and everyone's friend, a gilded youth, the other still locked in Puritan inhibitions. Longfellow spoke of Thoreau as one of the philosophers when they met again in 1848!

But there was a joker in this not unattractive college curricu-lum. The subjects regarded as important, such as rhetoric, the classics, and mathematics, were weighted when it came to marks. It was an academic device not unfamiliar today. Full credit for modern languages was less than for the classics. Channing's essays counted on a scale of 48 against 8 for ordinary recitations. Those who chose to broaden their curriculum had to pay, by lower final marks or much harder work, for not being orthodox.

Now, Thoreau was on a scholarship for needy students. He was expected to do brilliantly and so secure a livelihood. But he was also a congenital reader who must often have exceeded Hale's two or three hours a day in the library. If he did not graduate on the higher pinnacles it was because of ill health and absence, but also because he would not sacrifice his intel-lectual interest for high marks. It is incredible that a man who read as much Greek and Latin for pleasure immediately after graduating should have done anything but well in those sub-jects. And, indeed, the class mark book shows that, except for illness and absence, his record, except in English Composition, would have been toward the top of the class. But not at the top. He was too original to be a teacher's pet.

2

There is a pen picture of Thoreau while at Harvard which could hardly be bettered. One of his classmates, John Weiss, was the grandson of a German Jew of Germantown, Pennsyl-vania, and probably himself a little uncomfortable in the

Harvard Zion. He had a beard and burning eyes. Later he
made a reputation as a Unitarian minister and an outspoken
antagonist of slavery, was a wit, an explosive intellect, and a
man untouched by conventions. When, years later, in *The
Christian Examiner* of July, 1865, he reviewed the four published
books of his dead friend, with a classmate's 'late but ever-
deepening regard,' he began his criticism with reminiscences.
Some of his sentences have often been quoted, but not the most
significant passages:

> He would smile to overhear that word [career] applied to
> the reserve and unaptness of his college life. He was not
> signalized by a plentiful distribution of the parts and honors
> which fall to the successful student. The writer remembers that
> a speech which was made at a highly inflammatory meeting
> in Dr. Beck's recitation room, during the Christopher Dunkin
> Rebellion, claimed, in allusion to Dunkin's arbitrary marking,
> that 'our offense was *rank*.' It certainly was not Thoreau's
> offense; and many of the rest of us shared, in this respect, his
> blamelessness. We could sympathize with his tranquil indiffer-
> ence to college honors, but we did not suspect the fine genius
> that was developing under that impassive demeanor. Of his
> private tastes there is little of consequence to recall, excepting
> that he was devoted to the old English literature, and had a
> good many volumes of the poetry from Gower and Chaucer
> down through the era of Elizabeth. In this mine he worked
> with a quiet enthusiasm, diverting to it hours that should
> have sparkled with emulation in the divisions where other
> genius stood that never lived, like his, to ripen. For this was
> the class of C. S. Wheeler, of Hildreth, Hayward, Eustis; schol-
> ars and poets all, to whom the sky stretched a too eager di-
> ploma....
> But he passed for nothing, it is suspected, with most of us;
> for he was cold and unimpressible. The touch of his hand was
> moist and indifferent, as if he had taken up something when he
> saw your hand coming, and caught your grasp upon it. How
> the prominent, gray-blue eyes seemed to rove down the path,

just in advance of his feet, as his grave Indian stride carried him down to University Hall! This down-looking habit was Chaucer's also, who walked as if a great deal of surmising went on between the earth and him....

He did not care for people; his classmates seemed very remote. This reverie hung always about him, and not so loosely as the odd garments which the pious household care furnished. Thought had not yet awakened his countenance; it was serene, but rather dull, rather plodding. The lips were not yet firm; there was almost a look of smug satisfaction lurking round their corners. It is plain now that he was preparing to hold his future views with great setness, and personal appreciation of their importance. The nose was prominent, but its curve fell forward without firmness over the upper lip; and we remember him as looking very much like some Egyptian sculptures of faces, large-featured, but brooding, immobile, fixed in a mystic egotism. Yet his eyes were sometimes searching, as if he had dropped, or expected to find, something. It was the look of Nature's own child learning to detect her wayside secrets; and those eyes have stocked his books with subtle traits of animate and inanimate creation which had escaped less patient observers. For he saw more upon the ground than anybody suspected to be there.... In fact, his eyes seldom left the ground, even in his most earnest conversation with you, if you can call earnest a tone and manner that was very confident, as of an opinion that had formed from granitic sediment, but also very level and unflushed with feeling. The Sphinx might have become passionate and exalted as soon....

Now, it is no wonder that he kept himself aloof from us in college; for he was already living on some Walden Pond, where he had run up a temporary shanty in the depths of his reserve. He built it better afterwards, but no nearer to men. Did anybody ever tempt him down to Snow's, with the offer of an unlimited molluscous entertainment? The naturalist was not yet enough awakened to lead him to ruin a midnight stomach for the sake of the constitution of an oyster. Who ever saw him sailing out of Willard's long entry upon that airy smack which students not intended for the pulpit launched from port-wine sangarees? We are confident that he never discovered the

back-parlor aperture through which our finite thirst com-
municated with its spiritual source. So that his observing faculty
must, after all, be charged with limitations.... But Thoreau
was always indisposed to call at the ordinary places for his
spiritual refreshment; and he went farther than most persons
when apparently he did not go so far....

But he had no animal spirits for our sport or mischief. We
cannot recollect what became of him during the scenes of the
Dunkin Rebellion. He must have slipped off into some 'cool
retreat or mossy cell.' ... However this may be, Thoreau disappeared while our young absurdity held its orgies, stripping
shutters from the lower windows of the buildings, dismantling
recitation rooms, greeting tutors and professors with a frenzied
and groundless indignation which we symbolized by kindling
the spoils of sacked premises upon the steps. It probably occurred to him that fools might rush in where angels were not in
the habit of going. We recollect that he declined to accompany
several fools of this description, who rushed late, all in a fine
condition of contempt, with Corybantic gestures, into morning
prayers, — a college exercise which we are confident was never
attended by the angels.

Weiss's memory served him well. Thoreau was 'plodding'
through his early college years because his mind was still merely
romantic and conventional. He seemed to plod to the end of
his college course because he was reserved and ill at ease. He
had the superior smugness of the bright boy from a small town,
and his humor was dulled in an environment where the professors took their learning too seriously for him, and the Lowells
and Hales and Longfellows, and others of the privileged classes,
did not take life seriously enough for his moral tastes. Weiss
and those who knew him young read into his later books a lack
of the 'emotional affections' which belied him utterly. They
remembered his fishy handclasp and downcast eyes. When
Emerson began to talk of him as '*the* man' [9] of Concord, there
was surprise and incredulity.

3

What his contemporaries really meant when they said he did not distinguish himself at Harvard was what Americans always mean when they write of college careers. He was not known. Harvard in 1833–1837 was often called a 'seminary' by its president, but in no way resembled one. It was socially stratified, inclined to despise what the faculty regarded as intellectual endeavor, and not unfamiliar with riotous living. Commencement evening was a drunken festival. There were social sets and literary sets, to none of which Thoreau belonged. Alpha Delta Phi was founded in his day, and a group from this very secret society conducted the *Harvardiana*, to which he did not contribute. Athletics were non-existent, but the rule already held, if you were not pre-known (like the Lowells and Hales) when you came to Harvard, you must compete, *do* something, or remain in obscurity. Perhaps Thoreau chose obscurity; in any case it would have been thrust upon him. He was never a go-getter. This later protestant *à outrance* took no part in the student rebellions of his day. His own friends, with one exception, were inconspicuous. Lowell was a year behind him; Dana, back from two years before the mast, entered his class. William W. Story, the sculptor, was in '38; Horatio Hale, who began his study of Indian languages with Penobscot Indians in the Yard itself, was in '37. Theodore Parker was in the Divinity School. Charles Hayward of Thoreau's class (who died young) wrote a tragedy which was put on at the Tremont Theatre, and was the class hope in literature. Only Charles Stearns Davis, a scholar of brilliant promise and one of the *Harvardiana* group, was his friend among the well known in Harvard in his day. With him Thoreau went camping, and it was with Davis in his freshman year that he walked home to Concord, the last two miles in his stocking feet.

And yet he was no recluse. He had two room-mates in successive years. When he wrote or was written to of his life at
Harvard, there is nothing to suggest a morose individualism.
He was just a poor boy who remained obscure. His deep and
rich personality made no impression upon the Harvard world
because it was still unsealed, and Harvard gave no opportunity to release it. Literary promise was in high estimation,
but Thoreau was not yet literary, except for experiments in
conventional poetry; his talents were for scholarship.[10] 'He was
not known to have any literary tastes' in college, said his classmate David Greene Haskins years afterward.[11] When Professor
Channing asked him to discourse on 'The Literary Life,' he
wrote an essay on the pleasures of scholarship! And even his
scholarship tended to wander from the orthodox into a seventeenth-century literature unknown to his fellow students and
probably to his professors.

Socially, Thoreau did not really leave Concord while he was
at Harvard. He was just a village boy away from home, and if
his reading excited him, his life in Cambridge was dull. He
meant himself when he said in 'Walden' that the really diligent
student in Cambridge College 'is as solitary as a dervis in the
desert.'[12] He was lonely, but not in an unhappy sense. Like
most men with a happy family life, it was no hardship for him
to be alone.

4

But the myth that Thoreau owed nothing to Harvard should
be exploded once for all. A friend of his mother's told Edward
Emerson that he said his Harvard education was not worth
the outlay in cost and sacrifices.[13] It cost very little, though the
family sacrifices were not inconsiderable. What with the scholarship rents he collected himself, as Emerson had done before him,

and his economies, the remark sounds a little ironical. In a
passage in 'Walden,' [14] he outlines a kind of progressive education which would have been worth while, and would have cost
even less, because the students would have practised mathematics, science, and economics in helping to support themselves in the college. They 'should not *play* life, or *study* it merely
. . . but earnestly *live* it.' This is as far as he got with a theory
of education now being widely experimented with. His own
college essays are as empty of first-hand human contact as a
stale sermon.

What he got, specifically, from Harvard was something very
different and quite indispensable. He was disciplined in the
exactness, the accuracy, and the care for meaning which is the
essence of scholarship. And, more important still, he learned
to use a library. The Harvard library became his library, and
was constantly used by him throughout his life. For this latter
service, our most erudite American author should have been
grateful. He got more out of the library than from the association with the 'most cultivated of his contemporaries,' for which,
as he says in the same 'Walden' passage, no charge was made.
He did not associate with them — for reasons stated — but the
Harvard library stands behind his books. It overpacked the
Journal and the 'Week' with reading, some of it pedantic; yet
it is difficult to conceive of 'Walden' without a background of
an easy familiarity with the world's best books. At least one
of Thoreau's advantages over that other eccentric genius of
Concord, Bronson Alcott, was that, like Emerson, he had frames
of reference acquired at Harvard.

Harvard made a scholar of him, but nearly ruined him as a
writer. It took him approximately ten years to put his Harvard
rhetoric behind him, and write steadily on his own. Six years
after graduation he was still conscious of something gone wrong
in his training, and desirous of saving others from his difficulties.

When Margaret Fuller's brother was at Harvard he wrote him
a letter of educational reminiscence:

> Dear Richard, — ... What I was learning in college was
> chiefly, I think, to express myself, and I see now, that... my
> teachers should have prescribed to me, 1st, sincerity; 2d,
> sincerity; 3d, sincerity. The old mythology is incomplete with-
> out a god or goddess of sincerity, on whose altars we might
> offer up all the products of our... studies.... This is the only
> panacea.

The thirty essays that Thoreau liked well enough to keep for
his family and himself from his fifty-odd college exercises are
very dull reading. They are sincere, but it is the wrong kind of
sincerity. He was given such topics, all ethical in trend, as
'Energy in Men,' 'Shall We Keep Journals?', 'Punishment,'
'The Simple Style,' 'The Superior and the Common Man,'
'Mankind Classified,' and 'The Morality of Lying,' and he
answered the implied questions out of the philosophy and ethics
which were being taught at Harvard. All of his essays are
comments on his study or his reading. Only rarely, and then
in his last two years, is there a sentence which anyone in the
class, or the faculty, might not, and would not, have written.
Never did a highly personal author put less of himself in his
early writing. In his letters, he is already humorous, allusive,
and whimsical, though a little heavy-handed, but these essays
read as if they came from a barrel and were going back.

They were not intended to express his personality, in which
the tough-minded Professor Channing would not have been in
the least interested. Edward Tyrrell Channing was, and is, a
figure in Harvard history. He had the handling of more really
distinguished writers than any other American. Emerson,
Thoreau, Lowell, Edward Everett Hale, Charles Sumner,
Oliver Wendell Holmes — what a list! 'This department was,
in my time,' said Thomas Wentworth Higginson of the class

of 1841, in his 'Cheerful Yesterdays,' 'by far the most potent
influence in determining college rank. ... Never in my life
have I had to meet such exacting criticism on anything written
as came from Professor Channing, and never have I had any
praise so encouraging as his.' [15] The trouble in Thoreau's case
was that the inoculation did not take. What Channing tried to
teach Thoreau, as is evident from the essays and the criticisms
occasionally written upon them, was how to think out any
proposition logically, and how to organize it in words; and this,
of course, should be the first purpose of every teacher of composition. With such topics as have been cited, the response was
almost automatic for a boy brought up in moralistic Concord
and disciplined in the ethics of Harvard of the thirties. He knew
what was expected as well as Channing did. All he had to do
was to organize his writing. This he did excellently well, and
the expounding, arguing, clarifying would have been very good
practice for anyone, except Thoreau.

Thoreau's mind was not made to work that way, was already
not working that way, as some inconsistencies in his essays,
and many passages in his letters, show. It was an intuitive mind,
passionate in its attempt to capture a great truth in a few words,
but impatient of logical sequences. To expound platitudes
might be good forensic, but was not sincerity — was not himself.
The man who would hope a few years later that he had sometimes been able to attain obscurity was the youth who was asked
to iron out conventional moral deficiencies into a creaseless
pattern. The further away Thoreau got from the logical organization of material, the better he wrote. The 'Week' has no
structure except a sequence of days and moods. Its feeblest
portions are the rather pedantic literary pages in which Thoreau
was still writing Harvard essays. The Journal is constantly
incoherent, even in its best pages. The 'Excursions' ramble.
So does 'Cape Cod.' The two famous protests, 'Civil Disobedi-

ence' and 'Life Without Principle,' would neither of them pass a strict examination on coherence and emphasis. If any man alive could have taught Thoreau to have a beginning, a middle, and an end, it was Channing, but he failed.

He failed because Thoreau's thinking was highly emotionalized, lay deep even in youth, and could be lifted to the light by no steam shovel and derrick methods. His ore was in pockets, and when it was blasted out lay untidily in chunks to be selected afterward and put in the exhibition case of a lecture or a book. Much of it was very rich, so rich that he spent his energies on the lumps, and let the sequence of the display take care of itself. Only in narrative did his imagination flow smoothly, and they did not teach narrative at Harvard. He would have been a more successful writer if he could have learned from Channing how to make a rhetoric for his own highly personal thoughts. Thoreau was right. He should have been taught sincerity first, rhetoric afterward.

So far his experience was typical of any original mind under academic discipline. The college quite rightly assumes that genius is exceptional and is seldom hurt by obeying the rules. Unfortunately, however, Channing was only too successful in encouraging a kind of didactic, moralistic exposition which was inherent in Thoreau, though not a part of his genius. From his college exercises, the youth acquired a habit, hard to escape, of wringing a moral from his themes. There is much of this in his early Journal, and even in the 1850's he has an occasional relapse.

And if Thoreau did not take as high a ranking in Harvard as his family expected, one reason was that Channing, whose marks counted so heavily, did not estimate very highly his powers of writing. Thoreau's rating was never low, except for an instance which from its dating was probably his attack on formal education. He did as well, usually, as his promising classmate Weiss. But in comparison with Channing's favorite, Horace Morison, his marks were mediocre indeed.[16] Morison, in Channing's eyes, was the real writer of the class of '37. In later life he published a book of children's stories called 'Pebbles from the Sea Shore'!

5

But that Thoreau's own mind was emancipating, finding itself, expressing itself, is evident in his essay of May 15, 1837, 'Conformity in Things Unessential,' in which he did *not* give the expected answer. 'Duty' consists 'in conformity to the dictates of an inward arbiter.' It 'is one and invariable.' 'So far ... as duty is concerned, we may entirely neglect the distinction of little things and great. Mere conformity to another's habits or customs is never, properly speaking, a duty. . . . The fear of displeasing the world ought not in the least to influence my actions. Were it otherwise, the principal avenue to Reform would be closed.'

That is Thoreau himself, trying to come through. And it is Thoreau the person, not the student, who wrote in his Commencement speech of August 16, 1837, on 'The Commercial Spirit':

> This curious world which we inhabit is more wonderful than it is convenient; more beautiful than it is useful; it is more to be admired and enjoyed than used. The order of things should be somewhat reversed; the seventh should be man's day of toil, wherein to earn his living by the sweat of his brow; and the other six his Sabbath of the affections and the soul, — in which to range this widespread garden, and drink in the soft influences and sublime revelations of Nature.

The ideas in this passage undoubtedly came from Emerson's 'Nature,' as Sanborn, who quotes it in 'Familiar Letters,' suggests; but the phrasing begins to be Thoreau, and the radical application of a one-day week to the problem of leisure is a first taste of that truth by exaggeration which was to become his favorite weapon. Yet, like so many of his hard sayings, it was not an exaggeration of his own experience. He learned later how to keep himself going on six weeks' gainful work for a year, which is not far from one day in seven! The rest of his Commencement Address is rhetoric; this is sincere.

Oliver Wendell Holmes, in the book already mentioned, calls Thoreau half college graduate and half Algonquin,[17] a witty but inaccurate description. Thoreau was never more than ten per cent Indian in his psychology, and in 1837 he was a good ninety per cent college graduate, his traits of Indian and nature lover driven far back in his mind by college disciplines and an inrush of new ideas. Whether he was yet 'twice born,' as Moncure Conway later was to say of him, not being able to account by his parents for his strange genius,[18] is doubtful. But that the process had begun is sure. A questioning mind had been aroused in a boy who had independence, a gift for words, a love of nature, and little more.

Yet in one sense Thoreau was all college graduate. He had assumed a responsibility. Nowadays a college degree is like a dress suit, which indicates only a certain social and a much more uncertain intellectual standing. A B.A. meant much more for the twenty-year-old Thoreau. It has been said that he thought so little of the degree that he would not pay the five dollars necessary in order to secure it. What truth there is in the yarn has been twisted. He was voted his degree on Commencement morning, which meant that all his college dues had been paid. But the President was authorized to collect a dollar or more from anyone who desired a diploma. Thoreau was poor and Scotch; probably he refused to pay for parchment. 'Let every sheep keep but his own skin, I say,' was his remark to Emerson apropos of diplomas,[19] which may account for the story. But with or without a diploma the Harvard graduate in the early nineteenth century was a man of whom much was expected, and indeed from whom much was realized. If not in church and state, why then in private life, it was demanded that he should manifest his education. Thoreau's account of his doings since graduation for the class record of 1847 was apologetic:

> Though bodily I have been a member of Harvard University, heart and soul I have been far away among the scenes of my boyhood. Those hours that should have been devoted to study, have been spent in scouring the woods and exploring the lakes and streams of my native village.

No apprenticing to carpenters was possible for a college B.A.; no elementary school teaching was enough, if too long continued; pencil-making was *infra dig*. He had been wandering aimlessly through the scenes of his boyhood, while acting as local handyman, caretaker of Emerson's house, and amateur student of nature, and this was all, except for his work on *The Dial*, that he could show by '47, and as much as Cambridge and Concord, Emerson's group excepted, could tell of this Harvard graduate.

It may be added that as a last gesture of his Harvard career, he cut Mr. Quincy's levee, and never appeared at his classmates' 'evening entertainments' — a drunken revel according to Edward Everett Hale. On August 7 Emerson made this Commencement memorable by the most famous of all Phi Beta Kappa addresses, 'The American Scholar,' an event more to Henry's taste. We may guess that he was there.

5. HARVARD INTERLUDE

It is impossible to make Thoreau's college life interesting, for it was not interesting. He had his passions and excitements, yes, but they were for books; there is no record of any other intensities, and no warrant for inventing them, except on the dubious hypothesis that a youth whose mind was in a tumult at age twenty-two or twenty-three must have been equally stirred at nineteen or twenty. Harvard made him a scholar, Harvard also made him bookish, which is not quite the same thing. Yet it is clear from his letters, and from the passages in his later Harvard essays already quoted, that the conventions which he had lived by were cracked and perhaps broken before he left. He read Emerson's 'Nature'; and he lived for six weeks or more with Orestes A. Brownson. The impact of 'Nature,' which set so many youthful brains bubbling in the thirties, is part of a strange and difficult relationship between two extraordinary men, to be discussed later. While he was at Harvard, Thoreau could have known Emerson only as a lecturer and Concord celebrity. Brownson was his first personal contact with the free world in which move the dynamic and liberated minds of the great and the near-great.

Poor students in Thoreau's Harvard days were allowed at least one leave of absence to teach school in order to earn a little money. Thoreau's turn came in December of 1835, in his junior year, when, at eighteen years of age, he kept school for seventy pupils in Canton, Massachusetts. The Reverend Orestes A. Brownson, whose children were in the school, examined and recommended him to the school board, and took him into his own home. At their first meeting 'the two sat up talking till midnight,' and then 'struck heartily to studying German, and getting all they could of the time together, like old friends.' [1] Now this was the plodding Thoreau, the indifferent Thoreau, who at Cambridge walked with downcast eyes, and made few friends! He is said to have kept school for six weeks, but the class mark book shows that he was absent and without record until March 19, the beginning of a new term, and absent again, probably from illness, until April 29. It was at the end of this May that he 'left college,' presumably fearing that he would never be able to return. A disastrous year scholastically, it was rich in experience, since he may have spent as much as three months in the stimulating society of Brownson.

Brownson was no cut-to-the-pattern country minister. If he is not a figure in American history it is only because his raging discontent took him from camp to camp until he sought the safety of the Roman Catholic Church, where historians have left him, forgetting his prophetic activities in the cause of labor and a socialized democracy. He was a big fellow, about thirty-two or thirty-three years old when Thoreau met him, aggressive, enthusiastic, dissatisfied with the world as he found it, and avid for new ideas and reform. He had come under the influence of the educational Utopians, Robert Owen and Frances Wright; he had already helped in the support of the Workingmen's Party; then, feeling that moral reform must accompany political reform, had entered the Unitarian church, and attempted unsuccessfully to bring about some unity of action. He was a leader in the movement to make religion a moral and social force, and in touch with Doctor Channing and other apostles of 'newness.' Later, he was to go to Brook Farm, and then establish *The Boston Quarterly Review*, which was the pre-*Dial* of Transcendentalism, and a pioneer in economic reform. A hard-hitter, a powerful writer, a social radical, here was a human specimen very different from Concord Abolitionists and Harvard professors. Young people, like the impressionable Hecker brothers, rose up and followed him as if he were a belligerent Christ.

Canton was only a pausing place for this energetic progressive, whose calibre can be judged from a review in his own quarterly [2] of Carlyle's 'Chartism,' which Bernard De Voto calls the first proletarian review. It is an onslaught in good, set Marxian terms, though Marx must have been to him unknown. Carlyle is a blusterer. The laboring class in England has always been bought off with beef. Education must be accompanied by shorter hours and better feeding, and only revolution and violence will shake the grip of the middle class upon economic privilege. This kind of talk would have set Harvard buzzing, and Brownson was quite as radical in 1836. At the moment he was studying German, as was Theodore Parker, because in German theology was to be found dynamite to blow life into the dormant New England churches.[3]

The influence of Brownson upon the later Thoreau was much greater than has been supposed. From him he may very well have derived his distrust of Abolitionism, and his belief that self-reform should lead to passive resistance rather than become a practical method of improving society, as reformers like the Reverend W. E. Channing believed. The two never again come into vital contact. Like Professor Channing's logical structure, Brownson's socialism did not inoculate a mind congenitally individualistic. But the intellectual shock of such a contact must have been reverberating. Here was protest with body and blood in it, very different from the moral fervor of Aunt Maria and the Wards directed against slaveholders who lived in a South of which they knew next to nothing. Here was passionate interest in a language and a literature not for marks, or for linguistics, but for what they contained immediately applicable to life. Here was a man who was 'reckless, ultra,' [4] whose imagination dealt with epochs and masses, yet eager to sit up to midnight talking with a boy. Something happened here which revealed Thoreau, the diffident, to himself, and prepared him for Emerson, a greater man with a more congenial background, who was also eager to talk to youth — the right kind of youth. Brownson invited him into the society of active minds where age and position are no factors. What he missed in Harvard, he seems to have compensated for in part at least in these weeks. After that visit, the still reticent boy must have known that he could make himself acceptable to the intellectually emancipated, even though he was not doing too well at Harvard. Here is the letter he wrote to Brownson in December of 1837. As it was a statement of his qualifications for a teaching job, it is inevitably formal, yet some of the importance of this experience breaks through:

> Concord, December 30th, 1837.
> Dear sir, — I have never ceased to look back with interest, not to say satisfaction, upon the short six weeks which I passed with you. They were an era in my life — the morning of a new *Lebenstag*. They are to me as a dream that is dreamt, but which returns from time to time in all its original freshness. Such a one as I would dream a second and a third time, and then tell before breakfast....
> My apology for this letter is to ask your assistance in obtaining employment. For, say what you will, this frostbitten 'forked

carrot' of a body must be fed and clothed after all. It is ungrateful, to say the least, to suffer this much abused case to fall into so dilapidated a condition that every northwester may luxuriate through its chinks and crevices, blasting the kindly affections it should shelter, when a few clouts will save it. Thank heaven, the toothache occurs often enough to remind me that I must be out patching the roof occasionally, and not be always keeping up a blaze upon the hearth within, with my German and metaphysical cat-sticks.

But my subject is not postponed *sine die*. I seek a situation as teacher of a small school, or assistant in a large one, or, what is more desirable, as private tutor in a gentleman's family.

Perhaps I should give some account of myself. I could make education a pleasant thing both to the teacher and the scholar. This discipline which we allow to be the end of life, should not be one thing in the schoolroom, and another in the street. We should seek to be fellow-students with the pupil, and we should learn of, as well as with him, if we would be most helpful to him. But I am not blind to the difficulties of the case; it supposes a degree of freedom, which rarely exists. [It hath not entered into the heart of man to conceive the full import of that word — Freedom — not a paltry republican freedom, with a *posse comitatus* at his heels to administer it in doses as to a sick child — but a freedom proportionate to the dignity of his nature — a freedom that shall make him feel that he is a man among men, and responsible only to that reason of which he is a particle, for his thoughts and his actions.]

I have ever been disposed to regard the cowhide as a non-conductor, — methinks that, unlike the electric wire, not a single spark of truth is ever transmitted through its agency to the slumbering intellect it would address. I mistake, it may teach a truth in physics, but never a truth in morals.

I shall be exceedingly grateful if you will take the trouble to inform me of any institution of the kind described that you may hear of. As referees I could mention Mr. Emerson, Mr. Hoar, and Dr. Ripley.

I have perused with pleasure the first number of the Boston Review. I like the spirit of independence which distinguishes it. It is high time that we knew where to look for the expression of *American* thoughts. It is vexatious not to know beforehand whether we shall find our account in the perusal of an article. But the doubt speedily vanishes when we can depend upon having the genuine conclusions of a single reflecting man.

Excuse this cold business letter. Please remember me to Mrs. Brownson, and don't forget to make mention to the children of the stern pedagogue that was.

Sincerely and truly yours,

HENRY D. THOREAU.

P.S. I add this postscript merely to ask if I wrote this formal epistle. It absolutely freezes my fingers.

Rev. O. A. Brownson, Chelsea, Mass.[5]

If Harvard educated Thoreau, it seems to have been Brownson who first made his education personal and alive.

6. 'WHAT ARE YOU DOING NOW?'

THE VISIBILITY IS better when, in August of 1837, Thoreau comes back to Concord to stay. He had been home at frequent intervals during his college course, and in the spring of 1836 was invalided there, yet, though in his affections he had never left his native village, his mind had been abroad. Even in the letters sent to his Harvard friends while he was recovering from his illness, he had played the undergraduate, with that affectation of humorous intellectuality which bookish boys assume when they get to college:

Concord, July 5, 1836.

Dear Vose: — You will probably recognize in the following dialogue a part which you yourself acted.

Act I. Scene 1st.

T. Come, Vose, let's hear from a fellow now and then.

V. We-ll, I certainly will, but you must write first.

T. No, confound you, — I shall have my hands full, and, moreover, shall have nothing to say; while you will have bonfires, gunpowder plots, and deviltry enough to back you.

Or to another classmate, Charles Wyatt Rice, written that August:

Methinks I see thee stretched at thy ease by the side of a fragrant rick, with mighty flagon in one hand, a cold slice in the other, and a most ravenous appetite to boot. So much for haying.

Then he breaks into rather pedantic doggerel. He is feeling 'bluey.' The doctor has forbidden him to dig for arrowheads or chop wood — but the facts in this letter are drowned in its preciosity.

I think that this pose of the Harvard intellectual was a protective covering for a mind in conflict and not self-assured, since he dropped it after graduation except in his family, where (like so many others) he enjoyed playing the erudite and inscrutable son. You can see them around the evening table puzzling out the high-flung allusions to Concord politics in that letter in Cooper Indian style which he wrote to John at Taunton on November 11 of this year: 'The hearts of the Leevites are gladdened; the young Peacock has returned to his lodge at Naushawtuck.' He liked to show off and they enjoyed it, kept his pseudo-literary effusions, and probably read them to their friends. The two Wards, who were boarding at the Thoreaus, were much impressed by the brilliance of the Thoreau boys, and speak of them in their letters always with great respect. And Thoreau was not only precious when he came back from Harvard, he was argumentative and aggressive. Helen, the other real intellectual of the family, was troubled by a spirit in her gentle brother that she did not understand. She apologized for him when he aired his 'sacred opinions,' probably to shock the aunts. This, said the young bachelor of arts in a letter to which reference has already been made, was a 'gross injustice.' 'You know we have hardly done our own deeds, thought our own thoughts, or lived our own lives hitherto.' [1] And so with an editorial 'we' he asserts his dignity.

He was twenty, shortish, rugged of feature, but not homely, with fine eyes, and a finely cut mouth and pursed lips, fronted by a long, drooping nose over a slightly receding chin. Hands and feet were noticeably small. Some say his arms were short, some, his legs. From Ricketson's later caricature, it would appear that it was his arms that were short. Short or long, his legs pushed him ruthlessly through the brush regardless of those left behind, and must have seemed long to his companions. There seems to have been some disproportion in his figure which led all observers to speak of his height as below the Concord norm. Howells later called him a stumpish man. If we can trust a self-reference, he was five feet, seven inches.[2] It was his eyes and brow which, even as a youth, gave him distinction. They certainly were not yet the terrible eyes Emerson described in his funeral oration, but they must already have been piercing, like Emerson's own. Though he seldom looked at his friends when he talked, yet he was not morose, could laugh and heartily. He liked to ruffle his feathers and speak past the company.

The truth was, of course, that he had come home from college as obscure as he went, and with a mind upset by conflicting compensatory ambitions. He wanted to be a poet (to live like a poet even more than to write poetry) and will write Carlylese on the nature and functions of the poet hero for some years. 'Sartor Resartus,' which he had read while in college, had puffed his mind full of vague self-confidences. He passionately desired to have his own life and think his own thoughts. Emerson's 'Nature' had given him the ideal of spiritual individualism. 'My desire is to know *what* I have lived, that I may know *how* to live henceforth,' he set down in his November of 1837 Journal, like a moralizing schoolboy.

This Journal began with a question: ' "What are you doing now?" he asked. "Do you keep a journal?" ' His reply to Emerson, for the solicitous Emerson was quite certainly the questioner,[3] was to begin one; and his final answer, at death, might have been, 'I kept a journal.' But in 1837 the immediate difficulty could not be so simply answered. What was he to do?

2

The brief history of Thoreau's career as a teacher in Concord was no reply to the question, which was not to be answered by anything so relatively simple as the choice of a profession or the making of an income. He was clearly a youth for whom doing meant the attaining of spiritual and intellectual satisfaction. But in Concord, and in America generally, there was wide freedom to do anything anywhere except in the arts, letters, or other unprofitable pursuits where such satisfactions could be obtained. When he asked his mother, probably sometime in his senior year, what profession he should choose and she replied, 'You can buckle on your knapsack, and roam abroad to seek your fortune,' he had no answer ready. 'The tears came in his eyes and rolled down his cheeks. . . .' His sister Helen put her arm around him and kissed him, saying, 'No, Henry, you shall not go: you shall stay at home and live with us.' 4 Tears — and Thoreau! This of course was the age of Dickens when men wept easily — but not in Concord.

I think the story has been misunderstood. It was a little late to be homesick, but just the time for that sense of weakness and incapacity which all sensitive youngsters feel when they begin to compare what they want with what they can or are supposed to do. The idea that he must set off again from Concord with his problems all unsolved was too upsetting for an emotional nature, already, as we shall see, aroused and distraught. Must he leave home to work for Admetus while the Apollo in his imagination dies unborn? He said just this, without tears, to Lucy Brown a few years later when he thought he had learned to love his fate 'to the very core and rind': 'I am as unfit for any practical purpose — I mean for the furtherance of the world's ends — as gossamer for ship-timber; and I, who am going to be a pencil-maker tomorrow, can sympathize with God Apollo, who served King Admetus for a while on earth. . . . I shall hold the nobler part at least out of the service.' [5]

Like many another uncertain American youth, he began to teach school. In the September after his graduation, he took the 'town school' — that is, the public elementary school for children, 'announcing that he should not flog, but would talk morals as a punishment instead.' As he said to Brownson, he did not trust the cowhide. After a fortnight, a deacon, one of the school committee, 'walked in and told Mr. Thoreau that he must flog and use the ferule, or the school would spoil. So he did, — feruling six of his pupils after school, one of whom was the maid-servant in his own house' [6] — and resigned, telling the committee to keep the school themselves, for he would not accept interference. This naturally caused talk in the town.

Edward Emerson knew one of the pupils in later life, who still bore a grudge against Thoreau for his unjustified and inexplicable punishment.[7] He had cause to be unforgiving, since he was sacrificed to a principle. Thoreau had presumably intended to repeat the experiment of Alcott in his famous Temple School in Boston, just closed after four years, in which 'the spirit of love, the reverence for childhood, the ideal of the home,' [8] were the bases of discipline. When things went wrong, Alcott used to punish himself. The feruling of the six, however, was Thoreau's own idea. Since physical punishment has no relation to educational progress, let it be applied, if the deacon insists, to good and poor students alike, and so show up its futility, and also the deacon. All cry, and for one reason only, they are hurt! Concord was accustomed to eccentrics, but here was an independence made somewhat offensive by its mixture of contempt. In Harvard, he may have talked and written about rank and emulation, but this was a deed!

A deed, moreover, which left him dependent upon pencil-making, or another job in teaching. He seems to have preferred the latter, for in the autumn of '37 and '38 he tried to get a school in Maine, hoped for one in Virginia, and in April of 1838 had made up his mind to go west with John to Louisville unless they could get a school nearer.[9] Finally, in June of '38 he opened a private school in the Parkman house, where the Concord library now stands, and was asking John to join him. By September they were teaching together in the Academy, which had been closed since Phineas Allen, Thoreau's 'Preceptor,' had left. Some at least of the out-of-town boys boarded with Mrs. Thoreau. The first families of Concord, who, like the first families of Boston, distrusted public schools, sent their little boys, and soon there were twenty-five children, a waiting list, and relative prosperity for the brothers.

John was the executive and it was he, apparently, who inspired confidence. Henry took the classical courses, and higher mathematics. This time no one asked them to flog. John was charming with small children. He took part in their sports, talked to them like an affectionate big brother, wrote them letters, 'so much from one who loves little boys but not *brats*.'[10] The discipline was excellent, the school life so happy that moral lectures were not much needed for punishment, and the children learned surprisingly fast. School was opened each morning by one of the brothers with a talk transcending the daily lessons. Once a week there was what we would call nature study — trips on the river, searchings for arrowheads, birds, and flowers, with comments on natural history and the life of the Indians who had been children there before them. There was even a little amateur surveying. It was, indeed, a successful progressive school, much like the present-day *écoles foyers* of Switzerland, where they still cherish the doctrines of Pestalozzi.

Writing to John in July of '38, Henry says that he is in school from eight to twelve, and two to four. Afterward he reads English or Greek, strolls in the fields, and begins to study birds. By the autumn he is giving his older sister advice in 'the style pedagogical,' on how to teach Latin and mental philosophy — though with his tongue in his cheek. 'The fact is, mental philosophy is very like Poverty, which, you know, begins at home; and indeed, when it goes abroad, it is poverty itself.' Self-knowledge is better — but she might try Abercrombie's textbook! In February, he writes her in Latin. There is nothing to indicate that this school was not a happy compromise while he was musing upon his ambitions, except that he never mentions it but once, and then indirectly, in his Journal, and was too ready to give it up.

In early 1841, John's health began to fail, probably from the Thoreau taint of tuberculosis. He died the next year, but of an accident, by lockjaw. Henry also was not well, as his Journal shows. In February of '41, he was looking for land to buy.[11] In March, it was announced that the school would close in a few days, and it did, leaving the little Hosmers and Sewalls to look elsewhere for an education. But John and the school still have a part in this history. He was a youth of sweet and easy temperament, a little precious in his letters, like Henry in his college period, more than a little amorous, to judge from his advice to his friend Stearns not to kiss too indiscreetly: 'For my part I am exempt from all such temptations; as there is naught here save a few antiquated spinsters, or December virgins, if you will; and well may I sing, "What's this dull town to me? no girls are here."' One was to arrive in June of 1839, and it is questionable whether the amorous or the austere brother fell in love with her first.

It was neither ill health nor the difficulty of finding a colleague to carry on with which accounts for Thoreau's willingness to let a pleasant and successful means of livelihood slip through his fingers. The school had clearly not entered into his imagination, which was already leaping far ahead of elementary Latin and mathematics. His 'nobler part' he had kept out of this service, and even while he carried on the agreeable routine of the day with John, he was afire inwardly with 'newness' and the excitement of his friendship with Emerson. It was foolish from any common-sense view to give up financial independence and the respect of Concord, but respect for him now had wider meanings. By the end of his school career he had pushed beyond the horizons of the stiff little New England communities of Concord and Harvard. Life had become complex, including the family, the school, and Emerson's serene province. He dropped the school.

3

The distinction of all the Concord group — a distinction which Thoreau was soon to share — was the way in which their minds slid around every problem until they found its typical or universal aspects. It was this habit which made the more worldly Boston and Cambridge men — the Lowells, Holmeses, Longfellows — call them the philosophers. No one of them could so much as eat an apple without thinking of the relation of diet to morals. This was the preacher's habit, of course, but lifted out of the barrel where the clerical mind chased platitudes round and round. The Concord men had new ideas and tested everything by newness; that was the reason they welcomed youth and attracted youth. Thoreau had few new ideas, if any, but his mind was alive and his character responding. Yet he was reticent as to his own emotions, even in his Journal, for his brain was clogged with Harvard moralisms, inchoate poetry, and unclear ambitions. It needed a far more powerful influence than he had encountered to give him direction — and he found one in Emerson. But to draw him out, to make him speak what he was feeling, a woman was indispensable — not an aunt, sister, or mother, but one outside the family circle where, as he complained to Helen (punning was his vice), the 'long *family-arity*' had kept them fencing each other off with witty foils, and prevented them from probing their mutual natures.[12] This celibate and bachelor never opened his heart except to a woman. He found his first release in Lucy Brown.

At the aunts' house in the spring of 1837, where the Thoreaus were then living, a Mrs. Lucy Jackson Brown was boarding, a sweet-faced woman, whose husband, a business man, was in residence abroad, for a time at least as far away as Constantinople, while she at home brought up her young son and daughter. An older sister of Emerson's second wife, Lidian, and a sister of Doctor Jackson the pioneer anesthetician, she seems, like Lidian Emerson, to have had uncertain health, and was not happy. Thoreau is soon to write such letters to her as he never wrote to his family at any period — unaffected, emotional, self-revealing; but of their relationship in 1837 we have only two records. It was she who, talking of a lecture of Emerson's, was told by Helen that her brother Henry had like thoughts in his Journal. The Journal was produced from upstairs (journals were taken seriously in New England), the thoughts were read, Emerson told of the parallels, and Thoreau brought to see him. They probably had met before, for Thoreau had certainly heard him lecture in Concord or Boston,[13] and Mrs. Thoreau had used Emerson's influence in reinstating Thoreau in Harvard after his illness; but this was his introduction as a disciple. Within a year Emerson was speaking of him as '*the* man of Concord.' Since the Journal was begun in October of 1837,

Emerson was undoubtedly right in saying that their relationship began in that year.[14]

Lucy Brown was more than an intermediary in Thoreau's
youthful expansion; she was a principal. Her photograph
shows a lovely woman, slender, with a face finely modeled in
lines of intelligence, yet probably (she is looking down) charming when she smiled. In 1837, she was in her late thirties, lonely,
and an eager reader. She had been at the Thoreaus' before —
Emerson says she saw the young people there every day.[15]
Under her influence, Henry offered his first recorded tribute
to the power of sex. Those who know of Thoreau's life only
perfunctorily might add, and his last. They would be egre-
giously wrong. He owed very much to the influence of women;
it is true, he gave them little.

What he did was simple enough. He tied a straw around a
bunch of plucked violets and tossed them, with a poem, into
her window.

It was not a love poem. With young men like Thoreau, the
first impulse toward love usually comes from older women, but
they offer them their youthful problems, not their love. The
soul reveals its secrets to its first affinity. Henry's poem was
cryptic, which was a compliment, since it was an emotional
understanding that he longed for. A few years later this left-
handed love-making was to leave him disconsolate, but with
Lucy Brown he was safe. She was much older, therefore tolerant
of egoism; and she was lonely, and enjoyed a youth who would
bring his reading to her and listen to hers. Literary in her
tastes, she was not Transcendental, not even intellectual.
Emerson writes of the 'vivacity of her sympathies,' and calls her
'a person of uncommonly fine instincts — little cultivated.'
She was no more than a sister-in-law to him.[16]

With the violets went these stanzas:

SIC VITA

I am a parcel of vain strivings tied
     By a chance bond together,
Dangling this way and that, their links
     Were made so loose and wide,
                    Methinks,
     For milder weather.

The violets which stood for his vain strivings were encircled by
a wisp of straw which was

               The law
          By which I'm fixed.

What Mrs. Brown thought of the poem is not recorded. She
showed it to Emerson, who must have noticed that the boy had
been reading George Herbert, and probably said what he was
to say again and again later, that if Thoreau wished to be a
poet he must spend more labor on his poetry. Yet he must also
have felt the epigrammatic quality of the first two lines, for he
is to tell his friends for the next few years that Thoreau is an
oncoming poet of genius. 'Sic Vita' is prophetic of Thoreau's
future in letters, but not of the future Emerson then expected
for him. He is seldom to get further in poetry than a magnificent passage rich in intuition and heavy with charged words.
For endurance, he needed the freer motions of prose.

It is easy enough to see, however, what he is trying to tell
Lucy Brown, even though the pronouns are peculiar. His mind
is a parcel of vain strivings bound together by his circumstances,
and none of them have roots to grow from. That is, presumably,
what she thought of him — an ambitious boy, wishing to be
many things but too much bound by incapacity and circumstance to go through with any one of them. His ambitions wilt as
fast as they flower. But give him another year, and freedom, and
then his vain strivings will have strengthened his character, and

have made more virile the stock of talent in his mind. The boy she knows will droop. Not so with the man himself. In the meantime, she has nourished his confidences — that is why he gives her the poem.

'Sic Vita' went into *The Dial* in 1841. When he reprinted it in 'A Week on the Concord and Merrimack Rivers' he was better able to understand his youthful uncertainties. 'It is but thin soil where we stand,' he wrote by way of preface. 'We live on the outskirts' of 'a nature behind the ordinary.... Let us wait a little, and not purchase any clearing here.' So much for school teaching as a career to settle down in, and so much indeed for any of the careers traditionally open to a poor student who had been graduated from Harvard!

These parcels of vain strivings which sensitive youths, with a sense of power in them, hide under whatever pose or stoicism they are able to assume, are never untied without pain, confusion, and an appearance of failure. The longing to achieve is more emotional than reasonable. It is the custom to call such emotional problems a last phase of adolescence, and if a woman succeeds in making them articulate in the tortured youth, then we suspect a transient phase of sexual excitement. This useful psychology oversimplifies the case of Henry Thoreau. His problem of how to live was a life-long obsession.

What could he do in a community that would pay him only for work that his genius could not grow on? How could he earn enough to stay independent and alive, while learning how to live? Such egotistic questionings are not to be laughed at. All creative minds, and hundreds of thousands of minds that only wish to create, are downed by them again and again in youth. Mrs. Brown did not laugh at him. He talked to her of how to lift '*can't* to *can*, in practice and theory.' They had golden moments together when they thought 'grandly' and spoke with emphasis. He recalls them in a letter written to her in 1841:

What makes the value of your life at present? what dreams have you, and what realizations? You know there is a high table-land which not even the east wind reaches. Now can't we walk and chat upon its plane still, as if there were no lower latitudes? Surely our two destinies are topics interesting and grand enough for any occasion.

And in an earlier letter of the same year: 'If the fates allot you a serene hour, don't fail to communicate some of its serenity to your friend.'

The too literary tone of these letters does not hide the deep sympathy between the two. And this in turn stirred the beginnings of another insistent question, which was to be peculiarly Thoreau's. How shall a sensitive mind be sure of a friend — and is a friend a lover, and can a lover be a friend?

When questions like these became vital for Thoreau he fastened on them, refused easy answers, was still asking them, hurting himself and annoying his intimates, until in sight of his death. He stayed youthful, asking the unanswered questions of youth, and offering partial answers which were revised as often as stated. While others found wise or unwise compromises, this boy spent a lifetime untying his bundle of strivings, and was called Dolittle by his neighbors!

When the school closed in 1841, Henry was already planning how to solve the most immediate of his questions, which was how to do what he wanted. First of all, he must escape the routine of an unpalatable job. Escape would have been improbable without Emerson. It was Emerson who was instilling in the young people of the 1830's a courage to break through dead doctrines. To be a friend of Emerson's was to see plodding and respectable Concord in perspective. Strivings, even vain strivings, toward self-knowledge and self-expression then became as natural and sensible as pencil-making or teaching, and much more important. If Thoreau got sympathy from Mrs.

Brown, from Emerson he got confidence. But Emerson's young men, as Albee remarked years later,[17] all had trouble in choosing their careers. The gift of mingled discontent and hope he gave them did not mix easily with opportunity. Thoreau, thanks to Emerson, escaped from his dilemma of how to earn his living while learning how to live, but the problem of what to do with his genius he took on for life.

Not that it worried him too much in the first years out of college. There was, to begin with, not too much genius in evidence, though talent enough. And also, at first, he was busy with the schoolboys, whom he liked and got on well with, though he had the reputation of being a little stiff. 'Trainer Thoreau' they called him, a military title. Also he was still in that happy student stage when so long as you are learning anything you have the sense of progress. His first Journal is little more than a notebook of continued college reading. Later it becomes the heart of Thoreau, but in these years half of his real story must be picked up outside.

7. EMERSON

ALL THE CONCORD intellectuals kept diaries. Emerson's runs to ten volumes, and has not yet been published in its entirety. Alcott wrote millions of words and spent his old age in reading them over. Hawthorne set down his ideas for stories in the midst of careful narrative and character description. Ellery Channing began a nature journal, but his erratic mind flew off into literature, which was the only climate in which he breathed freely.

In this journalizing habit, the philosophers were no more singular than in the wearing of black clothes for formal occasions. Among the intellectually ambitious in New England, who were numbered certainly in the thousands, keeping a journal was a standard means of self-improvement. Professor Channing asked the young Thoreau to write an essay on the topic 'Of Keeping a private Journal, or Record of our Thoughts, Feelings, Studies and daily Experience, — containing abstracts of Books, and the Opinions we formed of them on first reading them.' Thoreau knew what Channing expected him to say. While keeping our scattered thoughts might be of little importance, to learn how to express them was essential. One

should settle 'accounts with his mind' every day. And that is
what Emerson and Alcott and soon Thoreau would be doing as
regularly as the storekeeper on the Mill Dam set down his sales
and purchases.

Self-improvement through knowledge in general and self-
knowledge in particular was the young Thoreau's first idea of a
journal. Pepys, who kept a journal because he wanted to,
might have answered that the way to settle accounts with your
mind was to write down everything you thought and did,
particularly the items decidedly not intended to improve your
morals. But this was not the New England conception at all.
These diarists, even the philosophers, were less concerned with
the motive power than with the baggage carried. There was a
naïve idea, which the young Thoreau swallowed whole and
never got rid of, that the more freightage of quotations and
abstracts from good books, and the more comment on what
people ought to think, the more self-improvement. Self-
expression for all of them, even Emerson, was the adequate
expression of what they thought they ought to think. Hence
these journals are frequently essays, but only occasionally human documents.

Emerson and Thoreau are both, on numerous occasions,
personal in their journals, but too often personal only as saints
are personal who record in their lives the worldly events which
led them toward salvation. Emerson's Journal is full of ideas
with the dew of intuition upon them, and of observations upon
men and events which illustrate those ideas. He is most Emerson
when lifting the personal toward universal truth.

We can only guess what the original of the early Journal,
which Thoreau began in October of 1837, may have been like.
The two little notebooks now in the Morgan library, which date
from his first two years out of college, contain only what time
had not already gleaned, as he says himself on the title-page,

by which he seems to mean that he copied for preservation only
what seemed worth while. These neatly written pages with
items carefully spaced are copies of what in his original Journal
seemed to him not temporal or trivial in value, but part of his
record of self-improvement. He kept nothing personal that
could not be adapted to a book or essay, and indexed his topics
for ready reference. Later, his Journal, still copied from notes
but no longer anthologized, became one of the most complete
records extant of the inner life of an individual, but in his early
twenties it would be a mistake to guess the whole youth from
what he regarded as successful paragraphs worth preserving.

He was by no means the consecrated prig that appears in
some of these early pages. You must approach this prickly,
reticent youth with some knowledge gained from his friends or
from his letters. That he liked some girls, or at least their souls,
that he was susceptible to the charming sympathy of older
women, and was often intensely happy, scarcely appears in the
record. Emerson wrote in *The Dial* of April, 1841: 'Now ... I
talk ... with a conscientious youth who is still under the do-
minion of his own wild thoughts, and not yet harnessed in the
team of society to drag with us all in the ruts of custom.' [1] The
description fits the Thoreau of '38, '39, and '40 exactly, but the
wild thoughts seem to have been refined out of his early Journal
as not conducive to self-improvement.

2

Two stirring transforming experiences came to Thoreau in
'38 and '39: he became a friend of Emerson and he fell in love
with Ellen Sewall. Yet in the Journal we have to fish for evidence of either. The powerful influence of Emerson, from whom
Thoreau got, it is safe to say, the fundamental ideas which gave
direction to his life, is everywhere evident, but seldom made

explicit. There is no direct comment upon Emerson the man until 1845, with only casual references before; yet the Great Fact of Existence, as Carlyle would have said, for Thoreau in his first years out of college was this friendship with Emerson. But if it is impossible to tell from the Journal of his formative years what he thought of Emerson, it is fortunately much easier to know exactly what Emerson thought of 'the boy,' as he called young Henry Thoreau. He writes about him often, and not infrequently transcribes what he writes in a less personal form for inclusion in his essays, where all was to be set down in aspects of eternity.

I wish I could subscribe to either of the common theories of this famous friendship, for the toil of describing it would then be much simpler. And it deserves minute describing, for it is surely one of the most interesting friendships of literary history, and loses nothing in piquancy by being triangular, with Emerson's wife, Lidian, as a factor of unsuspected importance. Unfortunately for brevity, it is not at all true, as Thoreau's contemporaries believed, that Thoreau was Emerson's man, picking up the windfalls of his intellectual orchard.[2] Nor is it true that Thoreau ever forsook the fixed principles of life and how to live it which he took from Emerson and interpreted according to his own genius. It was not the philosophy but the personality of Thoreau which rebelled against Emerson. Yet in the beginning, it is not Thoreau's part in this friendship which is hard to understand, but the enthusiasm of Emerson, the great man, the master.

When Thoreau came back from Harvard in 1837, Emerson was thirty-four years old, and at the height of his powers, though he had not yet reached out to his greatest influence. He was living now in the ample house which still bears his name, on the edge of the village, with grass, trees, and gardens around it and a brook behind. Its comfortable parlors were arranged

Ralph-Waldo Emerson
'The impression he made was not of a saint, his eyes were too piercing,
his mouth too humorous'
From a portrait in possession of Professor Townsend Scudder III

for both talk and seclusion. He had already written his testament for youth in 'Nature,' had challenged American provincialism in his 'The American Scholar,' was known as a poet, and, having made himself articulate, was deeply concerned with making equally articulate a young America that he believed could be made as intuitive, as idealistic, and as truth-loving as himself. Julian Hawthorne in his Memoirs describes him as misshapen and awkward, with a small head,[3] but other testimony is of a presence that disarmed criticism. The impression he made was not of a saint, his eyes were too piercing, his mouth too humorous, yet the many who came to see him and the friends he made on his lecture tours here and abroad unite, though sometimes grudgingly, in describing a quality which they too easily define as something godlike in the man. His Journal gives a more satisfying picture. It is distinguished by an eagerness to pursue everything of good report, a faith in and a hope for man, which does not rise upon the wings of abstraction into a nebulous enthusiasm, like Alcott's Orphic sayings, but is controlled by a sense of history, and warmed by affection. There can be no age barrier with a man like that. To be with him was to share his experience and be moved to pledge your own, for he had in a high degree that magnanimity which he somewhat generously attributed to Thoreau. Never was a great man so nearly (but not quite) devoid of egoism; never a born leader who so consistently identified his success with the success of the good will he inspired in those that heard him. And still young himself, his life was most of all in youth.

There were other aspects of Emerson not often noticed by those who approached him with reverential admiration, but well known to himself. He was a lonely soul who, though affectionate, found the expression of personal emotion difficult in the extreme. Spiritually he would give all that could be given in words and sympathy, but there was a grip upon his heart that he did not seem able to relax even with his much admired wife, Lidian, whom he married so as to have a com‹ panion in the home. He felt that he was cold; a psychologist today would say, I think, that in love, which gives and takes without movement of the mind, he was inhibited. He closed his eyes when he smiled, which may have been significant.

3

Henry Thoreau, after his Journal passages had given him an entrée to the Emerson home, must have been a reasonably frequent visitor, since the first reference to him in Emerson's Journal is warm and familiar in tone. On the evening of February 10, 1838, there was a meeting of Sunday School teachers, probably co-workers of Lidian's, at the Emersons'. Others came to these meetings and shared in a discussion which in that house was sure to have extensions toward the infinite. Edmund Hosmer, Emerson's farmer friend, was there that night, and also Henry Thoreau, who, having recently signed off from the church (as he said in 'A Week') and from every institution to which he did not belong, was presumably not interested in Sunday Schools as such. Hosmer had been saying that Christ was not to be differentiated from a human mind; but, frightened at his own audacity, flopped over to the other side of the argument and proclaimed him maker of the world and the Eternal God. 'Henry Thoreau,' Emerson wrote in his Journal, 'merely remarked that "Mr. Hosmer had kicked the pail over." I delight much in my young friend, who seems to have as free and erect a mind as any I have ever met.'

If Henry came to Sunday School meetings at Emerson's, it is certain that he was soon included in those far more significant conversations in which the hopeful intellectuals of Massachusetts's renaissance began to plan a new future for themselves and America. And indeed he is soon noted as a member of what was called, though not by themselves, the Transcendental Club. We hear too much of the cranks, the freaks, the latter-day saints who passed in and out of Emerson's door, although even the wildest reformers were more his kin than the respectable money-seekers of Concord. Thoreau was more likely to meet men and women who were not so much reformers as seekers like himself of a way of life. Every kind of idealist was attracted by Emerson, who was an apostle of a vitality in religious and moral and intellectual experience which should be as prepotent as the energetic materialism of the age. But his chosen kind were intellectuals like himself. What must have made his house a revelation to the young Thoreau were the fine minds, finely if somewhat vehemently moved, that he found there; and the free sweeping winds of interest which blew in from all over the world. Brownson had given him a whiff of intellectual freedom, but, except in economics, Brownson himself was a provincial in comparison with Emerson. Not only Greece and Rome, Dante and Goethe, were familiars in this home and its talk, but ideas from France, from England, most of all from Germany, which was just then in intellectual eruption. A few hundred yards of shaded streets, and Thoreau could pass from the price of pencils and the moralities of the Sunday sermon to a society that saw nothing absurd in trying to make a spiritual Athens of Concord, and of Boston minus State Street.

There was Margaret Fuller, often visiting in Concord, incredibly well read, emotional, voluble, versatile, with the woman's movement of the next half-century in her head. There was Alcott, whose talk spiralled into a Utopia that made sense in principle, even though obviously impossible. There was sometimes Theodore Parker, hammering his opponents with German scholarship, able to take the ideas this group discussed and use them to excite a multitude. There was George Ripley,

a born critic of literature, and Cranch and Very, Transcendental poets, and Brownson, who wanted to make Transcendentalism work for social justice, and Hedge the translator. There
was Sarah Alden Bradford, one of the best Greek scholars in
the country, and Elizabeth Peabody, the pioneer educator,
whose Boston bookstore was a focus for 'come-outers'; and one
could count on various Unitarian ministers, and rebel tutors
from Harvard. Emerson was not so much the head as the inspiration and balance wheel in this attempt to arouse the mind
of New England. Transcendentalism was only a nickname for
the conversation of these ardent and enlightened seekers, whose
first principle was freedom of thought so that the mind might
breathe fresh air. If not in '38, certainly by '39, Thoreau was
one of them, and the youngest. By 1840, his presence is promised as an inducement for Margaret Fuller to attend and inspire
the 'reptile wits' of 'the club of clubs.' [4] It was an extraordinary
adventure for a questing youth of twenty-two, still a provincial
of Concord, with Harvard pedantry in his head.

'Club' was a misnomer for this assemblage of seekers. This
group of young people (they were most of them in their late
twenties or early thirties) had really no common denominator
except that all of them were agreed that the days of Locke and
his limitation of knowledge to the perception of the senses were
ended (except in Harvard), and that the mind properly stirred
and lifted could go direct by intuition to the sources of absolute
truth. Even this is too specific, and Emerson's statement that
'they only agreed in having fallen upon Coleridge and Wordsworth and Goethe, then on Carlyle, with pleasure and sympathy' [5] is nearer the truth. Far from founding a cult, these
eager talkers were seeking only a release of the passionate truth
that each believed he found in his own mind. They were
propagandists, not doctrinaires, amateurs, most of them, in
everything but theology and morals, with a great man at the

center and amiable lunatics on the fringe. 'Mr. Alcott,' asked a squeaking Englishman, 'a lady near me desires to inquire whether omnipotence abnegates attribute?' [6]

It was not the morals and the metaphysics that interested the young Thoreau. Indeed, it is probable that Locke's principle of experiment through the senses, which he had learned at Harvard, survived with complete metaphysical inconsistency his conversion to truth by intuition, and produced that life-long conflict between science and Transcendentalism which made both his writing and his career so different from Emerson's.[7] Nevertheless, he accepted, with them, the principle of the validity of intuition, and this made it necessary to re-examine all that stirred in literature, art, music, and the depths of religion with a fresh interest like that of the physicist who, nearly a century later, was to find that the dull minerals in his collection were sources of radio-active energy. Indeed, these men and women who, like Henry Thoreau, passed in and out of Emerson's house or met together in somewhat too solemn assemblage, discussed not *a* new philosophy, for they were interested in *any* new philosophy; not *a* new literature, for they were interested in *any* new literature — as their organ *The Dial* explicitly stated but failed to realize. They were interested in 'newness,' in everything that quickened the mind, brought fresh blood to thinking. The sexual they neglected as completely as did the New England church, against whose grip upon convention they were protesting, although the more prophetic, of whom Henry Thoreau was one, foresaw that there was a newness here not yet grasped by the idealist imagination.

4

How familiar this is in the history of literature! A circle, a focus in some prepotent personality, an interest, a principle, and an influence often all out of proportion to the discussion from which it stems. The clash of lively minds is the seed bed of good writing; which grows, however, only in solitude.

This circle was as shifting as the curve of waves on the sands. Its foci were a Concord and a Boston that had suddenly become aware of culture on the march. It was intensely nationalistic, although the nation for all but Emerson and Alcott and Brownson was Massachusetts, not America, and the talk was all of how to vitalize provincial thinking and conventional emotions by ideas brought home to be absorbed in the blood and bones of what Margaret Fuller called 'dear New England.' No magazine ever published in this country has shown more awareness of Europe and European thinking than *The Dial*, which was the outcome of the search for expression of these disciples of newness; yet no American magazine has ever been more definitely focussed upon the needs, real or assumed, of its native land. And indeed, the first number of *The Dial* in 1840 — with its underscored ethics, its soaring idealistic optimism, its amateur art criticism, its professional theology, its slipshod poetry where the intuition outruns the form, and the impression made of a badly edited magazine in which the great and the would-be great and the merely enthusiastic all talk together — is a perfect representation of what must have happened when three or four of the devoted got together in Emerson's house, the young Thoreau silent, except for an apothegm now and then, in the background. Theodore Parker thought it a failure — naturally, for he was no amateur. Yet the best-edited magazines are seldom the most important. This one, which the so-called Symposium was really brought together to form, shows a rush of intellectual vitality, ranging from the naïve to the profound, which in 1840 was quite as important an American phenomenon as the much written-up conquest of the continent, then under way. Indeed, Henry Thoreau, who was inspired by *The Dial's* guiding spirit, Emerson, and found his voice in its pages, was soon to raise the questions, For what is the continent conquered? What are we to do with it worth the cost? — questions not yet answered.

We are not yet in *The Dial* years. But in '38 and '39 it was the society of minds which made *The Dial* into which young Henry, an apprentice school teacher, was rather surprisingly introduced. He might have made pencils, taught school, re-read the classics, and walked in the woods for a decade in Litchfield, Connecticut, or West Chester, Pennsylvania, without ever guessing that his time was explosive with such new thinking. It was in Emerson's house or in Emerson's company that he was really reborn from Concord and Harvard. Reborn and birthmarked, for from the tensity of these intellectual romantics he had to escape before he could do his best work. Margaret Fuller with a headache, Jones Very on the edge of an insane asylum, Brownson ploughing through the sects toward Roman Catholicism, Ellery Channing never off a high horse of preciosity, learned moralistic women, and Alcott saluting the stars — none of them exhaled the atmosphere in which a 'Walden' is made.

And from the eager and often naïve and still oftener shallow cosmopolitanism of this society he reacted also. Of all the more important devotees to the new ideas from abroad, only Emerson had seen Europe and European men, and of them all only Emerson and Margaret Fuller were to know anything really valid about their own country outside of New England and the transplanted New England in New York and Ohio. Thoreau's Journal shows that he broke through those timidities and ignorances which make the provincial unaware of the free movement of thought across world cultures. But it shows, also, that Henry never felt more stubbornly that he was a Concord boy with no manners than after a session with the Transcendentalists. And Emerson in an unpublished paragraph in his own Journal suggests the impression that this still rustic and painfully sincere youth must have made upon the assembled intellectuals: 'November 18, 1838. The manners of young men who are engaged heart and soul in uttering their Protest against society as they find it, are perchance disagreeable; their whole being seems rough and unmelodious; but have a little patience.' The reference is surely to Henry Thoreau.

5

What he had been given at the age of twenty to twenty-one was a great opportunity. But why? His college friends were surprised to find him an intimate of the intellectually great and near-great. He had shown no such adaptability at Harvard, had never shown it except in the brief friendship with Orestes A. Brownson. Many years later his classmate, David Greene Haskins, set down his own bewilderment in rather churlish language, from which one quotation has already been made. In 1838, when visiting Emerson, he found Thoreau already an intimate of the house. 'We could not do without him,' said Emerson. He was '*the* man of Concord,' and Carlyle must be (and was) told about him. Thoreau's short figure, said Haskins, was of course unchanged, but there had been a transformation. His familiar college voice had become so like Emerson's that with eyes closed it was difficult to tell which was speaking.[8] He was even 'getting up a nose like Emerson's.' [9]

This sounds as if Henry had been often enough with Emerson to fall into that unconscious imitation quite inevitable in a youth not yet formed. Even one visit with the great man had been known to make a life-long impression on the visitor; and even Haskins, when he left, found himself inclined to adopt Emerson's voice and manner of speaking. If Professor Chan-

ning had been a Barrett Wendell, Thoreau would probably
have come home from Harvard talking like *him*. His impres-
sionability is not hard to understand; but why was Emerson so
impressed, why was Carlyle to be told of this youth who had
written so far only some Journal and one poem ('Sic Vita')
which we know that Emerson had seen?

The easy and attractive answer that there was genius manifest in Thoreau at the age of twenty-one, will not hold water.
No one but Emerson — and possibly Helen and Sophia —
thought that Thoreau was even remarkable in 1838. There
was talent, and Emerson was the man to detect it, but talent
was in and out of Emerson's house all day long. It is quite
clear from various remarks in the older man's Journal and his
letters that he consciously assumed the rôle of protector and
(as we should say now) publicity man for a young and promising poet when he opened his house to Thoreau, backed *The Dial*
in order to give him (with others) an opportunity to publish,
and later took him into his home. 'My Henry Thoreau has
broke out into good poetry and better prose.' 'Henry Thoreau
... writes genuine poetry that rarest product of New England
wit.' [10] But he never thought that Thoreau was a great poet.
His article in *The Dial* for October, 1840, on 'New Poetry'
defines with perfect clarity the artless, intuitive, unpolished
verses which he calls 'portfolio' poetry, sincere utterances not
meant, and often not prepared, for print, and valued for
sincerity rather than art. Thoreau, and Channing, who was
the subject of that essay, were for him 'portfolio' poets, their
greatness, if any, still in the future. Later he was to advise
Henry to burn most of his youthful poetry, which he did and
regretted it.

No, it was not a crown of laurels which Emerson saw prophetically on Henry's head. There was a much sounder reason for
his sudden enthusiasm. When he greeted Whitman at the out-

set of a great career, he was later embarrassed by the blank
check given to the poet who was not then gray, and much too
good to his own reputation. He made no such statement of
unequivocal genius about Thoreau. This boy for him was the
free and erect mind close to nature he had been seeking in a
younger generation that would make a new America. He was
one of his own ideas — receptive and in the flesh. Thus began
their friendship — and their inevitable though distant alienation.

The reader interested in how human ties are made and
broken should read again that most seminal of all American
books, Emerson's 'Nature,' and see there how boldly, while
Thoreau was still a junior at Harvard, Emerson appeals to his
own times to give up their materialisms and redeem their souls
through nature. 'When a faithful thinker, resolute to detach
every object from personal relations and see it in the light of
thought, shall, at the same time, kindle science with the fire
of the holiest affections, then will God go forth anew into the
creation.' Thoreau, who had read the book by 1837, accepted
the challenge. He was ready to learn, as Emerson said in his
'Biographical Sketch,' that 'excellent wisdom . . . which showed
him the material world as a means and symbol.' Indeed, he
was to tell Moncure Conway later that 'he had found in Emerson a world where truths existed with the same perfection as the
objects he studied in external nature, his ideas real and exact
as antennae and stamina.' [11] And, furthermore, he was already
a youth who 'knew the country like a fox or a bird,' and fit, as
Emerson saw, to acquire the scientific skills which the philosopher believed should be kindled with holy affections.

Emerson envied this perceptive boy, for his own observations
were more profound than accurate. He seems never to have
noticed the common mountain laurel in Concord till Thoreau
showed it growing in his familiar woods. The young Thoreau

was a new eye and ear for him. He was more that that, for he seemed to be the very man to put into practice a new study of nature in its relation to man for which the scholar-idealist knew he had neither energy, inclination, nor time. He had, indeed, imagined a Thoreau before he met him, which is enough in itself to account for the warmth of his welcome. A remarkable passage in his Journal, not before noted in this connection, shows that while Henry was still a sophomore and unknown to Emerson except as the needy son of the worthy Cynthia Thoreau, the author of 'Nature' had laid down a set of specifications for a life task which reads like an account of the career of Henry Thoreau:

> If life were long enough, among my thousand and one works should be a book of nature whereof Howitt's *Seasons* should be not so much the model as the parody. It should contain the natural history of the woods around my shifting camp for every month in the year. It should tie their astronomy, botany, physiology, meteorology, picturesque, and poetry together. No bird, no bug, no bud, should be forgotten on his day and hour.[12]

It was Howitt's 'Seasons' that Thoreau used as a model for his first extensive nature writing five or six years later;[13] and there is no better description anywhere than in these last sentences of what he tried to do for Concord. What Emerson knew of the sciences mentioned he learned largely, though much later, from Henry. Was he clairvoyant? Or did he make Thoreau over into the image of his own imagining?

However that may prove to be, one needs only to read these lines in order to see how and why the young teacher and nature lover soon began to seem to Emerson *the* man in Concord, *the* man of all in the little village most likely to restore that contact with nature which, losing, men lost the strength of their intuitions and the vigor of their faith.

Thus, when Emerson said good-bye to the proud world and went home to Concord, where leafy and watery wildernesses came up almost to the village streets, he stated a problem, and found a youth to solve it. If we had only Emerson's comments on Thoreau as we have only the critical estimates remaining of certain Greek writers, we would never guess that the boy's most important book would prove to be more satire than natural history. We would suppose him to have been one of those 'portfolio' poets whose verses were native woodnotes wild scarcely reaching to art; and one whose function had been to guide his master to the symbols of material nature. Did Emerson become jealous of his disciple? No, he was too generous for that — yet, like all teachers, and he was one of the greatest, he loved best in his pupil the extensions of his own personality.

6

Here is the way their friendship ran in the first year or two:

February 17, 1838. My good Henry Thoreau made this else solitary afternoon sunny with his simplicity and clear perception. How comic is simplicity in this double-dealing, quacking world. Everything that boy says makes merry with society, though nothing can be graver than his meaning. I told him he should write out the history of his college life. . . .

On the twenty-fifth of April they walk to Emerson's favorite cliffs above the Sudbury River. Henry is frankly religious this time, which in a young man of his generation strikes Emerson with surprise, 'and has all the air and effect of genius.' Next, Emerson must have asked him what use he intended to make of his scholarship and is pleased to find the boy would rather raise melons and tramp the woods than join Emerson's intellectual friends in the forming of some new sect. By September, Thoreau is telling him Concord yarns. Emerson was enjoying the smut in Montaigne that year, and was ready to laugh at a good story. By October, he had begun to share Thoreau's secrets: 'Every day I am struck with new particulars of the antagonism between your habits of thought and action, and the divine law of your being.' ¹⁴ What was that divine law? Emerson seemed to know. In November, the youth begins to complain that he owns Walden woods as much as the proprietors, which was making very concrete what Ralph Waldo had stated as a principle in 'Nature.' Emerson, being a landholder himself, demurs, and advises Henry to work out of his system and into a poem 'this maggot of Freedom and Humanity in his brain.' Says Thoreau, how can he do this and remain sincere. The master, recognizing his own teaching, has to agree, but cannot have liked such ruthless logic.

Nevertheless, at that moment Emerson may have begun to see in his young friend the new man he hoped for, who would *live* in utter sincerity the doctrine he preached. Was he thinking of this when he said in that famous preface to *The Dial*: 'As we wish not to multiply books, but to report life, our resources are therefore not so much the pens of practised writers, as the discourse of the living, and the portfolios which friendship has opened up to us'?

They meet often. Emerson gives him new perceptions; Thoreau gives Emerson new eyes. The choice of a career, which is troubling the youth, seems to the older man illusion. That career is already self-determined. 'I have my own stern claims and perfect circle,' he says, apparently of Thoreau, in 'Self-Reliance,' which was the stoic's solution of how to pay for your board. Yet Thoreau was impressed by this somewhat Transcendental advice to take no thought for the morrow: '*May 1839*. My brave Henry here who is content to live now, and feels no shame in not studying any profession, for he does not postpone his life, but lives already.' Yes, and was about to fall in love, which shook for a while this stoicism. The walks continue, with Henry more and more the guide and nature man, and less and less the pupil-poet. And so the friendship proceeds, with a delicate perceptiveness on Emerson's part which must be credited to the greatness of his nature. 'If you have any leisure for the useful arts,' he writes, 'L. E. [Lidian] is very desirous of your aid. Do not come at any risk of the Fine.' [15]

I have touched but lightly upon the beginnings of this friendship between the spiritual aristocrat, a man of the greatest world, which is the world of the mind, and this stocky, stubborn, ill-clad village scholar, loved by no one so far except his family, promising little to the ordinary folks who knew him, and still less to the local great ones, Samuel Hoar and Doctor Ripley. All one can be sure of is that Emerson discerned in Thoreau a genius that was not awake until he touched it; that he felt an instant response of like-mindedness, and in his Olympian way overlooked the differences; that his magnanimity set about to create a poet, and found unexpectedly an interpreter as Transcendental as himself and far more sensitive to the realities of the American fields and woods, which were the visible face of that nature which he worshipped in spiritual form.

Years later, Henry repeated with amusement the Mill Dam story that Emerson had gone to the Adirondacks with a gun which threw shot from one end and a ball from the other. As a youth, he did not laugh at Emerson's ineptitudes in the forest, for the truth was he knew very little about the visible face of nature himself. Rather, he seems to have been a sponge drinking up ideas on which he was to feed. Yet it was a dangerous relationship — master and pupil — the master an elementary force as impersonal really as a sun-smitten cloud, the pupil so independent that he had already thrashed six to prove that he could not be made to thrash anybody — and, like most independents, longing for love.

8. A BOY'S MIND

EMERSON IN 1838 called him 'the boy,' and a boy he must
have seemed still in his sudden enthusiasms and perversities,
and his unwillingness to settle down in any of the 'recognized
professions.' If he liked to talk eternal values with Emerson, he
liked also to go fishing and to sing in the Concord chorus, and
tease the family at home. I suspect that one reason he went to
Walden Pond to stay was to find his way back to the relaxed
and realistic mood in which he seems to have lived in his early
youth before Transcendentalism made him too tense. For
there was no desire for tolerant leisure on the good earth among
the Concord intellectuals. The Emersons were said to walk
through Concord streets as if the earth was not good enough for
them;[1] Alcott, when he arrived in 1840, was feeling such a
veneration for the soil that rather than impair her purity by
fertilizing with 'foul ordures,' he would trust to love;[2] Margaret
Fuller was as tense as a steel cable. It must have been a relief to
escape from all the bustle about Utopia among the philosophers,
to find Aunt Louisa with her elbow on the Bible and her eyes
admiring the dried leaves and waxwork on the shelf.

Very little of this boyish playfulness gets into his first Journal, or at least very little remains in what he kept. Much of the record is pedantic, and still more of it dull. He could write such moralistic tripe about a fog as:

> So when thick vapors cloud the soul, it strives in vain to escape from its humble working-day valley, and pierce the dense fog which shuts out from view the blue peaks in its horizon, but must be content to scan its near and homely hills.

Yet there was a brain functioning, as is proved by an occasional epigram that no one without promise for the future could write: 'The words of some men are thrown forcibly against you and adhere like burs.' Or, in the midst of rhetoric, you come across one of those homely metaphors which were to make him famous, as, for example, in his first, and to judge from the fragments he kept, very dull lecture before the Concord Lyceum on April 11, 1838, in which he described some of his Concord neighbors as 'newly shingled and clapboarded,' but if you knock no one is at home.

What he did not do was to get much of himself in this Journal. It was not a picture of himself; it was an attempt to carry on self-education and record what was happening to his mind. Emerson, and still more Emerson's book, was working on his imagination. He compares himself to Zeno, bred a merchant if not a pencil-maker, who entered a shop one day, bought a book, and became a philosopher while his outward self went on about its business.[3] The book for Thoreau was of course 'Nature,' and as he mixed graphite with poetry, or taught school, or fell in love, his thoughts must have incessantly reverted to the problem of how to become the kind of scholar, the kind of man, which Emerson believed was to lead on the new generation. That is what he writes about in between nature sketches, quotations, and chunks of Harvard rhetoric.

2

It is not too much to say that Thoreau was made by two books, 'Nature' and the 'Bhagavad-Gita.'

The paragraphs of 'Nature' still chant with a music that is serene and sure:

> Our age is retrospective. It builds the sepulchres of the fathers. It writes biographies, histories, and criticism. The foregoing generations beheld God and nature face to face; we, through their eyes. Why should not we also enjoy an original relation to the universe? Why should not we have a poetry and philosophy of insight and not of tradition, and a religion by revelation to us, and not the history of theirs? Embosomed for a season in nature, whose floods of life stream around and through us, and invite us, by the powers they supply, to action proportioned to nature, why should we grope among the dry bones of the past, or put the living generation into masquerade out of its faded wardrobe? The sun shines to-day also. There is more wool and flax in the fields. There are new lands, new men, new thoughts. Let us demand our own works and laws and worship. . . .
>
> Let us inquire, to what end is nature?
>
> All science has one aim, namely, to find a theory of nature. . . .
>
> When we speak of nature in this manner, we have a distinct but most poetical sense in the mind. We mean the integrity of impression made by manifold natural objects. It is this which distinguishes the stick of timber of the wood-cutter, from the tree of the poet. The charming landscape which I saw this morning is indubitably made up of some twenty or thirty farms. Miller owns this field, Locke that, and Manning the woodland beyond. But none of them owns the landscape. There is a property in the horizon which no man has but he whose eye can integrate all the parts, that is, the poet. This is the best part of these men's farms, yet to this their warranty-deeds give no title. . . .
>
> In the woods is perpetual youth. Within these plantations

of God, a decorum and sanctity reign, a perennial festival is
dressed, and the guest sees not how he should tire of them in
a thousand years. In the woods, we return to reason and
faith. . . .

Yet it is certain that the power to produce this delight does
not reside in nature, but in man, or in a harmony of both. . . .

The world proceeds from the same spirit as the body of man.
It is a remoter and inferior incarnation of God, a projection of
God in the unconscious. But it differs from the body in one
important respect. It is not, like that, now subjected to the
human will. Its serene order is inviolable by us. It is, therefore,
to us, the present expositor of the divine mind. It is a fixed
point whereby we may measure our departure. As we degen-
erate, the contrast between us and our house is more evident.
We are as much strangers in nature as we are aliens from God.
We do not understand the notes of birds. The fox and the deer
run away from us; the bear and tiger rend us.

When Thoreau first read 'Nature' I do not know, probably
soon after it came out in 1836, since he gave a copy to a classmate the next year; but a comparison of the text with the
favorite ideas of his Journal shows how he read it. The lines
selected above from the whole essay he drank into the heart of
his being, and, indeed, all of the ideas contained in the section
of the little book, also called *Nature*, keep rising throughout his
life to blend with his own thinking. The next important section, *Beauty*, he was not ready for, his sense of beauty being still
too instinctive and unreasoned for metaphysics about it. *Language* he paused over, since it appealed to his interest in rhetoric.
But he slipped over *Discipline* and *Idealism*, which apparently
were too speculative for his realistic mind. He read carefully in
Spirit, which gave him a definition often used later; and then
clamped down upon *Prospects*, in which Emerson sums up his
expectations for the future. *Nature* and *Prospects* were Henry
Thoreau's New Testament. Upon them he built his philosophy,
such as it was; from them with help from the Hindu scriptures

he directed his life. I have noted as many as five parallels on a page of 'Nature' between this heart of Emerson and Thoreau's most characteristic passages.

In *Prospects* he found guidance for a possible career:

> The best read naturalist who lends an entire and devout attention to truth, will see that there remains much to learn of his relation to the world, and that it is... arrived at by... continual self-recovery, and by entire humility. He will perceive that there are far more excellent qualities in the student than preciseness and infallibility; that a guess is often more fruitful than an indisputable affirmation....
>
> For the problems to be solved are precisely those which the physiologist and the naturalist omit to state. It is not so pertinent to man to know all the individuals of the animal kingdom, as it is to know whence and whereto is this tyrannizing unity in his constitution, which evermore separates and classifies things, endeavoring to reduce the most diverse to one form.

And then, as its deep influence proves, he plunged into the magnificent conclusion of the essay:

> At present, man applies to nature but half his force. He works on the world with his understanding alone... and he that works most in it is but a half-man.... His relation to nature, his power over it, is through the understanding, as by... steam, coal, chemical agriculture....
>
> The reason why the world lacks unity, and lies broken and in heaps, is because man is disunited with himself. He cannot be a naturalist until he satisfies all the demands of the spirit. Love is as much its demand as perception. Indeed, neither can be perfect without the other....
>
> It will not need, when the mind is prepared for study, to search for objects. The invariable mark of wisdom is to see the miraculous in the common....
>
> What we are, that only can we see.... Caesar called his house, Rome; you perhaps call yours, a cobbler's trade; a hundred acres of ploughed land; or a scholar's garret.... Build therefore your own world.

This language of exaltation and confident idealism may be out of fashion, although for the young Thoreau it was like wine after the dogmatic platitudes of his preachers and teachers, but the ideas are not out of fashion. It is not too much to say that thousands of thoughtful men and women are beginning again today precisely where Thoreau began with Emerson's challenge before him. We have learned to control nature by our understanding — a control incredibly more effective than Emerson dreamt of — but not how to engender the spirit of love, and we are the victims of our own inventions. We can fly round the world, grow food in bottles, build or destroy an incredible city, but how to find happiness on a hundred acres, or how to make men's lives as excellent as their intellects, fatally eludes us.

Emerson challenged this thoughtful youngster at a moment in New England when thousands believed that the time had come to rebuild the world nearer to the heart's desire — or, shall we say, the Puritan heart's desire. It was not easy to accept his conclusion that 'the advancing spirit ... shall draw beautiful faces, warm hearts, wise discourse, and heroic acts, around its way, until evil is no more seen.' There was a shortage of beautiful faces, warm hearts, and heroic acts in Concord, which was Thoreau's house, his Rome — and a little too much discussion. Thoreau slid away from such philosophy as his mind had glanced off other metaphysics and moralities in 'Nature,' and met the challenge by turning to the woods and fields about which Emerson was so curious. What were the facts about these woods, which some day may flower into truth? [4] What *were* trees? What made crystal and leaf seek the same formations?

> *Nov. 28, 1837* ... It struck me that these ghost leaves [of ice crystals] and the green ones [of the grasses on which they formed] ... were the creatures of the same law. It could not

be in obedience to two several laws that the vegetable juices swelled gradually into the perfect leaf on the one hand, and the crystalline particles trooped to their standard in the same admirable order on the other.

This, though good science, is not profound philosophy, since the identity is not carried back toward any necessary spiritual law of the universe. Yet here Thoreau is already going beyond Emerson, who was more likely to slip on ice crystals than to study them.

Emerson had asked in 'Nature,' 'What is a woman? What is a child?' questions not to be answered by a solitude-loving youth. He preferred to study the unity in diversity of life from the progress of the seasons, or the habits of the shrub oaks.

3

As Henry sat at night in his attic room in the Parkman house, writing up his Journal, he was consciously or unconsciously preparing to be one of those voices of a new age for which Emerson was calling. This accounts for the pedantic seriousness of his self-improvement, and for his sudden sparks and flashes as the will to learn collides with an economic system more interested in good pencils than in new voices. Soon the preparation became fully conscious, but it was not a preparation for reforming the world. Even in youth, something held him back from the romantic confidence of Emerson's group of seekers who were inventing panaceas and slogans for a changed society. If Harvard had made him pedantic, the classics studied so zealously there had imbued him with that ideal of tolerant understanding so admirably described by Santayana in his 'The Genteel Tradition at Bay.' Why not learn how to live yourself before making all this fuss about reform? Why not get to know nature before explaining its significance for man?

These questions are not explicit in this early Journal, but they
are implicit whenever any of Thoreau's own thinking or observation creeps out.

Solitude is the first request he makes. 'I seek a garret' was his
first entry in the Journal of 1837. He wanted a room of his
own, and naturally, since he lived in a boarding-house with at
least five women, and was soon to be spending half the day and
sometimes all the day with other people's children. Emerson
in 'Nature' had urged his new man to seek solitude. It could
be had by looking at the stars. Henry was interested in a more
limited variety. He wanted a place where his thoughts and he
could '*domineer in privacy*,' as Burton said in lines Thoreau set
on the title-page of his Journal. When he was safe in his 'upper
empire,' bounded by three walls of yellow-washed boards and
one of yellow-washed plaster, with rats in the purlieus, he did
not, at first, have much to say and so resorted to quoting, and
writing brief Harvard themes on 'Discipline,' 'Truth,' 'Virgil,'
or 'Thoughts.' Wild ducks and arrowheads interest him; with
ice crystals he begins really to observe.

Self-expression is evidently boring him. 'But what does all
this scribbling amount to?' he asks after a while, like all honest
beginners, and writes 'Carlyleish' on the margin of a paragraph
of critical moralizing. 'How can a man sit down and quietly
pare his nails, while the earth goes gyrating ahead amid such
a din of sphere music?' sounds like Thoreau, but is really only
Henry paraphrasing Emerson. He can make, as I said, an
epigram, but cannot yet write good prose, probably because his
intellectual faculties are in an absorptive stage, and not yet
ready to give out, indeed do not know how to give out. Not
until 1839 is he capable of so Thoreauvian a remark as that our
concern should be with how we have happened to the universe
and it has demeaned itself in consequence — but it is clumsily
put. He has not yet assimilated the ideas he has been collecting.

Courtesy of the Concord Public Library

The Parkman house (left) at the corner of Main Street and Sudbury Road, now the site of the Concord Public Library

'It was in the Parkman house ... that Thoreau ... tossed his love under the grate like a broken toy'

His emotions, which are still simple ones, are much more articulate. The affectionate boy, easily stirred to a passionate devotion, who has been so much neglected in all the discussions of Thoreau, speaks easily in verse. He is ready for love, though he calls it friendship:

> I think awhile of Love, and, while I think,
>> Love is to me a world,
>> Sole meat and sweetest drink,
>> And close connecting link
>>> 'Tween heaven and earth.
>
> I only know it is, not how or why,
>> My greatest happiness;
>> However hard I try,
>> Not if I were to die,
>>> Can I explain.
>
> I fain would ask my friend how it can be,
>> But, when the time arrives,
>> Then Love is more lovely
>> Than anything to me,
>>> And so I'm dumb....

After this he began to moralize, but these stanzas are candid, naïve, and charming, and so Thoreau must have seemed at twenty-one to women like Lucy Brown and Lidian Emerson.

He loses a tooth, talks to his spinsterish family, goes to a party where he seems to have tried to introduce the humorous persiflage liked by the Thoreaus.[5] He hears a pulpit-thumping preacher in Academy Hall, preferring the grasshoppers outside in the sun as more *truthful*. On August 13, 1838, he gets an overdose of, maybe, Emerson:

> Men are constantly dinging in my ears their fair theories and plausible solutions of the universe, but ever there is no help, and I return again to my shoreless, islandless ocean, and

fathom unceasingly for a bottom that will hold an anchor, that it may not drag.

And a month later makes one of the worst puns in literary history apropos of his boots which had let in too much water from the cranberry swamps:

> Theirs was the inward lustre that bespeaks
> An open sole. . . .

His skating poem, called 'Fair Haven,'[6] registers pure happiness; indeed, one of the problems of this biography of a wrestling and often sarcastic spirit is to remind the reader that most of the time Thoreau was happy. He writes a bad essay on 'Sound and Silence' — really Carlyleish, does some good translations from Anacreon, sets down platitudes on the exalted function of the poet, and begins to grow sardonic over Concord commercialism:

> What have death, and the cholera, and the immortal destiny of man, to do with the shipping interests? . . . Some attain to such a degree of . . . nonchalance as to be . . . manufacturers of pinheads, without once flinching . . . for the period of a natural life.

No devotion to pencil-making is shown in this item. He dug for fat pine roots in old pastures, saw the 'illuminated pictures' of Babylon, noted that farmers and merchants walked differently on the street, and in June of 1839 met for the first time young Edmund Sewall, and a few weeks later fell in love with his gracious, high-spirited, and beautiful sister.

4

If the contents of this chapter seem unassimilated, it is because the ambitions of Henry in these two years just out of college were themselves a 'bundle of vain strivings' loosely held together, and his life a set of unrelated experiences in the home, in school, at Emerson's house, in the woods and fields. His head was humming with poetry, his affections were stretching toward love, his open mind was a spring into which ideas drifted like leaves. His emotions were as yet without self-consciousness, and the genteel morality of Concord and Harvard was still his idea of serious writing. He thought pretty well of himself as an intellectual, yet was impressive only when he was obstinate or naïve, which must have been often. I think he felt, rather than saw, the direction his life must take, but was much too happy to realize its difficulties.

Overflowing with thoughts,[7] he yet looked around for more, because he was living so intensely that his own thoughts choked his utterance. This description will do for any young writer. Thoreau's advantage lay in his resolve to find out *what* he was living before he made a book about it — to be, as he said to Emerson, first the idea itself.

And we may for convenience divide at this point Thoreau's productive life into two overlapping parts, in the first of which he was trying to learn how to do what he wanted without interruption, and in the other, when he had bought his freedom, was endeavoring to solve the problem of nature, a problem whose complexity Emerson never suspected, and whose extent required a long life even to begin.

9. TRANSCENDENTAL TRIANGLE

THERE WERE TWO Concords in which Henry Thoreau lived, of which the visible, material Concord with its shadowed streets, farms sloping to the river marshes, boys and girls on boating parties, gossips and traders at the Mill Dam, was certainly the more pleasant. Youth had a good time there.[1] It was not exciting, yet its rivers, woods, and lakes were the scenery of that wide margin of leisure with which Henry was determined to endow his life.

The other Concord was exciting, at least to sensitive minds. It flowed with that spiritual Musketaquid, ethereal grass-ground river, which Emerson said ran in the inner vision of such of his fellow townsmen as could see through the veil of use and wont which hid reality. This was its mystical aspect. But the eager, seeking minds passing in and out of Emerson's doors were far too alive to be often mystical. There is no comparing of small things with great in such communities where the heart beats fast. When a deep excitement of the mind finds a favorable environment, as it did in this Concord which was, indeed, a power plant of idealistic energy stepping up the spiritual voltage of the nineteenth century, an authentic moment in the history of civilization often follows. Athens, Florence, Lisbon, Weimar, Virginia of the statesmen, Concord — it is not our business to assess relative significances. No common mood or purpose, no equal level of skill or influence runs among them; but worldly or unworldly, sophisticated or unsophisticated, setting the pulse of centuries or only of decades, these rare communities are alike in their release of creative energy. It is exciting to live in them — whether in the rising glories of Athens or in Transcendental Concord where nothing moved quickly except the mind.

The new thing that got into the blood of the young Thoreau was this intellectual excitement rather than the proposals to reform an unspiritual world which they debated over apples and water at Emerson's. Old Doctor Ripley was right to distrust these 'modern speculators' who seemed to him to be offending not only religion but common sense.[2] After Henry had once sucked 'Nature' into his brain and become friends with Emerson, it was impossible to stay with the old orthodoxy, or believe with Locke that the senses apprehended all reality. Transcendentalism, as they were beginning to call it, became an intense conviction that the secret of life could be learned by him and in Concord fields. The Unitarian ministers who met in the Symposium and Margaret Fuller and the rest were excited about humanity, but Thoreau, the boy still at the edge of the circle, was excited about himself.

For him, this intellectual stir-about supplied the one thing needed for life in Concord — it made it seem important. If, in a cranberry swamp or in a garret, he could really satisfy his worthiest ambitions, then where was the sting of being a small-town boy with an undistinguished Harvard career behind him, and school teaching for his livelihood? Here, as with Wordsworth, were a new heaven and earth opening at home. Even the oppressive New England moralism into which his family, his professors, and his friends in the town all drifted when they grew serious (you could not escape it; not in Massachusetts of the thirties and forties), even this was lifted into a cause. For when, under Emerson's guidance, he began to realize that the intuitive soul makes its own religion and its own morality, unlimited possibilities for self-improvement spread ahead. Man was on the march again, and everything he had, or could get, would soon be used.

These powerful influences (except the moralism) were, of course, not from old Concord. They were imported by alien intellectuals from outside New England, from as far as Connecticut, and France, and Germany, and England. But in Concord, these outsiders found an environment in which they could make their own intellectual climate. Thoreau was the only one of their circle whose roots were deep in Concord soil. He was their Concord guinea-pig, and, indeed, he proved a pig in obstinacy. Yet at twenty-two and in 1839 when this chapter takes up his first love, he was already the 'transcendental brother' he called himself in 1840,[3] and looked, listened, studied, thought, and fell in love Transcendentally.

2

Nevertheless, his first love affair is boyish, charming, with an idyllic beginning and a tense middle, if a Transcendental end.[4]

The story is clear in its main outlines, in spite of Thoreau's reticence, which is not so reticent after all when his many references to what happened are relieved of their seeming impersonality. Sophia, who knew most of it, did her best to conceal what seemed to her too spinster mind a sacred record; but we know enough. It is a story which involves the Thoreau of both Concords, but first of all the affectionate, home-bred youth. And I give it more space than it may seem to deserve, because it was a crisis in Henry's life, after which his rich emotions began to turn inward and his ideals of love and friendship to lift to impossible heights.

The Sewall family, resident in Scituate, where the Reverend Edmund Quincy Sewall was minister, were of the old and consecrated New England strain, descended from Colonial worthies, among them Judge Sewall who kept the famous diary. They were intellectual Unitarians, and rightly conscious that in Massachusetts they were among the elect. Sewall was a Harvard graduate, well read in literature as in theology, and of real intellectual attainments. When his indifferent health kept him from the pulpit, he taught private pupils. In every sense, he was the head of the family, and it was in his study that the only fire burned on cold nights. His wife, sister of Prudence Ward, was a vaguer creature, affectionate and pliant. There was much visiting back and forward between the Sewalls in Scituate and the Wards in Concord, who were boarders at Mrs. Thoreau's. It was Prudence who taught the Thoreau young people botany and drawing. She discussed the nature of beauty with Henry, and was constantly writing to the Sewalls of Mr. John's and Mr. Henry's affairs, as if the Thoreaus had been relatives. She was a devoted friend to young people and a match-maker with a spinster's kindly persistence.

The Sewalls had three children, of whom two are important in this story. The older brother, Edmund, was about eleven in 1839. He was an intelligent and candid youth, one of those children whose souls seem to shine through their faces. When his mother brought him for a visit to the Thoreau household in June of 1839, Henry, whose school was just under way, seems to have been in a mood unusually sensitive to spiritual youth. Edmund later [5] became a pupil in the Thoreau school, and as a schoolboy caused no Transcendental emotions in Thoreau.

But on this first visit he inspired the poem 'Sympathy,'[6] written
with a warmth of emotion which, with the confusion of dates
in Sanborn's biography, accounts for the story believed by
Emerson (but not Channing) that it was a record of Thoreau's
first love for a woman.

This poem about a gentle boy had Edmund for its subject,
not his sister Ellen, who had last been in Concord in 1836, when
she was a child, and Henry presumably at Harvard. It was
Thoreau's habit to set down in his Journal the impact of a
poetical idea before the poem was written. As we know from
the letters of Ellen, the Thoreaus took young Edmund to their
favorite woods and waters. Some emanation from the youth at
this time touched Thoreau's sensitive imagination:

> *June 22. Saturday. 1839.* [Edmund was visiting the Thoreaus.]
> I have within the last few days come into contact with a pure,
> uncompromising spirit, that is somewhere wandering in the
> atmosphere, but settles not positively anywhere. Some persons
> carry about them the air and conviction of virtue, though they
> themselves are unconscious of it, and are even backward to
> appreciate it in others. Such it is impossible not to love; still
> is their loveliness, as it were, independent of them, so that you
> seem not to lose it when they are absent, for when they are
> near it is like an invisible presence which attends you.
>   That virtue we appreciate is as much ours as another's.
> We see so much only as we possess.

There was, to Thoreau's seeing, a spiritual beauty in the face
of this boy, and, as was to be expected, his intimations quickly
shaped themselves into a poem, which two days later he copied
into his Journal:

> *June 24.*   SYMPATHY
>
>   Lately, alas, I knew a gentle boy,
>   Whose features all were cast in Virtue's mould,
>   As one she had designed for Beauty's toy,
>   But after manned him for her own stronghold.

On every side he open was as day,
That you might see no lack of strength within....

So was I taken unawares by this,
I quite forgot my homage to confess;
Yet now am forced to know, though hard it is,
I might have loved him, had I loved him less.

Each moment, as we nearer drew to each,
A stern respect withheld us farther yet,
So that we seemed beyond each other's reach,
And less acquainted than when first we met....

If I but love that virtue which he is,
Though it be scented in the morning air,
Still shall we be truest acquaintances,
Nor mortals know a sympathy more rare.

This is clearly Transcendental love-making in search of someone so virtuous that the emotions of love lose their personal character. A dangerous kind of love-making for a young man of twenty-two, yet safe enough with a pure uncompromising spirit, settled not positively anywhere, for the love was only ideal.[7] But suppose such sympathy should flow out to a lovely and high-spirited girl!

3

She came in July of that year to visit Mrs. Thoreau and the Wards. Ellen Devereux Sewall, who was seventeen when her mother brought her to Concord, was, as all agree with a unanimity remarkable in a family, a girl with that irradiant beauty which is as much temperament and character as beauty of feature and of countenance. Her youngest daughter [8] tells me that even at seventy she was still charming, gracious, and beautiful. Her letters are playful, a little romantic, always affectionate, yet saved from insipidity by an eager love of experience and a quick sympathy with her friends.

In midsummer, she came to stay for three weeks. It was vacation time at the school, Mr. John and Mr. Henry were at her service, and, with Prudence as chaperone, she was shown the sights of Concord. Henry took her on the Assabet for her first boat ride and to see the giraffe in some travelling show. The letter to her father which tells of her experience is joyful. Her fancy was touched, sentiment of which she had plenty was stirred (she was an ardent reader of Dickens). It was too much to say that she was in love with either brother, but both fell in love with her.

Henry was already in a highly susceptible state, and tumbled immediately. Ellen arrived at the Thoreaus' by stage on the twentieth of July, and for that very day he copied into his Journal a lyric, which, if not written for her, described his playful and amorous mood:

> One green leaf shall be our screen,
> Till the sun doth go to bed. . . .

Four days later the intoxication has mounted:

> Nature doth have her dawn each day,
> But mine are far between;
> Content, I cry, for, sooth to say,
> Mine brightest are, I ween. . . .

And by July 25 the water is over the dam. 'There is no remedy,' he wrote in his Journal, 'for love but to love more'; then a significant silence until August 31, which was the day two brothers set off on their famous trip down the Concord and up the Merrimack.

That both brothers were in love, and with the same girl, as they rowed the rivers on that well-recorded trip, is certain.

Henry made his love articulate; John, as soon as they were home again, rushed off to Scituate, where he spent two nights and, Ellen's parents being away, walked on the hills with her without a chaperone. But that Henry and John confessed their love each to the other at this time seems improbable. The drama, of which their close friends were all later aware, was not, I believe, set until the following summer.

'You don't know how much pleasure Mr. John's visit has afforded us,' Ellen wrote to Prudence. 'I see you all in dreams often.' She is reading 'Sartor Resartus' — 'What a queer book!' — surely by Henry's suggestion. In December, John and Henry go to Scituate together, taking Aunt Prudence with them. Henry brought the poems of Jones Very as a present to Mr. Sewall, who probably did not like them, and, walking on the beach, began to compose the beautiful 'The Fisher's Son':

> I know the world where land and water meet. . . .
>
> My sole employment 't is, and scrupulous care,
> To place my gains beyond the reach of tides,
> Each smoother pebble, and each shell more rare,
> Which ocean kindly to my hands confides. . . .

John was busy with other gains. He sends Ellen, when he returns, not pebbles of thought, but opals for her mineral collection. She has read his letter to little Georgie 'again and again.' But she forgets to thank Henry for his 'original poems,' also sent her. It is true that she is trying, at his suggestion, to etherealize still more her pure spirit by a cold water plan, abstaining from both coffee and tea. 'This is an *experiment*, but it may *last*. I make no promises.' [9]

In June of 1840, she was in Concord again visiting. What she did with John is not recorded, but she was assuredly the 'free, even lovely young lady' who sat in the stern of Henry's boat on June 19, as his Journal notes, 'and there was nothing but she

between me and the sky'; or, as he puts it more ornately and
grammatically in the 'Week,' where both note and the poem he
made of the occasion were worked in later, 'unattended but by
invisible guardians.' She was the Maiden in the East here and
in his later Journal, and so he called the poem when it was
printed in *The Dial* in 1842:

> I'll walk with gentle pace,
> And choose the smoothest place,
> And careful dip the oar,
> And shun the winding shore,
> And gently steer my boat
> Where water-lilies float....

So far all seems to have been idyll, but the climax came
quickly. Grandma Ward and Prudence, with John to join or
accompany them, went down to Scituate in latter July of the
same summer. Aunt Prudence sat on the beach while the two
young people wandered. Unexpectedly, or so Ellen said,
John asked her to marry him. In surprise and confusion, so
she said later, she accepted him. But the engagement was of the
shortest duration. Her mother persuaded her that the match
would not do — the two Thoreaus were too Transcendental,
which we would call too radical — and Ellen was not only sure
that her father whom she adored would not approve, but doubtful already whether it was not Henry she liked best. So she
broke it off at once, and, as soon as the school where she was
teaching had closed in early September, she was packed off to
visit Uncle Henry Sewall in Watertown, New York. That great
gossip of the Ward correspondence, Laura Harris, wrote to
Mrs. Sewall on September 23: 'Eliza says she is afraid she
[Ellen] will get a lover, while she is gone. I believe in your
case she would not let her leave home for that very reason.'
Laura did not know that she already had two!

Ellen was certainly not unhappy, although I realize that

even an innocent and candid Sewall may have had her duplic-
ities. On August 25, after the engagement had been broken,
John had been sending her crystals for her collection. 'I intend
writing to John this week,' she puts in the P.S., which usually
contains her emphases. By October, she is saying of Concord,
'Oh, those were happy times,' such 'nice' times, to use John's
adjective. John had told her this and that. Was John going
chestnutting? Was Henry on a vegetable diet? 'What great
work is he engaged in now?' No one but herself will read the
letters that Prudence writes from Concord.

4

There is, in fact, something queer about this engagement.
John was, of course, no brilliant match for a Sewall, but he was
not Transcendental, though the Sewalls may have thought so.
He was a church member, if not too orthodox. Although the
letters after the broken engagement speak of John, what she
told her daughters when she was old was probably true. She
had yielded to the Thoreau in John, but wisely changed her
mind.

Henry was certainly puzzled and upset. In his Journal for
July of 1840, at just about the time when John went with
Prudence to the Sewalls at Scituate, he wrote this heavily
fraught passage:

> *July 19, 1840.* These two days that I have not written in my
> Journal, set down in the calendar as the 17th and 18th of July,
> have been really an aeon in which a Syrian empire might rise
> and fall. How many Persias have been lost and won in the
> interim? Night is spangled with fresh stars.

Which seems to be H. D. T.'s way of saying that he has had an
unexpectedly nasty knock, but can take it.

I believe that John told him that he was going to Scituate to try his luck with Ellen, and that this was the moment when Henry made the sacrifice which all his close friends seemed to know about. He gave first chance to the brother he loved more dearly than anyone else in the family, probably more dearly than anyone else alive.[10] But, if, as the circumstances indicate, Thoreau had been brooding only on his own chances with Ellen, the surprise must have been an unpleasant one.[11]

It is a family tradition that he did not know John was in love until after John's death in '42.[12] This, I am sure, is not true; but he may well have not known it before the 'aeon' in 1840. Later he was to illustrate some remarks about fate and accident in the 'Week' by significant lines: 'I heard that an engagement was entered into between a certain youth and a maiden, and then I heard that it was broken off, but I did not know the reason in either case.'[13]

The tradition that Henry sacrificed his own love to give his brother an opportunity is too well documented to be disputed. But if he gave a pledge, the broken engagement released him. John had tried and failed. 'Conscious-stricken without shame,' as he wrote later, he slowly determined to try his own fate with Ellen. The standard edition of the Journal contains no entries between July and January, but his friend Blake, who published the first selections, had seen the intervening pages and printed some extracts in his 'Autumn,' and I have been fortunate enough to see the whole of this unpublished section of the Journal, now in the hands of a private collector. We can only infer, but if the inferences are hard to interpret, this new evidence makes their trend unmistakable.

In August of 1840, by which time the engagement was presumably broken, he was joyful. '*August 7*. A wave of happiness flows over me like moonshine over a field.' Letters, I suspect, were being written between them. If so, Ellen was getting some surprises, for Henry was in love in his own peculiar and Transcendental way. 'My friend will be as much better than myself as my aspiration is above my performance,' he had written in his Journal for 1839, which showed the difficult moral heights up which he expected Ellen to follow him.

By this autumn of 1840, when Ellen was at Watertown, his fervor had increased, but is no less moral and mystic: '*Oct. 17.* In the presence of my friend I am ashamed of my fingers and my toes. . . . There is more than maiden modesty between us. . . . I have no feature so fair as my love for him.'

It is 'him.' However, the succession of entries, followed by a proposal of marriage, leave little doubt that 'her' was meant. This is confirmed by the poem shortly to be quoted, in which Ellen's eastern home, where 'flashed auroral light' is evidently identical with the house in an eastern city, called 'his house' in the Journal, which was 'incandescent to my eye.' There are, indeed, many passages in the Journal and the 'Week' where Henry's emotional experiences with women are memorialized under a camouflage of masculine pronouns. More of this later.

On the next day, he records what is apparently part of a letter, since 'you' in his Journal nearly always indicates a draft for either a lecture or a letter:

> *Oct. 18.* I cannot make a disclosure — you should see my secret — Let me open any door never so wide, still within and behind them, where it is unobserved, does the sun rise and set — and day and night alternate — no fruit will ripen on the common.

Poor girl, if she got such a letter it must have puzzled her, and yet Henry's meaning was clear to himself. When his friend Blake, years later, asked him for comments on friendship and love, he went into his past for an answer, copying freely from his earlier Journal:

> Love is the profoundest of secrets. Divulged, even to the beloved, it is no longer Love. . . . I require that thou knowest

everything without being told anything. I parted from my
beloved because there was one thing which I had to tell her.
She *questioned* me. She should have known all by sympathy.
That I had to tell it her was the difference between us, — the
misunderstanding.[14]

The beloved from whom he parted because she questioned
him was not, I believe, Ellen, but the resemblance between the
two passages proves that he expected this eighteen-year-old
girl to guess his love, and understand its esoteric quality, without being told!

If he wrote, he did not wait for an answer, since the Journal
for the next day is another reflection on the nature of his love,
with again 'him' for 'her,' and a clear reference to Ellen's
house in Scituate, the 'eastern home' of the poem which he is
soon to set down in his Journal:

> *Oct. 19* — My friend dwells on the eastern horizon as rich
> as an eastern city there. There he sails all lonely under the
> edge of the sky. But thoughts go out silently from me and belay
> him, till at length he rides in my roadstead. But never does he
> fairly come to anchor in my harbor. Perhaps I afford no good
> anchorage. . . . His house is incandescent to my eye, while I
> have no house, but only a neighborhood to his.[15]

Ellen may have written him before the next week, for the
tone changes from aspiration to melancholy. We know that
he must have written her proposing marriage about the time
of the following entry:

> *Nov. 1.* I thought that the sun of our love should have risen
> as noiselessly as the sun out of the sea, and we sailors have found
> ourselves steering between the tropics as if the broad day had
> lasted forever. You know how the sun comes up from the sea
> when you stand on the cliff, and doesn't startle you, but every-
> thing and you too are helping it.

This again suggests a draft for a letter, and the colloquial
tone, and the seeming reference to the hill which rose above

the sea and the Sewalls' house at Scituate, support the inference.
Ellen told her daughters that it was 'a very beautiful letter' she
received from him when he asked her to marry him. But if this
is part of that letter, as is probable, he could not have written
with much hope of a favorable reply, which makes one wonder
why he proposed at all, unless to satisfy some self-induced belief
that love so exalted as his should give the lady an opportunity
to prove herself worthy. He clearly had no hope of success,
since, copied carefully into his Journal under the date of
November 7, is the poem, already referred to, which expands
the story of the dawn of the sun of their love, and tells how
gloomily it has ended in night. And this poem was set down,
and therefore certainly composed, before he had received
Ellen's short letter which put an end to love-making, though
not to Transcendentalizing:

> I'm guided in the darkest night
> By flashes of auroral light,
> Which over dart thy eastern home
> And teach me not in vain to roam.
> Thy steady light on t'other side
> Pales the sunset, makes day abide,
> And after sunrise stays the dawn,
> Forerunner of a brighter morn.
>
> There is no being here to me
> But staying here to be
> When others laugh I am not glad,
> When others cry I am not sad,
> But be they grieved or be they merry
> I'm supernumerary.
> I am a miser without blame
> Am conscience stricken without shame.
> An idler am I without leisure,
> A busy body without pleasure.
> I did not think so bright a day

Would issue in so dark a night.
I did not think such sober play
Would leave me in so sad a plight,
And I should be most sorely spent
Where first I was most innocent.
I thought by loving all beside
To prove to you my love was wide,
And by the rites I soared above
To show you my peculiar love.[16]

This much can easily be read from the items of this heart-felt, if not too skilful, poem and the Journal entries quoted above. He had begun innocently and easily with Ellen, and found love extraordinarily distracting. The width of his love he had hoped to prove by the breadth of his sympathies, and its transcendent quality by soaring above the rites — which I take to be a reference to conventional church religion. But she does not sympathize with or understand him. She asks for his secret — in other words, what does he mean by his cryptic language (and can you blame her!). He expected love to rise like the sun out of the sea, and finds it landing him in a sad plight. Where there had been innocent pleasure now there was only gloom and confusion. This simple, direct, but by no means unintelligent girl asked him, I suppose, what he meant. And he replied, having got far beyond Transcendental friendship, that he wanted to marry her.

His letter and her reply to him have been destroyed, and also Ellen's burst of confidence to Aunt Prudence on the receipt of his proposal. But after she had come home to Scituate, she sent to Prudence a report of what had happened. 'Burn my last,' she says in this letter of November 18; then the inevitable postscript written in up and down scrawls:

Last week Tuesday [*Nov. 10, 1840*], the day I sent my last letter to you I received one from Father. He wished me to write immediately in a *short explicit* and cold manner to Mr. T. He seemed very glad I was of the same opinion as himself with regard to the matter. I wrote to H. T. that evening. I never felt so badly at sending a letter in my life. I could not bear to think that both these friends whom I have enjoyed so much with would now no longer be able to have the free pleasant intercourse with us as formerly. My letter was very short indeed. But I hope it was the thing. It will not be best for either you or me to allude to this subject in our letters to each other. Your next letter may as well be to Mother perhaps or Edmund. By that time the worst of this will be passed and we can write freely again. I do feel so sorry H. wrote to me. It was such a pity. Though I would rather have it so than to have him say the same things on the *beach* or anywhere else. If I could only have been at home so that Father could have read the letter himself and have seen my answer, I should have liked it better. But it is all over now. We will say nothing of it till we meet.

5

And so Ellen passes out of the story and into Thoreau's imagination. He told Sophia or his mother before his death that his whole life had been affected by her memory. But she appears again only in dreams, in literary references, and in cryptic passages of his Journal, the first perhaps in the January following the crisis:

> To sigh under the cold, cold moon for a love unrequited is but a slight on nature; the natural remedy would be to fall in love with the moon and the night and find our love requited.[17]

Which is just what happened eventually to all of Thoreau's passions for those he loved.[18]

It is impossible to feel distressed at Henry's failure to win this lovely creature whom he had known in a true sense only superficially. I doubt whether he wanted to marry her; for after the idyllic opening of their relationship she became more and more for him an experiment in the philosophy of love. How he felt about love can be seen in his fine poem called 'Friends, Romans, Countrymen, and Lovers,' written in 1840 or 1841, and included in the 'Week' among those poems and passages which record his passions.[19]

> Let such pure hate still underprop
> Our love, that we may be
> Each other's conscience,
> And have our sympathy
> Mainly from thence. . . .
>
> Implacable is Love, —
> Foes may be bought or teased
> From their hostile intent,
> But he goes unappeased
> Who is on kindness bent.

No one wins an Ellen Sewall this way, though a Margaret Fuller might be open to such an approach. A curious idea — to force (as he clearly did) an implacable love upon a girl whose sympathy for him had been evidently stretched in the imagination beyond any possible truth to fact — but entirely characteristic of the fiercely consistent Thoreau.

6

He learned something of love by these emotional upsets, and yet I do not believe that his failure to win Ellen was the crisis to which Margaret Fuller refers in a curious postscript to a literary letter written to Thoreau in October of 1841:

> The penciled paper Mr. E. [Emerson] put into my hands. I have taken the liberty to copy it. You expressed one day my own opinion, — that the moment such a crisis is passed, we

may speak of it. There is no need of artificial delicacy, of secrecy; it keeps its own secrets; it cannot be made false. Thus you will not be sorry that I have seen the paper. Will you not send me [for *The Dial*] some other records of the *good week*? [20]

The pencilled paper will probably never be found, but it is possible to guess as to what it contained. Thoreau had given it to Emerson, probably one of those scribbled note sheets so common among his manuscripts. It described a delicate situation which suggested secrecy, so a woman was possibly involved. It referred to a crisis in Thoreau's life which had some relevance to literature, else it is difficult to see why Emerson should have shown it to Margaret, who is writing in her capacity of editor. It was a record of the *good week*, which can only be John and Henry's week on the rivers.[21] There was a personal crisis in Thoreau's life of which, we know, Emerson was aware, and this was the fraternal rivalry for the love of Ellen, and Henry's withdrawal in favor of his brother. Of what happened afterward, Emerson was ignorant. The pencilled paper is lost, but there is striking evidence in Thoreau's books that this drama of two brothers had powerfully affected his imagination.

On September 4, 1839 (so it is dated in the 'Week'), the brothers were camped by a small brook flowing into the Merrimack. The topic of love, which came 'right into the middle of a prosaic Goffstown day' while they were rowing upstream, had been discussed at length. They lie awake listening to the murmurs of the brook. Then Henry dreams a dream:

I dreamed this night of an event which had occurred long before. It was a difference with a Friend, which had not ceased to give me pain, though I had no cause to blame myself. But in my dream ideal justice was at length done me for his suspicions, and I received that compensation which I had never obtained in my waking hours. I was unspeakably soothed and rejoiced, even after I awoke, because in dreams we never deceive ourselves, nor are deceived, and this seemed to have the authority of a final judgment.

But it was not in 1839 on the banks of the Merrimack that Thoreau dreamed his dream. It happened at a far more significant time, on the night of the twenty-fifth of January, 1841, ten weeks after Ellen had refused him, seven months after those two days in July which seemed 'aeons' to Thoreau, eight months or less before the pencilled note about the 'crisis.' The entry is in his Journal for that date:

> I had a dream last night which had reference to an act in my life in which I had been most disinterested and true to my highest instinct but completely failed in realizing my hopes; and now, after so many months, in the stillness of sleep, complete justice was rendered me. It was a divine remuneration. In my waking hours I could not have conceived of such retribution; the presumption of desert would have damned the whole. But now I was permitted to be not so much a subject as a partner to that retribution. It was the award of divine justice, which will at length be and is even now accomplished.

On the twenty-seventh he adds: 'In the compensation of the dream, there was no implied loss to any, but immeasurable advantage to all.'

It is surely not difficult to interpret this dream, and particularly the second and original version. He had relinquished Ellen to his beloved John, and John had lost her. Thus his high and disinterested hopes had been frustrated. But, as we know from the letters of Ellen's printed above, his own hopes for himself had been also frustrated, and his proposal had once for all ended a relationship between Thoreaus and Sewalls which John may have felt with justice had a promise for the future. Ellen, though she had broken the engagement, was still corresponding with him, still keeping Concord in her heart. Here is presumably the cause of the difference with his friend, who was his brother, and of that brother's unjust suspicion, as recorded in the dream, that he had not been treated fairly. No explanation of itself heals such wounds. Henry may have been conscience-stricken without shame, since, indeed, his part in the affair had been honorable, but if John felt that his younger brother, rushing in at the first opportunity, had made his prospects hopeless (and of course he had) there were grounds for a painful difference between friends so close in devotion that when a year later John died in the agonies of lockjaw, Henry suffered actual pains.[22]

There is no solution for such a misunderstanding except time — or an ideal one which satisfies a conscience accustomed to trust its intuition. Such a conscience was Henry's, and his imagination working through a dream gave him the ideal justice which alone could soothe and rejoice him. Waking, it would have been beyond his deserts, for he was to be a partner not a subject of this compensation. But dreams do not deceive, at least do not deceive those who have faith in intuitive truth. What was this ideal justice? I think the answer may be found, and again in that essay on Friendship in the 'Week,' which so often memorializes Henry's loves, and especially in the pages where this passage occurs:

> Friendship is not so kind as is imagined; it has not much human blood in it. . . . There may be the sternest tragedy in the relation of two more than usually innocent and true to their highest instincts. . . . As for the number which this society admits, it is at any rate to be begun with one, the noblest and greatest that we know, and whether the world will ever carry it further . . . remains to be proved . . . . Yet Friendship does not stand for numbers. . . . The more there are included by this bond, if they are indeed included, the rarer and diviner the quality of the love that binds them. I am ready to believe that as private and intimate a relation may exist by which three are embraced, as between two.[23]

Was this his ideal solution? I think it highly probable, for it is in strict accord with his Transcendental view of love in which

> We'll one another treat like gods,
> And all the faith we have
> In virtue and in truth, bestow
> On either, and suspicion leave
> To gods below.[24]

Neither John nor he was to have Ellen in the flesh, but he could dream of a higher relationship in which all could share all, the brother he loved, now no longer suspicious, united with him in a transcendent relationship with this pure feminine spirit, where no one would be the subject but all partners in a rarer, diviner love. Of such a compensatory philosophy was the ideal justice of his dream certainly compounded. This Transcendental triangle will seem naïve only to those who find youth's constant attempts to make love a religion and a morality more than faintly absurd. That it has its humorous aspect I do not deny.

7

The sublimation of very human emotion into Transcendental idealism is characteristic of the young Thoreau. It is impossible to understand the fire with which he wrote the classic arguments for solitude unless one understands the passion with which here and later he seeks a bond of rare and divine love, too rare, too divine for realization with those he loved. This little drama of brotherly love and a frustrated sacrifice is a vital part of his biography. It is not important that he afforded no harborage for the Maiden in the East. She was wise to sail elsewhere, marry a man she was certainly in love with, and become the mother of numerous children

Ellen Sewall with three of her children. Her beautiful hair has been smoothed down to make a seemly portrait
'She was wise to sail elsewhere'
Reproduced from a daguerreotype by permission

and a successful clergyman's helpmate.²⁵ It is of the greatest importance that in the rarefied emotional atmosphere of Alcott's and Emerson's Concord, Thoreau should have based his idealizing upon a first-hand experience with the pangs of love.

Ellery Channing, who knew him so well, wrote in his Journal of March, 1867:

> Nothing was more delightful than the enormous curiosity, the continued greenness, the effervescing wonder of this child of Nature — glad of everything its mother said or did. This joy in Nature is something we can get over, like love. And yet, love — that is a hard toy to smash and fling under the grate for good. Now, Henry made no account of love at all, apparently. He had notions about friendship.²⁶

It is to escape this serious misunderstanding, which makes of Thoreau a sexless Platonist, that this chapter and one other to follow are written.

10. IN SEARCH OF A PUBLIC

It was in the Parkman house on Main Street of Concord, where the public library now stands, that Thoreau, according to Channing, tossed his love under the grate like a broken toy, and went to his garret room to acquire notions about friendship. Yet in those years while he was Transcendentally courting Ellen and being rejected in a fashion which was not Transcendental at all, Henry's mind was by no means entirely occupied with either love or friendship. After school and his walks in the woods, he must already have set himself rigorous working hours upon his Journal. But the casual reader of the prose in this Journal would never suspect that the record was of a man who at least thought he was in love. The poetry of course is more revealing.

It is the diary of a boy preparing for a career — but what? Until early 1840, it consists chiefly of little essays of a paragraph each on such subjects as 'Despondency,' 'Aeschylus,' 'Self-Culture,' 'Vice and Virtue,' 'The Loss of a Tooth,' 'Evening Sounds,' 'Fear,' with a few nature descriptions, poems, and an occasional incident. The nature descriptions are not very good — he did not know enough, did not love nature enough yet, to make them good. The essayettes are pretty dreadful, most of them — condensed Harvard themes, less interesting than the reports on his reading which he sets down with them. You see what they are intended for when he selects a few such topics to expand into longer essays on Society, Sound and Silence, Friendship. They are to become lectures, such as 'The Service,' a defense of the martial spirit, and 'Sir Walter Raleigh,' the good warrior, which Margaret Fuller, quite properly, rejected for *The Dial*, or the critique on the Latin poet Persius, which she accepted for the first number, and which got Thoreau one lifelong admirer in Blake of Worcester, and has probably been read by few since.

Was he trying to make a writer of himself? The question has often been asked, when did Thoreau determine to become a man of letters. It is a false question, in which we insert the very different conditions of America of our day. Young writers with a gift for expression were not likely to plan to become men of letters in 1839 or 1840, for there was no such profession. A literary journalist might make a bare living, as Poe found to his cost; a novelist whose talent could overcome the handicap of pirated English books had a fighting chance. Cooper won; Hawthorne, thanks to political assistance, came through, though not on his books. But a poet and Transcendentalist, with an undeveloped gift for nature writing — where was his possible sustenance?

To become a writer was, however, in Thoreau's mind; his verses prove it, his Journal proves it. Even as early as 1838 he was criticizing his own style for being 'Carlyleish.' But he can scarcely have hoped to make publication his substitute for school teaching or any other work that brought a steady income. The youth who could write in October of 1840 (I quote from the unpublished Journal already mentioned), 'I have not read any great literary criticism yet. . . . The flowing drapery of genius is too often tucked up and starched lest it offend against the fashions of the time,' was predestined by his own talent for distinction in literature; but that, in America, did not necessarily mean a career.

There is a too common belief that a young writer's first great struggle is the decision whether to write for money or for fame. Nonsense! — his first struggle is to find something to say, and his second to discover some way of publishing it. The question of money seldom arises in the early stages. Having found something to say, his problem is to break into print, paid or unpaid. Hence the two conditioning factors for writing anywhere, any time, are the quality of the imagination and the nature of the market. Later comes the fork of the road — one way toward the competent and salable, the other toward the excellent and possibly unsalable. The completely successful man of letters is not he who writes for nothing, but rather the writer who learns how to do what he wants — and how to make readers pay for it. The predestined commercial writer is seldom a frustrated man of letters. His success in cash returns is due to a different set of qualities. Every author writes for money, for money represents an audience, and no creative mind writes for itself alone. The question is, how high a price will he pay for the money he gets. That became Thoreau's problem; but at first his concern was with what he had to say, and to whom and how he could say it. When this was solved, the question of how he was to get paid enough to allow him to go on writing followed, and in solving that in his own original fashion he broke out of obscurity into fame.

2

But there is no real comparison between the beginning of Thoreau's career as a writer and Poe's or Longfellow's, because his idea of what at age twenty-two he would have called the poet's job was entirely different from theirs. 'The poem,' he said, is drawn out from under the feet of the poet, his whole weight has rested on this ground.' [1] This idea came from 'Nature' and from his conversations with Emerson. By 1840 there is plenty of evidence that he knew what he was trying to do, even though vague as to how to accomplish it:

March 21.... There is this moment proposed to me every kind of life that men lead anywhere, or that imagination can paint.

Our limbs, indeed, have room enough, but it is our souls that rust in a corner. Let us migrate interiorly without intermission.

March 30. Pray, what things interest me at present? A long, soaking rain, the drops trickling down the stubble, while I lay drenched on a last year's bed of wild oats, by the side of some bare hill, ruminating. These things are of moment.

April 8. How shall I help myself? By withdrawing into the garret, and associating with spiders and mice, determining to meet myself face to face sooner or later.[2]

April 22.... I cannot turn on my heel in a carpeted room. What a gap in the morning is a breakfast! A supper supersedes the sunset.

Will not one thick garment suffice for three thin ones? Then I shall be less compound, and can lay my hand on myself in the dark.

June 15.... Our life is not all moral.... The science of Human Nature has never been attempted, as the science of Nature has. The dry light has never shone on it.

June 16.... Would it not be a luxury to stand up to one's chin in some retired swamp for a whole summer's day, scenting the sweet-fern and bilberry blows, and lulled by the minstrelsy of gnats and mosquitoes?

June 21.... I never feel that I am inspired unless my body is also. It too spurns a tame and commonplace life.

June 26. The best poetry has never been written, for when it might have been, the poet forgot it, and when it was too late remembered it; or when it might have been, the poet remembered it, and when it was too late forgot it.

He who resists not at all will never surrender.

When a dog runs at you, whistle for him.

Say, Not so, and you will outcircle the philosophers.

There was no indolence in the purpose which lies behind these sentences. In that admirable preface to the first number of *The Dial* in July of 1840, Emerson set down what he must often have said to Henry Thoreau. There was a revolution, he said, under way in New England. A new spirit was abroad among many who did not know each other's faces or names. It was in every form a protest against convention and a search for principles, and existed like an oak or a river because it must. As for literature, there is somewhat in all life untranslatable into language. He who keeps his eyes on that will write better than the others, and think less of his writing, and of all writing. What is great usually slips through our fingers. We wish not to multiply books, but to report life.

Here is Thoreau's direction for a writing career — to report life, and first of all his own life. 'I told Henry Thoreau that his freedom is in the form, but he does not disclose new matter,' Emerson said of him the next year. 'I am very familiar with all his thoughts — they are my own quite originally drest.' [3] Not altogether true then, or later, this is surely true of the Thoreau of the quotations above. He was reporting his life, as Emerson advised him to do. And he continued to report life; indeed in 'Walden' he describes himself as a reporter. It is certain that he never sharply differentiated his profession of authorship from his basic job of unveiling his life in order to understand himself and his environment. Far more than with most authors, writing was a report rendered to his friends and possible readers of what he had learned about life. And being a very busy man, with a tremendous task cut out for himself, he got little time for making these reports into merchantable books. Emerson's advice he took with a difference, coming to think more and more of writing, but less and less of publication, except as a means of supporting himself while his reporting went on. Indeed, if I should coin an epithet for Henry Thoreau it would not be the 'poet-naturalist' of Channing, but rather, a reporter of spiritual and physical reality.

3

With all this in mind it is easy enough to see what he meant by the couplet already quoted:

> My life has been the poem I would have writ,
> But I could not both live and utter it.[4]

His first task was to get something to report. Yet not one man in a million has ever written out his commentary on experience (which is a good working definition of the basis of literature) without the hope of publication. With the act of composition comes the speculation as to who will read and how. Writer and audience are like man and his environment, essentially inseparable. Hence, if cash return is in question, the market, or, if communication is what is sought, the possible audience, is the inevitable concern of the articulate man. That the audience, at least, was Thoreau's concern, certainly from 1837 on, is obvious to anyone who will look over this early Journal. He is not only phrase-making, organizing his thoughts under headings, and indexing his paragraphs, he goes further and writes considerable essays. And when one passes on to the forties and sees his real reporting under way, the pointed sentences are evidently meant to be picked up later and worked into a 'piece,' as we should say now.

Like every writer he was responding to his possible opportunities. Until 1840 he could have seen only one. There were no magazines in America which would publish aphorisms like those above, from a youth. There were no magazines which would publish essays on 'Bravery' or 'The Service' or 'Sir Walter Raleigh,' and pay for them. But there was the Lyceum. In so far as Henry was not recording his own studies and self-development, he was getting ready to become, like Emerson, a lecturer. It was his only outlet.

The Lyceum idea, introduced into New England a short time before, had spread with extraordinary rapidity among these people hungry for uplift. It was admirably adapted to a country made up of small, self-respecting communities, where a passionate faith in education had absorbed the energies released when the New England mind turned from perfectibility for the next world to intellectual progress in this one.

The system was simple. A group of citizens hired a hall, often the vestry room of the church, or the town hall, invited lecturers from outside, filled up, if they were able, the gaps from their own local talent, and issued a prospectus asking for subscriptions. By this means, a community of two thousand people like Concord could hear, if it wished, what its committee regarded as the best thought available, and conversely, if there were local thinkers, they could be guaranteed an audience. The local speakers donated their services, the imported talent was paid, from five dollars up to twenty-five, rarely more. When Thoreau himself was Curator of the Concord Lyceum in 1843–1844 he carried through the season with an expenditure of only one hundred dollars, for which sum he provided for his townsmen such talent as Emerson, Theodore Parker, Horace Greeley, George Bancroft, and others now less famous. Emerson got nothing, Parker three dollars, a Mr. Giles ten dollars.

Emerson, in his time, was by profession a Lyceum lecturer. Alcott, who was too nebulous for a mixed audience, developed his 'Conversations,' in which he conducted his own Lyceum by a monologue with some discussion. Margaret Fuller did the same for women. There can be no question that a literary career for the young Thoreau meant first of all lecturing. It is for lecturing that his early Journal prepares, and, indeed, he lectured in Concord his first year out of college, and most of the years afterward. In Concord he was not paid, but his place in the well-known series there soon got him invitations elsewhere. And throughout his life it is as a lecturer that he usually describes himself. He was a bad lecturer — never successful except with individuals, the kind of lecturer who keeps his nose in his manuscript and drives the words at his audience.[5] But until the year of his death he never found a dependable annual outlet with a cash return for what he wrote, except through lecturing.

Like Mark Twain, like Emerson, Thoreau is a writer formed by the practice of appealing directly to an audience. This was his first idea of publication. This was the market in which, even before he knew what he was going to do with his life, he was preparing to sell his intellectual wares. At first his idea of a lecture was a Harvard essay. But after the brilliant idea of reporting his search for reality in himself and in nature had flashed from Emerson, he began to store up in his Journal, as in a munitions dump, sentences and paragraphs charged with his own peculiar thought and imagination. These were to be discharged at his audiences, like strips of cartridges, as soon as he could provide a machine gun. But he was no Emerson, of the grave, eloquent voice, the noble presence. His projectiles hit like duds. It was only in print that they began to explode.

The lecture, regarded as a literary form, had a definite appeal to a mind like Henry Thoreau's which it is a little hard for us to understand. Why did he keep at it after demonstrated failure? Surely not for the little cash it brought in, since he could readily make more by surveying or in the graphite shop. It appealed both to him and to Emerson because the lecture was a direct contact between the intuitive personality and his audience. It was the ideal method (when successful) for transmitting the intuitions of Transcendentalism. When the great Unitarian, Channing, was interviewed by young De Tocqueville, later to be author of the famous book on democracy, he made an illuminating remark. The disciples of 'newness,' he said, proposed to get back to that seventeenth century when ordinary men were made to feel a direct contact with their God. Of this (though not of understanding the complexities of the tariff) he felt the masses to be capable.[6] Emerson and Thoreau his disciple and Alcott all proposed to transmit, face to face, the results of their seeking of spiritual reality to men and women who might never read what they had to say, *could* never read it when (as with Thoreau and Alcott) publication was difficult or impossible.

Emerson had faith in the written word and the skill which managed it, and Thoreau, as soon as opportunities offered, came to his opinion, but Alcott distrusted all rhetoric, all skills of style and expressiveness, believing in a kind of induced electricity between speaker and hearer. There was a great deal of truth in his contentions. The Concord shoemaker who so deeply admired Emerson was accustomed to say that he understood very little but came away uplifted. Thoreau could not uplift with the spoken word, and perhaps that is the reason why of the three he became the best writer in prose. The clue to his oft-expressed 'meanness' in these early years is perhaps to be found in his sense of failure in communication, even as a lecturer. He had the stuff in his Journal, but he could not get it out. As he said again and again, he had to work for Admetus because he could not sell himself as Apollo. Audiences sought uplift, and did not get it from his radical perversities; or they wished to be amused, in which he obliged them only when he read them the accounts of his journeys in the woods or Cape Cod or of his life at Walden Pond.

Nearly everything Thoreau wrote was originally conceived as a lecture. 'A Week on the Concord and Merrimack Rivers' is a thin thread of narrative tying together a bundle of commentaries, of which several had actually been used as lectures. 'Walden' is a series of lectures upon the experiment of living alone at Walden, and what happened there. Much of it was given first as separate lectures. The 'Excursions' are all lectures. So are 'Civil Disobedience' and 'Life Without Principle.' 'Cape Cod' and 'The Maine Woods' and 'A Yankee in Canada' are lectures, worked up a bit afterward. Strange that a form in which he was not successful should have determined the nature of his literary output. Not strange, however, if one remembers that the lecture revised for print keeps the freedom of direct, personal address, with an air of casual utterance, while at the same time the author has had to write as well as he can since his audience is now unknown. In 1837 Henry was an apprentice in the profession of Lyceum lecturing, where were many brilliant stars that have long ceased to shine. He submitted to the discipline of print; they did not, or if they did, were unable to carry over into written style the color and flavor of their spoken words.

<h2 style="text-align:center">4</h2>

A lecture unpublished dies with the memory of the hearers. Print lasts. In breaking into print Thoreau was extremely lucky. The so-called Transcendental Club had wished for an organ to express their ideas of the 'newness' upsurging in New England. *The Dial*, founded in 1840 and first edited by Margaret Fuller, was the result, but by no means carried out the hopes of the circle. It was too literary for Theodore Parker, who thought Thoreau's much revised 'Persius' a 'foolish article,' and hoped he would write for the newspapers and so 'keep out of mischief' and *The Dial*. [7] It disappointed Alcott, who found too much about the arts and too little 'wise, humane, and brave sincerity.' [8] And naturally, for the imaginations which really created it, Emerson's and Margaret Fuller's in particular, were more fertile than the minds of Unitarian ministers and less mystical than Alcott and the seekers.

It is clear that Emerson, whose influence was major, was drawn into one of the very few institutions to which he ever lent his name by his strong desire to establish a medium of publication in which new minds, like Thoreau's, like Ellery Channing's, like Margaret Fuller's, could find a place to publish and establish their influence in print. He wanted them there, and was content to let 'our Journal share the impulses of the time, it cannot now prescribe its own course.' [9] It was to have, as Margaret Fuller said, perfect freedom to publish the 'newness' of youth. When Carlyle complained that the contributors were 'soaring after ideas,' Emerson answered: 'It is yet a fact for literary history, that all the bright boys and girls in New England ... take the world so.... The boys ... do not wish to go into trade.... They are all religious, but hate the churches: they reject all the ways of living of other men, but have none to offer in their stead.' [10] This is perfect of Thoreau, except that a way of living by 1842 was already forming in his mind. *The Dial*, Emerson wrote to Carlyle only eight days after the meeting of the Symposium when the magazine was planned, 'will give you a better knowledge of our young people than any you have had.'[11] By young people he meant first of all Thoreau. 'My Henry Thoreau,' he wrote in his Journal, 'will be a great poet for such a company, and one of these days for all companies.'

That Thoreau published so little in the magazine until Emerson began to edit it himself in the spring of 1842, was due to the vigilant editorship of Margaret Fuller. She regarded Henry as a somewhat 'bare hill' still unwarmed by the breezes of spring,[12] which was not true, but also as an unformed writer, given to incoherences, exaggerations, and diffusion, which was perfectly true. She rejected kindly but firmly the formal lecture-essays he tried to pass off on her. When Emerson took charge he had better luck, getting fifteen contributions into volume III, not counting his selections from the Sayings of Confucius, the Laws of Menu, and the Romaunt of the Rose. Here were some of his best poems, like 'The Inward Morning,' translations from the classics, and his 'Natural History of Massachusetts,' which revealed for the first time the charm of his nature description, while showing to the informed reader that his knowledge of natural history was still extremely sketchy. When, with the April number of 1844, *The Dial* gave up its struggle to live upon a handful of subscriptions, Henry was definitely an author; he had broken into print.

For *The Dial*, local as it was, with constant references to the taste and opinion of Boston, and never read perhaps by more than five hundred to a thousand readers, was yet the kind of magazine that made young writers known.[13] It was amateurish, it was too 'eclectic and miscellaneous,' as Emerson said of it retrospectively in his memoir of Margaret Fuller; 'each of its readers and writers valued only a small portion of it.' It was far stronger in criticism than in what is usually called creative writing. For the Transcendentalists could not write fiction, witness Channing's attempt in his 'The Youth of the Poet and the Painter' to tell a story by letters;[14] and aside from Emerson (often) and Thoreau (occasionally) and Channing (once) they could not write memorable poetry. Indeed, except for Emerson's contributions, a few of Thoreau's, and perhaps one or two others, there is nothing reprintable from the four volumes. Yet it had one great merit which, in the low and dependent state of American literature and American journalism at the time, was of really great importance. In spite of what Emerson called the too 'bookish' source of the agitation of these writers who 'found the air in America getting a little close and stagnant,'[15] there was a self-reliance, an optimism, a passionate interest in the soul and mind of America, which made these numbers, for all their New England provincialism, the first upstanding and confident exponents of an American mind. Of course, it was not the all-American mind, it was the Boston and Concord mind. Nevertheless, it was home-grown, if nurtured in European ideas, and it was confident.[16]

Thoreau's debt to *The Dial* is great. No other magazine would have published him in 1840. *The North American Review* was stodgy and Anglophile; the few magazines in New York and Philadelphia which paid for contributions and sometimes, like *Graham's Magazine*, paid those who owned them, belonged in a different intellectual climate from his. He will have to learn how to write for them. The New England propaganda periodicals, like Brownson's *Boston Quarterly Review*, were not to his taste, nor he to theirs. *The Dial* allowed him to work off his accumulations of classical scholarship, and gave him a chance to try in print a new kind of lecture in his 'A Winter Walk,' which disgusted Emerson because of its perverse eccentricities, but opened a line for Thoreau. *The Dial* was not afraid of his metaphysical poetry, which came from a deeper spiritual level than was being tapped (except by Emerson) elsewhere in American verse.

Best of all, he was given an experience in editing. While he was living at Emerson's he not only helped him edit the magazine, but himself edited the April number of 1843. The handling of manuscripts from the reader's point of view, the realization that great minds often make little mistakes, and the idea of an article as something not merely to be written but to be read, are of the greatest value to any young writer, but especially to a self-absorbed original. It is shortly after 1843, as nearly as we can date the moment, that Henry begins to think of how to make books of his reportings on life.

In February of 1841 he was still the solitary writer, excusing in his Journal the lack of consecutiveness by a fate which makes aim that way:

> When I select one here and another there, and strive to join sundered thoughts, I make but a partial heap after all.... A man does not tell us all he has thought upon truth or beauty at a sitting.... Sometimes a single and casual thought rises naturally and inevitably with a queenly majesty and escort.... Fate has surely enshrined it in this hour and circumstances for some purpose. What she has joined together, let not man put asunder. Shall I transplant the primrose by the river's brim, to set it beside its sister on the mountain?

In other words, he was finding it too hard work to combine his scattered paragraphs into anything coherent and printable, and so hoped that they could wait for posterity as they were. But by 1843, when he is editing *The Dial*, he writes to Emerson that Lane's essay could be made more universal and attractive, and that his dialect is sometimes abominable. The editor had begun to realize that composition and publication often serve different ends. He was beginning to feel professional.

Finally, Thoreau had gone beyond his lecture audience. Carlyle was reading *The Dial* in England. The Boston papers, picking Alcott's Orphic sayings partly because in the first number he alone signed his contribution, were abusing the Transcendentalists for (as Aunt Maria said in a letter) cracking the brains of sensible men. A new writer got the sense of having broken through to communication at last, even if there was a kick rather than a plaudit at the end.

5

Now came the problem of subsistence. When *The Dial* was launched Henry was a school teacher with an adequate job and income. It was not important that his accepted contributions were unpaid. By '41 the school had ended, and his project for buying the Hollowell Farm where he could keep himself alive while writing and lecturing had been defeated by the obstinacy of a farmer's wife, who would not sign a deed when the payment, except for ten dollars, was to be on credit. Emerson came to the rescue. While experimenting with the theory that dabbling in the soil would put health in his body and roots to his thoughts, he had overworked himself, and found, like many another, that manual and intellectual labor seldom mix well. Also, he was off lecturing for weeks or months at a time and wanted a friend, caretaker, a handyman about the house, and a helpmate for 'our too pensive, careful & melancholy wife.' There had been a boy, Alexander McCaffery, to do the chores for his board and education, but he had been called home. Now Henry, a 'scholar & a poet & as full of buds of promise as a young apple tree' was to have 'his board &c for what work he chooses to do.' [17] Yet most of all, I think, Emerson proposed a rescue. Only a short time before he had offered to shelter the impecunious Alcotts, an offer which the sensible Mrs. Alcott declined. And here was a compensation for his failure to help Alcott, that was at the same time a convenience. His 'dear Henry' was, so he believed, a poet for the future, and at the same time a jack-of-all-trades, a friend of the children, and reliable to the death. So Thoreau came to the Emersons' on April 26, 1841, to stay, wrote Emerson to Carlyle, 'for a twelvemonth.' He lived there two years.

But there was no monetary compensation, and, though Thoreau earned a little outside, after two years the need of ready cash became imperative. By February 16 of 1843 he is writing to Emerson that he is 'meditating some other method of paying debts than by lectures and writing, — which will only do to talk about. If anything of that "other" sort should come to your ears in New York, will you remember it for me?' Emerson remembered and thought over the problem.

By this time it was obvious that *The Dial* was not destined for even the least of commercial successes. It had never paid its contributors, it would never be able to pay its contributors. Furthermore, the poet whom Emerson had taken into his household, and who in September of 1841 had been 'in the mid-sea of verses',[18] and 'full of noble madness,' [19] was by February of '43 writing to his friend and master: 'As for poetry, I have not remembered to write any for some time; it has quite slipped my mind. ... You see it takes a good many words to supply the place of one deed.' He was in debt, his poetry was drying up, he had to find a new way of solving the problem of sustenance.[20]

What Emerson said and did can be deduced with reasonable certainty from what followed in the next six months. He got for Henry, not a job so much as an opportunity. He arranged with his brother William, the business man of the family who lived on Staten Island, to take on the young poet, who had broken into one magazine, and might break into others which were more remunerative, as a tutor for his son Haven.[21] William Emerson, 'very gentlemanly, very amenable, very clear-headed, but a mere business man,' as Margaret Fuller described him, does not figure in this history. Henry might as well have been living on the moon for all the note he took of the family with whom he spent six months. And with reason, for though he was conscientious in his tutoring, it is clear that Emerson had sent him to the neighborhood of New York with the idea that this was his chance to find markets for his prose if not his poetry. In January, as a hopeful preliminary, Hawthorne, who was drawn to Thoreau from the first, had him to tea at the Old Manse to meet O'Sullivan, editor of *The Democratic Review* of New York, who 'made a point of asking me to write for his Review, which I shall be glad to do.' [22]

On May 1 he was off, supplied with introductions by Emerson both to his youthful admirers in New York, Tappan, Waldo, and others, and to men of influence like Brisbane (who bored Henry with his Fourierism), Henry James (who fascinated him), and Horace Greeley, editor of *The Tribune*. The illness which, as so often, weakened him in February had passed, but bronchitis caught him on Staten Island, followed by a period of physical lassitude — another spot on the lung, one supposes. Nevertheless, his abundant letters from this only period when he lived away from Concord are full of his main purpose. 'I am sure that you are under sacred protection,' wrote the optimistic Emerson.[23] 'You must not count much upon what I can do or learn in New York. I feel a good way off here,' Thoreau replied; but as soon as his chest was clear he set about his projects earnestly, spending what William Emerson gave him upon bus trips uptown, and a new pair of pantaloons for $2.25.

Ellery Channing, who came to live in Concord just as Thoreau left, had been saying to Emerson that Henry should not see Concord again for ten years, should grind up fifty Concords in his mill. That was Emerson's idea also. This boy must break through into a less provincial (and more remunerative) world. And Thoreau did make a few steps in this direction. O'Sullivan bought a little essay — a very dull and perfunctory one — called 'The Landlord' for his *Democratic Review*, and ordered a review of an extraordinary book by a German called Etzler, which, after some haggling, he published.

'What with Alcott and Lane and Hawthorne, too, you look strong enough to take New York by storm,' Henry wrote to Emerson on May 23, still confident that Concord might conquer New York. But as might be expected he is less cocky with his family: 'As for money matters,' — this is June 8 — 'I have not set my traps yet, but I am getting my bait ready.' Yet he produced little, even in his Journal, in these months. 'In writing, conversation should be folded many times thick,' he wrote to Emerson.[24] The folding was difficult.

His time was not wasted, for his personal contacts were rich. He made a lifelong friend of Horace Greeley, and sent home word portraits of the notables he met which show far more power than anything in his *Dial* prose. But as a contributor he was not succeeding, and so he told his mother:

Castleton, Tuesday, August 29, 1843.
    Dear Mother, — ... I may yet accomplish something in the literary way; indeed, I should have done so before now but for the slowness and poverty of the 'Reviews' themselves. I have tried sundry methods of earning money in the city, of late, but without success: have rambled into every bookseller's or publisher's house, and discussed their affairs with them. Some propose to me to do what an honest man cannot. [Had someone, as Greeley did later, asked him to do an 'intimate' portrait of Emerson at home?] Among others I conversed with the Harpers — to see if they might not find me useful to them; but they say that they are making $50,000 annually, and their motto is to let well alone. I find that I talk with these poor men as if I were over head and ears in business, and a few thousands were no consideration with me.... But it is a very valuable experience, and the best introduction I could have.

He tries to sell subscriptions to *The Agriculturist*, but gets nothing out of it except a trip to the Croton Reservoir. Al-

though he was to earn a certain sum by winter, he admits to
Emerson in a September letter: 'Literature comes to a poor
market here; and even the little that I write is more than will
sell.' He has tried six magazines — only *The Ladies' Companion*
pays. 'My bait will not tempt the rats, — they are too well fed,'
he writes to his mother on October 1, although he holds together remarkably well as regards the 'outward linen and
woolen man; no holes more than I brought away.' As for *The
Ladies' Companion*, 'I could not write anything companionable.'
He reads in the library, watches the crowds, finds more to hate
than to love in the city. Perhaps he can get a teaching job for
Helen and himself, but the pay is poor, even here.

6

How familiar this is to anyone who has been young and hopeful in literature, or older and in a publisher's or an editor's
chair. Youth, scornful one moment, depressed and mean in
spirit the next, going the rounds, with only its promises to sell,
bluffing a little, pretending to have bluffed more — finding
doors closing quickly, kind words but no jobs, perfunctory
interest but no acceptances, a market which proves to be only
a business for those who edit and print and sell, a welcome only
for those who can write something 'companionable' — but for
an original mind not yet master of itself, nothing so profitable
even as lecturing. And for this home-lover, instead of the family
circle and the Valhalla at Emerson's, only the 'polite William
Emerson,' and Haven — 'I am not attracted toward him but
as to youth generally. He shall frequent me, however, as
much as he can, and I'll be I.' [25]
Haven could not have much enjoyed this tutor, sick of body,
sick for home, who 'loitered' through the neighboring fields, as
in Concord, took his fill of such ocean as he could see from

Staten Island, while the inner conviction grew that not in twenty lifetimes could he grind up one Concord in his mill. Concord was his destination, there was no sustenance for him in New York. His expedition into the outer un-Transcendental world had failed. The philosophers at home might talk too much about their spiritual reality ('Mamma,' said the child of Emerson's Journal, who was Louisa Alcott, 'they have begun again!'), but the reality which had a price in New York was out of his reach, and of his desire. He was homesick. Even Lane's absurd letter from Fruitlands, where Alcott and he were busy creating a mystic's paradise, offering fourteen acres of wood, 'a very sylvan realization, which only wants a Thoreau's mind to elevate it to classic beauty,' [26] even this cockney description of nature, which should have given Thoreau pain, seemed to him friendly and cheerful.

Thoreau was too busy and too unwell to do much journalizing on Staten Island, but an unpublished manuscript in the Huntington Library [27] contains notes of his set down in this period, which, if they represent his real interests, and of course they do, are enough in themselves to show how unlikely it was that his peculiar genius would make any headway in commercial New York. His contemporary, Poe, was writing criticism shrewder than Henry's and publishing it, and philosophy which, if more sensational, was quite as far above the popular brand. Poe was a born journalist, who knew how to push literature into the crevices of current interest, but, financially, even he failed. Thoreau, who did not know how to make compromises, had little chance. Among his Journal notes are some remarkable sentences, but they do not suggest a 'companionable' success:

> Who can see these cities and say that there is any life in them. I walked through New York yesterday [*Sept. 23rd*] — and met no real and living person.

Thursday 12th [*Oct.*] It is hard to read a contemporary poet critically for we go within the shallowest verse and inform it with all the life and promise of this day. We are such a near and kind and knowing audience as he will never have again.

Tuesday 24th [*Oct.*] Though I am old enough to have discovered that the dreams of youth are not to be realized in this state of existence yet I think it would be the next greatest happiness always to be allowed to look under the eyelids of time and contemplate the perfect steadily with the clear understanding that I do not attain to it.

You must store up none of the life in your gift — it is as fatal as to husband your breath. We must *live* all our *life*.

7

And so by Thanksgiving of 1843 he came back to Concord with a lecture on Ossian for the Lyceum, determined to live *his* life. He had learned what a more worldly man than Emerson could have told him in the beginning, that a poet, a critic, a Transcendentalist, and a man insisting on his own way, might get an entrée but could never make a living from New York magazines. The problem, indeed, was to reconcile the active, which was so strong with him, the contemplative, and the creative, without paying too much in dependence or privation for the experience. Teaching was ended, lecturing was a reed, magazine writing for pay promised only an occasional contribution, and that for the writing which contained least of himself. The answer was to find a way of living one's whole life so cheaply that there would be time and energy left over to learn how to record it in print.

This, then, was the real result of Emerson's attempt to foist him upon the greater world. The greater world had no need of him, and he in his turn found that, for him, the greater world was Concord. And so, having been an author without pay, and having learned how to place an occasional manuscript with insufficient pay, he came home to take up from a new angle his problem of how to live and how to stay alive while living. He had learned that in order to do what he wanted in writing he would have to publish himself. And this inevitably led him to Walden Pond.

I must repeat the significant economic fact of the last paragraph. With these New England Transcendentals, even with the practically minded Thoreau, it is very difficult to remember in the midst of their spiritual efflorescences that they were subject to the same law of the necessity of food and shelter and loose change in the pockets as any Poor Richard or Deacon Brown. More subject, in the case of Henry, who credited or debited his mother with one half a cent on an item loaned or borrowed, and who proudly wrote to his class secretary protesting that no one was to consider him a subject for charity — on the contrary, he was ready to give charity himself. And here he was back again, just where he had been in 1841 when the school closed, more ambitious, more able, more determined to work for Admetus as little as possible, disillusioned as to the possible rewards of literary labor, but determined to write and to eat and to clothe himself, and to have books and friends and leisure at his own cost. But how? It has been the problem of every creative, original mind since the days of the Greeks, and probably since tools gave some freedom to the mind of man.

II. TWO WOMEN

I<small>T IS THE WINTER</small> of 1841, before his stay at Emerson's and his adventures in New York. Thoreau, sitting, doubtless, in his attic room under the sloping roof of the Parkman house, was writing down his melancholy, as his idyllic love for Ellen Sewall drifted more and more rapidly into the past. Having put his 'sober play' and 'sad plight' into rhythm and sent his version of a proposal of marriage to Watertown, to be refused with brevity, he was turning elsewhere for the feminine sympathy he craved:

> *Jan. 4, 1841.* I know a woman who is as true to me and as incessant with her mild rebuke as the blue sky. When I stand under her cope, instantly all pretension drops off — for she plys me like wind and rain to remove all taint. I am fortunate that I can pass and repass before her as a mirror, each day. And I prove my strength in her glances. She is far truer to me than to herself. Her eyes are such bottomless and inexhaustible depths as if they were the windows of the Nature, through which I caught glimpses of the native land of the soul.[1]

Such passages as this are warnings not to make the biography of Thoreau a history of ideas. The reader who knows his Thoreau may answer, why not? — it is the ideas of Thoreau, or at least his phrasings of them, that have been planted so deeply in fertile minds that even now they are sending up fresh crops. Yet it is precisely this view which makes the existing biographies unsatisfactory. It is really not Thoreau's ideas which give to his best writing an authentic originality — it is his attitudes. His ideas are all borrowed; the originality is in the blending; and the secret of the blending is to be found in his own temperament expanding in his New England environment. Therefore the attitudes (and they were sometimes poses) of this youth, his loves, his hates, his scorns, his prejudices, and his inhibitions, are vital for biography, since they determine the uses he made of his thinking.

By 1843, when he came home disappointed in journalism but eager to write books, his philosophy of life was fixed, if not yet entirely articulate. He was to learn nothing more except that it is easier to make a philosophy than to carry it out, and much easier to carry it out than to explain the not-me of the world inside and outside of Concord by means of it. This philosophy of his is recorded, not always intelligibly, in the Journal in which he reported his life, and sent off daily, as he said, on a sheet postpaid to the gods: 'I am clerk in their counting-room, and at evening transfer the account from day-book to ledger.' [2] I shall pursue it through his quirks and puckers and preciosities, and occasional magnificent eloquences, in a later chapter, where I shall attempt to show that Henry, by his twenty-sixth year, if he had not ground up Concord in his mill, had assimilated Emerson and the Hindus and was ready to be Thoreau.

Yet how little they know of a man who know only what he thinks, not how and why! There is nothing in Thoreau's philosophy, for example, to explain the fierceness of his embrace of solitude and the passion of his reactions toward human love. There is nothing to account for the passionate intensity of his love for nature.

I shall not apologize, therefore, for devoting this chapter to a

Henry Thoreau who is feeling not thinking; a tender and charming Thoreau, his 'prickles' all subsided, whose emotions were
expanding as fast as his intellect and were always to color it.
This Thoreau was, I think, never visible except to women.
Only women could draw out from its hiding the tender, shy,
and passionate spirit, which in his writing is always just below
the surface even of his satirical passages. The conception of
Henry Thoreau as a woman-hater and a sexless philosopher is
easy to shatter. He was a woman's man, frustrated in his relationships with women by circumstances and his own independent, ambitious temperament.

There were at least four women in Thoreau's life, not counting his mother and sisters. With two he was in love, and one of
these was Ellen. One, at least, was in love with him. Two of
these women may be said to have saved him from the cold intellectuality of Concord which makes the Transcendentalism of
the eager spirits gathered there in the early forties seem so
brittle, so inhibited today. For *The Dial*, which was their organ,
was free in everything but this — there is no passion except of
the intellect in its pages.

2

The woman he knew so well, who was truer to him than to
herself, must have been the lonely invalid who looks down so
sweetly in her picture,[3] Lucy Jackson Brown. Mention has
already been made of her affection for the young poet, then a
senior at Harvard, who tossed 'Sic Vita' with a bunch of
violets into her window. In the winter of 1841 she was as often
before living at the Thoreaus', since Henry fixed her stove-door
as she talked:

> Last winter, you know, you did more than your share of
> the talking, and I did not complain for want of an opportu-
> nity. . . .

Not in a year of the gods, I fear, will such a golden approach to plain speaking revolve again.[4]

She seems to have left the Thoreaus and gone home to Plymouth in that spring when the school closed and Henry shifted his abode across the Mill Dam to the Emersons'. There the presence of her sister, Lidian, would have kept talk of her warm, even when she was not visiting them. She was his first literary confidant, which accounts for the bookish references in his letters and also for his frank confessions, as to an understanding mind, of what he hoped to do:

> Concord, January 24, 1843.
>
> Dear Friend,—... We always seem to be living just on the brink of a pure and lofty intercourse, which would make the ills and trivialness of life ridiculous. After each little interval, though it be but for the night, we are prepared to meet each other as gods and goddesses.
>
> I seem to have dodged all my days with one or two persons, and lived upon expectation, — as if the bud would surely blossom; and so I am content to live. ...
>
> I am very happy in my present environment [he was at the Emersons'], though actually mean enough myself, and so, of course, all around me; yet, I am sure, we for the most part are transfigured to one another, and are that to the other which we aspire to be ourselves. The longest course of mean and trivial intercourse may not prevent my practicing this divine courtesy to my companion. Notwithstanding all I hear about brooms, and scouring, and taxes, and housekeeping, I am constrained to live a strangely mixed life, — as if even Valhalla might have its kitchen. We are all of us Apollos serving some Admetus.

We must not smile at the elevated diction of this letter — it is quite as American as the flat familiarity of a later generation. These affectionate, deeply serious women were bringing out the best in Henry, making him forget his poses, and recognizing his

spiritual cravings. They were trying so hard to be worthy of
their souls, even in the kitchen of the Valhalla where Emerson
dwelt:

> Concord, Friday evening
> January 25, 1843.
>
> Dear Friend, —... I don't know whether you have got the
> many [letters] I have sent you, or rather whether you were
> quite sure where they came from. I mean the letters I have
> sometimes launched off eastward in my thought; but if you
> have been happier at one time than another, think that then
> you received them.... Why, I will send you my still fresh
> remembrance of the hours I have passed with you here, for I
> find in the remembrance of them the best gift you have left to me.
> We are poor and sick creatures at best; but we can have well
> memories, and sound and healthy thoughts of one another still,
> and an intercourse may be remembered which was without
> blur, and above us both.
>
> Perhaps you may like to know of my estate nowadays....
> One while I am vexed by a sense of meanness; one while I
> simply wonder at the mystery of life; and at another, and at
> another, seem to rest on my oars, as if propelled by propitious
> breezes from I know not what quarter. But for the most part
> I am an idle, inefficient, lingering (one term will do as well as
> another, when all are true and none true enough) member of
> the great commonwealth, who have most need of my own
> charity....
>
> Don't think me unkind because I have not written to you.
> I confess it was for so poor a reason as that you almost made a
> principle of not answering. I could not speak truly with this
> ugly fact in the way....

After this the warmth, but not the fact, of the friendship
lapsed. Even though Lucy Brown came to live in a house built
by Emerson across the road, the intimacy was transferred to
the younger sister.

3

It is difficult to learn much of Lidian Emerson, so much is
she overshadowed by her husband, who, indeed, did little himself
to encourage her personality beyond the home. We know that
she was a constant invalid, deeply religious rather than intellectual like her sister, conscientious to a fault, and with a sur-
passing love for flowers and gardening. The tolerant Emerson
found her sympathetic but unconverted to 'newness.' She
thought it wicked to go to church, which must have pleased
Thoreau, yet suffered from her doubts, and in her childhood
was subject to religious terrors. Lidian was witty, a little shy,
with a sense of duty to the home and the household which was
prevailing. When she had a new order to give in the kitchen,
she said, she felt like a boy who throws a stone and runs.[5]
Emerson, who called her 'mine Asia,' says frankly that he
thought of his first wife, Ellen, as one to travel with, which
means, I suppose, as an emotional sharer of experience, but of
Lidian as a companion in the home. Yet from the home she
constantly retreated to her family in Plymouth, leaving a long
succession of governesses and helpers in charge. There was,
seemingly, a neurosis of some kind at the root of her ill health.
Certainly Emerson was never truly intimate with his Asia,
and was aware of his frequent aloofness, his coldness with her,
and so was she. He led, he said rather bitterly of himself, 'a
bachelor existence,' and apologized more than once in his letters
for his lack of warmth to her. He was better, he said, as a father
than as a stove! [6]

There was an extraordinary politeness in the Emerson household, which many have commented on,[7] that set Thoreau's
prickles quivering. He lived, however, with the women, Lidian
and Lucy and Sophia Foord and Mary Russell,[8] and with the
children in house or garden, making toys and instruments for

little Waldo, and helping Lidian, in an atmosphere that was evidently less formal when the master was absent. He also was shy (though not too shy to read from his 'The Service' to Emerson's spiritual 'Sister,' Caroline Sturgis[9]). 'One of our girls said,' so R. W. E. notes in 1843, 'that Henry never went through the kitchen without coloring.' The wife and the young protégé must have been quickly drawn together, for they were constantly in each other's company. Thoreau's room in the house (it has now been made into a bathroom) was at the top of the front stairs and hence on the main-travelled way of the home.[10] While for Emerson it was 'much to know that poetry has been written this very day, under this very roof, by your side,'[11] he saw little of Henry in his first stay. His walks seem to have been with Ellery Channing, and the very excitement of his first boat ride with Thoreau shows that excursions with him did not happen often. The philosopher at home seems to have kept much to himself.

Thoreau's attitude toward Mrs. Emerson, say the editors of Emerson's Journal, was of respectful attention. At first, yes, as befitted the difference in their ages, but long before the two years of his residence ended there was a change. It is probable that the sudden death of little Waldo in January of 1842, followed by the death of Henry's beloved John in the same month, brought them closer together. Yet the presence of the warm-blooded youth in this polite household, so warm in its thinking, so cool in its decorum, is a better explanation of what happened. Lidian must have found Thoreau as sympathetic and as interesting as had her sister, but the new relations were more intimate, and she, behind her shyness, seems to have been a far more emotional person. Books did not concern her so much as her inner life, and humor was in her gift. While Emerson was in New York lecturing in '43 she wrote him of one of the famous Conversations held in the house:

Mrs. Ralph Waldo Emerson with one of her children
'*You must know that you represent to me woman*'
From a daguerreotype taken in 1847

Concord, February 20, 1843.

... The subjects were: What is Prophecy? Who is a Prophet? and The Love of Nature. Mr. Lane [Alcott's English friend who bought Fruitlands in order to devise something better than family life] decided, as for all time and the race, that this same love of nature — of which Henry was the champion, and Elizabeth Hoar and Lidian (though L. disclaimed possessing it herself) his faithful squiresses — that this love was the most subtle and dangerous of sins .... Henry frankly affirmed to both the wise men that they were wholly deficient in the faculty in question, and therefore could not judge of it. And Mr. Alcott as frankly answered that it was because they went beyond the mere material objects, and were filled with spiritual love and perception (as Mr. T. was not), that they seemed to Mr. Thoreau not to appreciate outward nature. I am very heavy, and have spoiled a most excellent story. I have given you no idea of the scene, which was ineffably comic, though it made no laugh at the time; I scarce laughed at it myself, — too deeply amused to give the usual sign. Henry was brave and noble; well as I have always liked him, he still grows upon me.

But she grew upon him even more. Indeed, from various references in his Journal, it seems probable that he was already deeply stirred. A year before the date of this letter he was inserting, without relevance, in the daily record of his Journal, 'Where is my heart gone? They say men cannot part with it and live.' [12] Lidian was the first outside the family to whom he wrote from Staten Island:

Castleton, Staten Island, May 22, 1843.

My dear Friend, — I believe a good many conversations with you were left in an unfinished state, and now indeed I don't know where to take them up. But I will resume some of the unfinished silence. I shall not hesitate to know you. I think of you as some elder sister of mine, whom I could not have avoided, — a sort of lunar influence, — only of such age as the moon, whose time is measured by her light. You must know that you represent to me woman, for I have not traveled very far or wide, — and what if I had? I like to deal with you, for I believe you do not lie or steal, and these are very rare virtues. I thank you for your influence for two years. I was fortunate to be subjected to it, and am now to remember it. It is the noblest gift we can make; what signify all others that can be bestowed? You have helped to keep my life 'on loft,' as Chaucer says of Griselda, and in a better sense. You always seemed to look down at me as from some elevation, — some of your high humilities, — and I was the better for having to look up. I felt taxed not to disappoint your expectation; for could there be any accident so sad as to be respected for something better than we are? It was a pleasure even to go away from you . . . as it apprised me of my high relations; and such a departure is a sort of further introduction and meeting. Nothing makes the earth seem so spacious as to have friends at a distance; they make the latitudes and longitudes.

You must not think that fate is so dark there, for even here I can see a faint reflected light over Concord, and I think that at this distance I can better weigh the value of a doubt there. Your moonlight, as I have told you, though it is a reflection of the sun, allows of bats and owls and other twilight birds to flit therein. But I am very glad that you can elevate your life with a doubt, for I am sure that it is nothing but an insatiable faith after all that deepens and darkens its current. And your doubt and my confidence are only a difference of expression.

This is a tribute of which any woman might be proud — yet notice its restrained emotion — she is much older (she was, in fact, fifteen years older), but the Jackson women in spite of invalidism kept youthful looks. She was timeless like the moon, her influence measured by its light. For him she represents woman. What she replied I do not know, but it is evident from Henry's next letter on June 20 that something has unlocked her heart, perhaps his tender reference to her religious doubts, perhaps the manly fervor of the letter quoted above. Certainly she responded as Ellen did not, as Mrs. Brown probably could not, to Thoreau's craving, so often expressed, for a friendship which lifted as it grew warmer, which was Transcendental yet intensely human:

Staten Island, June 20, 1843.

My very dear Friend, — I have only read a page of your letter, and have come out to the top of the hill at sunset, where I can see the ocean, to prepare to read the rest. It is fitter that it should hear it than the walls of my chamber. . . . I feel as if it were a great daring to go on and read the rest, and then to live accordingly. . . . I am almost afraid to look at your letter. I see that it will make my life very steep, but it may lead to fairer prospects than this. . . .

My dear friend, it was very noble in you to write me so trustful an answer. . . . The thought of you will constantly elevate my life. . . . I think I know your thoughts without seeing you, and as well here as in Concord. You are not at all strange to me.

I could hardly believe, after the lapse of one night, that I had such a noble letter still at hand to read. . . . I looked at midnight to be sure that it was real. I feel that I am unworthy to know you, and yet they will not permit it wrongfully. . . .

My friend, I have read your letter as if I was not reading it. After each pause I could defer the rest forever. . . . What have we to do with petty rumbling news? We have our own great affairs. Sometimes in Concord I found my actions dictated, as it were, by your influence, and though it led almost to trivial Hindoo observances, yet it was good and elevating. . . .

I send my love to my other friend and brother, whose nobleness I slowly recognize.

HENRY

After two years under his roof, it is only slowly that Thoreau recognizes the nobleness of his 'friend and brother,' Emerson! Surely it was because of lack of opportunity, not doubt. Lidian, not Emerson, has been the great influence in his emotional life, and this letter, with its over-tensity of feeling, is a cogent explanation of the Platonisms of the essay on Friendship. Here is a source more important than his reading for his obsession with love which is friendship and friendship which is love, and also,

I am sure, of many passionate passages in his Journal where the substitution of a 'she' brings them close to these letters. It was the beginning also, I fear, of a lifelong frustration. For Lidian was a wife and mother, and she was certainly enough awake emotionally to recognize that his letter, for all its ethereal morality, was perilously close to love, by any definition. Her letter had been an exhortation by a dear friend to live a life worthy of him and of her — but it was read, though Henry would have denied it, as a love letter is read.

Certainly, she took fright. I believe she must have written him a cooling epistle. His next recorded letter to her was not written until October 16, and deals precisely with the 'petty rumbling news' which was to be unnecessary between them. He tells her that W. H. Channing has published his 'Present,' he asks whether they have gone berrying or to the Cliffs, and how are the flowers and the hens, says he has been reading Quarles, and sends a critique for her and for Mrs. Brown. How are Edith, Ellen, and Elizabeth Hoar? And nothing more!

4

She would have been abundantly justified if a cooling letter was written, could she have read the remarkable confession called 'A Sister,' which is preserved in a manuscript now in the Huntington Library, dated by Sanborn as of 1848 to 1850, and containing passages used later in 'Walden.' 'A Sister' was therefore written either at Walden Pond, when his Journal was pointing toward 'Walden,' or in the years just succeeding, one of which was spent, by her request, in companionship with Lidian:

A Sister.
One in whom you have — unbounded faith — whom you can — purely love. A sweet presence and companion making the

world populous. Whose heart answers to your heart. Whose
presence can fill all space. One who is a spirit. Who attends
to your truth. A gentle spirit — a wise spirit — a loving spirit.
An enlargement to your being, level to yourself. Whom you
presume to know.... The stream of whose being unites with
your own without a ripple or a murmur. & this spreads into a
sea.

I still think of you as my sister.... Others are of my kindred
by blood or of my acquaintance but you are part of me. You
are of me & I of you I cannot tell where I leave off and you
begin.... To you I can afford to be forever what I am, for
your presence will not permit me to be what I should not be....
My sister whom I love I almost have no more to do with. I
shall know where to find her.... I can more heartily meet her
when our bodies are away. I see her without the veil of the
body.... Other men have added to their farms I have annexed a soul to mine.

When I love you I feel as if I were annexing another world
to mine.... O Do not disappoint me.

Whose breath is as gentle and salubrious as a Zephyr's
whisper. Whom I know as an atmosphere.... Whom in thought
my spirit continually embraces. Unto whom I flow.... Who
art clothed in white. Who comest like an incense. Who art
all that I can imagine — my inspirer. The feminine of me —
Who art magnanimous

It is morning when I meet thee in a still cool dewy white
sun light In the hushed dawn — my young mother — I thy
eldest son.... Whether art thou my mother or my sister —
whether am I thy son or thy brother.

On the remembrances of whom I repose — so *old* a sister art
thou — so nearly hast thou recreated me ... whose eyes are
like the morning star Who comest to me in the morning
twilight.[13]

Even if we knew of any other woman of whom these fervid
passages, with their curious incoherence in relationships and
their approaches to hysterical emotion, could conceivably have
been written, the parallels to Thoreau's letter to Lidian, and

the known intimacy between them in '47–'48, as well as in '41–'43, would make it substantially certain that Mrs. Emerson was intended. I leave to psychologists of love what Thoreau's state exactly was. But certainly he was deeply moved, though he would have admitted only such a Transcendental meaning as can be found in Emerson's letters to *his* 'Sister,' Caroline Sturgis Tappan, so much warmer emotionally than his letters to his wife. He had evidently intended, as in the essay on Friendship, to conceal the personal references by 'thou' and 'art,' and there are many revisions apparent in the manuscript. But no revision could make 'A Sister' publishable without revealings. Its place in a manuscript made up of passages not sequent, either by number of page or by subject, suggests that these pages were not meant to be a part of the Journal which he expected the public some day to read.

There is, as it happens, direct evidence in other pages of the manuscript that this essay was personal. I can only guess at the significance of one isolated sentence: 'I would not that my love should be a trouble or a disgrace to my friends,' though the inference seems clear enough. But in another place is what seems to be his own guarded statement of what lay behind 'A Sister.' The page is torn at the top:

> By turns my purity has inspired and my impurity has cast me down.
> My most intimate acquaintance with woman has been a sisters relation, or at most a catholic's virgin mother relation — not that it has always been free from the suspicion of lower sympathy. There is a love of woman [page torn] with marriage — of woman on the [page torn] She has exerted the influence of a goddess on me; cultivating my gentler humane nature; cultivating & preserving purity, innocence, truth, [end of page]
> [Succeeding fragment; marked 1850 by Sanborn.] Woman is a nature older than I and commanding from me a vast amount of veneration — like Nature. She is my mother at

the same time that she is my sister, so that she is at any rate an older sister. . . . I cannot imagine a woman no older than I. . . . Methinks that I am younger than aught that I associate with. The youngest child is more than my coeval.[14]

It is impossible to believe after reading these passages that Thoreau was immune to love, nor hard to understand after his experience with young romance and this religious passion for a conscientious married woman, why his emotional life in the future was likely to take the common course of love frustrated, toward sublimation. But that is the last chapter of his emotional history. He was to find first, and at least one other woman was to discover from him, that 'implacable is love.'

There would seem to be little doubt, whatever the psychologists say, that Thoreau was what the common man would call in love with Emerson's wife, although I suspect that the intensity of the relationship did not reach its peak until during and after his second stay at the Emersons'. It was so easy for him to Transcendentalize this emotion, and so impossible for his Concord imagination to conceive anything not Transcendental in his relations with his benefactor's wife, that it is useless to look for open confirmation on his part. When they were thrown together while Emerson was lecturing in '47 and '48 he writes to Emerson in England: 'Lidian and I make very good housekeepers. She is a very dear sister to me.' 'Lidian is too unwell to write.' There is no further mention of her, either in his Journal or his published letters, but that she is often if not always the mysterious friend of the Journal of the fifties who is cold, who disappoints, who will not meet with heart as well as mind, I have little doubt. More of this later.

12. FRIENDS AND ACQUAINTANCES

MY TRUEST, SERENEST MOMENTS are too still for emotion; they have woollen feet.' So Thoreau wrote in January of 1841 when he was just recovering from one emotional experience and about to become involved in another. No statement of mood could be truer of this obstinate, sensitive youth, who was played upon by all the high seriousness of the 1840's and desired, like the early Quakers, quiet in which to feel his intuitions of spiritual truth quietly form and quietly evolve. Already in 1841 he was seeking his inward light, but in the visible Concord he was still a small-town youth, unsure, diffident, reaching toward friendship with noble minds, and then drawing back with an unmannerly shrug. These are the years when he begins to make what might be called important friends, yet his first reaction with people at ease in a broader world than Concord or Harvard is distress — often followed by rather clumsy sarcasm.

There is an interesting self-portrait from this period which explains a good deal. The elaborate ornithological record kept by his brother John went, at his death on January 11, 1842, to Henry, who added a few items (not being then much interested in birds), and used it for a notebook.[1] In this, is an early draft of the 'Walk to Wachusett,' which was published in 1843; and immediately succeeding it and in different ink, as if begun, and then taken up again, and finally dropped, what I believe was an attempt (his only one) at an autobiographical story. The date is probably 1842, since the handwriting is identical with the Wachusett pages:

> It may be well if first of all I should give some account first of my species and variety. I am about five feet 7 inches in height — of a light complexion, rather slimly built, and just approaching the Roman age of manhood. One who faces West oftener than East — walks out of the house with a better grace than he goes in — who loves winter as well as summer — forest as well as field — darkness as well as light. Rather solitary than gregarious — not migratory nor dormant — but to be raised at any season, by day or night, not by the pulling of any bell wire, but by a smart stroke upon any pine tree in the woods of Concord.

He was about twenty-five, the Roman age of responsibility; therefore the description should do well enough. The five feet, seven inches is puzzling, for the impression he made was of a shorter man. So he seemed to Howells, who visited him in 1860:

> He came into the room a quaint, stump figure of a man, whose effect of long trunk and short limbs was heightened by his fashionless trousers being let down too low. He had a noble face, with tossed hair, a distraught eye, and a fine aquilinity of profile ... but his nose failed to add that foot to his stature which Lamb says a nose of that shape will always give a man.[2]

Restore the freshness of youth to this figure, and add the finely curved lips, beautiful in repose, but puckered probably, like the rest of the Thoreaus when he spoke; think of the face still unbearded, and keep the trousers, designed for scrub oaks, not for drawing-rooms.

Then there is the reminiscence of Hawthorne's daughter, Mrs. Lathrop. He 'used to flit in and out of the house with long, ungainly, Indian-like stride, and his piercing large orbs, staring, as it were in vacancy.' [3]

As Emerson said, he would enter a room, discharge what he had to say, and leave without chance for conversation. Emerson never speaks of his clothes, nor does Thoreau until after he had become a partner of the Transcendentalists who met so often in Concord. His aunt made his first homespun; later, he got it from Vermont and had his clothes made up for utility, not show, by Mrs. Hosmer, a village sempstress. His boots were never blacked, he wore a low collar like Emerson, and could be and often was mistaken for a farmer. No wonder that in the presence of these lecturers, ministers, conversationalists, editors, and women who knew and were known by their Boston, he began to feel mean and uncouth and took his revenge by savage attacks on manners. His one objection to school teaching was that you had to dress up for it.

When the Tyrolean singers came to Concord in '41 Thoreau was deeply impressed — for if his taste in music was literary, it was passionate; but what concerned him most, to judge from his Journal, was his indecision when a lady came in late looking for a seat. He did not give her his. 'No, be true to your interests, and sit; wait till you can be genuinely polite, if it be till doomsday, and not lose your chance everlastingly by a cowardly yielding to young etiquette.' He wrote two pages about it. She thought he was rude, and so did he — and tried to philosophize himself out of his sense of social maladjustment.

Hence, among the friends of his three worlds, the intellectuals, the Concord family circle, and the farmers, he was always a little on edge with the first, and his uneasy words about them must often be discounted, as you would discount the report of a formal dinner by a man who arrived by mistake in a business suit.

But unease with the well-mannered and worldly passed,

though the scars remained. The youth did make way among the notables of Concord and elsewhere, long before the well-known chapter describing his visitors at Walden. Even in 1841 he was not so much of a bare hill as Margaret Fuller thought, and his comparison of himself with Wachusett Mountain (that lovely peak one sees from the Harvard hills) as standing alone without society, was half a pose.

2

His relations with Emerson ripened slowly. There was too much veneration at first, then too much unease in the presence of the smiling serenity of the great man, who never wavered in his faith in Thoreau's genius or in his certainty of its limitations. Thoreau is always 'valiant Henry,' 'my brave Henry' — seldom, except in moments of irritation, a realized human being. When in 1841 Thoreau had settled down in the little room at the head of the front stairs, he was ready to 'approach a great nature with infinite expectation and uncertainty, not knowing what I may meet.' He soon felt 'expanded and enlarged,' and he was not deceived by Emerson's superior calm when off his guard into thinking him complacent. 'When I see a man with serene countenance in the sunshine of summer, drinking in peace in the garden or parlor, it looks like a great inward leisure that he enjoys' — but actually 'the man of principle gets never a holiday'; — and never really relaxes, he adds later, into frank, familiar converse. Yet it was not an easy relationship. Emerson was an acknowledged great man, Henry was determined to make at least his soul and mind great. 'Between the sincere there will be no civilities,' he wrote. But it was hard for the younger man to be sincere without pressing his own differences, and 'no greatness seems prepared for the little decorum, even savage unmannerliness, it meets from equal greatness.' Emerson clearly did not like to be argued with. He was still a preacher. Nor did he like to descend from his own heights to meet the warmth of aspiring personalities: 'I would have [my friends] where I can get them, but I seldom use them. . . . Though I prize my friends I cannot afford to talk with them and study their visions lest I lose my own. It would indeed give a certain household joy to quit this lofty seeking . . . and come down into warm sympathies with you but then I know well I shall mourn always the vanishing of my Mighty Gods.' [4] No wonder Emerson told Hawthorne that, much as he loved Henry, he suffered inconveniences by having him under his roof. No wonder Henry felt him to be remote.

Yet the inexplicable thing is how very few references, direct or indirect, are to be found in Thoreau's Journal to the man in whose home he was living for over two years, and to the routine of Emerson's house, except where it concerned the women and children. It must be, as Emerson's Journal also indicates, that they saw little of each other, except at work. Emerson retired to his study, Thoreau was busy in the garden, or walking the woods alone, or at home on Parkman Street, or cultivating independence in his hall bedroom or the barn. He could not have been present often at the Emersons' frequent entertainments. It is impossible not to feel that Emerson was a little irritated when he found he had acquired a philosopher who was not content to be intuitive but must challenge everything. Less experienced in human nature than in thought, he did not realize that this was the natural attempt of a pupil to break away from the dominance, not from the ideas, of his master. Less familiar with artists than with preachers, having known in a familiar environment only Hawthorne, whose books he could not read, he was puzzled by the creative instinct, which must worry ideas, as a dog worries slippers, until they are shaped like something eatable. So in the summer of '44 he writes: 'Henry Thoreau's conversation consisted of a continual coining of the present moment into a sentence and offering it to me.' He is like a boy who rolls a snowball and 'flings it at me. . . . He has no troublesome memory, no wake, but lives *ex tempore*, and brings to-day a new proposition as radical and revolutionary as that of yesterday, but different. The only man of leisure in the town. . . . If I cannot show his performance much more manifest than that of the other grand promisers, at least I can see that, with his practical faculty, he has declined all the kingdoms of this world. Satan has no bribe for him.'

This is mixed praise and blame for not getting somewhere. Emerson is urging the village Thoreau to use his leisure (though not in the village way) and will shortly push him off to New York, as narrated in the last chapter. The youth's delays, and the tensions and obstinacies that accompanied them, were beginning to annoy his friends.

It was in the year before that the highly intelligent Elizabeth Hoar, who was to have married Emerson's brother Charles, was heard to say, 'I love Henry, but do not like him.' Emerson, who quoted her, knew what Elizabeth meant. These young men, he commented, owe us a new world, but have not yet acquitted the debt. When after two years' intimate residence Thoreau left for Staten Island, Emerson wrote in his Journal merely, 'Henry Thoreau is gone yesterday to New York.'

3

Yet the two Journals give a somewhat false impression of a friendship that was noble, sweet, and rewarding. As happens with writers who are often reserved in person, letters reveal what may never have got into conversation. The death of little Waldo Emerson, Thoreau's favorite, on January 27, 1842, had brought them closer together, although it was Lidian who admitted him to the intimacy of grief. His own loss of John in the same month softened him still more. 'As for Waldo, he died as the mist rises from the brook. . . . He had not even taken root here,' Henry wrote to Lucy Brown. And so when Emerson has gone to New York and it is Thoreau's duty to tell him the news of the household, his gratitude comes easily in the written word.

It is January 24, 1843, and the letter begins by teasing Lane and Wright, Alcott's English admirers, who are always railing at the Transcendentalists and calling for more action. Alcott has gone to jail for refusing to pay his taxes. 'I vum,' says Staples, the jailer, who afterward was to know Henry better, 'I vum, I believe it was nothing but principle, for I never heerd a man talk honester.' Lane tries to get Henry to agitate with him against the state, but Henry's principles are not yet touched. His ideas might come from others, but his rebellions had to be self-made. At the moment these reformers with their communities like boarding-houses and their idea of nature as a virgin whom a touch would ravish, did not interest him. Then comes the heart of his letter:

> I will not write — what alone I had to say — to thank you and Mrs. Emerson for your long kindness to me. It would be more ungrateful than my constant thought. I have been your pensioner for nearly two years, and still left free as under the sky. It has been as free a gift as the sun or the summer, though I have sometimes molested you with my mean acceptance of it, — I who have failed to render even those slight services of the *hand* which would have been for a sign at least; and, by the fault of my nature, have failed of many better and higher services. But I will not trouble you with this, but for once thank you as well as Heaven.

Had he gone off too often to make pencils for pocket money, or been walking or journalizing when house or garden needed attention? Probably his apologies are mere overscrupulousness, for Henry was impeccable in payment of his debts. But that he meant every ounce of his gratitude is shown by his poem 'The Departure,' written probably when he was on Staten Island:

> This true people took the stranger,
> And warm-hearted housed the ranger. . . .
>
> And still the more he stayed
> The less his debt was paid.

Concord, February 10, 1843.
Dear Friend, — . . . I will tell you what we are doing this now. Supper is done, and Edith — the dessert, perhaps more than the dessert — is brought in, or even comes in *per se*; and round she goes, now to this altar, and then to that, with her monosyllabic invocation of 'oc,' 'oc.' It makes me think of 'Langue d'oc.' She must belong to that province. And like the gypsies she talks a language of her own while she understands ours. . . . And now she runs the race over the carpet, while all Olympia applauds, — mamma, grandma, and uncle.

Yet the second part of this letter, written two days later, begins, 'How mean are our relations to one another! Let us pause till they are nobler,' and is an essay on friendship, high-flown, rhetorical, which might have been sent to a stranger. It is not until five years afterward, when Emerson was in England, that Henry can write, 'Dear Waldo, — For I think I have heard that that is your name.'

4

The perfect dilettante in literature, William Ellery Channing, was in Concord off and on in '40 and '41, but his associations were chiefly with Emerson, in whose shadow he lived. Thoreau knew and liked him, and Channing, who liked hardly anyone very long, not even his wife, Margaret Fuller's sister, whom he married in '42, or his dog, loved Thoreau for the rest of his life.

He had seen enough of him by May of '43 to thank him for his many benevolences and to ask him to look after his new house.[5] Later he was to write an imaginary dialogue with Thoreau, Emerson, and himself speaking, which, in spite of (and sometimes because of) borrowings from their Journals, is so precious, so strained, and so pseudo-intellectual that one wonders how Thoreau in his later years, when he had shed his literary bravado, stood his companionship. Sometimes, of course, he didn't, and went off in his boat, leaving Channing on the shore. Yet this is to be one of his great friendships as distinguished from his loves. Here, in the last fifteen years of his life was his most constant companion.

Perhaps Emerson's description when Channing in '41 was *his* young friend and promising poet, is the best introduction to, and explanation of, the lasting quality of the companionship offered. After all, there were not many men in Concord with so much of English and still more of classic literature active and quotable in their minds:

> He is very good company, with his taste, and his cool, hard, sensible behaviour, yet with the capacity of melting to emotion, or of wakening to the most genial mirth.... The conversation always begins low down, and, at the least faltering or excess on the high keys, instantly returns to the weather.... There is in him a wonderful respect for mere humours of the mind, for very gentle and delicate courses of behaviour.[6]

This is why Thoreau liked Channing — being forthright to roughness himself, he craved intellectual consideration from others, and readily forgave lack of achievement in a man who had character, and eccentricity in one who sacrificed his life to follow his will-o'-the-wisp intuitions. He approved of a man who said that the excuse for cows was that they made paths in pastures; and never criticized Ellery's nature love, which was as sincere and as dilettante as his poetry. But when the 'high keys' of the conversation faltered, and Channing let it down by telling smutty stories, as happened, probably, more than once, Thoreau froze.

And Channing, too, was a protestant *à outrance* against materialism, convention, and sometimes common sense. His interest was in the life of the mind, and this he had pursued by running away from Harvard, where his famous name made his desertion of the arid scholarship he found there a little scandalous, and living for a while in a hut on the Illinois prairies. All of these disciples of 'newness' sought solitude when they were in trouble — it was their romance. And afterward he let his wife teach school while he cultivated his garden and walked with Emerson. He had all the impulses of Thoreau but less stamina, a weaker imagination; most of all, a character as shifting as clouds on a windy day. He got from Thoreau a sense of the reality of outward circumstance which he never possessed himself, but Thoreau's integrity in creative thinking he could not borrow — for at best he was only an honest dilettante. The most that can be said for him he said for himself in 'The Youth of the Poet and the Painter,' his autobiographical story in letters, published in *The Dial*.

5

Hawthorne came to live in the Old Manse with Sophia Peabody, his bride, in July of '42. Doctor Ripley had died in September of 1841, so it was natural that Mrs. Ripley's brother should get Thoreau to help him in putting the garden in order. Henry became one of Hawthorne's first, and was one of his few, acquaintances in Concord. It was a true relationship from the beginning, for these two men, as different otherwise as day from night, had a sympathy for everyday human nature which the Transcendentalists lacked. Hawthorne liked to sit in bar-rooms; Thoreau would have enjoyed doing so, and liked inns, and farmers, and loafers on the river. Hawthorne was impressed by a character as individual as those he liked to create, nor was his interest due to any previous knowledge of Emerson's protégé, for he spells his name (as did Alcott on first meeting) 'Thorow,' which certainly shows no familiar acquaintance. 'He is ... a young man with much of wild, original nature still remaining in him,' he wrote in his Notebook (these were the years when Henry was feeling savage and could eat woodchucks); 'and so far as he is sophisticated, it is in a way and method of his own. He is as ugly as sin [but Hawthorne's taste in male beauty was decadent Greek], long-nosed, queer-mouthed, and with uncouth and somewhat rustic, although courteous manners, corresponding very well with such an exterior. But his ugliness is of an honest and agreeable fashion, and becomes him much better than beauty.... For two or three years back, he has repudiated all regular modes of getting a living, and seems inclined to lead a sort of Indian life.' Emerson keeps him 'for the sake of what true manhood there is in him.... He is a good writer ... giving the spirit as well as letter of what he sees.' [7]

By winter they were skating together, in a trio described in Rose Hawthorne Lathrop's 'Memories of Hawthorne':

> One afternoon, Mr. Emerson and Mr. Thoreau went with him [Hawthorne] down the river. Henry Thoreau is an experienced skater, and was figuring dithyrambic dances and Bacchic leaps on the ice — very remarkable, but very ugly, methought. Next him followed Mr. Hawthorne who, wrapped in his cloak, moved like a self-impelled Greek statue, stately and grave. Mr. Emerson closed the line, evidently too weary to hold himself erect, pitching headforemost, half lying on the air.[8]

This daughter of Hawthorne's, Rose Lathrop, says her father liked Thoreau best of all men in Concord, which may be true, though opportunity never allowed their friendship to ripen. If so, this is a tribute to Thoreau's personality, for Thoreau disliked fiction, had 'heard of' the minister with the black veil, but seemingly never took the trouble to read his friend's books, which, with a writer, is a strain on friendship.⁹ 'I should like to have him remain here,' Hawthorne said before the New York journey; 'he being one of the few persons, I think, with whom to hold intercourse is like hearing the wind among the boughs of a forest-tree; and with all this wild freedom, there is high and classic cultivation in him too' — an excellent description.

6

The youth, now twenty-six, was getting around, but his intimate relations were still with the women in Emerson's household and his own family. The letters he writes home from Staten Island are newsy, considerate, and warm. He never shows off with his family, goes Transcendental, or overwrites, except for a puff of rhetoric now and then to Helen. Sophia hears about shrubs and flowers, John senior of a new credit establishment, Mrs. Thoreau about the Ward family, and how to get about New York, his health, which was bad all this year, and his underwear:

> Methinks I should be content to sit at the back door in Concord, under the poplar tree, henceforth forever. Not that I am homesick at all, — for places are strangely indifferent to me, — but Concord is still a cynosure to my eyes, and I find it hard to attach it, even in imagination, to the rest of the globe, and tell where the seam is.

There was, I am sure, some strain, nevertheless, in these family relations. Just before Thoreau went to Emerson's, boys from the school were boarding at the house as well as the Wards, and there were always casual mealers-in. It is true

that when he wrote 'As for these communities, I think I had
rather keep bachelor's hall in hell than go to board in heaven,'
he was probably thinking of the Brook Farm community just
under way, which he was to refuse to join. But the emphasis
falls on boarding,[10] and is continued, almost viciously, on the
nineteenth of March, 1841:

> No true and brave person will be content to live on such a
> footing with his fellow and himself as the laws of every house-
> hold now require.... I am impatient to withdraw myself from
> under its roof as an unclean spot. There is no circulation there:
> it is full of stagnant and mephitic vapors.

Too much women's prattle may account for this outburst, and
an overdose of bourgeois Concord. One remembers that when
Alcott held a Conversation at Mrs. Thoreau's house on May 3,
1839, on 'Futurity,' Emerson was there and said the people
were stupid.[11] The Thoreaus and their friends were not stupid
in a worldly sense, yet town gossip, education, and reform
absorbed and satisfied them. A visitor to the household recalls
how Henry used to steal down from his attic room, when one
of his sisters played the piano they had gone without butter
and coffee to buy. More often he must have stolen up.

Also, being young and a man, he seems to have needed a more
virile jollity than he got at home. It was not only to escape
society that he was trying to buy the Hollowell farm in these
months. George Ward, Prudence's younger brother, wrote his
mother on February 22 of this year of 1841:

> Henry will have to take care that he don't hurt himself
> seasoning — a very common occurrence. When he gets settled
> on his farm — I should like to look in upon him... & sing with
> him & John — 'In good old ——[12] times'.... We will 'do up'
> the glee & other matters with as hearty a will at least, as ever.

The Wards were always hoping that Henry would become
normal! George saw him in New York: 'I think he is getting to

view things more as others do, than formerly; & he remarked he had been studying books — now he intended to study nature & daily life. It would be well.' It was Dennis, another Ward brother, who pitied Mr. Emerson because he seemed to have 'so many new ideas & notions in his head & yet cannot find any language to express his thoughts by which any manner of man can comprehend him.' And 'Some of us poor plain headed folk stand a chance of getting our brains dislocated,' wrote George again, in general disapproval of 'newness.' For all his affection, Henry, with so much 'newness' bubbling in his brain, may well have found home talk sometimes trying; and if he was to view things more as others do it was not in that direction.[13]

However, the sudden and terrible death of John must have renewed Henry's strong family sense, if indeed it had been really weakened. Some slight coldness between the brothers may have remained as a result of the Sewall affair, for they went on no more excursions together, and do not seem to have spent much time in each other's company; nor are there references to John in Henry's letters. If there was a strain, it did not diminish Henry's love. In January of 1842 John caught his hand on a nail while jumping a fence and tore the flesh and muscles, from his wrist to his fingers.[14] Lockjaw set in and in spite of help from Boston he died in agony on January 11,[15] with Henry beside him. He was twenty-seven, two years older than Henry.

When Henry resumes his Journal on February 19 he is master of himself, but this was such a shock as he had never suffered before. You can see the tensity mounting on the monthly anniversaries for some time. 'I feel,' he says in February, 'as if years had been crowded into the last month.' He was ill. 'My soul and body have tottered along together of late, tripping and hindering one another.' The result was that elevation which comes to fine minds in the presence of irreparable loss and grief. He poured it out to Lucy Brown:

> What right have I to grieve, who have not ceased to wonder? ... For a great grief is but sympathy with the soul that disposes events.... The same everlasting serenity will appear in this face of God [nature], and we will not be sorrowful if he is not.

Then with more simple humanity:

> I do not wish to see John ever again, — I mean him who is dead, — but that other, whom only he would have wished to see, or to be, of whom he was the imperfect representative. For... we treat or esteem each other... for what we are capable of being.

A little later he discharged his grief in a poem, which he sent to Helen in a letter from Staten Island. But a balance-wheel was taken from the delicate machinery of Henry's mind when John died. He had been a cheerful spirit, a Good Genius, who, as Henry said in the 'Week,' happily prevailed over the neurotic fears and strainings of his brother. There is a note of something like despair when, after broodings about death and loss, the path to the uncertain future must be taken again. It is seldom that one finds in the Journal such uncontrolled utterance:

> *March 11, Friday, 1842.* [John died on January 11th.] My life, my life! why will you linger? Are the years short and the months of no account? How often has long delay quenched my aspirations! Can God afford that I should forget him?... Why were my ears given to hear those everlasting strains which haunt my life, and yet to be prophaned much more by these perpetual dull sounds?... Why, God, did you include me in your great scheme? Will you not make me a partner at last?

This is neither impudence nor bravado. He had decided to resign himself to the will of God, like a plant or stone, when suddenly instinct rebels. God has made him a representative of the creative spirit. It is a prayer to be put to work, from the lips of a man convalescing from a great grief.

7

Bronson Alcott, that garrulous archangel, can scarcely be reckoned as more than an experience in these years. It was not until he returned, a broken reformer, from spiritual farming at the Fruitlands community, and had shaken off his English friends, that the two became friends. 'Clean daft,' Prudence told her brother George he would consider the Englishmen, and Thoreau, with his sense for soil and necessity, thought Alcott a little daft till he grew to know him better. Mrs. Alcott was a friend of the family, writing witty letters from Fruitlands which Thoreau must have read. The house was 'a refined kind of pig sty — which however is rendered quite endurable by our agreeable men and inexhaustible library.' She is 'on a mission of duty among the higher intelligences who admit me some-times at their debates when the carnal things are to be dis-cussed (or rather dissected).' Prudence had sent her an 'irre-sistible cap.' [16]

Louisa Alcott's idealized portrait of Thoreau in her first novel, 'Moods' (1864), was based upon his familiar association with her father which lasted for twenty years. Her Adam Warwick is a wandering scholar devoted to nature, intensely independent, rich because he makes his own wants few. He is 'violently virtuous,' brusque, 'clings to principles; persons are but animated facts or ideas; he seizes, searches, uses them, and when they have no more for him, drops them.... For life to him is perpetual progress [Thoreau had no "wake," said Emer-son], and he obeys the law of his nature as steadily as sun or sea.' So the young novelist saw him, and the description fits him at any period. But it may have been the young schoolmaster she was remembering when she sends Adam on a river excursion, camping at night with his friends, and falling in love with a young girl who later marries another while still loving Adam — in the end both lose her. The household must have known the story of John, and Henry's sacrifice.[17]

8

To this expanding circle in Concord must be added the acquaintances, and one friend-to-be, he made in New York, when he adventured thither from Staten Island. His employer, William Emerson, lived on the Richmond road, inland and seaward of Stapleton, a one and a quarter hour's walk from the quarantine village of Castleton. A ferry from Port Richmond took Thoreau across the bay to New York. The sea and the ships coming in and out of the harbor got into his imagination, but otherwise Staten Island was a blank. Even the immigrants interested him only as specimens of a different race, like the Irish who were building the railroad along Walden Pond. He had not Whitman's feeling for 'en masse,' or his sense of a continent growing, for his imagination was stubbornly New England and unconcerned with geographical space. And neither did the ships sailing toward Europe and the East tempt him. His eyes were still fixed on Concord, and his brain busy with the unsolved problems of what nature meant to a Transcendentalized mind.

But in New York there were celebrities and disciples of Emerson. Henry James, father of the novelist and the philosopher, apostle for Swedenborg in America, pleased him best, because he seemed to speak a language he understood. 'I have been to see Henry James, and like him very much. . . . It makes humanity seem more erect and respectable. I never was more kindly and faithfully catechized. . . . He is a man, and takes his own way, or stands still in his own place. I know of no one so patient and determined to have the good of you. ... He wants an expression of your faith, or to be sure that it is faith, and confesses that his own treads fast upon the neck of his understanding.' [18] Ellery Channing, two years later, described him as 'a little fat, rosy Swedenborgian amateur with the look of a broker and the brains and heart of a Pascal.' Channing would always make his phrase. Thoreau, who knew nothing of brokers, characteristically did not trouble about the outer shell of a man he liked. Yet his pen portraits are sharply etched:

> W. H. Channing [Christian socialist and editor]... is a concave man, and you see by his attitude and the lines of his face that he is retreating from himself and from yourself, with sad doubts.... He would break with a conchoidal fracture. You feel as if you would like to see him when he has made up his mind to run all the risks.[19]

Then there was Albert Brisbane, who talked nonsense about solar evolution, said Emerson, but whose Fourieresque insanity was better than New York insanity. He was busy propagandizing for that communal socialism which was becoming a religion among social reformers. Horace Greeley was converted. It was Fourierism that finally captured Brook Farm, and shocked some of its supporters when they discovered that its French founder had risky ideas about free love. Brisbane, father of the notorious editorial writer of our day, had all his son's energy and skill of delivery, but with canalized principles instead of opportunism:

> Brisbane... looks like a man who has lived in a cellar, far gone in consumption. I barely saw him, but he did not look as if he could let Fourier go, in any case, and throw up his hat.[20]

Horace Greeley, although their first meeting was casual
enough, became by far the most important of his new acquaintances. He was to be Henry's best publicity agent after Emerson,
and most perspicacious admirer, for, a great journalist, he
knew good writing when he saw it, and in spite of his reverence
for the unworldly Transcendentalists, tried to give Henry
always what he needed most, cash and an outlet for his work.
We can think of him in '43 in his light suit like a miller, with
chalky face:

> Horace Greeley, editor of the *Tribune*, who is cheerfully
> in earnest, at his office of all work, a hearty New Hampshire
> boy as one would wish to meet, and says, 'Now be neighborly,'
> and believes only, or mainly, first, in the Sylvania Association,
> somewhere in Pennsylvania; and, secondly, and most of all,
> in a new association to go into operation soon in New Jersey.[21]

There was too much about associations, communities in the
talk of these men, for Thoreau. He liked the individualist,
Henry James, best.

He heard the great Quaker reformer, Lucretia Mott. The
meeting pleased him — the women 'looking all like sisters or
so many chickadees,' and the square coats and expansive hats
which came from house to house, and had a history. It was
'Transcendentalism in its mildest form.' [22] Already, and long
before Emerson, he sensed the dangerous quietism of the
Quakers, which was to be content with solidity and reform, and
let the spirit speak too mildly.

Indeed, his final conclusion as to all these idealists is a distrust of reformers:

> Staten Island, October 18, 1843.
> Dear Helen, — ... My objection to Channing and all that
> fraternity is that they need and deserve sympathy themselves
> rather than are able to render it to others. They want faith,
> and mistake their private ail for an infected atmosphere; but let

any one of them recover hope for a moment, and right his *particular* grievance, and he will no longer train in that company. To speak or do anything that shall concern mankind, one must speak and act as if well, or from that grain of health which he has left.... I have the jaundice myself; but I also know what it is to be well.

Here is the social critic of 'Walden' unsheathing his wings. He has learned in New York what he guessed in little Concord, that reformers usually suffer from stomach-ache, and that 'Physician, heal thyself' was a social principle.

New York itself made little impression upon him. The city, he wrote Emerson, was 'a thousand times meaner than I could have imagined. It will be something to hate.... The pigs in the street are the most respectable part of the population. When will the world learn that a million men are of no importance compared with *one* man?' This is spoken through his long nose, tilted upward, and if it is not the 'village pedantry' of which Emerson warned Henry James in introducing him, then it is the exaggeration of bravado.[23] Indeed, the mass in New York frightened him a little, though he only slantingly admits it. As with the Irish in Concord, here was something not amenable to, perhaps destructive of, his philosophy. Whitman, when they met later, was struck by this individualist's snobbishness. 'It must have a very bad influence on children,' Henry wrote to his mother, 'to see so many human beings at once, — mere herds of men.'

His instinct was all for Concord: 'My thoughts revert to those dear hills and that *river* which so fills up the world to its brim.... How can it run heedless to the sea, as if I were there to countenance it? George Minott, too, looms up considerably, — and many another old familiar face. These things all look sober and respectable.... Staying at home is the heavenly way.' The New Yorkers were interesting, and yet 'the heavens

THOREAU

are not shivered into diamonds over their heads,'[24] as had happened to him on many a Concord hill.

And so, trailing memories of a larger, but to him less significant, society, he went back. From now on he lived in Concord — or in his memory and imagination.

13. PICTURE OF A MIND

I HAVE SPOKEN of Thoreau as a twice-born man, quoting
Moncure Conway, who could not understand how this rare bird
was hatched in a Concord yard. Perhaps we all in youth are
reborn at intervals whose frequency depends upon the tissue of
the spirit. Thoreau's rebirth was after he joined the Emerson
circle. It might be dated in August of 1841.

The maturing of his thought and the sharpening of his talent
for expression are evident in his Journal for that year, during
part of which he was at the Emersons'. In September he was
'in the mid-sea of verses,' but there he was self-deceived; it was
prose that he was really mastering, prose rhythms, prose phrasings; and you can see the growth of his control over metaphor,
in which he excels all moderns.[1] He felt his power increasing,
writing in February: 'We do not acquire the ability to do new
deeds, but a new capacity for all deeds. My recent growth does
not appear in any visible new talent. . . .' Where he was going,
what he had found out about himself, how to live, and what to
live for, does not appear in any full statement. But one can
gather handfuls of sentences from his Journal (as he did himself
when he came to write the 'Week,' and particularly from this

summer of 1841) which will show what this growth amounted to. All authors collect ideas. They are the legendary wheat grains of the Pharoahs, which will grow whenever the time comes to plant them. Thoreau's kernels were germinal, and some of them had already sprouted. There is no continuity in the passages I assemble below from '41 to '42, but if they do not chart his mind, they picture it:

> I have been breaking silence these twenty-three years and have hardly made a rent in it.

> What is called charity is no charity, but the interference of a third person.... Shall I defraud man of the opportunities which God gave him, and so take away his life?... I will not stay to cobble and patch God's rents, but do clean, new work when he has given me my hands full.... We go about mending the times, when we should be building the eternity.... Help implies a sympathy of energy and effort, else no alleviation will avail.

> The fickle person is he that does not know what is true or right absolutely, — who has not an ancient wisdom for a lifetime, but a new prudence every hour.

> If I am well, then I see well. The bulletins of health are twirled along my visual rays, like pasteboards on a kite string.

> I think I could write a poem to be called 'Concord.' For argument I should have the River, the Woods, the Ponds, the Hills, the Fields, the Swamps and Meadows, the Streets and Buildings, and the Villagers. Then Morning, Noon, and Evening, Spring, Summer, Autumn, and Winter, Night, Indian Summer, and the Mountains in the Horizon.

> Poetry cannot breathe in the scholar's atmosphere.

> I make my own time, I make my own terms. I cannot see how God or Nature can ever get the start of me.

> One does not soon learn the trade of life.

I find incessant labor with the hands, which engrosses the attention also, the best method to remove palaver out of one's style.

God does not sympathize with the popular movements.

What am I good for now, who am still marching after high things, but... to bring wood and water, and count how many eggs the hens lay?... I will not aspire longer. I will see what it is I would be after. I will be unanimous.

Those authors are successful who do not *write down* to others, but make their own taste and judgment their audience.

I must confess I have felt mean enough when asked how I was to act on society, what errand I had to mankind.... Yet my loitering is not without defense.... I wish to communicate those parts of my life which I would gladly live again myself.

How often must one feel, as he looks back on his past life, that he has gained a talent, but lost a character! My life has got down into my fingers.

The really efficient laborer will be found not to crowd his day with work, but will saunter to his task surrounded by a wide halo of ease and leisure.... Those who work much do not work hard.[2]

These pithy sentences are still rhetorical but no longer rhetoric, and very different from the notes on reading and moral reflections of his first years out of college. There was some truth in what he said to George Ward in New York in 1843, that he had been studying books but now intended to study nature and human life. But his debt to books has not yet been fully recorded, had not, even in 1843, reached its full extent, and these epigrammatic sentences are reflections of reading even more than life.

2

They refused to let Henry Thoreau take books out of the Harvard library until he went to the President and argued, very sensibly, that, with the railroad, Concord was now as near the library as Boston had been in the past. After that he had no trouble, and showed his gratitude in 1852 by contributing five dollars to a fund to purchase volumes for poor students, 'which is more than I have earned in the past three months.' 3 In 1841 he had Emerson's rich library to browse in; in 1843 he read deeply, if briefly, in the libraries of New York. And even in his poverty he kept adding to his own carefully selected library of classics, science, travel, poetry, which contained about four hundred volumes at his death.

Thoreau was a scholar. He knew the right books, knew them to the core, and how to use them. In comparison with his scholarship Lowell's is often impressionistic, Poe's and Whitman's mere bluffing, Emerson's broader though, in the classics, not so deep. But he was also a man of letters, who knew that poetry cannot breathe in a library. The right books were those that were right for him. His search for the eternal truths, with which all the Transcendentalists were busy, made him almost immune to contemporary literature unless it contained facts or ideas which pointed the way of timeless wisdom. For his own times, except in travel and science, he trusted to his experience, and sought his own current impressions of contemporary man. There can be no other American man of letters who read so little American literature. Even in Emerson, after 'Nature' and the first essays, he read but passingly. Longfellow and Irving are quoted in a college notebook but neglected afterward. Melville (except for 'Typee'), Hawthorne, Poe, Lowell, Whittier — if he read them at all, there is no repercussion in his Journal. Of all the authors of the so-called Golden Age, Emerson excepted, only Whitman caught his attention — Whitman the singer of the democratic 'en masse' and the magnificent body of man, as Thoreau was the praiser of the individual, the power of the *one* man, the might of the spirit in harmony with nature of which its body was a part. They are the two poles of American idealism in literature.

In contemporary British, French, German literature he was almost as eclectic. From De Quincey he learned some of the secrets of an eloquence that was not preaching, from Carlyle nothing but the knowledge that others sought spirit in matter, from Howitt the idea of a book on the love of nature,[4] from Gilpin the artist's view of natural beauty, from Tennyson nothing, from Goethe the conception of a universally curious man of letters, from Coleridge what he learned from Carlyle, earlier and more profoundly, from Scott nothing except a fleeting taste for medieval romance, from Wordsworth assurance in his Transcendental nature-love. His true sources were in his own life, or in the great classics of the past.

There are several excellent treatises on Thoreau's literary sources. If I seem to oversimplify by depicting his mind as swung from its track by only four great influences, the reader can learn of less significant pressures upon this indefatigable student by consulting a bibliography, and noting later references in this biography. Thoreau read whenever he was able, for hours at a time on many days.[5] Much of his reading was for knowledge; of what he read for wisdom and delight only a little went under his skin, but that went deep.

3

Thoreau's literary masters were Emerson, the English prose and poetry writers of the deeply religious English seventeenth century, the Greek dramatists and Homer, and the Sanskrit sacred writings, especially the Vedas, Menu, and most of all the 'Bhagavad-Gita.'

From those wrestlers with the word and the spirit, Donne, Herbert, Vaughan, Quarles — and from the eloquent writers in prose, like Sir Thomas Browne and the makers of the English Bible, he borrowed much. All of these writers caused English to say spiritual things with passion and worldly things with poetic significance. There he got some of his rhythms, especially in poetry, and his way of making sentences that were not so much statements as pictures of a deeply felt reality. The habit of the great English prose of the seventeenth century to express itself by sentences rather than by paragraphs, became his habit. It was natural for him to imitate it, because his belief in the value of intuition filled his Journal, as it filled Emerson's, with 'sayings,' each coining a fresh idea or observation. This Puritan in morals was most strongly moved, not by Milton, whom he merely admired, nor by Bunyan, but by the churchmen, the lovers of the beautiful in religion, and most of all the Platonists, whose poetry was almost as good Greek as good Christian. They meant much more to him than Shakespeare, who was too unspiritual, perhaps too direct, for a mind always seeking the shadow of reality behind outward appearance. Disliking metaphysics, he was irresistibly attracted by the curious twists of language of these so-called metaphysical poets, who tried to pack philosophical meaning into the plainest statements. Not subtlety of doctrine but subtlety of expression, by which the feelings of man in the presence of God in nature become articulate, was his aim as it was theirs.

There was a further kinship in that these seventeenth-century men were writers in a fresh world of new religious vitality, new science, new expectations of man; a wider, richer society than the New England 'newness,' in less dangerous conflict with materialism, but with purposes and opportunities having much resemblance. They were creating the symbols by which the religious felt and thought, and had a language still plastic to mould; and so did the New Englanders; not so plastic, not so mouldable, because worked upon through two centuries of intense literary activity, yet a language released and freshened by the exigencies of a new continent. Thus the seventeenth century deeply affected Thoreau's modes of expression, as it had earlier affected Emerson's, and gave him confidence. I cannot see that it influenced his thought. His style gained force, but often lost clarity from what it fed upon. Its real vices came from the stale eighteenth-century habits of the early nineteenth century.

From the Greeks, he got one thing chiefly — phrase-making. His close study of Greek, fortunately conducted in Harvard under two good teachers, one of whom, Jones Very, was a poet, and carried on steadily through his Walden period, and as recreation through his life, taught him, I think, how to write a sentence that was not a rhetorical arrangement of words, but an arrow from the bow of the imagination, barbed, feathered, aimed, quivering, made for the target. The Greeks to him were the great writers, as the Hindus were the great thinkers. They were his literary masters, felt as such, constantly analyzed and admired:

Jan. 29, 1840 . . . Aeschylus had a clear eye for the commonest things. His genius was only an enlarged common sense. . . . If his hero is to make a boast, it does not lack fullness, it is as boastful as could be desired; he has a flexible mouth, and can fill it readily with strong, round words, so that you will say the man's speech wants nothing, he has left nothing unsaid, but he has actually wiped his lips of it.

As so often with a writer's criticism, this is at least as good a description of what Thoreau tried to do and often did with his own writing as of Aeschylus. 'Enlarged common sense' and 'strong, round words' and a phrase that 'wipes the lips' of all that can be said — who would not be glad to find such happy phrases in trying to describe Thoreau at his best. It was Greek, which he mastered at Harvard, that taught him to escape from Harvard's preacher-rhetoric.

Of Emerson's influence I have already written. Upon Thoreau's thought it was profound, upon his style it was deleterious. The habit of composing by sentences or brief paragraphs inconsecutive as the flashes of perception which they recorded, he probably borrowed from him, although, as said before, it is a natural method for an intuitive diarist. The plan of selecting and arranging these paragraphs in a loose pattern about a theme, he certainly learned from Emerson, who had always composed that way. It is entirely different from the method of essay development he had learned at Harvard; and is closely related to the idea, which he got, of course, from Emerson, of the validity of the recorded flash of intuition. Instead of reasoning out a theme, one sets down with careful articulation the idea which springs rich and true from the mind's sudden contact with spiritual reality. But one idea does not make an essay — if it is to be rich there must be time for the intuitive mind to complete its work. Then, when the occasion for delivery comes, the writer opens the door of his storehouse, searches for the articulate thoughts that belong together, fits them in an order, and writes an essay or gives a lecture which is a necklace of like-colored jewels on a slender thread of continuity.

Emerson, with his preacher's training in organization for an audience, and his habit of distilling from the fact instead of recording it, made his famous essays successful by just this process. But it was much harder work for Thoreau, who could not flow from conclusion to conclusion as did the preacher-philosopher, or indeed, except in 'Walden' and one or two of his essays, deal with a single idea at all, but must labor to make each sentence live in a rhythm and sequence of its own and create its own meaning. For Thoreau was a seeker, like Emerson, but, unlike Emerson, a seeker who never achieved certainty except as to the worth of what he thought. Nature, and man too, for him were the golden bottles in which reality was stored. He could not take the stoppers out, like God and Emerson, but, rather, was forever delaying while he studied their intricate designs of appearance and behavior. These preliminary studies filled his notes, which were kept on backs of letters, scraps of paper, anything on which you could write, and finally transferred to his Journal, which he often tried to index. Then, while he was making his books, his Journal was ransacked, until the author was finally entangled in such a mass of papers as one finds in the work sheets for 'Walden,' now in the Huntington library. No literary man with whom I am acquainted ever worked amidst greater self-made difficulties. With his Concord self-sufficiency, he plunged into a day-by-day record of his life-search for truth and seldom could find a good way of getting out.

4

While form is in question, let us add to Thoreau's disabilities the intangible influence of all the loose, smart, diffuse, precious writing of the early nineteenth century, forgotten, except by scholars, because so many masters of literature used it with genius. No writer escapes from his times, not even Thoreau, who read newspapers and magazines much more than he admitted. The affectations of Thackeray, the ramblings of Dickens, the pretty word pictures in the magazines, the strained humor of Carlyle, the literary, O so literary! moralizings, invokings, describings of the Willises, Curtises, Griswolds, etc., etc., etc., from which even *The Dial* critics were not free, the constant preaching, the winking allusiveness, the attitude as of one standing apart from his subject and daubing it with words — there is something of all this in Thoreau at his worst, and a little of it in Thoreau at his almost best, as in the humorous passages in 'Walden' and the 'Week.' For an exaggerated instance of such viciousness, see the imitations in a college magazine, such as *The Yale Literary Magazine* of the forties. But Channing, a literary man with nothing to write about except his reading, supplies an even more relevant example, for he was close to Thoreau, and exhibits his worst weaknesses by imitating him with just that touch of excess added which unintentionally creates burlesque. I have spoken before of the dialogue of Emerson, Thoreau, and himself, which he had prepared for a book, and finally used to pad his memoir of Thoreau, published in 1873. Having been given access to Emerson's Journal and Thoreau's, he supplemented them by his own memories of the conversations as they walked, and let the whole go as a record of friendship in the years just before and after 1850.

TO WHITE POND

T. Above our heads the night-hawk rips; and, soaring over the tallest pine, the fierce hen-harrier screams and hisses; *cow, cow, cow*, sounds the timorous cuckoo: thus our cheerful and pleasant birds do sing along else silent paths, strewn with the bright and bluest violets, with Houstonias, anemones, and cinque-foils. Academies of Music and Schools of Design, truly! and to-day on all the young oaks shall be seen their bright crimson leaves, each in itself as good as a rich and delicate flower; and the sky bends o'er us with its friendly face like Jerusalem delivered.

E. And Mrs. Jones and Miss Brown ——

T. No, indeed: I declare it boldly, let us leave out man in such days; his history may be written at nearly any future period, in dull weather.

C. Yet hath the same toiling knave in yonder field a kind of grim advantage.

T. The grime I perceive, and hear the toads sing.

E. Yet the poet says,—
> 'Not in their houses stand the stars,
> But o'er the pinnacles of thine.'

T. And also listen to *my* poet:—
> 'Go thou to thy learned task,
> I stay with the flowers of Spring;
> Do thou of the Ages ask,
> What to me the Hours will bring.'

Oh, the soft, mellow green of the swamp-sides! Oh, the sweet, tender green of the pastures! Do you observe how like the colors of currant-jelly are the maple-keys where the sun shines through them? I suppose to please you I ought to be unhappy, but the contrast is too strong.

C. See the *Rana palustris* bellying the world in the warm pool, and making up his froggy mind to accept the season for lack of a brighter; and will not a gossiping dialogue between two comfortable brown thrashers cure the heartache of half the world? Hear the charming song-sparrow, the Primadonna of the wall-side; and the meadow-lark's sweet, timid, yet gushing lay, hymns the praise of the Divine Beauty. And — were you ever in love?

T. Was that the squeak of a night-hawk?

C. Yes, flung beyond the thin wall of nature, whereon thy fowls and beasts are spasmodically plastered, and swamped so perfectly in one of thy own race as to forget this illusory showman's wax figures? . . .

E. I think you said we were going to White Pond? [6]

This is terrible, yet it can be parallelled, though not equalled in badness, by passages from Henry's Journal. And even in 'Walden' this 'show off' of the nineteenth-century intellectual is occasional, in the 'Week' frequent. Melville and Thoreau (and Carlyle more than either) were subject to it as if it were an influenza. Melville, who is often insufferable, escaped into a sea sublimity that absorbed the verbose play of his words; Thoreau, by an increasing grip upon his subject, brought his rhetoric slowly into an exact accord with reality.

5

But these criticisms are digressive. The last of Thoreau's important literary sources had very little influence upon his style, unless to encourage his habit of 'sayings,' fascicles as he called them, composed of concentrated wisdom. Yet it may be said to have given the final direction to his life, and hence to his works.

It has been asserted that Thoreau's debt to the Hindu scriptures might be described by Coleridge's line:

> O Lady! we receive but what we give.[7]

This was probably true when, presumably in Emerson's library in the summer of 1841, Henry began to study 'The Laws of Menu,' and to extend a reading in Hindu literature which he seems to have begun in college. There he found confirmation of ideas which had long been his own, instinctive at first, then made articulate by the idealism of 'Nature.' Now he discovered that great teachers, a great literature, a great race had seen beneath outward appearance. They had purified their hearts in order to feel the presence of God in nature, they had learned simplicity of living and seen diamonds sometimes shiver in the skies above their heads. They had penetrated the shell of external verisimilitude and felt reality behind. Their poets and preachers spoke with the authority of enduring tradition. For the enlightened among them, happiness and success were merged into a longing for reality. Their asceticism was not the cold putting aside of New England Puritanism in its stale nineteenth-century phase, or the intellectual passion for moral perfectibility of the Transcendentalists, or even Emerson's confident faith in the superior strength of the ideal. It was a way of life and a search, rather than a doctrine of progress:

They have put a golden stopper into the neck of the bottle.
Pull it, Lord! Let out reality. I am full of longing.[3]

The first effect upon Thoreau of this reading was a mounting
excitement. He had found fellow minds. His own undefined
longings were shown to be on the side of the angels:

> I cannot read a sentence in the book of the Hindoos without
> being elevated upon the table-land of the Ghauts.... The page
> nods towards the fact and is silent.... The impression which
> those sublime sentences made on me last night has awakened
> me before any cockcrowing....
>
> Any book of great authority and genius seems to our imagina-
> tion to permeate and pervade all space.... Its influence...
> bathes the huckleberries on the hills, as sometimes a new influ-
> ence in the sky washes in waves over the fields and seems to
> break on some invisible beach in the air. All things confirm it.
> It spends the mornings and the evenings.....
>
> The simple life herein described confers on us a degree of
> freedom even in the perusal.... Wants so easily and gracefully
> satisfied that they seem like a more refined pleasure and replete-
> ness.[9]

In 1841 when these recordings were made, to be used later
in the 'Week,' he knew little of Hinduism; indeed, he never
knew, or cared to know, much. The elaborate process of self-
effacement through asceticism until the personality merged
into the godhead, interested but did not attract his Western
mind. He was like his New England predecessors, the Puritans,
who took what they needed from the book of the Oriental
religion of Israel and the Greek-Oriental religion of Christ,
and let the rest go. What he needed was assurance that the
relations of self to God in the sensuous world were as vital as he
felt them to be. This he would have got in theory from any
barrel of sermons, but the inner conviction was lacking in the
church as he knew it, and there was not only no force in the
Christian statement of reality, since the great sayings were stale

in his ears, but also the Bible lacked that simple pantheism of the Hindus which made the barriers between man and nature so low that the imagination dwelt with ease on either side. His own intuition had been that an inner spirit flowed through man and his environment alike, and unified the world, and in the Hindus he found it made articulate as the beginning of a creed. All this was vague so far — an inspiration, no more than a benediction from a faith with immeasurable experience of man in its past.

With Emerson the inspiration went no further. His mind, trained in theology, knew immediately the limitations of his possible belief. There was no progress, no social perfectibility in the Hindu faith. Henry was as obstinately Western as he was, perhaps more so, for he had a zest for labor with the hands quite strange to Emerson, for whom thought was a sufficient activity. But Thoreau's unmetaphysical mind let him sink deeper into the Hindu books with little regard for contradictions. This Word carried on into his life far more powerfully than with Emerson. He was a young man dubious on the threshold of a career, aprickle with unsatisfied ambitions, a hard worker in a strenuous country, whose aims he already doubted but whose energy was just an extension of his own. He liked to see the trains run, the goods of the North sliding southward, the soil upturned for the crop, and life kept clear and vigorous and happy with fresh-running blood.

But he was a rebel against acquisition, which was the vice of New England. For two years, as Hawthorne said, he had followed no recognized profession. 'The gods have given me these years without any incumbrance,' he said himself; 'society has no mortgage on them,' by which he meant that he had been living for the sake of the good life, and not with the idea of gain. He must have agreed, if he read it, with what Death in the Katha-Upanishad said to the world: 'What can the money-maddened simpleton know of the future? "This is the only world" cries he; because he thinks there is no other. I kill him again and again.' [10] And yet the dilemma, inescapable for a Yankee in the 1840's, remained. He wished to *be*; he wished to find his life, which meant find himself before taking his part in action (before uttering it as a poem, as he said, being a writer and thinking of action as expression). But in order to *be*, in New England which had no monasteries and no tolerance of roadside pundits with begging bowls, he had to *do*, which so far had meant being handyman for Emerson and the village, Apollo in the service of Admetus.

6

This was a real, not a metaphysical problem, whose solution, which determined his later life, I am sure that he found in that great moral and religious parable, the 'Bhagavad-Gita.' Menu, Confucius, the Vedas, the Upanishads — from all these he drew wisdom, and might have drawn the same lesson. But the 'Bhagavad-Gita' was explicit, and, like Emerson's 'Nature,' went deep down into his consciousness and gave him a new birth.

I do not know just when he read the dialogues of Krishna and the king Arjoon, but he had certainly read them before he finished the 'Week,' in which they are mentioned, and before he began the writings which afterward took form as 'Walden.' Probably he read the book just as he was going to the pond to live, since Emerson, in June of 1845, was writing with tremendous enthusiasm to his correspondents about the Gita, which had just come into his hands, and quotes without comment in his Journal a paragraph about action versus inaction. [11] At least we know the book in which Thoreau read it — Charles Wilkins' translation of 1785, the first edition in English, with a fine

preface by Warren Hastings. As with 'Nature,' Thoreau took
what he needed and let the rest go by.

In the second lecture he found his own particular problem of
being versus doing dramatically discussed.[12] Arjoon is hesitat-
ing whether to enter a battle in which he must meet and slay
his friends. Is it not nobler to withdraw from the world and let
the vain show of things pass by the reflective spirit? Is not
understanding better than action, which here leads to slaughter?
But the god Krishna spoke, and Thoreau took his answer to
heart:

> A man's own calling, with all its faults, ought not to be for-
> saken. . . . Wherefore, O Arjoon, resolve to fight. . . . Every
> man is involuntarily urged to act by those principles which are
> inherent in his nature. . . . So the man is praised, who, having
> subdued all his passions, performeth with his active faculties all
> the functions of life, unconcerned about the event. . . . He who
> may behold as it were inaction in action, and action in inaction,
> is wise amongst mankind.

And Thoreau comments on Warren Hastings' quotations:

> What, after all, does the practicalness of life amount to?
> The things immediate to be done are very trivial. I could
> postpone them all to hear this locust sing. The most glorious
> fact in my experience is not anything that I have done or may
> hope to do, but a transient thought, or vision, or dream, which
> I have had. I would give all the wealth of the world, and all
> the deeds of all the heroes, for one true vision. But how can I
> communicate with the gods, who am a pencil-maker on the
> earth, and not be insane?[13]

Action and inaction, says Krishna, have in the long run
the same justification, since God is in both and the issue is
always in him. The influence of a thought and a deed are
alike in the end. A man must search out 'those principles which
are inherent in his nature,' and do accordingly. The man of
action must act (in Concord, Henry found this a justification

for the slayers of the harmless muskrats on the river). 'Abandon all thought of the consequence,' says Krishna, for good and evil are essentially the same in a world which is an emanation of a unitary spirit.

What lesson here for a pencil-maker? The obvious answer was to stop worrying because society did not seem to have any use for his talents, and find out where the principles inherent in his nature led him, and how to follow them. What was his own genius? He could answer easily that it was to live in the present (without a 'wake'), and to live close to nature where the phenomena of God were freest from human error and easily studied by a man who could always be summoned by a rap on a Concord pine tree, to live without regard to the effect of his actions on his career, and to report the results of his living for the benefit of his fellow men. This was to *be*, and also to *act*, a compromise approved by the wisdom of the ancients, and acceptable to a Yankee nonconformist who objected not so much to the strenuosity of his neighbors as to the ends they sought thereby, which he thought tricked them again and again.

'The wise man . . . seeketh for that which is homogeneous to his own nature.' This is the dominant idea which Thoreau took from the 'Bhagavad-Gita.' His sardonic humor, his passion for nature as an experience, his indignation with the stupidities of the state — all these would have been heresies in the eyes of a pundit. The Yankee did not become an Oriental. He took the idea he needed, became a twice-born Yankee, but remained a Yankee still. And because he was a Yankee, he put his idea to work on the great problem of the restless American race, the problem of the choice of a career.

The guidance of the 'Bhagavad-Gita' came after his resolve to go to Walden pond, but Walden provided a solution in exact accord with the principles of the great book, and of this Thoreau was well aware. Wild nature was homogeneous to his

own nature, self-knowledge was best obtained in an environment where solitude was possible. Leisure for contemplation,
and time for the study of nature in New England, which already
began to reveal itself as of an infinitely greater complexity
than the Hindus (or even Emerson) suspected, could be bought
by simplicity of living.

How deeply this lecture sank into his mind is proved by the
quotations he made from it, and the many parallels in his most
vital writing. Says Krishna: 'The man who is incapable of
thinking, hath no rest.' Says Thoreau, in the passage most
frequently quoted from 'Walden': 'The mass of men lead lives
of quiet desperation.' Says Krishna: 'The man who, having
abandoned all lusts of the flesh, walketh without inordinate
desires, unassuming, and free from pride, obtaineth happiness';
which is Thoreau's doctrine of simplicity made articulate in
dozens of often quoted passages. Wisdom is to live in this way,
unwisdom is restlessness in the chains of the world.

It was upon a mind still uncrystallized, but mature, flexible,
and creative, that the powerful doctrine of the Hindu moralists
broke and precipitated the resolve to be 'unanimous' in his
desire 'to live deliberately, to front only the essential facts of
life, and see if I could not learn what it had to teach, and not,
when I came to die, discover that I had not lived. I did not
wish to live what was not life, living is so dear; nor did I wish
to practice resignation, unless it was quite necessary.... I
wanted ... to drive life into a corner, and reduce it to its
lowest terms, and, if it proved to be mean, why then to get the
whole and genuine meanness of it ... or if it were sublime, to
know it by experience, and be able to give a true account of it
in my next excursion.... Be it life or death, we crave only
reality. If we are really dying, let us hear the rattle in our
throats and feel cold in the extremities; if we are alive, let
us go about our business.... Time is but the stream I go

a-fishing in.   I drink at it; but while I drink I see the sandy bottom and detect how shallow it is.   Its thin current slides away,
but eternity remains.   I would drink deeper; fish in the sky,
whose bottom is pebbly with stars.'

Some of the eloquence, more of the resolve of this famous
passage from 'Walden,' he drew direct from the great Hindus.

So much for the waves of influence, some washing over, some
into, the mind of Henry Thoreau as he sat in his garret chamber, or his bedroom at Emerson's, or worked on the new house
the Thoreaus were building in these years of 1841, '42, '43, and
'44, the truly formative years of his life.   Afterward he was
never to waver in his principles and his interests, though, in
applying them, he learned the hard lesson that unless absorption
in the eternal spirit is your aim — and it was certainly not his,
any more than any Yankee's — knowledge, even self-knowledge, is sure to be frustrated.   But he carried with him always,
and added to his gusto for living, the deep spiritual warmth of
the East.

14. WALDEN POND

The name of Henry Thoreau will always be associated with Walden Pond because he carried out successfully there one of those experiments in living which have caught the imagination. But irony is mixed with his fame, for that crystal-clear lake, wood-surrounded, by the shore of which he sought nature and solitude, became a railroad amusement park and is now a reservation of the state of Massachusetts, where the memory of the poet-naturalist is celebrated by public baths, water slides, and boats for amorous couples.

Yet Walden in its cup of the hills above, and only a mile from the edge, of Concord is still beautiful; and Thoreau's sojourn there in his cabin by a cove, if less significant than St. Francis' retirement among the birds and beasts, or Christ's retreat to the wilderness, is, nevertheless, one of the memorable gestures of the spirit of man.

Many of Thoreau's own contemporaries, like Lowell and Alger, thought that the escape to Walden was a pose, or sheer eccentricity. Even his youthful admirer, Hecker, called him in later years a consecrated crank.[1] And admirers of Thoreau since have been too ready to think and write of his Walden adventure as the bravado of a perverse idealism, or as a hermit's challenge to a society which had to carry on with the responsibilities he left behind. Robert Louis Stevenson, with this in mind, thought he was a skulker.[2]

Actually the retreat to Walden was just what Channing in his biography called it, the result of economic forethought. It was common-sense expedient, as logical as his friend Stearns Wheeler's journey to Germany to study the new learning, or his classmate Dana's voyage around the Horn to California in search of better health. It was an idea long cherished which became a reality when his speculations as to what he wanted to do crystallized and the right opportunity came at the right moment.

Of course, the results of his going were more extensive than his original purpose contemplated. His plan went no further than to find a way in which a poor scholar, who was a skilful handyman, could live in independence with time enough to do what he wanted, and a wide margin of leisure in which to reflect and enjoy. His intent was, first, to make a satisfactory life for himself, and, next, to go on with his reporting of experience for his contemporaries. But the result was a challenge to his neighbors that became a challenge to a rapidly industrializing world — a challenge to each individual in any race, under any circumstance, to discover, as the Hindu said, his own peculiar genius, and, having learned what he wanted to do, to learn how to do what he wanted. It was the challenge which, three quarters of a century later, the one hundred per cent American, Lewis' George F. Babbitt, was to say so bitterly that he had understood too late.

Henry Thoreau had numerous precedents for seeking a hermitage. The young people in search of 'newness,' who had read Coleridge and Carlyle and Wordsworth and had been inoculated with the German philosophy of spiritual nearness

to God through nature which was God's cloak, were all romantically inclined toward solitude. Stearns Wheeler had
lived alone in the woods, and Henry is supposed to have spent
six weeks with him. Channing had lived on the prairie. J. G.
Zimmermann's much read book on 'Solitude' was suggesting a
retreat for solitary reflection as a cure of souls.[3] Emerson's
'Nature' had been conceived in the groves. Wordsworth and
Coleridge sought wildness in England and Scotland and Wales.
Nor should it be forgotten that no Transcendentalism was
needed to draw the young, nature-loving American of the
early nineteenth century toward the life of the Indian in the
woods. Thousands with no spark of philosophy in them had
yielded to the attraction of waste spaces and the independence
of a self-sustaining life. Even in the forties they were still drifting off Westward, not to be pioneers or land speculators, but
to escape from the money system or the pressure of stale morality or the idea of progress by getting rich.

All of this counted with Thoreau, yet his idea of Walden had
a much more commonplace origin. On the first page of his
Journal, he longs for a room of his own. If nature was a recreation and afterward a business for him, the independence of
relative solitude was a necessity. He had work to do of a kind
not recognized as such in Concord, and he had to find a better
place than a boarding-house in which to learn how to do it,
and some more time-saving method of earning a living than
pencil-making, teaching, or living at Emerson's.

2

His first idea was a farm. In the winter of '41 he was trying
to buy the Hollowell Farm on credit. The school was soon to
close, some new experiment in subsistence was inevitable,
unless he was to teach elsewhere, or make pencils and live in a

boarding-house indefinitely. He had his seeds ready, and some tools, as he says in 'Walden.' George Ward's letter, quoted above, suggests that he intended to go in for subsistence farming in a small way, without livestock or bulky crops, eked out presumably by lecturing and writing. It would have been more sensible to rent, as he once thought of doing, from a man who had 'four acres as good soil as any outdoors.' But at this time he was willing to 'contemplate to drudge' that he might own a farm, if he could get one. The Hollowell place was not to be improved. He hoped to get it before the owner had cleared up its delicious wildness, and there seek nature and seclusion where life might pass 'simple and true and natural'; or find some other spot where many things 'would be impossible to be done.' 'How many books I might not read!' [4] There was evidently to be a money-crop, which would take not too much time, yet free him from day-long hard labor. Sanborn says that he also thought to buy Weird Dell, the orchard side of Fairhaven Hill, the Cliff Hill, or the Baker Farm.[5] Apparently the scheme was deep set.

When the school closed on April 1 of 1841, he was still landless, but his fancy kept on building:

> *April 5.* I only ask a clean seat. I will build my lodge on the southern slope of some hill, and take there the life the gods send me. Will it not be employment enough to accept gratefully all that is yielded me between sun and sun?... If my jacket and trousers, my boots and shoes, are fit to worship God in, they will do. Won't they, Deacon Spaulding?

That was the difficulty. If it was not to be a farm, how to get the next boots, jackets, and trousers out of a lodge on the hill. And so he looks for a job, and gets a day's work and seventy-five cents for 'heaving manure.'

> *April 7. Wednesday.* My life will wait for nobody, but is being matured still irresistibly while I go about the streets and

chaffer with this man and that to secure it a living.... This staying to buy me a farm is as if the Mississippi should stop to chaffer with a clamshell.

Brave words — or rather bravado. The truth is that economically he was in a tight place.

What have I to do with plows? I cut another furrow than you see. Where the off ox treads, there it is not, it is farther off; where the nigh ox walks, it will not be, it is nigher still. If corn fails, my crop fails not.... Is not my sand well clayed, my peat well sanded?

But fine words butter no unwelcome facts. The chaffering stopped only when Emerson offered him a refuge. It was a refuge only; the idea of supporting himself in the country when opportunity offered, never left him. He talked or wrote of it to all his intimates, and began to think, not too hopefully, of his beloved Walden:

Dec. 24. Friday. [At Emerson's.] I want to go soon and live away by the pond.... It will be success if I shall have left myself behind. But my friends ask what I will do when I get there. Will it not be employment enough to watch the progress of the seasons?

The answer was in the negative. Only a native in a tropical climate could merely watch the progress of the seasons and survive. Three months later he is still planning:

I am led about from sunrise to sunset by an ignoble routine, and yet can find no better road. I must make a part of the planet. I must obey the law of nature,

which was too abstract to be helpful.

He had no idea of starving in his attempts to live a complete life and to make himself a productive writer. To starve or to be dependent was simply *not* to live a complete life. Only weak men would take such ways. As he wrote to Horace Greeley in 1848, when his problem had been half solved:

> Unless the human race perspire more than I do, there is no occasion to live by the sweat of their brow. . . . We are too often told of 'the pursuit of knowledge under difficulties,' — how poets depend on patrons and starve in garrets. . . . Why should not the scholar, if he is really wiser than the multitude, do coarse work now and then? Why not let his greater wisdom enable him to do without things?

But neither coarse work as a handyman or pencil-maker nor his domestic duties at Emerson's met his specifications for a life where the getting of a living was not too expensive in time and energy. And so he went to New York, as has been recorded, to pay his debts, open a market for his writing, and make a fresh start.

3

When he came back in late 1844, it was with the same resolve. He was pencil-making now, and helping his father build the Texas house across the railroad, called Texas because of its distance from the Mill-Dam. He was certainly earning enough to pay for his board and other expenses and put aside a little. Probably it was in this interval of craft-work that he developed the flotation process for graphite described by Edward Emerson,[6] which made the Thoreau powder so much finer than its rivals that when electrotyping was invented in 1848–1849 the demand for their graphite soon caused the family business to be really profitable, and enabled them to give up pencil-making and peddling of their wares. This is undoubtedly the origin of the story of Henry's boast to Emerson that having made a perfect pencil he determined never to make another. His last pencil-making was in the early fifties, when he paid off his debt for the publication of the 'Week' by some thousands of pencils, sold at a sacrifice. After that pencil-making stopped because powdered graphite brought in more money. Less Transcendental than the perfect-pencil story, the truth is in better accord with Thoreau's common sense.

Emerson has a record of a conversation in March of 1844 which is revealing:

> Henry Thoreau said, he knew but one secret, which was to do one thing at a time, and though he has his evenings for study, if he was in the day inventing machines for sawing his plumbago, he invents wheels all the evening and night also; and if this week he has some good reading and thoughts before him, his brain runs on that all day, whilst pencils pass through his hands.

'I constantly return,' so Henry wrote to Hecker, the God-drunk youth then living at the Thoreau's Parkman house, 'from every external enterprise with disgust, to fresh faith in a kind of Brahminical, Artesian, Inner Temple life. All my experience, as yours probably, proves only this reality.' [7] He was not only inventing machines, he was also building the Texas house, which he is said to have designed (it is no credit to his artistic faculties), and the cellar of which he dug and stoned. If this did not satisfy his desire for an esoteric reality, it at least gave him useful experience in building. The house is a plain box, with a disproportioned doorway in one side, which apparently led to the pencil-shed, now attached to another side of the building. A grapevine, a syringa bush, and some fruit trees planted by Thoreau still flourish there.[8] Building, moulding plumbago, and pencil-making, a walking trip in the summer of 1844 with Channing through the Hoosacs and the Catskills, later recorded in the 'Week,' and longing for a chance to do what he wanted — this is the record for 1844 and up to the spring of 1845, when his chance came. But two happenings, one of which seems, but was not, trivial, were hardening his mind toward escape.

4

In April of 1844, on Town Meeting Day, young Edward Hoar, then a student in Harvard, went with Thoreau on a long day's excursion up the Sudbury River. They caught some fish (fishing was Henry's vice — there he still practised killing), and cooked them on a stump in the woods. In spite of this precaution the dry April grass of the forest floor caught, wind whirled the fire, and it was soon out of control. Having given the alarm and exhausted himself by running, Thoreau sank down to watch the progress of the flames. If you believe the account in his Journal, his reflections were all sardonic.[9] It was only property that these owners of the forest cared about — the lost beauty made no difference to them. As for the flames, they were but 'consuming their natural food.' It was the 'trivial fishing' that weighed on his conscience! But actually he was deeply hurt, as is evident from his over-emphatic sarcasm. He, the nature lover, had destroyed the woods (a hundred acres or more) that he loved best. And he was not so indifferent, as he pretends to be in 1850, to the remark made for him to hear as the fire fighters went home — 'a damned rascal'; or to the 'burnt woods' which was often called behind his back afterward as he went through Concord. If he had not been with Samuel Hoar's son, says Sanborn, he would probably have been prosecuted. Ask for reminiscences of Thoreau in Concord now, and you will be taken back a generation to the memories of his townsmen, who were surprised at his fame because they thought him shiftless, worthless, not a good citizen. Press further and you come again and again to this fire in the woods. The Harvard graduate who wore old clothes, wouldn't choose a career, and could be met loafing wherever there were pine trees, ponds, or rivers, had, as everyone expected, made trouble. He had burnt up property. Miss Sarah R. Bartlett of the Concord library says that her great-aunt never liked Thoreau because she had blackened her fingers for years on the charred wood they brought in from the wood-lot. Such village wounds fester. For unsocial as Thoreau pretended to be, and often was, Concord was his home, the center of his universe, his first love and his last.

And also it was in April of 1844 that, with the end of *The Dial*, Transcendentalism lost its voice and Emerson's young men their easy outlet toward fame. Thoreau had been a frequent contributor to the last numbers. Now his one sure means of reaching an audience by print was closed; nor had New York promised others. It was time to take stock of what he had, what he could do. There is very little Journal for '44 and early '45, very little time obviously for anything intellectual. And time was needed if he was to shape his scattered notes into anything resembling a book. He describes the condition of his manuscripts in a passage that is undated but belongs to the Walden period:

> From all points of the compass, from the earth beneath and the heavens above, have come these inspirations and been entered duly in the order of their arrival in the journal. Thereafter, when the time arrived, they were winnowed into lectures, and again, in due time, from lectures into essays. And at last they stand, like the cubes of Pythagoras, firmly on either basis; like statues on their pedestals, but the statues rarely take hold of hands. There is only such connection and series as is attainable in the galleries. And this affects their immediate practical and popular influence.[10]

He had his statues, but they did not yet take hands. He had his notebooks full of the life blood of his thought. It had flowed into lectures and essays, yet Henry Thoreau, the whole man, was still inarticulate in print. He must find time to make the statues take hands. This also drove him toward a new way of life, and indeed he told Channing that at least one item of his 'private business' at Walden Pond was to complete a book.

5

Emerson liked to contemplate nature without bothering too much about its details, and shared Henry Thoreau's love for Walden Pond and its woods, so near and yet so wild. On the 4th of October, 1844, he wrote to his brother William that he had met at Walden Pond two or three men come 'to sell and to buy a field.' They asked him to bid as a possible purchaser. William, the business man, must have wagged his head over his brother's simplicity, since someone had evidently seen an opportunity to sell a briar patch to a philosopher! 'As ... for years I had a sort of daily occupancy in it, I bid on it and bought it, eleven acres, for $8.10 per acre.' Next day some of his 'gossips' came to the place and said the field would be no good if Heartwell Bigelow cut down his pine grove. This sounds like Thoreau's common-sense advice. 'I bought, for $125 more, his pretty wood-lot of 3 or 4 acres — and so am landlord and water-lord of 14 acres, more or less, on the shore of Walden, and can raise my own blackberries.' [11]

What he had bought was a clearing above a little cove on the lake side, where young pitch pine and all the usual scrub of a New England cut-over were growing. This lifted by a terrace to an extensive level field adjoining a high-road — too extensive as Henry found when after clearing its briars he planted two and a half acres of beans. At the left, as one looked in from the lake, was the wood-lot of 'tall, arrowy white pines, still in their youth.' On the right, if one can trust the memory, said to be good, of the artist who in 1880 sketched the site as it appeared in 1847, was a rail fence with woods behind.[12]

It may very well have been Channing who suggested to

Emerson that he let Thoreau use the land, and build his own
home there. Henry, it is to be remembered, had just built a
house. 'I see nothing for you in this earth,' he wrote on March
5, 1845, to Thoreau from New York where, with Margaret
Fuller, he was writing for *The Tribune*, 'but that field which I
once christened "Briars"; go out upon that, build yourself a
hut, and there begin the grand process of devouring yourself
alive. . . . Eat yourself up; you will eat nobody else, nor anything else. Concord is just as good a place as any other. . . .'
Then, writing as if with the pen of Carlyle, 'I saw Teufels-
dröckh a few days since. . . . Says he, "That fellow Thoreau
might be something, if he would only take a journey through
the Everlasting No. . . . He is too dry, too composed, too chalky,
too concrete. Does that execrable compound of sawdust and
stagnation L. still prose about nothing? and that nutmeg-
grater of a Z. yet shriek about nothing?"'' [13]

There was too much tendencious talk in Concord for Thoreau — too much of Lane, too much of Alcott (if Z. was meant
for Alcott). 'Mr. Alcott and Mr. Wright,' wrote Emerson to
Margaret Fuller, 'cannot chat or so much as open the mouth on
aught less than a new Solar System and the prospective education in the nebulae.' [14]   The erect philosophers, gravely eating
russet apples while they waited for a solemn saying, as George
William Curtis describes them at Emerson's house in 1845,
might have driven less fidgety men than Thoreau toward the
long silences of Walden. [15] Channing was forgetting how much
he talked himself, and was too inclined to think that Henry
had only intellectual problems. But he already loved the man,
and his intuition told him that what was needed was an atmosphere of his own. Also, he had changed his mind about
grinding fifty Concords in a mill. Thoreau had not got far
with one. His life still lingered.

The letter was well-timed. At the end of March, Thoreau

began work near the briary field in the clearing above the shores of Walden. He had needed cheap or free land and the means of living on it. The land was Emerson's, the cabin was within his own capacity, and the location was ideal. It was not a farm, but there was a field in which he could raise food and a money-crop. It was near enough Concord for a man who did not propose to lose touch with his friends, far enough and remote enough to simulate, when necessary, a wilderness. Nor was the agreement with Emerson one-sided. The philosopher could count on a friend in his forests, and the next year he began to plan with Henry's aid a lodge to be built on a ledge across the lake. Furthermore, Henry cleared his briary field, and was later to plant pines upon it. It is probable that the bargain was, that Thoreau should clear the field, build his house in the clearing below, and, if and when he had enough, leave or sell his improvements to his landlord.[16] He was, as always, paying his way.

Emerson surely never thought of him as a dependent or a parasite. 'If any man assist me in the way of the world, let him derive satisfaction from the deed itself,' Henry wrote a little truculently at Emerson's in September of 1841, and when they were talking in 1846, 'He is grateful,' notes Emerson, but does not flatter; 'you must leave him to designate who is the benefactor.' 'He thinks that which he took of you was no more yours than the air which he breathed in your house.' And in June of 1845, just before Thoreau went to Walden: 'You think he [a man] has character; have you kicked him? Talleyrand would not change countenance; Edward Taylor, Henry Thoreau, would put the assailant out of countenance.' It is difficult to be a benefactor to a man with the obstinate independence of a woodchuck and the sensitiveness of a thoroughbred horse. If Emerson succeeded, it was because he knew that Thoreau was right. They exchanged gifts.

6

The cabin Henry built in the spring of 1845, far from being in the dense forest as May Alcott drew it after Thoreau's death,[17] or in an open field as the *Concord Freeman* sketch shows it, was sheltered by a young pitch pine, and amidst a tangle of brush, but open to the sun and to sight from both lake and high-road. Prudence Ward's matter-of-fact description dispels all illusions of wilderness:

> Jan. 20, 1846.
> ... Henry T has built him a house of one room a little distance from Walden pond & in view of the public road. There he lives — cooks, eats, studies & sleeps & is quite happy. He has many visitors, whom he receives with pleasure & does his best to entertain. We talk of passing the day with him soon.[18]

Walden woods were still quite wild, and at night wild life moved freely through them. Walden Pond looked like an Adirondack lake, but the hut on Emerson's land was, as Channing said, a bivouac, rather than a hermitage, and the oft-told story that Henry, posing as a hermit, used to help himself stealthily to doughnuts from his mother's kitchen, has no point. Of course he did, but not stealthily. He was not trying to live *out* of the world; he was trying to live without being inconveniently dependent upon the world.

His description of how the hut was built, the beans planted, and his life organized, is a classic of 'Walden' and need not be repeated here. No annotation is required except to name the friends who helped him with the final raising. There was Channing, who says in the manuscript notes in his own copy of 'Walden' that the axe was his, young George William Curtis, then living with Edmund Hosmer, and afterward an editor of real distinction, Alcott, who was born on a farm and knew how

Courtesy of Mrs. Adams Tolman

*The Walden Pond Hut, from a crude wood drawing
from memory, published in the* Concord Freeman
'*It had no lock to the door, no curtain to the window, and belonged to nature nearly
as much as to man*'

to work, and Edmund Hosmer, the philosophic farmer, under whose roof near Walden Henry later spent so many evenings of high converse over the great mythologies of Scandinavia. Hosmer must have approved of the briary field and the problems it presented to an agriculturist, for it was he who said to Lidian Emerson that 'it was a piece of weak indulgence in the good God to make plums and peaches.'

The cabin itself was so excellently built, that it stood at least two movings after Thoreau's death, was in perfect condition so far as frame and covering until 1868, and ended by transubstantiation into the fabric of a garage.[19] I like Channing's description of it in his biography:

> It was just large enough for one, like the plate of boiled apple pudding he used to order of the restaurateur... in a jaunt to the city.... It was... a sentry-box on the shore, in the wood of Walden, ready to walk into in rain or snow or cold.... It was so superior to the common domestic contrivances that I do not associate it with them. By standing on a chair you could reach into the garret, and a corn broom fathomed the depth of the cellar. It had no lock to the door, no curtain to the window, and belonged to nature nearly as much as to man.[20]

When Henry was receptive to visitors he left a chair outside. When visitors came in good weather his pine grove was his reception room.

And so, moving the furniture he needed, some of which he had made himself, in a hay rigging, and getting his boat, also, from the river to his cove, he entered into residence on the fourth of July, 1845, to be reporter of Walden Pond for two years and three months.

> When I was fairly established in my house I hummed to myself rhymes, without invoking any Muse that is in regular standing.
>
> > I seek the present time,
> > No other clime,

Life in to-day, —
Not to sail another way, —
To Paris or to Rome,
Or farther still from home....
My feet forever stand
On Concord fields....[21]

There was a pencil drawing of a man taming a mouse on the closet door.

The book 'Walden' is tendencious as well as descriptive, yet so excellently descriptive that it would be an impertinence to add to its account of Henry's life at the pond, except to fill in the blanks he leaves, and to note what others said of it. This life was, of course, not continuous. He went off in the second summer for a trip to the Maine woods, in good weather he seems to have been in Concord almost daily, and, after his better judgment led him to plant, in the second year, only one third of an acre of beans, he spent much time with his friends, family, and neighbors.[22] He lectured, took on odd jobs in the village to help his expense account, experimented, but not very far, with the disciplined turning inward of the mind of the Yogi, read much, and studied. He wrote at least one long review, of which more later, kept an extensive Journal, of which only a little is printed in its original form, the rest having been used later in 'Walden,' [23] and worked on his book, the 'Week.' He became his own man at last, and immediately (as so often happens in a world where all freedom is relative) began his lifelong slavery to an observation of nature too minute for its objectives. But he was never a hermit, except when snows shut him in, or heavy rain, or his own absorption in work. To go and see Henry Thoreau was a Concord recreation.

Here is an account of a day there, written by Joseph Hosmer of Chicago, son of Edmund, for the *Thoreau Annex* (supplement,

Pencil drawing by May Alcott of Thoreau's cabin on Lake Walden. Thoreau in his boat at the foot of the path
'Walden woods were still quite wild'

we should call it) which the *Concord Freeman* published, with the picture already mentioned, on May 6, 1880.

In early September of 1845, on Henry's invitation, Hosmer spent the day at Walden. Thoreau, he said, seemed to regard the hut as a retreat and a camp rather than a home. The house, not yet furnished, for the chimney and fireplace were built later, 'stood in the open field, some thirty rods from the lake, and in full view of it.' The king-post was an entire tree, extending from the bottom of the cellar to the ridgepole, 'upon which we descended as sailors do into the hold of a vessel.' A meal was cooked outside in a hole made in the earth and inlaid with stones. They ate roasted horn pouts, corn, beans, bread, salt, etc. 'I gave the bill of fare in English and Henry rendered it in French, Latin, and Greek.' Meal was mixed with lake water for bread and spread upon the surface of the stones. Thoreau's pet mouse refused to appear — a relief to the biographer, who does not find in the Journal evidence of the birds and beasts who by tradition were usually crawling over or perching on Thoreau. But he told of the woodchuck he caught in a trap, and carried two miles away rather than knock his brains out. It never returned.

7

Joseph Hosmer was a literal-minded man, thus all the better able to see how much common sense there was in the self-sustained, easy-going life Thoreau was leading. The scope of Thoreau's purpose, however, eluded him. Henry was 'one of the most practical of men, but without imagination or fancy and what was not real was unworthy of his thought.' 'Walden,' when it appeared, must have puzzled Joseph, since he had evidently heard at the pond itself only of catching pouts, growing beans, and living at next to nothing a year.

No imagination in that — imagination wrote romantic verse or worked for progress in Chicago.

The Transcendentalists saw a very different Thoreau when they visited the pond, and to get at the truth we must allow for the subjective prejudices of both literalists and idealists. Alcott, whose friendship with Thoreau kept maturing in January and February of 1847 until he came to spend every Sunday evening at Walden, wrote down in his Diary for March of this year a characterization of what seems to be a different man:

> Thoreau's is a walking Muse, winged at the anklets and rhyming her steps. The ruddiest and nimblest genius that has trodden our woods, he comes amidst mists and exhalations, his locks dripping with moisture, in the sonorous rains of an ever-lyric day. His genius insinuates itself at every pore of us, and eliminates us into the old elements again. A wood-nymph, he abides on the earth, and is a sylvan soul. If he could but clap wings to his shoulders or brow and spring forthright into the cope above sometimes, instead of beating the bush and measuring his tread along the marsh-sides and the river's sedge and sand, and taking us to some Maine or Indian wilderness, and peopling the woods with the Sileni and all the dryads!
>
> But this fits him all the better for his special task of delineating these yet unspoiled American things, and of inspiring us with a sense of their homelier beauties — opening to us the riches of a nation scarcely yet discovered by her own population.

At Walden, Thoreau lived both of these lives. He was the intensely practical man, so concerned with facts that Hosmer thought he had no imagination, and he was also the walking muse, ruddy and nimble, skeptical of Alcott's eternal vacuities, but discovering the 'yet unspoiled American things.'

But it is only fair to take Thoreau's own account of what was in his mind when he came to Walden, and to take it, not from his book which became a tract for the times, but from what he set down in his Journal two days after he had settled into his house.

> *July 6, 1845.* I wish to meet the facts of life — the vital facts, which are the phenomena or actuality the gods meant to show us — face to face, and so I came down here. Life! who knows what it is, what it does? If I am not quite right here, I am less wrong than before; and now let us see what they will have.... Even time has a depth, and below its surface the waves do not lapse and roar. I wonder men can be so frivolous almost as to attend to the gross form of negro slavery, there are so many keen and subtle masters who subject us both.... One emancipated heart and intellect! It would knock off the fetters from a million slaves.

And the next day:

> We are the subjects of an experiment how singular! Can we not dispense with the society of our gossips a little while under these circumstances?

Hosmer was right. This poetical-minded Yankee was practical. He wished to prove, as he said in 'Walden,' that 'the student who wishes for a shelter can obtain one for a lifetime at an expense not greater than the rent which he now pays annually.' Alcott was also right. Thoreau wished to live near American nature, so little known as yet by the transplanted Europeans who called themselves Americans. Yet he was quite wrong when he said later in the same passage that this 'West Indian,' as he called Thoreau, had no sky to his world. It was precisely to get at reality, whether of earth or sky, to 'live deliberately' until he could find what for him were 'the essential facts of life,' that Henry had with economic forethought made Walden a laboratory where he could subsist without endowment or undue perspiration from time-consuming labor. Unlike Alcott, who was a congenital preacher and teacher, unlike most New Englanders of either the Transcendental or moralistic strain, he wanted (for a time, at least) to learn, not to teach. 'For most men, it appears to me, are in a strange uncertainty about it [life], whether it is of the devil or of God, and have *somewhat hastily* concluded that it is the chief end of man here to "glorify God and enjoy him forever."' And many others, as he said elsewhere in 'Walden,' propose to creep 'down the road of life, pushing . . . a barn . . . and one hundred acres of land, tillage, mowing, pasture, and wood-lot! . . . It is a fool's life, as they will find when they get to the end of it, if not before.'

15. OUTWARD MORNING

WITH A NIGHT IN JAIL

I F I WRITE of Thoreau's Life in the Woods (the subtitle of his first edition of 'Walden') it will not be to duplicate the engaging narrative of the book. That famous book, although ostensibly an account of his experiences at the pond, is really the history of what he learned there. It is his cockcrow, his lecture to his townsmen first, and then to the world in due order, though I doubt whether he felt sure the world would hear him.

What seems to me the most interesting effect of his seclusion at Walden is quite opposite from the accepted picture of a hermit withdrawing into his inner self. The inner self seems, it is true, to have been his first concern. He worked his feet 'downward [I am quoting from 'Walden'] through the mud and slush of opinion, and prejudice, and tradition, and delusion, and appearance . . . to a hard bottom . . . which we can call *reality*,' [1] until he felt he had become a 'Realometer' to register the depths of shams and appearance. But when he had gained this sense of reality, he began to use it on his external life, on the state, on his friends. He began to escape from his egocentricity, which is sometimes almost offensive in his early Journal. From subjectivity he began to move toward objectivity. His subjectivity began to break up like the ice in Walden in the spring, and strong new interests in the objective world of men and nature flowed up and over.

The simile must stop here, for the subjective in Thoreau never entirely melted. He will always descend again and again into the aqueous region of the intuition, in which the light from the visible world shows faint and transformed through blocks of crystal. Yet at Walden, having realized the satisfactions of self knowledge, he takes a new grip, which was to become a too tight grip upon outward reality. Having lived 'as deliberately as Nature,' his invigorated mind begins to be shocked, sensitized, or fascinated by what has been going on outside while he has been wrestling with his own problems.

First, like any young rebel, he tells society what he thinks of it; and then goes about his business, which is to study what he loves best — wild nature, which was for him the veil behind which reality moves. And soon the texture of the veil becomes more engrossing than the Transcendental reality behind it. The social thinker, the scientist, and the artist concerned with form as well as meaning, all awoke in Thoreau at Walden.

The process was complex, but can be easily separated into sets of everyday happenings which, while he was living them, did not seem as important to Thoreau as his own musings. That not too cryptic poem of the early forties, 'The Inward Morning,' is his poetic self-picture of a mind such as his was then, probing inward, absorbing, analyzing his own genius, seeking to interpret life in terms of himself:

> Packed in my mind lie all the clothes
> Which outward nature wears,
> And in its fashion's hourly change
> It all things else repairs.
>
> In vain I look for change abroad,
> And can no difference find,

> Till some new ray of peace uncalled
> Illumes my inmost mind. . . .
>
> How could the patient pine have known
> The morning breeze would come,
> Or humble flowers anticipate
> The insect's noonday hum. . . .

The morning breeze had come, though I should hesitate to call Henry's prickly mind a humble flower, and it had left him his own man, confident in self-knowledge, happy in the interweaving of the active and the contemplative life. And so the outward morning began.

2

First of all, his contacts with his human kind were suddenly broadened. I do not mean those night-long talks with the Concord intellectuals while the pine boughs brushed his wind-swept roof, nor the sociability of his outdoor sitting-rooms where he was host to his family and their Concord friends. It is probable, of course, that since he had escaped from Mrs. Thoreau's garrulity and the gossip of reform of his sisters and his aunts, and could escape at will from the windy speculations of Emerson's friends and Alcott's monologues, he liked them all better, and his friends more keenly appreciated him. It is not from the Walden period that we collect anecdotes of his gruffness and aggressive bravado.

No, it was another Concord that soon began to engage his liking and his imagination. A country-dweller now, a farmer (in a small way), a hunter without a gun, and a fisher for his sustenance — most of all, when work and thought were finished, a wanderer with time to stop and talk, he fell easily into relations with the simple people who lived by their hands. He had known few simple people well — perhaps only old George

Minott, the farmer on the hill opposite Emerson's, who was as native to Concord soil, and as unconscious of thinking, as a shrub oak tree in his pastures. And there was farmer Hosmer, but he was scarcely simple. But now when he sauntered riverward or forestward, or walked to and fro from Concord, he met his neighbors as one of them.

There was Therien, the French-Canadian woodchopper, a Homeric peasant, 'who made his last supper on a woodchuck,' and had a philosophy far older than Thoreau's. There were roving hunters and workers on the railroad, and farmers and their wives who stopped by his bean field, and young people from the village who talked to him more freely than at home. And there were the memories of the past inhabitants of Walden woods, Hugh Quoil, the drunken, tragic Irishman, who was at Waterloo, and slaves and rascals much like the rascals he was to get to know so well on the rivers. The taste he acquired for simple and uncomplicated natures was new to him — it was to be powerful in later life. He had a kinship here not granted to Emerson. The sketches of these men which Francis H. Allen has brought together in his excerpts from the Journal, called 'Men of Concord,' show Thoreau at his most humane and most human.

3

The second push forward of new interests was in a different direction. It was a new attitude toward the wild nature in which he lived. While he had always loved nature, he had too often moralized it, or been content with pleasant and dilettante description. Now, as the reader of 'Walden' knows, he began to be intensely curious as to the behavior of the wild. Some of the most readable of his nature descriptions are in 'Walden' because curiosity had not yet swamped him in detail. It is still recreation, not a business that he is pursuing. It was still recreation which took him on August 31, 1846, the anniversary of the trip on the rivers, to the Maine woods, despoiled of pine but otherwise still virgin, in search of the heart of the wilderness on Mount Ktaadn. Having tasted wildness at the pond, he was no longer content with walks to Wachusett or the Catskills but must pry out the realities of the wilderness itself.

Still more significant are the hours which Thoreau spent in an exacting study of the depths, flows, colors, seasons, ice, and fishy denizens of Walden Pond, to the last exactitude. Even if there was an ample margin of leisure when his beans were cultivated and his writing, study, and contemplation done for the day, this expenditure of so much of his hard-won time on a geographer's business is unexpected. And yet he took it so seriously that his map of the depths of Walden (important to no one but himself) was inserted in the first edition of his book. This was not living in nature, not contemplating nature, not certainly a search for the meaning of nature. It was measuring nature. Walden Pond was put through as elaborate a physical test as a recruit for the army. No more could be said of it when he was through, except what a chemist, biologist, or geologist might have added. Here is a new Thoreau.

4

Next, as his objective interests increased, he encountered the economic state, which, in a theoretical form, with its ideas of material progress, he had already met head on within the covers of a book.

J. A. Etzler was 'a native of Germany' of whom little was known by Thoreau except that he had published 'The Paradise Within the Reach of All Men, Without Labour, by Powers of Nature and Machinery. An Address to All Intelligent Men.

In Two Parts.' Actually, he was an immigrant living in Pittsburgh, where his book was published in 1833. It concludes with a petition to the Congress and to Andrew Jackson to legislate his Paradise into being. The second English edition of the 'First Part' of his Utopian scheme, published at London in 1842, had been sent for sale to America, where Utopian colonies were so popular. The book came to *The Dial* for review, and some 'rude and snappish speech' was made about it by Emerson, which Henry professed not to remember. Perhaps the younger man, leafing it through, had told Waldo that here was his optimism worked out in dollars and cents. In any case, when Emerson was in New York, in February of 1843, he asked Henry to review it. Henry promised to try, but there is no indication that he wrote anything until June or July, when he was on Staten Island. And then he sent the article to O'Sullivan's *Democratic Review*. O'Sullivan objected to some of Thoreau's opinions, but published it finally in his November number.[2]

Etzler's proposed Paradise was to be created by means described in the sequel to his first book.[3] Thoreau had not seen this sequel, but the idea was sufficiently expounded in the Address to All Intelligent Men. The wind, the waves, the tide, the sunshine, were to be harnessed for power and the power was to be used by a vast co-operative (shares at twenty dollars apiece) to make comfortable living possible for all by 'a short turn of some crank.' There were to be prefabricated houses of seven thousand private rooms, synthetic cloth for clothes, public parks of great beauty, communal cooking, tractors (he did not call them that) for easy agriculture. 'Man is powerful but in union with many. Nothing great, for the improvement of his own condition, or that of his fellow-men, can ever be effected by individual enterprise.'

Thoreau's imagination expanded with Etzler's. He did not

so much challenge the German's mechanical dreams, most of which have been now, in principle, realized, as doubt the moral soundness of the whole scheme. Etzler, indeed, seemed to him more practical than Utopian. What he questioned was the values he proposed to extract from living. 'The chief fault of this book is, that it aims to secure the greatest degree of gross comfort and pleasure merely.' The physical calculations of Etzler are not to be disparaged, but what of the moral characteristics of the men who are to inhabit this Paradise? What calculations have been made for them? 'In this matter of reforming the world, we have little faith in corporations; not thus was it first formed.' 'Nothing can be effected but by one man. . . . We must first succeed alone, that we may enjoy our success together.'

Thus, at his first contact with the new ideas of the perfection of society by the control of nature, Thoreau jumps forward a full three quarters of a century and makes the criticism of a scientific civilization which is so common today. Power over the earth, power over water, power in the air, power by socialization, and yet the same individual, his eyes and understanding shut 'by preconceptions,' untrained in self-knowledge, unable to estimate the far more important power of love, which 'the wisest men in all ages have labored to publish . . . yet how little is it actually applied to social ends!' A sentence of fire for the twentieth century.

I have gone back several years in Thoreau's development in order to show how consistently his ideas of self-perfection reacted against a mechanical Utopia, whose details intrigued and encouraged his imagination. But his criticism is still lightly satiric, for this Paradise did not touch him or Concord. It was a practical dreamer's project to provide new values for humanity, against which he opposed his already firm belief that progress began with the individual, not society, and was a sham until it was determined which among the commodities of living were true values and which were merely valued by erroneous preconceptions. He did not wish, either for himself or for others, a diversion of energy to the mechanics of living, until he and they had learned what was really wanted, 'living is so dear.' So might the modern say who sees the airplane intended for transportation drop a high explosive invented for industry upon a tank devised for agriculture. It was better to live without science and its power plants than to let machinery run ahead of self-knowledge and self-control.[4]

Thus by 1845 he had already encountered the ideals of the Industrial Revolution, and responded by an energetic caveat. But he had also and in a much more personal fashion come into conflict with the economic state as it was organized in his own Concord. The utilitarians of Concord paid him grudgingly for teaching, and would have helped him to get rich if he had kept his brains on graphite, yet disapproved of him heartily when he tried to do what he wanted — an occupation which seemed to them idleness because it made no reckonable profits, indeed, had led to the burning of their woods. His answer was the defiant challenge of this Walden experiment, by which he hoped to show that one man, at least, by reducing his wants and employing his 'coarse labor' where it would make him most independent, could escape the job-to-make-money system without practising any resignation of which he was not easily capable. He called the first chapter of 'Walden,' the book he made of it, 'Economy,' with a pun on the word, for his economy was really a theory of economics. As a treatise, this chapter is limited in scope, but unlike most of the vast library of nineteenth-century speculation on the economic man, it still has validity.

5

Next in his important objective experiences was a briefer, but more sensational, conflict with the political state. When young, he had been, like Emerson, of Whiggish tendencies, anti-Jackson, anti-Democratic so far as he had been anything political at all. After that curious letter in pseudo-Indian language to John, there is not the slightest indication of interest in politics as such until the slavery issue began to force itself upon his attention. He never voted. But as this issue, with all it involved for the Union and for a citizen, mounted toward an irrepressible conflict, politics began, as today, to involve the least politically minded. Thoreau heartily wished that government would take care of itself while he went about his business, in which he was typically American. But government, the weak, easy-going government of the American thirties and forties, began to get itself into trouble. Pocketbooks were touched by the tariff, patriotism was involved by states' rights, conscience was stung by slavery. In its blundering action more and more interests were trampled on. Finally, government trod on Thoreau.

In 1838 he had protested a tax levied for the benefit of the established church, but was allowed to 'sign off.' That issue was dead. But in 1846 it was not so easy to be a neutral. Texas had been annexed in 1845, Polk had been elected on an imperialistic platform, the Mexican War, which in one of its aspects was a war to extend the slave-holding area into the Southwest, was formally declared on May 13, 1846. Thoreau's Abolitionist family must have been abuzz with anti-slavery talk.

In late July, when blueberries (he makes them huckleberries, perhaps to suit the altered date in 'Walden') were ripe, and men were sitting in their shirtsleeves on account of the heat, Henry walked from Walden early one evening in to Concord to get a mended shoe from the cobbler's. Shoes were always an important item in his economy. He had not paid his poll-tax for some years — for six, he said in 'Civil Disobedience' when it was published in 1849 — probably not since 1843 when Alcott set the example and was arrested.[5] Taxes, as such, he paid readily, but the poll-tax he felt to be the specific imposition of the political state — a state which, as he says in the 'Walden' version of the story, buys and sells men, and women, and children, meaning slaves. In 1846, the Mexican War stiffened his resistance. 'When a sixth of the population of a nation which has undertaken to be the refuge of liberty are slaves, and a whole country is unjustly overrun and conquered by a foreign army, and subjected to military law, I think that it is not too soon for honest men to rebel and revolutionize.' So he wrote in 'Civil Disobedience' — so he felt when they arrested him on that July evening. He had quietly declared war with the state, after his fashion, by refusing to let his dollar buy 'a man or a musket to shoot one with ... though I will still make what use and get what advantage of her [the state] I can, as is usual in such cases.'[6]

Was it perhaps Thoreau's unpopularity as a setter of forest fires which led the authorities to choose him as an example from among the passive resistants to the state? Did they fear that Alcott and others more important might begin stirring up trouble again because of 'principle'? At all events, he was 'seized and put into jail,' and had a most interesting night there with his cell companion, who was an alleged barn-burner, and (later) thoroughly enjoyed the idea that the poor Walden student had made the state 'run "amok"' against him, it being the desperate party which could make its will prevail only by force and with no permanent results. 'I do not hear of *men* being *forced* to live this way or that by masses of men.' Not Yankees, at least, who lived by principle — certainly not a minority made up of Thoreaus. 'I saw that the State . . . did not know its friends from its foes.' [7]

Julian Hawthorne in his 'Memoirs' tells a different story. He reports there that Thoreau lost his temper when he was jailed. This seems to be true. Sam Staples, his jailor, interviewed many years later, said Henry 'was mad as the devil' when he turned him loose in the morning.[8] Thoreau was a great rationalizer of his emotions when the time came to philosophize them! Unhappily, the famous story of Emerson's visit to the jail must also be rewritten.[9] 'Henry, why are you there?' he is supposed to have said, to be answered, 'Why are you not here?' If there was such a question, it came later, after Henry's release, for Sam locked up his prisoners early, took his boots off, and wouldn't unlock them again even after the fine was paid. The phrasing also must have been different. Emerson knew precisely why he was there, since both Transcendentalists insisted upon the prerogatives of the individual in defiance of the will of the rulers of the state. That is what Henry really meant by the state — its rulers. He was not intransigent against his duties to society, but against the intransigence of rulers in what he regarded as the essential right of the individual to preserve his moral integrity. With this Emerson, of course, agreed. The issue between them — and it was real — was on what grounds a man should take his stand. Thoreau had found Alcott's previous arrest on principle a rather admirable gesture until the archangel began talking about it as if it were a revolution. Now that Thoreau was arrested, Emerson felt much the same way about him. He told Alcott in July of 1846, as Alcott records in his Journal, that it was 'mean and skulking, and in bad taste.' 'I defended it,' says Alcott, 'on the grounds of a dignified non-compliance with the injunction of civil powers.'

But Emerson's private comment was made in his Journal for

the same month: 'Mr. Webster told them how much the war cost . . . and sends his son to it. They calculated rightly on Mr. Webster. My friend Mr. Thoreau has gone to jail rather than pay his tax. On him they could not calculate.' It was perhaps bad taste and a little mean for Thoreau to make an issue over a poll-tax, and thus, while great problems were being thrust upon the idealists who were on the side of the angels, to fight over a straw, and raise the question whether his friends and sympathizers, and Emerson among them, whose influence was so much greater than his own, were not also and merely stiff-necked obstructionists. Nevertheless, the state could not calculate on any subservience from Henry Thoreau.

He was in jail only one night, yet long enough for the valuable experience of seeing his townsmen from the point of view of those condemned for not conforming to the rules by which Concord lived. Then, according to Jane Hosmer, 'When his mother heard of his arrest, she hastened to the Jail, then to the Thoreau house in the Square, at which Misses Jane and Maria Thoreau then lived, and one of the latter [Aunt Maria in disguise, says Annie Russell Marble in her biography], putting a shawl over her head, went to the jailer's door, and paid the tax and fees to Ellen Staples, her father the jailer being absent.' [10] Either Henry forbade his mother to pay, or she had not enough money at hand.

And so, by no act of his own, but unjailable again except for a new offense, Henry came out, got his shoe, and went huckleberrying, while his neighbors first looked at him and then at one another, 'as if I had returned from a long journey. . . . This is the whole history of "My Prisons."' Yet he was a little inclined to agree with Emerson that, in itself, it was not too noble a history. 'One cannot be too much on his guard in such a case,' he wrote in 'Civil Disobedience,' from which the quotations above are taken, 'lest his action be biased by obstinacy or an undue regard for the opinions of men. Let him see that he does only what belongs to himself and to the hour.' And so, having made his gesture, withheld his tax for six years, and got his reactions out of his system in a thundering essay, he paid in 1849 his poll-tax of $1.50, as the tax-book now in the Middlebury College library shows, and let the state look elsewhere for a victim!

6

'Civil Disobedience,' the lecture which Alcott liked so much, was written in 1848 as a commentary upon his jailing, of which it contains an account much more extensive than the narrative in 'Walden.' It was published in May of 1849 in Elizabeth Peabody's symposium of papers from old *Dial* contributors, called *Aesthetic Papers*, which was to be followed by others if the public responded, which they did not. 'Civil Disobedience' attracted no attention at the time, but has since gone round the world. It was Gandhi's source-book in his Indian campaign for Civil Resistance, and has been read and pondered by thousands who hope to find some way to resist seemingly irresistible force.

The extraordinary effectiveness of Thoreau's essay on resistance to the power of the state is not due to any dramatic necessity in the cause that produced it. Here it has the Anglo-Saxon quality of understatement. No tyrant, no dictator, no Oriental despotism is even thought of by this Concord citizen of the most easy-going of republics. He assumes a democratic system. He assumes majority rule. He assumes a weak government, not a strong one. He does not exaggerate his act of rebellion, laughs at it a little, wonders if he has been too obstinate; then clamps down suddenly on the principle involved, which is good for all weathers. The most liberal government becomes a tyranny when it denies the right of the individual to be responsible for his intellectual and moral integrity. It can overrule him, yes, but he must somehow resist. If he is a crank, an opponent of order, which is essential to the state, if he is a self-centered egotist, he will suffer, and let him suffer. If, however, his integrity is based on values indispensable to a self-respecting man, then resistance is also indispensable, and will become a power unconquerable in the long run, even by force.

The political weakness of this argument is obvious. It leaves one of those wide margins that Thoreau liked in his thinking as well as in his life, and this time a wide margin of possible error. For if the individual is to determine his own rights, what authority is left to distinguish between enlightened resistance to the rulers of a state, and anarchy, which will inevitably dissolve the state itself? Thoreau would have answered that you must have faith in man, you must believe that an intuition of what is necessary for survival is a reality in human nature. And it is the only possible answer.

But this was not the lesson which thousands have learned since from 'Civil Disobedience.' The metaphysics of politics concerns them as little as it concerned Thoreau. The conflict of man against the state is real, no matter what one thinks of its rules. It wanes, it waxes — we have reached or are nearing again one of its periodical crises. There will always be those who are faced with the sacrifice either of their just rights or their security. How can those who are determined to resist oppose, with any hope of success, a régime of irresistible force? Thoreau, writing in an America soon to be in the throes of a great rebellion, was not at that time, nor for any time, thinking of mass rebellion where motives are mixed and the objective is always power. He was concerned with the individual whose power can only be his own integrity. For him he counsels passive resistance, and this is the answer which has made his essay famous:

A very few... serve the state with their consciences... and so necessarily resist it for the most part; and they are commonly treated as enemies by it.

It is not so important that many should be as good as you, as that there be some absolute goodness somewhere; for that will leaven the whole lump.

A wise man will not leave the right to the mercy of chance, nor wish it to prevail through the power of the majority.

It is not a man's duty, as a matter of course, to devote himself to the eradication of any, even the most enormous, wrong [so much for professional reformers]; he may still properly have other concerns to engage him; but it is his duty, at least, to wash his hands of it, and, if he gives it no thought longer, not to give it practically his support.

Action from principle... changes things and relations; it is essentially revolutionary.

If the injustice is part of the necessary friction of the machine of government, let it go, let it go: perchance it will wear smooth. ... But if it is of such a nature that it requires you to be the agent of injustice to another, then, I say, break the law.

I was not born to be forced. I will breathe after my own fashion.... If a plant cannot live according to its nature, it dies; and so a man.

I am as desirous of being a good neighbor as I am of being a bad subject.

There will never be a really free and enlightened State until the State comes to recognize the individual as a higher and independent power, from which all its own power and authority are derived, and treats him accordingly. I please myself with imagining a State at last which can afford to be just to all men... which even would not think it inconsistent with its own repose if a few were to live aloof from it, not meddling with it, nor embraced by it, who fulfilled all the duties of neighbors and fellow-men.

And until such a state arises, he is ready to resist, when necessary, brute force. While he cannot expect successfully to oppose the force itself, his resistance may be effective because it may change the minds of the men that exercise it. And therefore it is not futile quietly to declare war upon your state.

History abundantly proves that such disobedience can be effective. There is perhaps no power in the world today able to overcome aerial bombs and machine guns but intellectual and emotional resistance in Thoreau's sense, by brave men, clear of mind, and able to endure until their conviction becomes infectious.

How would the author of 'Civil Disobedience' act if he were alive today? His revolution was a one-man revolution against a feeble state, concerned for its own prosperity. The dictatorial state, with torture at its command, and a fanaticism as strong and far less reasonable than Thoreau's, presents very different problems. His answer, I should say, to the totalitarian idea would be, that such massed individuals as support these states may for the time being be impregnable, are like avalanches, which no man can hope to resist. The citizen will have to step back and, protecting integrity by any concessions possible to it, endeavor to make the nobler moral fervor prevail. But he would disobey rather than rebel, and wrestle with weakness in himself rather than use violence against the despot in the enemy. Gandhi took such a position. He struck at the pocketbook of the state, not at its armies. He refused to conform, but did not attack his rulers.

7

Thoreau's mind at Walden turned outward in at least one other way, far less sensational, but most important for his own career. He began to organize his reporting of experience into statements complete up to date, and get ready to publish his first real book. The first months at Walden, while he was building his cabin and cultivating, and later harvesting, his beans, must have been too crowded with necessary labor to permit more writing than the records of his experience in his Journal. The days when he sat in a muse from morning till the sun began to decline (not many, I imagine) sound like interludes between hard physical labors, when the mind was set free from a languorous body for dreamy thought rather than creation. 'Tell children,' said Emerson, surely in answer to Henry in the spring of '46, 'what you say about writing and laboring with the hands. I know better.... The writer must live and die by his writing.' Experience exists to him only as 'colors for his brush.' ¹¹

But after autumn and the bean harvest and the chimney built, and the November-December plastering of the first year, when he had to go home for a while to let the walls dry, and when winter had set in, there must have been leisure enough and enough unexpended energy. Since by July of 1846 the 'Week' was ready for publication, its first completed draft can probably be dated in the spring of that year, when he said he had planted fewer beans and more 'sincerity, truth, simplicity, faith, innocence.' These took less time to weed.

There had been other writing. By December of 1845 he had composed a lecture on the 'mean and sneaking life you live' in Concord, and in 1847 read 'The History of Myself' at the Lyceum, which included, according to Sanborn, a considerable part of 'Walden.'

Before midsummer of 1846 he had written his essay on Carlyle, also a lecture, the use as such being stipulated in the agreement for publication he made through Greeley and Rufus Griswold in *Graham's Magazine*. It was not printed until 1847, and its publication involved a characteristic row over payment. The essay itself has never been estimated at its true worth. Here is Henry applying his mature philosophy of life and literature to a contemporary, a European, and a dweller like himself close to the founts of intuition. It is supposed to be an appreciation, and seemed so to Carlyle, who wrote to Emerson, 'A vigorous Mr. Thoreau' who 'recognizes us, and various other things, in a most admiring great-hearted manner.' [12] Vigorous, yes, and admiring in its way, yet if turned upside down, a severe criticism of Carlyle for being an impressionist who plays with highly colored ideas, and a humorist who relies upon his humor to weariness. It is Carlyle's appeal to youth that Thoreau likes; he finds little solid ground underneath, and a tendency to exaggerate whatever idea moved the author's emotions. Intuitive, an exaggerator, a humorist himself, he saw what Carlyle's critics have failed even today to recognize, that, as with Emerson, the ideas which come to him exist only as 'colors for his brush.' In the Carlyle essay, as in the 'Civil Disobedience' and the preliminaries of 'Walden,' he begins to look out from his inner vision at the leadership of his own times.

Much of the remainder of his writing time he must have devoted to his Journal, in which he was preparing for 'Walden,' and to his book, 'A Week on the Concord and Merrimack Rivers.' In 1845, he gave a lecture on 'Concord River' which was assuredly part of the 'Week,' very probably the first chapter, with its piscatorial and alluvial passages. The 'Week' was the only one of his Excursions that burst its narrow scope of narrative and observation, and became a book. Both brothers kept diaries on the trip,[13] as Henry records, but the 'Week' never gets as far as the White Mountains, which were a part of their excursion. Instead, Thoreau adopted a scheme of Days, each on the river, which is the only plan for a book, aside from mere chronology, he ever made — except for 'Walden,' which is bound together by an idea. I believe that his deep love for John, the tension which rose between them over Ellen, which must have colored the memory of those intimate days on the rivers, and John's sudden and terrible death, gave to his many tentative records of the voyage a significance and a worth which no casual tramping over the Catskills or on Cape Cod with Ellery could equal. He must have brooded upon his narrative as an experience never, alas, to be repeated. And as he brooded his inner life attached itself to those memories, enriched them, and set its own memorial next to the record. For all this he had time at Walden.

At Walden Pond the first stage of this enrichment by accretion was completed. A book was finished and offered for publication, which was certainly not a mere narrative Excursion, though he used the word in his first title, but such an organized history of the imagination of Henry Thoreau afloat upon the rivers as we have, with later additions, in the standard text. He read this version to Emerson in the early summer of 1846, who wrote in July: 'In a short time, if Wiley and Putnam smile, you shall have Henry Thoreau's *Excursion on the Concord and Merrimack Rivers*, a seven days' voyage in as many chapters, pastoral as Isaak Walton, spicy as flagroot, broad and deep as Menu. He read me some of it under an oak on the river bank the other afternoon and invigorated me.'[14] Wiley and Putnam, who did not smile, were New York publishers with whom Emerson had dealings. He probably had sent them the manuscript himself, as he was to send it again and later to New York and Philadelphia, also without success.

'A Week on the Concord and Merrimack Rivers,' as curious and interesting a compilation, whether viewed as literature, psychology, or Americana, as any written on this continent, I shall discuss later. But that it was Thoreau's first reaching out to an audience which he hoped would take all of him that could be put into words, seems obvious. The esoteric musings, the 'Hindoo practices,' the self-seekings at Walden Pond were real enough. But these feelers toward the world beyond his egocentricity seem to me more significant for the biography of a man whose most famous book was to be a criticism of society.

16. CLIMAX AND TRANSITION

Concord, Sept. 25th, 1847.

Dear P —— ... Mr. Emerson is going to Europe soon to *lecture* there, and in consequence Henry has sold his house to him, and is going to reside in his family this winter.... Mrs. —— ¹ is going to keep a coffee shop, by *subscription* that they dignify with some french name, which I have forgotten, but it may well be asked, what is in a name, neither food nor clothing. Forgive this malevolent speech, but I do love to hear things call'd by their right names, and these *Transcendentalists* do so trans- mogrophy. (I have written that at a venture not knowing exactly the meaning of it myself, but shouldn't I be as tran- scendental as the rest of them?) so transmogrophy their words and pervert common sense that I have no patience with them. Mr. Alcott's going to Europe for the present seems to have blown over, he and H —— is building an arbour for Mr. Emer- son, but H —— says, A —— pulls down as fast as he builds up, (quite characteristic) but it is rather expensive [and] somewhat tedious to poor Henry, to say nothing of endangering life and limbs for if there had not been a comfortable haystack near that he availed himself of by jumping into, when the top rafter was knock'd off, it might have been rather a serious affair. I do not know but I exaggerate a little, but at any rate jump he had to, and I believe it *was* in a hay mow. I hope they will find as soft a

landing place, one and all, when they drop from the clouds, this
expression is rather ambiguous you may take it as you list —
but my letter is becoming quite too transcendental. I will
descend a little.... [2]

Thus the garrulous Aunt Maria, who loved orthodoxy and
Henry, but disapproved of 'newness,' wrote to her gossip,
Prudence Ward.

Thoreau left Walden Pond on September 6 of 1847, as unaccountably (so he says in his Journal) as he went there: 'There
was a little stagnation, it may be. About 2 o'clock in the afternoon the world's axle creaked as if it needed greasing.' 'Perhaps it seemed to me that I had several more lives to live, and
could not spare any more time for that one.... I did not wish
to take a cabin passage, but rather to go before the mast and on
the deck of the world.' [3]

All of which means that, having tried his experiment and di-
gested its meaning, got one book done and another under way,
he 'wanted a change.' Often in later years he longed to be back
at Walden, yet he was no hermit by nature, and as Occidental
in his resolve to get all he wanted from life as he was Oriental in
his desire to escape from busyness. So when opportunity
knocked on his cabin door he was ready to go. Emerson was
going abroad to lecture in England. Emerson wished to have
him come to his house again, 'for company' for Mrs. Emerson;
to be this time a head of the household, handle the family affairs, financial and otherwise, act as friend to the children, and
look after the place. Now he was to come, not as a struggling
youth who might be saved for poetry, but as a colleague of *The
Dial*, a writer who had written a book that Emerson thought
first-rate, and a mature man who had learned how to stand on
his own feet. Hugh, the gardener, was there to do the rough
work. But it was actually Lidian who invited him, as it had
been Lidian who said she could not spare Henry when it was

The rustic summer-house designed and erected for Emerson
by Alcott and Thoreau
'H—— says, A—— pulls down as fast as he builds up'
From an etching in Homes of American Authors, *1853*

proposed that he should go to Staten Island.[4] And so, probably in October, he moved into the little room at the head of the stairs.

The hut at Walden was left to the chipmunks and the stars. But soon Hugh, the gardener, who also had ambitions toward a place of his own, moved it to the bean field which he proposed to turn into an orchard, and with eighty dollars borrowed from Emerson [5] began work on an addition. 'Irish like,' he dug the cellar so close that the old hut began to topple; then got drunk and ran away from both Walden Pond and his wife. That was the end of human life on the lot by the pondside. Nature soon took back her own, aided by Henry, who planted pines in the bean field.

Thoreau had been telling Emerson that he would rather go to Oregon than to England. 'What seeks he,' Emerson wrote in his Journal, 'but the most energetic Nature?' His perverse friend, who after two years in the woods wanted only larger forests to live in, was a little irritating. He seemed to him this year 'sometimes only as a *gendarme,* good to knock down a cockney with, but without that power to cheer and establish which makes the value of a friend.'

2

Oregon was just tall talk. What Thoreau really wanted was to tackle the literary world again, to get on its deck. As for the 'power to cheer and establish which makes the value of a friend,' his letters written to Emerson abroad of his love and cheer and comfort for the family left behind must have made the sage regret his remark. A chestnut bur, hiding its sweetness, Thoreau was to most men. It was presumably in this year that Lidian became the Sister of whom he wrote.

Emerson sailed in October on the *Washington Irving* packet, leaving Henry to begin what he called a 'solid time,' an experiment that worked so well that he stayed on until the lecturer's return the following July. With Lidian, who was ill much of this year, he ran the house, helping her shyness to prepare for guests who sometimes never turned up, and in his free time wrote lectures in his hall bedroom. 'The Rights and Duties of the Individual in Relation to Government' was lying on his desk in February, to become later the famous 'Civil Disobedience.' He read his 'Ktaadn' adventure to 'quite a large audience of men and boys,' the intrinsic interest of the piece seeming to make up for his always bad delivery. He was amused by a peace meeting where Deacon Brown and others signed a pledge to 'treat all mankind as brothers henceforth,' remarking, 'I think I shall wait and see how they treat me first.' With Alcott, he built the rustic arbor, fortunately beside a haymow, and offended the Great Conversationalist by laughing at his wildwood architecture. 'He is very grave to look at,' wrote Thoreau, and behaved 'as if I had still some of the animal heat in me.' [6] Thoreau had — plenty. Alcott was hospitable to travelling thoughts but would not 'toe the line' — come down to earth, I suppose Thoreau means. There was too much Connecticut philosophy in him. 'After all,' this to Emerson, 'I think we must call him particularly *your* man.' 'There stands the dear Henry,' Emerson replied to his letter on January 11, 1848, 'erect, serene, & undeceivable,' inserting after the 'dear Henry' as if by afterthought, ' — if indeed anybody had a right to call him so, —.' [7]

In the meantime negotiations for the publication of the 'Week' continued. Emerson had promised to inquire in Philadelphia and New York 'before we begin to set our own types. . . . Thoreau is mainly bent on having it printed in a cheap form for a large circulation.' [8] His friend, William Henry Furness, to whom he wrote, could do nothing in Philadelphia, and by the

Phila... Nov 26. 54

My dear friend,

we depend upon hearing the NY Lecture here.

I was glad to see Mr. Thoreau. He was full of interesting talk for the little while that we saw him, & it was amusing to hear your intonations. And then he looked so differently from my idea of him [something so.—] He had a glimpse of the Academy as he will tell you — I could not hear him lecture for which I was sorry. Miss Caroline Haven heard him, & from her report I judge the audience was stupid & did not appreciate him

With much love

R. W. E.   W. H. Furness

our

From a letter of William Henry Furness to Emerson,
with a sketch of Thoreau's profile
'His nose . . . was like the prow of a ship'

end of '47 four publishers at least had declined it. In the spring Thoreau still likes it 'well enough to mend it,' and indeed had written in January, for inclusion in the chapter called 'Wednesday,' the famous essay on Friendship, and read it to Alcott. Emerson urged him to print at his own expense, so finally the contract for his first book was signed with James Munroe, the Boston publisher and bookseller, 'my *publisher*, falsely so called,' as he names him later, who had mishandled *The Dial*. The book was ready in 1848, for that is the copyright date in the proof sheets, but not actually published until May of 1849.

Thoreau had fifty dollars on hand from Greeley for his magazine writings, twenty-five or fifty dollars coming in, and still more in prospect; [9] also (if Aunt Maria was right) what Emerson had paid him for the Walden house. A sheet of manuscript in the Huntington library shows that after he went home from Emerson's he was lending money to his mother, paying his father sums up to twenty dollars, working in the pencil-shop sometimes all day, and still had a balance due him from Emerson. 'It is five years that I have been maintaining myself entirely by manual labor,' he wrote to Greeley, and now his pen was actually earning something. When the 'Week' is done, 'I shall get leisure for those shorter articles you want, — then look out.' Even so cautious a spender as Henry felt that the time had come to back himself for fame. And so he agreed to pay for his book.[10]

3

And not only agreed, but in the confidence of approaching publication began to get ready another book for printing. When the 'Week,' that 'purely American' voyage, as Alcott somewhat inaccurately called it, came off the press, the advertising pages carried this announcement:

WILL SOON BE PUBLISHED

WALDEN,

OR

LIFE IN THE WOODS

'Walden' was written by early 1849. In spite of the additions
made from the later Journal, it was a real book by then, and it
is probable that the work-sheets in the Huntington library, with
their many variants and twelve thousand words not in the
published version,¹¹ represent only a revision and amplifying
of the 'Walden' which Aunt Maria's letter proves was being
made ready for the press in 1849:

Concord, Feb. 28th. 1849.
Dear P ——... Today Henry has gone to Salem to read another lecture they seem to be wonderfully taken with him there,
and next month he is to go to Portland, to deliver the same, and
George wants him to keep on to Bangor they want to have him
there, and if their funds will hold out they intend to send for
him, they give 25 dollars, and at Salem and Portland 20 — he is
preparing his Book for the press and the title is to be, Waldien
(I dont know how to spell it) or life in the Woods. I think the
title will take if the Book dont. I was quite amused with what
Sophia told me her mother said about it the other day, she poor
girl was lying in bed with a sick head ache when she heard
Cynthia (who has grown rather nervous of late) telling over her
troubles to Mrs. Dunbar, after speaking of her own and Helen's
sickness, she says, and there's Sophia she's the greatest trial I've
got, for she has complaints she *never will* get rid of, and Henry is
putting things into his Book that never ought to be there, and
Mr. Thoreau has faint turns and I don't know what ails him,
and so she went on from one thing to another hardly knew
where to stop, and tho it is pretty much so, I could not help
smiling at Sophia's description of it. As for Henry's book, you
know I have said, there were parts of it that sounded to me very
much like blasphemy, and I did not believe they would publish
it, on reading it to Helen the other day Sophia told me, she

made the same remark, and coming from her, Henry was much surprised, and said she did not understand it, but still I fear they will not persuade him to leave it out.

Henry must often have wished himself back in the woods or at Emerson's. Cynthia, nervous and conventional, Helen, rigidly moral and dying of tuberculosis, Sophia with her headaches, so admiring and yet so easily shocked, Aunt Maria and her sarcastic Toryism — they were all passing his book around and begging him to take out this or that. He had addressed it to his fellow townsmen, but his first reaction was from the family. The devastating implications of his economic theories slid off their minds — they had none of them been fattened by prosperity — but blasphemy (by which I suppose Aunt Maria meant his doubts about Christianity) was another matter. Even his friend and fellow intellectual, George Ripley, was to attack in *The Tribune*, with a gravity made emphatic by his praise of the style, the free-thinking of the 'Week.' It was not safe to be radical in all directions in Concord in the 1840's.

Thoreau seems to have shown 'Walden' to neither Emerson nor Alcott, perhaps because so much had been done to help him publish his first book that he preferred to talk less, and do more himself, about the second. In the twelve months from, say, early '48 to early '49, he certainly reached the climax of his creative achievements, and probably of his powers. He had finished the last revision of the 'Week' and written his first draft of 'Walden' in these months, and was ready for anything except what happened — the flat failure of the first and the deferring of the publication of the second for five years. This delay in printing what was to prove his masterpiece is one of those casualties in the life of a man of letters which change the course, if they do not alter the character, of genius.

4

After he left Emerson's, Thoreau went to the Texas house
among the vines and trees planted by his own hand. In September of 1849, however, his father was ready to go back to the
inner village again, and this time as owner of the 'yellow house'
(now called the Thoreau-Alcott house) on Main Street, which
he bought from Daniel Shattuck for $1450. With Thoreau's
assistance he 'reformed' it, moving there in August of 1850. A
pleasant house, better proportioned and larger than the one
which father and son had built together, it testified to the increasing prosperity of the family. Electrotyping was creating
an eager demand for first-quality ground graphite, which sold
for a while at ten dollars a pound, though by the mid-fifties two
dollars seems to have been the standard price. The Thoreau
firm had got as much as six dollars a gross for good pencils, and
at retail some at least sold for twenty-five cents apiece. But the
competition was severe, the imported Bavarian clay, of the
existence of which Henry had learned in a Scotch encyclopedia,
was expensive, and the Thoreaus soon went over entirely to
supplying the electrotype market with the dust which Henry's
craftsmanship had made of such excellent quality and easy
production. These processes were always kept secret, for the
Thoreaus had no money to fight infringements of a patent.
Sanborn says that it was never good form to speak of either
pencils or graphite in the household, and no one was admitted
to the workroom. The spectacle of this fearless antagonist of
the abuses of industrialism protecting the trade secrets of what
for a while was a monopoly, is amusing to the point of irony!
Reforming the Yellow House consisted in part at least of building a wing for the graphite business.

There are interesting glimpses of him in these climactic years
when he seemed to himself and others about to become an

established American writer. Very little of his Journal remains from '48 and '49, and most of that is fragmentary and not included in his published works. Probably the bulk was ground up in the mill of the 'Week' and 'Walden.' Letters and the journals of others, however, help to keep in touch.

Emerson, of course, was away until July of 1848, but this absence, like his previous one, is the cause of Thoreau's very best letters. 'I have almost never written letters in my life,' he wrote with his usual exaggeration, 'yet I think I can write as good ones as I frequently see,' and he did. But Emerson was disappointed when he came home, to find the 'Week' still unpublished and Thoreau once again working for his father, tramping the woods, and apparently pointed toward no career except to 'travel in Concord.' Henry, he said in his Journal, led poetry into the woods and left her there in want and madness. Even Ellery seems to have begun to doubt his friend: 'His effects can all be produced by cork and sand: but the substance that produces them is godlike and divine.' [12]

Less intimate companions felt more truly the strength that Thoreau had brought back from Walden. When he lectured in Salem at Hawthorne's invitation, Hawthorne's daughter remembered his 'enormous eyes, tame with religious intellect and wild with the loose rein, making a steady flash in this strange union of forces.' They frightened her dreadfully at first. Yet his 'countenance had an April pensiveness about it.' [13] Her mother said that he had 'risen above all his arrogance of manner, and is as gentle, simple, ruddy, and meek as all geniuses should be; and now his great blue eyes fairly outshine and put into shade a nose which I once thought must make him uncomely forever.' [14] Hawthorne himself took him to dinner at Longfellow's afterward, apologizing for the liberty: 'You will find him well worth knowing; he is a man ... with a certain iron-pokerish-ness, an uncompromising stiffness in his mental character, which is interesting, though it grows wearisome.' [15] Later, Longfellow notes drily: 'At dinner, Hawthorne, Thoreau, Channing, and Sam; — all the philosophers.' But the two had dined together a few days earlier, on November 16, when Longfellow had gone to Concord to meet Emerson's 'meek philosophers,' meaning Alcott, Thoreau, and Channing. There is an unmistakable touch of condescension in the relationship. [16]

A less complimentary description of Thoreau, as he appeared at a Conversation of Alcott's in Boston, dates from 1848. Mrs. Ednah D. Cheney, a lively young woman of wit and intellect, saw him there and noted that he was 'getting up a caricature nose like Emerson's. Yet he has something in himself, — else he would be altogether disgusting and ridiculous [young women, with the exception of Ellen Sewall and Louisa Alcott, never seemed to have liked Thoreau]; as it is, 'tis funny. I really enjoyed it all the evening, and wanted to say to him, as the child did to Judge Smith, of Exeter, — "Man, talk more!" He was not a living man, — he was a phenomenal creature.' [17]

Channing, as vigorous as ever, accompanied him on walks which were now growing more regular and businesslike, and Thoreau, rather surprisingly, was sometimes a tactful intermediary between the temperamental Ellery and his wife, from whom he was soon to separate. Channing and he in '49 took their first excursion to Cape Cod.

It was this year that his sister Helen died. Both Congregational and Unitarian ministers were at the service. In the interval, while they were preparing to move the coffin, Henry wound his favorite music box and let it play tender, minor strains. [18]

5

The most useful friend of this creative period was Mumbo Jumbo, as Ellery called him, the soon-to-be-great editor,

Horace Greeley. Greeley had a respect amounting to veneration for the Transcendentalists and Concord, but his mind was essentially practical, and he belonged to the new generation of editors who were to make New York the literary center of the country. No matter how noble and unworldly the utterance, he believed in getting it printed and paid for. In Thoreau's case, since his publisher's sixth sense told him that there was a cow needing to be milked, his respect and real affection led him to undertake the difficult task. In this he seems to have been completely disinterested — a literary agent who took only his expenses, a publicity man who worked for his friend's reputation and not for his own firm. *The Tribune* was no medium for Thoreau, who was a magazine and book writer, not a journalist; therefore Horace Greeley's efforts were directed to placing his young friend where his talents could find a steady market. 'I want one shorter article from your pen that will be quoted ... and let the public know something of your way of thinking and seeing,' he wrote.[19]

There was some difficulty in extracting Thoreau's manuscripts, for the Concord author seems to have felt that his one sure market was the Lyceum, and that publishing his lectures would leave him without ammunition. Greeley got the Carlyle essay and placed it in *Graham's Magazine*, and later the Ktaadn story, which he sold to Sartain for the *Union Magazine*, and did his best to persuade Thoreau to write brief critiques of his eminent Concord friends, but vainly; Henry would not commercialize his friendships. His prestige availed where Thoreau's own efforts had been unsuccessful, and his knowledge of the tricky magazine trade, where free contributions were the rule and engagements to pay were often not kept, enabled him to extract by drafts and bullyings actual cash which he sent faithfully to Thoreau, deducting only his costs. Perhaps the greatest tribute ever paid him in his distinguished career was Thoreau's later request for a loan of seventy-five dollars. The prickly porcupine had at last found a man who was both honest and shrewd.

It is a compliment to Thoreau's discrimination that even if he felt the sometimes vacuous Alcott to be Emerson's man, not his, affection never slackened. Two more different temperaments never spent profitably so much time in each other's company — the one, for all his underlying idealism, in love with visible nature and a shrub oak tree, the other passionate about nothing but pure and tenuous ideas. Yet Alcott sowed seed wherever he went, which ripened in minds more realistic than his own. He was 'the sanest man,' said Thoreau writing of him in 'Walden,' meaning undoubtedly that he dealt only in fundamentals; yet 'with no venture in the present'; one who peddled ideas for a better future, 'prompting God and disgracing man.' It took insight as well as humor to understand that Alcott's conspicuous failures, his progressive school, for instance, were due to the bad timing of an overconfident optimist rather than to any lack of good sense.

Yet even optimists get discouraged. In one of the conversations in this year of '48 between the arch-idealist and the young man who had gone to Walden to make himself into a 'Realometer,' Alcott asked the question which Thoreau put to himself whenever he felt that the world preferred his pencils to his ideas. Were not all the Transcendentalists inefficient? They had attracted no 'maid from the farmer's hearth or youth from farm or workshop' to their houses, and seemed indeed to have little 'positive and real existence here in this world, in this 19th century ... in this little centre of Concord, Mass.' Between them and their townspeople only the vaguest relations existed. They were ghosts, spectres, rumors, and their dealings with men were ridiculous in the eyes of banks and bar-rooms. A great life should 'shine abroad and educate,' but they were merely fabulous.[20] Alcott remained 'fabulous' to his townsmen until they borrowed a few coals of his genius to warm the office of the Concord school superintendent. But it may be significant of the fertilizing power of his intensely suggestive mind, that it was soon after this year that Henry began to put together 'Walden' as an open challenge to his townspeople, for whom he was only a rumor of a Harvard graduate turned loafer and handyman.

Another friendship of life-long durability, and far more intimate, began at this time. Harrison G. O. Blake of Worcester was, as Emerson said, 'a terribly conscientious man, "a man who would even return a borrowed umbrella."' [21] After reading Thoreau's letters to him — many of great length — I should sharpen the description by calling him, rather, a conscience-bound man. He had been in the class of 1835 in Harvard, knew Thoreau by sight, and met him later through Emerson in Concord. Did he feel any longings for the society of his friends? Blake asked. 'No, I am nothing,' Thoreau replied, being in one of his 'mean and low' moods. 'I would know of that soul which can say "I am nothing,"' wrote Blake. [22]

It was the wrong approach, but when in '48 Blake read for the second time the article on Persius in *The Dial* and wrote a congratulatory letter, the friendship began. Thoreau was of the age and in the situation when a writer and thinker begins to yearn for admirers. He had praise and respect from his peers, creative intellects like himself, but so far no maid from the kitchen, youth from the farm, or, what was more to the point, no unknown reader of his own intellectual class had become a disciple. Men who preach, and in spite of his dislike of the clergy Henry was often a preacher, seek disciples, sometimes unconsciously. Blake himself had been a Unitarian minister possessed by doubts which had shifted him into the less responsible job of teacher and tutor. To Thoreau he offered the veneration of a trained though second-class intellect.

His conversion was sudden. When he was concerned with theological matters, said Emerson to Fields, 'he believed wholly in me ... but one day he met Thoreau and he never came to my house afterwards.' [23] 'Speak to me in this hour as you are prompted,' Blake wrote to Thoreau in '48. For fourteen years Thoreau spoke to him of moral courage and the way of life. The result was a series of lay sermons in the form of letters, which undoubtedly helped Blake's somewhat shaky morale, but are the dullest reading Thoreau ever provided except in his attempts to be too scientific with nature. Into these letters Thoreau wove from his Journal some interesting passages, but usually selected the most moral, least life-inspired of his reflections, and usually toward the end of each letter broke down into the real Thoreau, perverse, zestful, humorous, with an impatient lift of language which makes all that precedes seem as flat as it usually is. It was Thoreau's weakness, and the weakness of the New England tradition, to pontificate whenever someone pushed the moral button. Stevenson, that Scotch moralist, did the same, but carried his eloquence more successfully into tracts on spiritual behavior. He was a born preacher. Thoreau was not; he had to be humorous or passionate or ironic or contemptuous in order to write his best, and no one of these moods, except passion, goes well in the pulpit — and Thoreau's passion was the wrong kind.

Blake was a solid friend, and proved a devoted editor when, after Thoreau's death, he put together the first organized anthology of Thoreau's Journal in the volumes called 'Early Spring in Massachusetts,' 'Summer,' 'Winter,' and 'Autumn' — although curiously enough he emphasized nature and not morals in these books, and is largely responsible for the idea that Thoreau's chief eminence was as a naturalist. Yet he was the first of that new circle of inferior minds, worshipful rather than stimulating, that were to be substitutes for real friends in the remainder of Thoreau's life.

6

Thoreau had three kinds of friends. Such men as Ellery Channing were like the members of his own family, intimate, easy, deeply affectionate, though Channing's intellectual persiflage kept that relationship from ever being merely familiar. He had love for Thoreau — we can only guess that the affection was returned, in kind if not in degree. Intellectual comprehensions between them were quicker and deeper than with the family, yet, as with Elizabeth Hoar, and the much more *simpática* Lucy Brown, or with Hawthorne and Alcott, there was no tension of feeling, no stir beyond friendship in the ordinary sense of that term. Such friends Thoreau loved as equals.

Blake belonged to a different category, which soon begins to broaden. His friend, Theophilus Brown of Worcester, joined it later, and Daniel Ricketson, the Providence Quaker, who knew so much of Thoreau's later life, and many correspondents who lacked only time and opportunity to become, like these men, recipients of Thoreauvian advice, and good companions. The worship of such friends was sweet to a man who had only tasted success; yet it did not turn his cool judgment. He could at any moment have gone back to Walden and forgotten them.

The third classification is much more puzzling. It includes his brother John, and Lidian Emerson, and Emerson himself — and, of course, the brief apparition of Ellen Sewall. It was of these that he wrote his lifelong series of outpourings on what he called friendship, sometimes coolly analytical, often passionate, sometimes morbid with self-hurt. The painful alienation between Emerson and Thoreau began a few years later than the dates of this chapter. Yet it is probable that one of these tense emotional friendships — with Lidian, his 'Sister' — reached its height in these years of the high tide of his creative imagination — and that its ebb and frustration have much to do with the new Thoreau shortly to emerge from these years of climax and transition.

More of this later. But other women beside Lidian were now feeling the emotional intensity of this 'phenomenal creature,' who had by no means as yet taken nature and the shrub oaks for his love. If they do not belong among his passionate friendships, they themselves seem to have been passionately involved. The evidence is obscure, but conclusive as to the facts, if unsatisfactory as to the identity of the woman or women involved. It is certain that one at least came dangerously under the spell, either of the 'enormous eyes' that frightened Mrs. Lathrop, or of Henry's persuasive sincerity.

I have already quoted part of Aunt Maria's gossipy letter of February 28, 1849, in which she describes the devastating effect of 'Waldien' upon the family. The letter continues:

> By the way have you heard what a strange story there was about Miss Ford, and Henry, Mrs. Brooks said at the convention, a lady came to her and inquired, if it was true, that Miss F —— had committed, or was going to commit suicide on account of H —— Thoreau, what a ridiculous story this is. When it was told to H —— he made no remark at all, and we cannot find out from him any thing about it, for a while, they corresponded, and Sophia said that she recollected one day on the reception of a letter she heard H —— say, he shouldn't answer it, or he must put a stop to this, some such thing she couldn't exactly tell what. . . .[24]

There are two candidates for the doubtful honor of having committed, or having tried to commit, suicide on Henry Thoreau's account. And let it be said before discussing their identities that Thoreau's remark, recorded in his Journal some years later, at least suggests that Mrs. Brooks' friend spoke with some real knowledge. 'Hearing that one with whom I was acquainted had committed suicide,' he wrote on August 5, 1852, 'I said I did not know when I had planted the seed of that fact that I should hear of it.' As he was not responsible, he resented being told!

Ann Frances Ford was the daughter of Colonel Nathaniel and his wife Ann Kendall Ford of Dedham, who was a first cousin of Prudence Ward, often visited by the Wards, and frequently mentioned in their letters. The daughter Ann was a delicate girl when first described, her fragility contrasted with the glowing health of Ellen Sewall. There was every likelihood that she should have met Henry while Prudence Ward, who so admired the Thoreau young men, was living in the Thoreau household. Every likelihood, also, that Prudence would pass on to the Fords as she did to other members of the family circle her interest in the 'deep things' Henry was writing. And, knowing the moral earnestness of the young woman of early nineteenth-century New England, an admiring letter from Ann to Henry would not be surprising. In 1846 and 1847, she was sinking rapidly into that fatal tuberculosis so common, so little admitted until too late by the New England families of this generation, when hot stoves and airtight rooms were completing what the climate began. In January, Laura Harris is taking flowers to 'Fanny,' who has had two hemorrhages, yet is off visiting. When she finds her, she notes her 'bright eyes and delicate bloom.' Her cough is incessant, yet she is very cheerful and apparently unconscious of her situation. In February she was no better, in May, better, on August 2, 1847, dead of consumption, 'aged 18-0-0.' [25]

Someone beside Sophia might have known of a correspondence which Henry said he must put a stop to, someone might have said, and perhaps reported to the family friend, Mrs. Brooks of Concord, that Ann died of a broken heart — Ann might have said so herself, for like so many of her contemporaries she refused to accept the dread warnings of consumption. The gossips could have made it suicide.

But the circumstances are improbable. The girl seems too young for so serious a relationship. As it happens, there was another Miss Ford, whose conditions of life fit much better into the puzzle. She may seem too old, as Ann was too young, for such an involvement with Thoreau, but it was older women whom he attracted most easily.

Sophia Foord, often called by Emerson and others Miss Ford, and probably so pronouncing her name, was, in 1845, when we first hear of her, about forty-three years old (born in Milton, Massachusetts, in 1802), and hence fifteen years older than the twenty-eight year old Thoreau, and a contemporary of Lidian's. She was giving little Louisa Alcott lessons in botany in the woods in 1845, and telling her about the bones in her body.[26] In 1846 (and probably in 1845), she was teaching the little Emersons and little Alcotts in Emerson's barn. On May Day she prepared a May pole and rode with it from the Alcotts' house to the Emersons', accompanied by Bronson and the children, all singing 'Merrily we go.' In August of that year she took the children 'gipsying,' not for the first time, and those who gipsied in Concord woods were likely to meet Henry Thoreau.

In September, Lidian being away, James Freeman Clarke's mother and her son asked for board at the Emersons', and it was arranged that Miss Foord should move into the schoolroom while Thoreau built a room for them in the barn. In October, she left the Emersons' quite ill, 'and we have very unfavorable accounts of her today. She is much respected by all her friends.' So Emerson. She returned, but on April 1, 1847, left them for good, writing Emerson from Milton in July of the days spent 'under your roof.' [27]

These meagre details concerning Louisa Alcott's teacher and the Emerson schoolmistress for much of the time from 1845 to

1847 barely indicate that Sophia was interested in botany and that the children liked her, but in relation to what follows they are significant. For the best part of two years she must have seen Henry Thoreau often enough to come under his curious spell which drew, when it did not rebuff, intellectual women. For her, as for so many New Englanders, there may well have been a glamour upon Emerson's home and upon Emerson's circle, on whose woody border wandered he who was so often called a Pan. If this was the Miss Ford of the lady's story, she had opportunity to fall in love. Teachers of youth, females particularly, are vulnerable in their forties.

If it were she, poor woman, who engaged in a correspondence which Henry said he must stop, and if it was she who was said to have committed suicide for his sake, it is not surprising that Henry would 'make no remark at all' upon the story. It is inconceivable, even upon the evidence thus far stated, that he should have led her on. If his heart was engaged, it was elsewhere. But there is another story, which he called this time 'tragic,' and which proves, at the least, that some woman, as close to Emerson and Thoreau as Sophia Foord, much closer than Ann Ford, was fatally involved in the life of Thoreau, and might have had reasons for tragically ending her frustration.

In a letter written by Thoreau to Emerson, who was in England, is a mysterious reference upon which Sanborn, its editor, makes no comment, nor has it ever been mentioned by Thoreau's biographers: [28]

Concord, November 14, 1847.

Dear Friend, — ... I have had a tragic correspondence, for the most part all on one side, with Miss ——— . She did really wish to — I hesitate to write — marry me. That is the way they spell it. Of course I did not write a deliberate answer. How could I deliberate upon it? I sent back as distinct a *no* as I have learned to pronounce after considerable practice, and I trust that this *no* has succeeded. Indeed, I wished that it might burst, like hollow shot, after it had struck and buried itself and made itself felt there. *There was no other way.* I really had anticipated no such foe as this in my career.

Who was this woman so persistent and aggressive that she had to be bombed out of the way of Henry's career? For there is nothing kind in this letter, but rather a defensive egoism aroused by some opposing egoism. This is no Lidian, no Ellen, and no Ann Ford. The original of this letter is apparently lost, after being published by Sanborn in *The Atlantic Monthly* for June, 1892, with a note saying that it had been given him with others in 1882, the year of Emerson's death, and again in his 'Familiar Letters' of Thoreau in 1894. I believe that the blank of 'Miss ——' was not filled in the original, for Sanborn has inserted other names missing in the correspondence. Yet in default of a certainty, a biographer may be permitted to guess at his own risk. Miss —— was surely not Ann Ford, who had died three months before, two months before Emerson left for England, and whose death must have been long since known to the Thoreau family. Nor would Emerson have had the slightest interest in her, or indeed in any of the Ward-Thoreau family connection, which regarded him as Henry's famous but perversely nebulous friend. The Miss —— of whom Henry wrote was a concern of Emerson's, a close concern, otherwise in a letter of news about Emerson's affairs in Concord it would have been an impertinence on Thoreau's part and an incredible breach of his reticence to have mentioned a proposal of marriage, presumably intended to be confidential.

Only two names among the known women who might have asked Thoreau to marry them in this year of 1847 seem possible to the biographer, Sophia Foord and Margaret Fuller.

The idea that Margaret Fuller, the strong-minded apostle of culture and woman's rights should have proposed matrimony to the penniless hermit of Walden — seven years younger than herself — is not so ridiculous as it seems. They had been closely associated in the days of *The Dial*, and it is evident, both from their correspondence and from her references to him, that he constantly stirred her interest and curiosity. She did not like him,[29] called him an 'enemy,' but it was the kind of dislike which may be a facet of love. She told him, in a letter already quoted, that he was still a bare hill, unwarmed by spring, and her refusals of his contributions are couched in a language so sympathetic as to have the warmth of that uplifting friendship which Thoreau himself regarded as the worthiest form of love. It is probable that her aggressive personality repelled him as it repelled Emerson, whom, indeed, she drove into an extraordinary confusion by asking for a more emotional relationship than he was willing or able to risk.[30] She had a way of inviting confidences, especially of those younger than herself; young girls adored her almost pathologically; and she had probably, as we have seen, been made a partaker in Thoreau's own secret of love and struggle. But, though intellectually stimulating to him, she did not open his heart, and apparently was not satisfied. This may be deduced from one of the paragraphs in the essay on Friendship, which is generally supposed, and with some reason, to have Margaret for its subject. No other likely candidate has been suggested:

> I know a woman who possesses a restless and intelligent mind, interested in her own culture, and earnest to enjoy the highest possible advantages, and I meet her with pleasure as a natural person who not a little provokes me, and I suppose is stimulated in turn by myself. Yet our acquaintance plainly does not attain to that degree of confidence and sentiment which women, which all, in fact, covet. I am glad to help her, as I am helped by her; I like very well to know her with a sort of stranger's privilege, and hesitate to visit her often, like her other Friends. My nature pauses here, I do not well know why. Perhaps she does not make the highest demand

on me, a religious demand. Some, with whose prejudices or peculiar bias I have no sympathy, yet inspire me with confidence, and I trust that they confide in me also as a religious heathen at least, — a good Greek. I, too, have principles as well founded as their own. If this person could conceive that, without wilfulness, I associate with her as far as our destinies are coincident, as far as our Good Geniuses permit, and still value such intercourse, it would be a grateful assurance to me. I feel as if I appeared careless, indifferent, and without principle to her, not expecting more, and yet not content with less. If she could know that I make an infinite demand on myself, as well as on all others, she would see that this true though incomplete intercourse is infinitely better than a more unreserved but falsely grounded one, without the principle of growth in it. For a companion, I require one who will make an equal demand on me with my own genius. Such a one will always be rightly tolerant. It is suicide, and corrupts good manners, to welcome any less than this. I value and trust those who love and praise my aspiration rather than my performance. If you would not stop to look at me, but look whither I am looking, and farther, then my education could not dispense with your company.

It sounds like an apology, and indeed is followed by an apology, a poem, written in the early forties, and published in *The Dial* of '42, but inserted significantly in this essay which was written not many weeks after his letter to Emerson:

> My love must be as free
>   As is the eagle's wing,
> Hovering o'er land and sea
>   And everything.
>
> I must not dim my eye
>   In thy saloon,
> I must not leave my sky
>   And nightly moon....
>
> I cannot leave my sky
>   For thy caprice....

'Saloon,' by which he meant 'salon,' certainly suggests the Conversations made so famous by Margaret Fuller.

But this early autumn of 1847, when this tragic correspondence must be presumed to have been consummated — if it had been earlier Emerson could have been told of the affair before he sailed — was a critical moment in Margaret's career.

She had gone abroad with her friends, the Marcus Springs, in 1846. In September of '46 the crisis came in her romance with the German Jew, James Nathan, with whom she had lived such intense hours in New York, and who was to refuse to return her letters, and then publish their pathetic-exultant lines after her tragic death. She had heard by September that he was married to the daughter of a rich man in Hamburg. By 1847 she had healed her wounds, but was depressed and at loose ends. In the spring at Rome she met, under intriguing circumstances, the Marquis Ossoli, a follower of Mazzini, and a man much younger than herself, about Thoreau's age, in fact, and also at loose ends, thanks to a quarrel with his family over his liberalism. Margaret, that stout-hearted defender of everything liberal, who yet was very much a woman, must have seemed to him a portent and symbol of the new age to which he wished to belong. If she was plain to excess, she was impressive.

At all events, with few preliminaries, he asked her to marry him. Although she went off to Venice to think it over, there is no evidence that she seriously considered such an unsuitable marriage. She was in need of money; he had none. She was his elder, a professional woman of letters, while he was nothing but the gentle and untrained son of a decaying family. And it was precisely in this summer, or earliest autumn, when she was disillusioned with Europe, disappointed in love, yet capable, so it seemed, of attracting young men, that the correspondence with Henry, still at Walden, might have begun. For, as she wrote to Emerson, she was estimating far more highly than ever before the qualities of her home-bred friends, the possibilities of American genius, American youth.

Rome, October 18, 1847.

... I please myself, too, with remembering some ardent souls among the American youth, who, I trust, will yet expand and help to give soul to the huge, over-fed, too-hastily-grown-up body.... But I dare not expect too much of them. I am not very old; yet of those who, in life's morning, I saw touched by the light of a high hope, many have seceded. Some have become ... mere family men... others are lost through indolence and vacillation. Yet some remain constant.

What she wished is made even clearer in another letter:

Rome, Dec. 20, 1847.

Nothing less than two or three years, free from care and forced labor, would heal all my hurts, and renew my life-blood at its source. Since Destiny will not grant me that, I hope she will not leave me long in the world, for I am tired of keeping myself up in the water without corks, and without strength to swim. I should like to go to sleep, and be born again into a state where my young life should not be prematurely taxed.[31]

And she was Margaret Fuller, always ready to join anything from a community to a Conversation for the cause of Excelsior! One could easily reconstruct from her journals, letters, essays, the kind of Transcendental, moralistic, let-us-lift-ourselves-by-our-boot-straps letters she might have written to Thoreau. And so he wrote — to someone — an everlasting 'no' — short, like Ellen Sewall's letter to him, and explosive with the emphatic negative of a young man asked to sacrifice his sacred individualism for a woman.

The mysterious letter would have reached Thoreau after October 5, when Emerson sailed. His answer, over which he did not deliberate, should have been sent, with its hollow shot, by early November certainly. In October, Margaret Fuller had come back to Rome, and seen Ossoli again. In November, she writes (not to Thoreau) that she is 'free.' By the end of November or earliest December she has yielded to Ossoli, and is living with him — technically if not actually. In December, she writes that she is 'happy.' But a child had been conceived in the first week of the month. In January, she is 'frightened and miserable.' She has discovered that she is pregnant. When the old Marquis dies they are married. Two years later, in July of 1850, they came home with the child and all were drowned in a wreck off Fire Island. It was Thoreau that Emerson commissioned, acting in the absence of available members of the family, to go to the beach and search for the belongings of the drowned Ossolis and Margaret's *chef d'oeuvre*, her history of the Roman revolution.

I insert these speculations upon Margaret Fuller because they provide, at the least, atmosphere for the much underestimated personal magnetism of Thoreau, who was, in any case, much more involved with her dynamic personality than has been generally supposed. Someone, not Ann, who died when she was eighteen, wanted to marry him. I hope it was Margaret. It would make her storm-tossed life more interesting with this sudden reversion to the high intellectual optimism in which she and the other *Dial* enthusiasts had hoped to make Boston and Concord a new world of lofty companionship, shot through with duty, but not without the 'rarer and diviner love' which Thoreau in his essay on Friendship said could embrace three as well as two. And it would bear new witness to the deep personal experience which underlay the eloquence of this essay on Friendship, written as a lecture in that same January when Margaret was frightened and miserable abroad. The lines already quoted would then have been intended as an explanation to Margaret of the bursting 'no,' which, if aimed at her, might have helped to drive her toward a liaison most surprising in a blue-stocking, a Transcendentalist, and a New Englander.

I fear, however, that this was a New England tragedy of a grimmer and drabber variety. Those who study the curious psychology of the abundant letters between Margaret Fuller and Emerson in Professor Rusk's recent edition will agree that Margaret was capable of this assault upon Walden. But the probabilities favor Sophia Foord as the tragic heroine, both of the proposal and of the alleged suicide. She was an intimate of Emerson's household at this time, part of that court of service which Lidian always gathered about her, to which Henry himself in these years belonged. If it were she that was pressing marriage upon him, and she whom he rebuffed, Thoreau would naturally have informed Emerson of what happened as soon as it took a form which made action on his part unavoidable; and, indeed, both his letter and Emerson's reply suggest that the older man was not unaware of a situation developing beneath his roof. For he did reply, although his significant words have been omitted from the published version of his letter from England of December 2, 1847: 'You tell me in your letter one odious circumstance, which we will dismiss from remembrance, henceforward,' he wrote.[32] It is improbable that he would have used the word 'odious' of Margaret, who remained his close friend and correspondent until her death. But that Miss Sophia Foord, fifteen years older than Henry Thoreau, should have pursued him under the roof of the Emerson Valhalla may well have seemed odious. Poor woman, singing 'Merrily we go' beneath her May pole, whether frustration led to suicide, or whether her serious illness was renewed and when she died gossip said it was because of her known obsession with Henry Thoreau, her story is both tragic and pathetic. She would not have been comforted could she have known that Henry saw no reason why he should be told of a death for which he was surely not to blame.[33]

Thoreau's sudden spurt of creative power and (rarer for him) constructive power in these years, his friendships, his attraction for others, indicate a high-water mark of living. In all but one aspect, and that the deep, devoted love of nature which has always been made the most of in his career, he is now at his height. He has reached the end of his first phase, and already there are signs of change and sublimation, which the blow to his hopes for fame when the 'Week' failed, and the still more serious putting off of 'Walden,' and very probably the end of his intimacy with Lidian, all further. Thoreau the nature writer and naturalist is a succession product of the creative powers, and particularly of the emotional experiences, described so far in these chapters. This familiar Thoreau belongs after, not before, 'Walden' and the 'Week,' which deserve a more intimate consideration before he takes the stage.

17. TWO BOOKS

In May of 1849, about the twenty-sixth, James Munroe published 'A Week on the Concord and Merrimack Rivers,' and thus the child, conceived ten years earlier,[1] at last saw the light. Authors are very much alike in the history of their hopes, so it is fair to assume that May and June were lit with expectation, for copies were on their way to England, where Clough and Froude read the book, and had been sent to the reviewers, to Thoreau's influential friends, and to admirers like Blake. Thoreau had bought his ticket in the lottery of fame.

It was a unique book, 'an American book, worthy to stand beside Emerson's Essays,' as Alcott justly said in his Journal, and read it all day on the twenty-seventh, and again on the twenty-eighth. It was an original book in its plan of days and in the best of its subject matter, one of the few really original books to appear so far on this side of the Atlantic. Beside it, Irving's mellifluous 'Sketch Book' seems and is an excellent *pastiche* from European models; nor do Hawthorne's narratives convey the same strong sense of a New England mind viewing its country and its culture. And it was a beautiful book, with passages, to use Emerson's phrase, as fresh as the wild flag, and a poetry of description which sometimes has the simplicity and memorable quality of great art, and often no important source except the writer's native sensibilities.

Alcott felt this when in his Walden cabin Thoreau read him portions of the manuscript:

> The book is purely American, fragrant with the lives of New England woods and streams, and could have been written nowhere else. It... is written in a style as picturesque and flowing as the streams he sails on.... There is a toughness too, and a sinewy vigor, as of roots and the strength that comes of feeding on wild meats, and the moist lustres of the fishes in the bed below. It has the merit, moreover, that somehow, despite all presumptions to the contrary, the sod and sap and fibre and flavour of New England have found at last a clear relation to the literature of other and classic lands.... Egypt, India, Greece, England, flow from the poet's hand as he scoops the waters for us from the rivers.[2]

Alcott would have been a more perceptive reviewer than those who went into print about the 'Week.' Yet he guessed wrong, as friends too often will, when he said: 'It seems likely to become a popular book with our people here.' It did not. And Thoreau himself guessed wrong when he thought that if the book were cheap enough it would circulate widely. Both men failed to consider the nature of the audience to which the 'Week' in its published form was too obviously addressed. It was not that *'hypaethral'* book, 'open to the heavens above, *under the ether*,' smelling, not of the study and poet's attic, but of the fields and woods, which Thoreau regretfully described when he recorded its failure with the public.[3] It may have been just that in its earliest versions; it is still such a book in its fluvial passages down which barges sail through an eternal summer as in Constable's paintings, and in its pauses for a philosophy that is not crabbed but youthful with the sincerity of first impressions and outdoor thoughts.

But the child had been too long aborning. The 'Week,' as we have it, is like many books of that seventeenth century which was a spiritual home for both Emerson and Thoreau. It is an anthology carried upon a frame of story, and into that anthology are tucked, one by one, sometimes with the excuse of an association and sometimes with no excuse at all, the best of Thoreau's poetry — which was well enough — and those lectures, essays, critiques, which were the fruits of his scholarly hours, the products of his adult education. Particularly in its last chapters, these stored-up manuscripts are dropped like coins into an open purse. This 'unroofed' book, as he called it, which was intended to convey outdoors to its readers, became perilously like a library of the shorter works of Henry Thoreau. Sometimes these essays weave out of the fabric of the narrative into patterns of insight so true, and so personal, that the great Greeks and the great Hindus are felt to be yielding all that they have for the New England mind. Sometimes the intimacies of his own past became a pattern for philosophy, as in the essay on Friendship. Yet too often the pauses in the camps at night, or the moorings on the river bank, are filled with such essays on Chaucer, Ossian, Persius, or Goethe, as any good student might have written, or critiques on poetry, prose, and the art of reading ill set in this vacation scenery, or lengthy quotations from the Colonial history of the rivers, where antiquarianism overflows the voyage.

The book was designed to be autobiography, in which the writer, as he said of Goethe's 'Italian Travels,' would give an exact description of things as they appeared to him, and their effect upon him. He wrote it as a history of his own imagination, floated upon the realities of a voyage with his beloved brother, and organized by days, to each day its own experiences, its own interests, and its own moods. Such a book might well have reached beyond his friends to a wider public. But as the freightage of erudite philosophy and criticism increased, the character of his possible audience changed. Although the book could still be readily appreciated by friends of his Transcendental circle, too much of it was now over the heads or beyond the interests of the general reader. One had to be either a scholar or a Transcendentalist to take, in a book by an untried author, such doses of digressive and difficult reading.

This was unfortunate. If the 'Week' had been English, Harvard-bred readers and their like might have assimilated analyses of religion, discussions of the Greek tragedies, and descriptions of the poetic mind as seasonings to a charming and 'hypaethral' book. Its digressiveness, its overstuffed quality as of a pudding into which the pantry has been dumped, its high allusiveness, are no more apparent than in many a famous volume. But the American academic world, and even the society of college graduates who read, was colonial then, and is still somewhat colonial in its tastes. For them the 'Week,' in spite of Lowell's pleasant words, was, and indeed still is, too American in its New England familiarity and too presumptuous in its handling of the sacred cows of scholarship. The failure of the 'Week' when it was first published, must be charged to the failure of the audience to whom he finally addressed it, as much as, I think far more than, to its own defects in composition.

And yet, of course, it has not failed. No book can be said to have failed, even in its first printing, that gave so much pleasure to its few readers then, and to so many readers over its century of life. It is a book where skipping is possible, yet full of delights, with stretches of eloquent, unstrained writing, simpler in tone, and less epigrammatic than 'Walden,' as naturally beautiful as the banks of the Concord, and vivid because written by an already incomparable observer. The humor of 'Walden,' often hardening into scorn, and the pervasive intellect of that book which is always valuing its own values, are not to be found in the 'Week,' which is kindly, speculative, and tender toward human nature, whether found on the rivers, or in poets' studies, or at the Cattle Fair in Concord village. And the infinite suggestiveness of Thoreau's mind is at its best in this book, which more truly represents the literary portions of his Journal than any other. Being young in spirit, his thoughts race ahead of him, and are set down tentatively as if life will test them:

> In all her products, Nature only develops her simplest germs. One would say that it was no great stretch of invention to create birds. The hawk which now takes his flight over the top of the wood was at first, perchance, only a leaf which fluttered in its aisles. From rustling leaves she came in the course of ages to the loftier flight and clear carol of the bird.

> I love to see the herd of men feeding heartily on coarse and succulent pleasures, as cattle on the husks and stalks of vegetables. Though there are many crooked and crabbed specimens of humanity among them, run all to thorn and rind, and crowded out of shape by adverse circumstances, like the third chestnut in the bur, so that you wonder to see some heads wear a whole hat, yet fear not that the race will fail or waver in them; like the crabs which grow in hedges, they furnish the stocks of sweet and thrifty fruits still. Thus is nature recruited from age to age, while the fair and palatable varieties die out, and have their period. This is that mankind. How cheap must be the material of which so many men are made!

Alcott was right. This book, even though Thoreau digressed Transcendentally in defiance of Professor Channing's rules of rhetoric, is an American masterpiece. It is indigenous, in spite of its comments on literature and religion abroad; it is a record of our native imagination in one of its phases, and a charming and whimsical portrait of the New England scene. One has only to compare the 'Week' with Howitt's nature descriptions in order to feel the difference between the well-done but mediocre, and the imperfect but excellent. Howitt's books show the mellow ease of a cultivated mind to whom writing has become second nature. But Thoreau's overstuffed masterpiece is bursting with vigorous health. 'Heal yourselves, doctors; by God I live.' [4]

2

The history of the 'Week' since its publication includes many imitations as well as multitudes of delighted readers. Its history for Thoreau's own time is, however, pathetically brief. On the whole, it was well received, better received than 'Walden,' for there were no reviews as severe as Lowell's of the latter book. Greeley, here, as later when 'Walden' appeared, was the first to provide publicity. George Ripley, of Concord, who reviewed regularly for *The Tribune*, was commissioned to feature the 'Week' and did so as early as June 13, in one of the long reviews which *The Tribune* gave quite regularly to what it regarded as the book of the week. He called it 'very near' that rare thing, 'a really new book — a fresh, original, thoughtful work.' Ripley thought, and with some justice, that Henry's scholarship was a little ostentatious, his prose excellent, his verse bad prose. But he stuck fast in Thoreau's Transcendental-Oriental pantheism. The author had said that the works of the Brahmins were not inferior to the Bible, of which sacred book he seemed to be somewhat ignorant. This was shocking. The times being what they were, and possible readers outside of Emerson's circle what *they* were, this was enough seriously to affect the sale of the book. The review must have helped Thoreau's reputation, and seriously damaged his chance to become a publishable author.

From England, Froude wrote, 'In your book . . . I see hope

for the coming world.' Froude, however, was also an author, with new books of his own! *The Athenaeum*, on October 27, indicated more accurately how little success Emerson's boosting of the 'Week' in England was to have with possible publishers. It printed a supercilious review, inspired by dislike of Emerson and Carlyle. The 'Week' was 'imitations of an imitation' (original not specified). A few things suggested a man with a habit of original thinking; yet the matter was for the most part 'poor enough.' Lowell followed by December in the *Massachusetts Quarterly Review* with a long appreciation, which is often quoted as an instance of his quick recognition of genius. The family were pleased — 'so just and pleasant — and some parts of it so laughable,' wrote Aunt Maria,[5] and it must have pleased Thoreau, for it was the first lengthy consideration of his work. Yet one feels that it was a chance to write, rather than a chance to praise a fellow graduate, that got Lowell into action. The first four pages are fluff of the smart style of contemporary essay writing, into which Henry himself sometimes fell. The rest is tribute. 'He is both wise man and poet.' Yet as for the 'Week,' 'its being a book at all is only a happy fortuity,' a just remark. Of the Hindu pages he was scornful, being ignorant and therefore superficial. Thoreau's poetry was ill-rhymed, his prose 'conscientiously and neatly done,' a grudging estimate which detracts from the oft-quoted characterization of the wine-like quality of his style. The essay, as a whole, is a little patronizing, unaware of the book's central theme of escape from utilitarianism, yet sensitive to a new talent, as if Lowell felt more justly than he could understand. Alcott was a better man at estimating the real values of Thoreau.

Yet neither Ripley's qualified praise nor Lowell's somewhat flippant enthusiasm helped the 'Week' to find readers. Like many another original book, it had to make its own way and slowly. How slowly Thoreau himself records in 1853:

For a year or two past, my *publisher*, falsely so called, has been writing from time to time to ask what disposition should be made of the copies of 'A Week on the Concord and Merrimack Rivers' still on hand, and at last suggesting that he had use for the room they occupied in his cellar. So I had them all sent to me here, and they have arrived to-day by express, filling the man's wagon, — 706 copies out of an edition of 1000 which I bought of Munroe four years ago and have been ever since paying for, and have not quite paid for yet. The wares are sent to me at last, and I have an opportunity to examine my purchase. They are something more substantial than fame, as my back knows, which has borne them up two flights of stairs to a place similar to that to which they trace their origin. Of the remaining two hundred and ninety and odd, seventy-five were given away, the rest sold. I have now a library of nearly nine hundred volumes, over seven hundred of which I wrote myself. Is it not well that the author should behold the fruits of his labor? My works are piled up on one side of my chamber half as high as my head, my *opera omnia*. This is authorship; these are the work of my brain. There was just one piece of good luck in the venture. The unbound were tied up by the printer four years ago in stout paper wrappers, and inscribed, —

H. D. Thoreau's
Concord River
50 cops.

So Munroe had only to cross out 'River' and write 'Mass.' and deliver them to the expressman at once. I can see now what I write for, the result of my labors.

Nevertheless, in spite of this result, sitting beside the inert mass of my works, I take up my pen to-night to record what thought or experience I may have had, with as much satisfaction as ever. Indeed, I believe that this result is more inspiring and better for me than if a thousand had bought my wares. It affects my privacy less and leaves me freer.

Nor was its financial history more fortunate. Henry had borrowed a hundred dollars to guarantee the publication of the

book in 1849. By November of 1853 when the account with
Munroe was settled, he had paid this publisher 'falsely so
called,' two hundred and ninety dollars 'directly out of pocket,'
which seems to mean that Munroe had received three hundred
and ninety dollars in all, plus the proceeds from two hundred
and fourteen books actually sold. Furthermore, 'I was obliged
to manufacture a thousand dollars' worth of pencils and slowly
dispose of and finally sacrifice them' in order to pay back the
hundred-dollar debt. This must have been several thousand
pencils, since they sold at six dollars a gross.

He confesses he was hard put to it, for on the way to New
York to peddle pencils, probably in '49 when the book was
clearly a failure,[6] he came near speculating in cranberries 'to
raise the wind to pay for "A Week on the Concord and Merrimack Rivers."' And in '52, for reasons not stated, he borrowed
seventy-five dollars from Horace Greeley, an action unprec-
edented for Thoreau. As his own salesman he took in fifteen
dollars for books sold before the edition came home to roost
(and a little more afterward), and this was 'the pecuniary value
of the book' — a sad tale for budding aspirants in the field of
letters. And highly important for the later career of Thoreau,
who, by abundant testimony, was abnormally sensitive to debt
or dependence, and who lost confidence in publishing as a
source of income before 'Walden' proved too late that he might
hope to publish a book without having to pay for the privilege
of doing so.[7]

But one lesson in human nature he did learn, and records
it in a Journal of 1849, now in the Huntington library:

> I had a friend, I wrote a book, I asked my friend's criticism,
> I never got but praise for what was good in it — My friend be-
> came estranged from me and then I got blame for all that was
> bad, — & so I got at last the criticism which I wanted.[8]

This was Channing, who 'rejects it altogether,' [9] said Emerson, speaking of the 'Week.' Later, Channing wrote disparaging remarks on the style upon the margins of the copy of 'Walden' which Thoreau gave to him. 'Chatted,' he said, is a 'vile word.'

3

Reputation will often make its way in the teeth of failure. After the account with Munroe was settled and before March of 1854, Thoreau had arranged for the publication of 'Walden' through the rising firm of Ticknor and Fields. Emerson's influence may have counted, but even more the nature of the book. It is addressed to his townsmen, but in effect was written for the audience of all intelligent men and women interested in life and how to live it, and its central problem was no Transcendental idea of escape into the spirit, but a concrete proposition, challenging everyone with ears to hear: 'A man is rich in proportion to the number of things he can afford to let alone.' No load of critical essays, no surplusage of erudition, no elusive and allusive intricacy of structure assumes in the reader a scholar's mind and a scholar's interests. It was, and is, a book for anyone interested in how to live a good life and open to the appeals of wild nature, good books, good talk, provocative thinking, and the companionship of an interesting mind. His new publishers were real publishers. No money seems to have been called for from the author, and two thousand copies were sold. It was, however, not until eight years later that they took over and reprinted the 'Week.'

'Walden,' like the 'Week,' is autobiography, but autobiography used to drive home an idea like a nail in a pine tree. 'Mr. Thoreau,' said *Graham's Magazine* in its review in September, 'it is well known, belongs to the class of transcendentalists who lay the greatest stress on the "I." ...' 'Well known' in

1854 must have made Henry smile. But the rest was true enough, nor was the author's apology in the first chapter for being so personal at all necessary. The book was a testament of an experience. It was 'I' or nothing, if the readers were to be convinced. The 'Week' has a plan which often breaks up under the weight of interpolations. 'Walden' is bound together, unified, given point by its governing idea. It has no digressions, though sometimes too much detail. If the 'Week,' as Lowell said, became a book only by happy fortuity, 'Walden' was planned as a book,[10] written with one theme in mind, and made to conform in style, subject, and material to the deliberate purpose of the author. This is a great reason for its success. It is a controlled, complete work of art.

'Walden' is by no means all of Thoreau. There is a very different book (alas, never to be completed) to be found scattered through his later Journal. Yet it contains the essence of what he had to say by way of comment on his times. It is his book on society as distinguished from the accounts of his excursions in wild nature. 'Civil Disobedience' and 'Life Without Principle' could be deduced from it. The scholar and the poet are visible here only in their fruits; the naturalist and poet of nature only in their preliminaries. 'Walden' tells his townsmen how they ought not to live, how one man lived and was happy. Later, Thoreau will follow his peculiar genius further, describing his own chosen pursuits in superb passages; yet before he could become the positive Thoreau outright, he had to get the negative Thoreau, the challenger, out of his system. He had to establish his relations to a society which would not let him do what he wanted, and did so in 'Walden.'

The dominant idea of 'Walden,' which is simple, has been abundantly misunderstood. Thoreau's problem is the poor student's (or artist's or scientist's) who wishes to study, investigate, create, in a society which will not pay him enough for the proceeds of his labor, and is not interested in his brand of happiness. His solution is self-reliance, simplification of living, willingness to labor with the hands if necessary, resignation of everything not essential to his particular temperament, and a shrewd study of how he can provide for his sustenance with the least waste of time. Thoreau's own estimate of time needed was a month to six weeks out of a year.

This solution is worthless, however, unless it brings with it an expansion of every taste, interest, vocation, and avocation which is possible to the experimenter, wished for by him, and practicable in a life of disciplined simplicity. 'Walden' calls for more life, not less. Nor is Thoreau's particular solution prescribed, like a reformer's panacea, to everyone, but only to the discontented who live lives of quiet desperation. 'Strong and valiant natures, who ... spend more lavishly than the richest, without ever impoverishing themselves ... those who are well employed,' can take care of themselves. He writes for that 'most terribly impoverished class of all, who have accumulated dross, but know not how to use it,' and 'the mass of men [alas, how much more numerous!] who are discontented, and idly complaining of ... their lot or of the times, when they might improve them.' [11] 'I desire that there may be as many different persons in the world as possible; but I would have each one be very careful to find out and pursue *his own* way, and not his father's or his mother's or his neighbor's instead.' [12] The book is the story of how he, a poor scholar, and discontented, found *his way*, and how he enjoyed it.

The idea that 'Walden' is a study in asceticism is quite wrong. If Thoreau was an ascetic (though not always) in his eating, if he was an ascetic in physical love, nevertheless he was passionate in most of his pursuits, an epicure in many of the delights of the senses, and a propagandist for life that tingles from the brain to the toe-tips. He was unmarried and childless, which made his problem easier to solve economically, but no less a problem. Marriage — in a cabin with a bean or corn field — was raising poor whites all along the frontier, even as Thoreau wrote, and such simplicity solved no problems. If you wish to get married, if you love good wine, if you must live in a library, or go to Europe, or belong to a country club — these are merely the terms of your problem. The principle is the same — simplify in what is not necessary for your content. And if your needs are spiritual and intellectual, do not starve them in order to feed less durable pleasures. Learn in any case what *you* can do in order to live the life you really desire while earning what you have to earn. Industrialism has made the problem of the man with a soul as well as a stomach more acute because it sells only for money, which must somehow be had. Thoreau's solution was to reduce his wants, grow beans for cash, build his house with his own hands, and be willing to be solitary as long and as much as solitude did him good. What is yours?

4

There were excellent reasons why 'Walden' was begun in the middle forties, put together in the late forties, and published in the early fifties.

The first reason for its writing I have already touched upon. Thoreau, in his Walden years, was outward bound; he had been forced to consider what society meant to him and what he meant to society. The challenge of 'Walden' was his answer.

But the more important reason was inwoven in the history of the country. The decade of the forties was a turning point in American social and moral development. The opening of the West, the rapid spread of railroads, most of all the development of the machine, had given the North and East — and

New England particularly — a preponderance over the agrarian economy of the Southern planters. There was an extraordinary increase in production. New wealth and new wants grew. Texas land, California gold, and the Western trade were exploited all together in the same few years, and the railroads and the rapidly increasing merchant marine carried the new products to and from everywhere. Free — or nearly free — land became a new social factor. Settlements in fresh regions were now possible without the crushing hardships of earlier Western emigration. Labor, which had been turbulent, and whose problems Thoreau mentions more often than politics, was quieted by the drain to the frontiers. The cry, as the Beards say,[13] was changed from wages to ownership, perhaps by design. Socialism, so much in every thoughtful mind in the forties, was put off for generations.

Naturally, the intellectual and spiritual activities centering in New England were subtly affected by the vast if fluctuating increase in prosperity. The Concord intellectuals were optimists, even when they most deplored the uses made of prosperity. An Emerson in Carlyle's England, where industrialism was grinding the lower classes, is incredible. Thoreau in his 'Civil Disobedience' never so much as imagines an American state — or an American economy — that would be forced to torture or to crush. His state is afraid of the citizens, afraid that they will escape without paying.

But the widespread speculation, the immense increase in material prosperity, which, in spite of the frequent panics, was characteristic of this fabulous age, was changing the moral mind of America. It was destroying quickly the ideals of conduct formed by the old ethics of damnation. It was producing no new ones, except the freedom, which became the duty, to get rich. There was a boom in New England in the very years when 'Walden' was being made into a book. Materialism spread, but what spread even faster was an intoxication of gain, a rapid expansion of the instincts for power, possession, sensual enjoyments. Genteel literature ignored this, but wherever the writer truly observes — whether a Mark Twain, or a recording journalist, or a letter writer, or a diarist — the facts show through. Historical fiction is feeding fat upon them today.

Against all of this Thoreau rebelled, as he naturally would. His bitter remarks on Australian and Californian gold are to be found in 'Life Without Principle,' and his comments on the intoxication of ownership everywhere in his writings. 'Walden' is a protest against his friend Horace Greeley's 'Go West, Young Man,' though it was not to the West itself but to the spirit in which men went there that he objected. His creed of simplicity is a protest against the get-rich-quick of free land and industrialism. Against land or industry he held no brief. But their exploiters who, he believed, were also self-exploiters to their hurt, were vigorous, successful, and also imaginative, real enemies, well worth fighting. The West, the machine, prosperity were all ideals — ideals captured by their greed.

The 'Week' had contained the literary and philosophic reflections of a youth sensitive to new thought but indifferent to his surroundings, except in so far as they were pregnant with the realities of nature or reminiscent of a past when men's experience, so he felt, came closer to a vital reality than in the streets and homes of Concord. 'Walden' was his recognition of a human present which he could no longer escape. It was a cockcrow (so he called it) to warn his neighbors that their souls were being enslaved. He wrote in terms of Concord farms and shops, not of manifest destiny in the West and the factories, but his near sight was clear sight. If he had gone West with Margaret Fuller he would never have written so truly, for, though she saw the degradation of morals and of morale, she, like Emerson, shared the intoxication of progress, and believed that these evils were transitory. 'Walden' is the story of a pioneer who stayed at home, who did not go bust in the panics, or get rich in the booms, who could, therefore, ask what this drunken prosperity would mean when all the railroad tracks were laid on Irishmen's bodies, when the emigrants were plowed into their own fields, and when the speculators, made rich by gambling, would have to ask, 'What next?'

The newly prosperous had their answer ready, and it was to become a slogan in the great days of expansion after the Civil War. They said, more land, more money, bigger cities, harder work, more power over nature; the future belongs to the millionaire, so let us all get rich together. Thoreau said, 'No.' 'When a man is warmed ... what does he want next? Surely not more warmth of the same kind, as more and richer food, larger and more splendid houses, finer and more abundant clothing, more numerous, incessant, and hotter fires, and the like. When he has obtained those things which are necessary to life, there is another alternative than to obtain the super-fluities; and that is, to adventure on life now, his vacation from humbler toil having commenced.' [14] He was wrong, of course. That was just what they were going to want, down to the last improvement in oil furnaces. The adventure in life which must not be deferred because living is so dear, was never to begin for the discontented mass of Americans trying to catch up with the Joneses, although some 'strong and valiant natures' would find abundant satisfactions in their competitions, being in-capable of sucking anything else from the marrow of life. But more and more thoughtful and disillusioned Americans were to agree with Thoreau as the buoyant nineteenth century was merged in the dubious twentieth. 'Walden' had been, and remained, a tract for the times.

'Walden' was ready for publication in 1849. 'The Communist Manifesto' of Marx and Engels was published in 1848. There is no coincidence in this significant paralleling of dates. The same diseases of the profit system had impressed the American recluse and the German scholars. But three thousand miles and a philosophic abyss lay between Thoreau's solution in terms of morality and individualism, and the Communist rule of the proletariat. If Thoreau provided no technique by which society as a whole could escape from wage slavery, at least his challenge to Americans did not imply a dictatorship.

5

'Walden' was an artful tract, in the exact sense of that adjective. A true story is always the best argument, and this book was an autobiography. From the account of the hut and the bean field, with their statistics of cost and profit down to the last half cent, through the frank explanations of why he went to Walden and what he learned there, the outline of this book is straightforward narrative throughout. Nor does its story suffer in point because of the chapters about the friends who came to talk with him, or his neighbors in the woods, or the lake in its moods, or the books that he read, or the thoughts that he pondered through long winter evenings and in sunny musings. For these were all parts of his biography, and described the nature of the man who wrote, and the nature of his profitable happiness at Walden. These gave his escape from society and its pressure a meaning that could be estimated by the reader; made him feel that a man and not a theory wrote the book.

Yet much of the art of 'Walden' inheres in its style. Thoreau's style in this book is most consistently at its best. Still rhetorical in the fashion of the early nineteenth century and sometimes what Aunt Maria would have called transmogrified in its

flights to capture spiritual ideas, it is nevertheless able to re-
count in the tersest and most vigorous of American prose the
simplest facts of daily experience, making them real, vivid,
and significant. Yet it is able also to rise with the life of his
imagination to magnificent poetic paragraphs:

> Suddenly an influx of light filled my house, though the
> evening was at hand, and the clouds of winter still overhung it,
> and the eaves were dripping with sleety rain. I looked out the
> window, and lo! where yesterday was cold gray ice there lay
> the transparent pond already calm and full of hope as in a
> summer evening, reflecting a summer evening sky in its bosom,
> though none was visible overhead, as if it had intelligence with
> some remote horizon. I heard a robin in the distance, the
> first I had heard for many a thousand years, methought, whose
> note I shall not forget for many a thousand more, — the same
> sweet and powerful song as of yore. O the evening robin, at the
> end of a New England summer day! If I could ever find the
> twig he sits upon! I mean *he*; I mean *the twig*. This at least is
> not the *Turdus migratorius*. The pitch pines and shrub oaks
> about my house, which had so long drooped, suddenly resumed
> their several characters, looked brighter, greener, and more
> erect and alive, as if effectually cleansed and restored by the
> rain. I knew that it would not rain any more. You may tell
> by looking at any twig of the forest, ay, at your very wood-pile,
> whether its winter is past or not. As it grew darker, I was
> startled by the honking of geese flying low over the woods, like
> weary travellers getting in late from Southern lakes, and in-
> dulging at last in unrestrained complaint and mutual consola-
> tion. Standing at my door, I could hear the rush of their wings;
> when, driving toward my house, they suddenly spied my light,
> and with hushed clamor wheeled and settled in the pond.
> So I came in, and shut the door, and passed my first spring
> night in the woods.

Or it can be epigrammatic, or humorous, or tender, or hard.

And thanks to his style, there is the unmistakable presence
on every page of 'Walden' of a personality, a man like a rock

in his immovable principles, like an oak in his toughness, like a wild flower in his sensitiveness, like a woodchuck in his persistence, like a hawk in his flights. It is not always possible, as Elizabeth Hoar said, to like Thoreau, but you can never escape from his personality, nor from admiring and respecting it. His egocentricity was justified, at least in literature, for he pervades this book as no lesser ego could have done. There is never a page which is not Thoreau's and no other's.

'Walden' is assuredly one of the great modern books, which is not to say that it is perfect. In spite of its doctrine of simplicity, the writing itself is never entirely simple. Its tone is of a satirically humorous detachment which is definitely literary, and sometimes consciously rhetorical. This was a good level from which to descend into straightforward description or to rise into eloquence; yet it is an attitude, sometimes almost a pose, never for long allowed to relax. It is the attitude, pose if you please, which had become, and which was until our times, the convention of the personal essay in the English tradition, from the Augustans downwards. Nothing in such an essay can be said without due consideration of the effect upon the reader, who is conscious all the time that he is reading, not mere statements, but literature. Here, as I have said, Thoreau did not escape from his times. He did escape from the dangers of his own rhetoric by lifting his homely subject matter upon an idea until it demanded a style. Nevertheless, like Charles Lamb, like Carlyle, like Hazlitt, like Emerson, like De Quincey, Thoreau, even in 'Walden,' is best when read a chapter, or even a paragraph, at a time. There is a strain to write well in this book, which the modern reader, conditioned by journalism to familiar speaking, is sure to feel, though his own taste may prove to be more to blame than Thoreau. Like carefully prepared food, this style needs a slow and zestful consumption. Some modern readers also find too much detail, and particu-

larly too much description in 'Walden.' I did once, but on
every re-reading my criticism diminishes. Thoreau would
not be Thoreau without the details of his insatiable observing.

6

Praise of 'Walden' on its publication in 1854 was hearty but
by no means unanimous. Greeley had offered to announce it
in *The Tribune*, whether Ticknor, its publisher, did or not, and
was better than his word. It was announced as 'Walden: Or
Life in the Woods' on the ninth of August, 1854, and was
available at G. P. Putnam's at one dollar, on the tenth. But
on Saturday the twenty-ninth of July, Greeley had already
printed an excellent summary of those parts of the book which
gave the autobiographical outline of the Walden adventure.
'By the courtesy of the publishers,' said the writer, 'we are
permitted to take some extracts in advance of the regular
issue,' followed by three and a third columns of small type
dealing with life at Walden, visitors, expenses, etc., about two
thousand words in all. Thoreau's thoughts and comments do
not appear in this survey, except by implication, but the
implication of course is there, for it is impossible to quote at
length from 'Walden' without presenting the mind of Thoreau.
This advance publicity in the newspaper, most widely read by
those most likely to be found sympathetic to Thoreau, was of
greater importance for the success of the book than any review.
The two extracts already published by Thoreau himself in
Sartain's Union Magazine of Literature and Art were vignettes
merely;[15] here was the work itself, presented in its most interesting aspect, with nothing included that might frighten the orthodox reader.

Lowell did not express his opinion of 'Walden' until 1865,
after Thoreau's death. The essay on Thoreau which he wrote

then is ostensibly a review of Emerson's edition of Thoreau's letters, called 'Letters to Various Persons,' but it is inspired by 'Walden' more than by the other six volumes he said he read in preparation, and would have been pointless without that work. In this full length critique he somewhat revised his earlier opinion of his fellow graduate.

And indeed it is a much deeper-going criticism, the most brilliant essay yet written on Thoreau, and the most sensitive estimate of his purely literary gifts. It also says, and says well, all that could be said against Thoreau the man, the philosopher, the experimenter in the economics of self-dependence and in the virtues of relative solitude. Thoreau, Lowell wrote, was a man 'with so high a conceit of himself that he accepted without questioning, and insisted upon our accepting, his defects and weaknesses of character as virtues and powers peculiar to himself. . . . He had little active imagination; of the receptive he had much.' He was 'not by nature an observer.' He loved not so much the True as the 'Out-of-the-Way.' He insisted 'in public on going back to flint and steel when there is a match-box in his pocket. . . . He confounded physical with spiritual remoteness from men. . . . His whole life was a search for the doctor. . . . Thoreau had no humor, and this implies that he was a sorry logician.' His return to nature was a sentimentalism. 'He was not a strong thinker, but a sensitive feeler. . . . His shanty-life was a mere impossibility, so far as his own conception of it goes, as an entire independency of mankind.' [16]

These sentences, ranging from truths through half-truths to absurd misconceptions, account for the indignation aroused by this essay among Thoreau's friends and admirers, who quite failed to note the tribute to his achievement in literature which as usual did not make up for the detraction. 'There is no writing comparable with Thoreau's in kind, that is comparable with it in degree. . . . We have said that his range was narrow, but to be a master is to be a master.' His friends raged because, indeed, Thoreau himself, and 'Walden' in particular, invite, though they do not justify, such warped interpretations of the man.

But how to account for Lowell's almost stupid misunderstanding of the shanty-life of his acquaintance, or for his deafness to the humor of 'Walden,' his blindness to the nature which Thoreau was trying to interpret, his curious idea that this Puritan life was a search for the doctor? The explanation, in part, is to be found in the beginning of his essay, a humorous and incisive account of the Transcendentalists, men who were struggling for fresh air in thinking, but who 'stood ready at a moment's notice to reform everything but themselves.'

Lowell, that genial worldling, who so soon outlived his brief fervor of reform and slid so comfortably into the genteel age, seems to have thought that Thoreau, like the other Transcendentalists, was trying to reform him and his kind, for he had become a successful compromiser in an age of compromise, to whom this criticism of society from the backwoods of Concord sounded like fanaticism. 'While he studied with respectful attention the minks and woodchucks, his neighbors, he looked with utter contempt on the august drama of destiny of which his country was the scene, and on which the curtain had already risen.' By destiny, Lowell clearly means the 'manifest destiny' of the exploitation of the West, whose more sordid and unfortunate aspects Thoreau had prophesied two generations before their time of realization.

I can only suppose that Lowell had more resemblance than he would have admitted to Aunt Maria. The brag in Thoreau undoubtedly offended his gentility — for he was genteel and Thoreau was not, but the tone of persiflage could not have troubled him, it was too much like his own. No, like Aunt Maria, he felt blasphemy in the book. Not blasphemy against

Christ and Jehovah, but against all the valuable ideals of cultivated living which Thoreau shook so harshly by questioning whether a deeper sincerity must not come first. What was to become of an American civilization just escaping from crudity and ugliness if the uncompromising idealists of simplicity, who really preferred a cabin to a mahogany dining table, were to have their way? He was right in one sense — a society of Thoreaus would have no theater, no light conversation, no amenities of living — music perhaps, but no art except the primitive, religion but no ritual, society but none in which a gentleman who was not a Puritan and an intellectual could ever be at ease. Emerson would have understood what Lowell meant. Thoreau was a gendarme, not a gentleman. Yet Lowell was utterly wrong in his final estimate, because he did not understand that 'Walden' was a defense of a principle, rather than a plan to live in the woods. And so he attacked, as a fanatical absurdity and a pose, that clear-sighted view of the dangers of a false economics and the perversion of values in American living which keeps 'Walden' a timely book. The quills of the Concord porcupine were to keep on pricking after the critic's amenities and his halfway Americanism had lost their power to charm.

There is little question that Lowell's essay, afterward collected in his 'My Study Windows,' and widely read, is chiefly responsible for the nineteenth-century estimate of Thoreau as an egotistic eccentric, a misanthrope, and a crank. As every literary editor knows, it is the depreciation in a review, if pointed and effectively descriptive, which catches the reader's attention and remains in his memory. Lowell's taste was admirable, and he could not and did not miss the unusual quality of Thoreau's writing, but the man irritated him, and it was the man he reviewed.

The further history of 'Walden,' how it picked up admirers, one by one, all over the world, became a textbook for the British Labor Party, won its place as a world classic of literature, and was relegated by our American academic colonials to the humble position of accessory reading about nature, does not concern us here. Yet in one of its aspects it has earned a place in our American history. Thoreau spoke in it for the young generation of the early forties who were determined to live and to think in a new way. He also spoke against the dilettantism of so many of this generation who wished to talk and write rather than to do, and against the youth of the later forties and early fifties, who, as Margaret Fuller said, had sold out to material prosperity. Like 'Leaves of Grass,' his book has become social history as well as literature — less romantic social history than Whitman's masterpiece, and more truly prophetic.

Indeed, the full significance of 'Walden' has never been felt until today. It is only in our generation that the industrial revolution has reached a point where man is in real danger of becoming a machine thinking like a machine, and where the increasing regimentation of society and the standardization of the ways of life make doing what you want a heroic achievement. It is only in our generation that the old Puritan morality of America, with its generally accepted ideals of conduct, has lost its power to control, so that men and women are moving on their own momentum, confessedly in search of new ideals. And it is only in our own time that bodily comfort and the satisfactions of pride have been elevated into what is frankly called the American standard of living. 'Walden,' with its doctrine of 'simplify, simplify,' is no longer blasphemy, except to the school of economists who think that *all* the world's ills can be cured by production. But it is still radical, and because it records one great individualist's heart-felt and brain-felt experience, it is still eloquent.

7

I do not wish to close this brief discussion of a great book with the impression that it deserves its life in literature for its social message only. There is a fervor in it not explained by its preaching. 'I long ago lost a hound, a bay horse, and a turtle-dove, and am still on their trail,' the author wrote in one of its early pages. 'Many are the travellers I have spoken concerning them, describing their tracks and what calls they answered to. I have met one or two who had heard the hound, and the tramp of the horse, and even seen the dove disappear behind a cloud, and they seemed as anxious to recover them as if they had lost them themselves.' The identification of these fabulous animals with Edmund Sewall, John Thoreau, and Ellen Sewall, which seems to have begun with Prudence Ward, is both naïve and absurd. For no one of these three was Thoreau, by any stretch of the imagination, still searching. When Uncle Edward Watson, meeting him after he had waded through the shallows to get to Clark's Island, asked him what he meant by saying he had lost a horse, a hound, and a dove, Thoreau replied, 'Have not you?' which was answer enough.[17] He had been writing in the context of this famous passage of how he desired to spend his life, how he had tried 'to stand on the meeting of two eternities, the past and future, which is precisely the present moment,' how he had hoped to anticipate nature herself. In the symbolic language of the Persian poets which he so often read, he is clearly describing a search for no lost maid or boy, but for that sense of the spiritual reality behind nature, which again and again in his Journal he deplores as something felt in youth, but never quite regained.

And 'Walden' itself owes its poetry to a spiritual quest, of which it is a record quite as much as of an economic experiment. For Thoreau went to Walden in pursuit of that eternal

desire of ambitious youth, 'to live deep and suck out all the
marrow of life' — beans, hut, and simplifying were all a means
to an end, a technique of experiment. He went on the trail
of that sense of spiritual reality which all the Transcendentalists
believed was a priceless possession of youth, and which had
certainly been his possession. He hoped to reawaken his inner
life, recover his lost 'intimations of immortality,' and he succeeded, as the book tells. Reality itself, whatever that was, he
never found, but spent the rest of his life in the study of its
tracks and trails in visible nature.

～ II ～

Naturalist and Nature Writer

18. SURVEYOR OF CONCORD

THOREAU IN 1848 had come home for good — home from Walden, home from Emerson's house, home to Concord. His brief trips away will be more frequent, but at last he was really settled in the family home. He goes to Cape Cod three times for journeys which eventually make a book; he goes twice more to the Maine woods, and to Canada, to Minnesota, to his favorite near-by mountains, and on many surveying and lecturing trips outside of Concord. Yet, even though once in Boston Harbor he was tempted to let the winds blow him abroad, his most important travels from now on are in Concord. Always a saunterer in its woods and a drifter on its rivers, his intellectual being now turns home for its chief activities. His thoughts range even more widely as his reading of travel books, scientific manuals, and histories widens, but his best energies go into the ever complicating task of research in the Concord environment — no end to the knowing.[1] Still a student of the classics and the great religions, he adds science to his adult education and finds no final answers to his insatiable questioning. Once a speculative observer, he becomes a measurer of the phenomena of his own and his neighbor's fields. For the making of pencils he substitutes the conscious making of perfect sentences — in which he attained equal skill and from which he got far greater satisfactions.

By August 29 of 1850 he was living in the reformed yellow house on Main Street, and making far less fuss about the desperations of domestic experience. The family was smaller, of course — Sophia, John senior, Cynthia as talkative as ever, and Aunt Louisa Dunbar to speak for religion. There seem to have been no permanent boarders, unless Mrs. Dunbar, Cynthia's sister, be counted as one, but some transients, and a household table open to recommended visitors to Concord, or residents, like Sanborn, who wanted meals. Once, for nearly a month of cold weather, Henry had to sit downstairs with the family in the evening, and again he takes resolutions for greater privacy. But he was older, his daytime hours were more definitely his own, so that he seems to have tolerated — and often enjoyed — the company the visitors gave him at meals and on brief excursions. The family goes often with him now in his boat. There is little complaint except of Ellery, his constant walking companion, whose dilettantism did not accord with Thoreau's new naturalist mood. There was no longer a family financial problem to prick his conscience. Graphite was yielding the Thoreaus a good income and easily, too. While he took no responsibility for business until after his father's death in 1859, he was always at hand to help with suggestions, and even devised a machine so small and so light that Sophia could run it. Economical as always, he used the backs of the 'J. Thoreau and Son' correspondence for his own Journal notes, and these sheets indicate how steady and profitable was the business of supplying the electrotypers. There was even an attempt to establish an agency in New York.[2]

2

His own financial problem was almost solved. All he needed was a reliable source for a little income in addition to the variable and unreliable returns from lectures and magazine articles. In books as an asset he had emphatically lost confidence. The 'Week' had let him down, and out for many dollars. 'Walden' was on the shelf, ready for publication, but with no takers. The answer to his problem was surveying.

It was just such a common-sense solution as those who knew him best might have expected of Thoreau, and why it did not occur to him earlier is hard to understand, unless the cost of good instruments prevented. He had bought in 1840 a levelling instrument and circumferentor combined, with which John and he had given their boys lessons in elementary surveying. And surveying was among the trades he claimed in his Harvard class book record for 1847: 'I am a schoolmaster, a private Tutor, a Surveyor, a Gardener, a Farmer, a Painter, I mean a House Painter, a Carpenter, a Mason, a Day laborer, a Pencil-maker, a Glass-paper-maker, a Writer & sometimes a Poetaster. ... My steadiest employment is to keep myself at the top of my condition.'

Perhaps it was the disagreeable experience of making the many thousand pencils sold as a sacrifice to pay for the 'Week' which led him to use some of the money recorded as earned or borrowed in the years of the late forties to buy the expensive instruments now in the Concord Library, and set up as a professional surveyor. He was ready at least as early as November of 1849, when the first of his surveys in the Concord library collection was made of the wood lot of Isaac Watts. Before the date of the last document in this collection, a land survey for William Munroe on December 1, 1860, he had become surveyor-in-chief for Concord, noted for the accuracy and the detail of his work, and for the neatness and legibility of his maps, which are in striking contrast to the disorder of his notes and some parts of his Journal. He was employed to lay out roads, to 'walk the bounds' of the town with the selectmen, and later to prepare a mass of documents, involving hydraulic engineering, for a suit over the flooding of the Concord hay meadows by industrial establishments on the lower river.

And what a man for the job! He knew already the Concord farmers' lands as well as they did, and their wood lots even better, since he had often to guide them out of their own forests. He had boated over every foot of the rivers, and every acre of marsh land when the spring and autumn floods made lakes of the Concord valley. He knew the abundant swamps of Concord to their quaking hearts, and the haunts of the muskrat and wild duck as well as the hunters. His stout legs, which had never weakened except in his February attacks of bronchitis, and his tough clothing, plowed through scrub and brambles that would have halted a deer. And this was an outdoor job, with amenities, such as the opportunity to note the blooming time of flowers, to flush rare birds, and to check the habits of the trees, while earning a living. No hardship in the work for a man like Thoreau, except the coarse food the farmers gave him, which was too meaty for his asceticism; and the coarser conversation of his often dull employers and his thick-headed assistants.

By such employment, which was occasional but sure to recur, he earned somewhat better than the dollar a day which was his wage as an odd-job man. He wrote to Blake that he had made seventy-six dollars in seventy-six days, in some of which he had not worked. That his charges were not high can be seen in a receipted bill now in the Middlebury College library:

Concord, April 29th, 1851.
Cyrus Stow to H. D. Thoreau, Dr. — To surveying a *woodlot* in the east part of Concord, making a *Plan*, and calculating

two Areas; also — to laying out a street and House-lots near the middle of the town — & making a Plan of the same —... seven dollars.

$7.oo.

He had calculated in 'Walden' that thirty or forty days of labor in a year would support a man, and had written to Greeley that a month of rude labor a year had actually maintained him. As a rule, he surveyed much more than thirty days a year, but there was plenty of time left for lecturing and help about the house. The rest of the year was his own.

3

Except for his inevitable colds, Thoreau was in excellent health, engrossed by a new and fascinating task of becoming a student as well as an interpreter of nature, as content (at least in 1850) as his temperament would permit in his relations with his friends, entirely self-conscious now of his vocation as a writer, although doubtful of his means of publication. He was shaping his powerful sentences with a complete understanding of his peculiar technique, and able to carry over into them an ecstasy from his contacts with nature in which the easy emotion of youth was controlled by maturity. Emerson noted in early 1851: 'Nothing so marks a man as bold imaginative expressions. Henry Thoreau promises to make as good sentences of that kind as anybody.' And Henry himself had said to him that 'a thought would destroy like the jet of a blowpipe.' ³ He was perfecting the blowpipe, though by no means always to destroy.

Nevertheless, except in moments of ecstasy, or in those vigorous hours when he 'inhabited' his body 'with inexpressible satisfaction,' he was often unhappy. 'If I could wholly cease to be ashamed of myself, I think that all my days would be fair.'

'I feel ripe for something, yet do nothing, can't discover what that thing is. I feel fertile merely. It is seedtime with me. I have lain fallow long enough. . . . A sense of unworthiness . . . possesses me . . . I regard myself as a good deal of a scamp. . . . Yet I question sometimes if there is not some settlement to come.' 'There is some advantage in being the humblest, cheapest, least dignified man in the village. . . . There is many a coarsely well-meaning fellow, who knows only the skin of me, who addresses me familiarly by my Christian name.' 'I am getting used to my meanness, getting to accept my low estate. O if I could be discontented with myself! If I could feel anguish at each descent!' [4]

Alas for divine philosophy! Here were all circumstances, his Concord environment included, shaping his life toward the opportunities for rich saunterings and fertile leisure which he said he desired so much more than fame — yet he is ruffled because Sam Staples sends him on errands and common fellows call him by his first name. But if unphilosophic, the reasons for his lowness were very human. Thoreau, for all his disclaimers, was intensely ambitious. He wanted to live right, and also to get credit for what he did with his living, but although he had solved his economic problems, in the eyes of the world he was, if seen at all, only an unsuccessful lecturer and obscure writer, in the eyes of Concord an odd-job man, said to have published a book, and now promoted to surveying. And while he was 'fertile' he still did not know what crops to grow. Even his friends were discouraged, assigning to lack of push what was really due to the misfortune of unsuccessful publication. In July of 1851 Emerson wrote in his Journal: 'Thoreau wants a little ambition in his mixture. Fault of this, instead of being the head of American engineers, he is captain of [a] huckleberry party.'

Engineer! — First his friend had advised poetry, and now

engineering, to which, of course, surveying might have led. The biting, realistic philosophy of which Thoreau had already given examples had never appealed to this great idealist. And yet in the sentences preceding this often-quoted remark, Emerson was again returning to an idea for Henry's career which he had set down the year before. 'I think we must one day have a naturalist in each village as invariably as a lawyer or doctor.... Henry Thoreau ... would find ... employment.' [5] Did this profession, in which, indeed, he gave Thoreau too much credit for competence, also in his eyes want in ambition? Very probably, for natural history was a minor, not a major, among Emerson's interests, and Thoreau, who from now on teaches him so much about flowers and birds, served him here very much as he served the farmers whose wood lots he surveyed. For both he made the environment in which they lived more precise according to the needs of each. Even 'Walden,' when it finally appeared, seems to have appealed to Emerson for its evocation of natural beauty rather than its timely economic message. 'The little pond sinks in these days as tremulous as its human fame.' [There was a drought that summer, but Thoreau with characteristic accuracy notes that the pond did *not* sink.] 'All American kind are delighted with "Walden."' [6]

The gentle disparagement of Emerson's 'huckleberry party' belongs to the years before 'Walden' was published and coincides with Thoreau's far more severe self-criticism. It was the deferring of his success for five years after the failure of the 'Week' which was certainly a cause of his friends' suspicion that he was content with surveying and journal-keeping and more concerned with huckleberries than with fame; it was probably a cause also of Thoreau's own feeling of 'meanness.' He was lying fallow, and for what? He was fertile, but for what? Although the author of a great book of protest, it lay unpub-

lished, and he seemed to have no future in literature of that
kind.

In this passing period of uncertainty the suggestion which
Emerson must have made years before and now renewed seems
to have caught Henry's imagination. He would follow his own
genius still further and make a profession of his nature love.
In his Journal, which from 1850 seems to be preserved in its
complete form, there is an entirely new emphasis on observation. Nature, for the first time, becomes its chief subject.
Science takes the place of the classics. It is clear that he had
resolved to know nature well enough at last to write importantly
and with truth.

Thwarted love, of which more later, lowness of occupation
(New England, he said, would rather have his surveys than his
thought),[7] uncertainty as to a literary future, were all driving
him toward this new ambition, which was like the old ambition
to criticize the values of living in that it involved self-expression
in the best style he could command, but unlike it in that it was
positive not negative, and required that a student of the classics
had to begin over again with new studies if he were to become
the historian of the environment of Concord. 'Yesterday,'
wrote Emerson in 1850, 'Thoreau told me it [Nature] was more
[interesting] . . . and persons less.' He had said so before, but
this time he meant it.

With the exception of passionate returns to the follies of
society, especially when slavery and John Brown stirred him to
the roots of his being, this nature study was the chief concern
for the rest of his life. And it was the dependable income from
the craft of surveying, plus the easier circumstances of his
family, which made these exhaustive studies and the fourteen
volumes of Journal which recorded them possible without
serious interruption in order to raise cash by less congenial
means.

19. HOW HE LIVED

F ROM EARLY 1850 on, Thoreau's published Journal is a continuous, day-by-day, dated record, which does not seem to
have been often true even of the original volumes which he
gutted for 'Walden' and the 'Week.' ¹ Settled down at home in
Concord, he seems to have found both time and inclination to
make his Journal a more complete daybook of his 'account with
the gods,' and his increasing interest in natural phenomena
gave him abundance of material. Thoughts are still recorded as
fully as before, but observation and excerpts from his reading
fill the heavy majority of his pages. With a few gaps, the record
runs straight and full to just before his death.

In this decade it is possible for the first time to follow him
day by day, through every incident, reflection, or observation
he chooses to record. The man, indeed, is here; but in such a
minute record, so repetitive in its detail, so interrupted in sequence by change of theme, so inflated by rewriting — for one
incident may be recounted three times in order to get it brief
and right — that only a hearty admirer can be expected to
read all he wrote.

When he was weary he hoped that there would be such admirers, who would take and read his unrolling Journal as an autobiography in which a sincere man gave himself, without the artifices of arrangement and compression, entire to the world. When he felt inventive and vigorous, and surely whenever he realized how many thousands of mental acres he was plowing and harrowing, he would consider the possibility of another book which would bottle the best of his vintage. It was to be a book on the Seasons, on the Natural History of Concord, or on his travels at home.

Only those who have been through these voluminous diaries know the extent and complexity and inconsecutiveness of their records. To their thousands of pages must be added his commonplace books packed with quotations, his 'Index Rerum,' assembled from his early Journal, his bibliographies of books to be read, his broad sheets of tables in which the blooming time and locality of flowers are set down, his notes for the phenomena of the seasons scribbled on loose sheets, and a mass of manuscript quotations for use in a proposed history of the American Indian never even begun.[2] We are about to see, in the words of 'Walden,' ironical indeed when paraphrased to apply to its author, 'a poor immortal soul ... crushed and smothered under its load' of millions of words.

And yet while tables, lists, citations, and quotations remained tentative, that is not true of the Journal itself. While as a whole it is an agglomeration of experience, consecutive only in chronology, in its parts it is finished writing. No paragraph but is carefully turned, no sentence that is not carefully and often finally written. For those who will search for it, the best of Thoreau, after 'Walden,' is to be found in this calendar of his life.

Let us watch him at work with legs, eyes, and quill pen, remembering that in the early fifties he is still descriptive, not analytical, in his nature studies, for he does not know enough yet to be steadily analytical. He is reaching, indeed, a happy balance where his spiritual perceptions of 'the sweet mystery' of nature are weighted by exact observation but not yet sunk under the innumerable details which his eyes, often against his will, are later going to force upon his attention. He can still say, 'My desire for knowledge is intermittent; but my desire to communicate with the spirit of the universe . . . is perennial and constant.' [3] In these early fifties, when science was running like a subtle wine through his Transcendentalism, he had developed no methodology of study to impede the easy flow of his imagination. He knew enough of nature to see wholes clearly; as the infinite details of life grew more complex to his understanding, his vision narrowed and shortened. Soon he was studying Gray, whose botany, first published in 1848, and first mentioned by Thoreau in 1851, made plant study possible on a sound scientific basis.[4] After Gray, it became increasingly difficult for him to look at a flower except in terms of science. The reader of his later Journal can check both the gain and the loss.

2

When he came home to Main Street to live the rest of his life, his days free from surveying, and they were numerous, were carefully planned. In the forenoon he usually read, studied, and sometimes wrote. In the evening, to judge from many references, he chiefly wrote up his Journal from the almost undecipherable notes taken in the fields,[5] sometimes by moonlight, adding paragraphs of reflection and comment on his observations or upon things in general as he wrote. An epigram or a brilliant paragraph of applied psychology will often be stuck in the middle of a nature narrative, which resumes later.

The afternoon was his sacred time. Every free day he walked, or boated, from three to four hours; sometimes he would

'weather' the 'danger' of the supper hour and stay out until
sunset and after. If the moon was full, he shifted his excursion
to midnight, walking occasionally until dawn.

Starting westward usually, from some instinctive desire to
turn away from Boston and toward the mountains that ho-
rizoned Concord, he walked the hill and lake region of the town,
skirted the marshes, plunged into the swamps, or if his expedition was fluvial, rowed or paddled upstream to Fair Haven
bay, or pushed past the hemlocks on the Assabet. His shoes,
kept supple with tallow, were good for rough going — in winter
he kept three varieties of footgear for use according to the
weather — cowhide boots for dry snows and bare ground,
light boots and India rubbers for thaws and spring weather,
rubber boots for slush.[6] His homespun coat and trousers were
strong against brambles and the tough shrub oak of Concord
brush. He wore a neckerchief instead of a collar, and a hat
with the lining gathered in midway to make a shelf for flowers
and plants, which were kept moist by 'the darkness and the
vapors that arise from the head.'[7] It was not only his dislike
of manners which made him reluctant to salute ladies when he
met them!

He did not meet them often in his walks. From the home on
Main Street it was only a step across the street to the river,
where Ellery Channing's boat or his own was tied; and from
the back door he could easily make his way into the country
past the Texas house or across lots to the road back of Emerson's which led toward Walden. Avoiding roads, when possible,
if he had to follow them he kept on their margins. Usually he
crossed fences, navigated pastures by the cow paths winding
through juniper and wild apple, and as soon as possible bored
into the woods and swamps. He tried to keep a hedge, a grove,
or a brush patch between himself and the farmers' houses —
sometimes Channing and he, when they went on an all-day

Snow fields of Concord
'*No one can follow its fox trails in clothes presentable in Concord parlors*'
From the N. C. Wyeth painting in Men of Concord

walk, played a game to see how many farmhouses they could pass without being observed. The farmers, indeed, saw him on his daily walks only by chance, and then when they were working in the fields or their wood lots. But in his boat he could not hide, and so became the familiar of Melvin, the muskrat hunter, and Goodwin, the one-eyed fisherman. Often the Concord country-dwellers must have wondered when his short figure emerged from one thicket to plunge into another, or when he stood eyeing an elusive bird. One farmer, seeing him musing before a willow, mistook him for his drunken father in a trance.

Usually he carried a stick notched for measuring, a stout cord, a strong knife, and under his arm an old music book for pressing plants. After 1853, when he had wanted one long enough to satisfy his Puritan's conscience, he bought a spy glass for birds and carried that also. It was good for ducks, almost useless for small fowl. He could never catch in its small field the mysterious night warbler, whose song bothered him for so many years, even when it sang in twilight; nor the 'seringo,' so-called, which may have been a Savannah sparrow, but was more probably several species confused in their brushy hoppings and singings. It is hard enough to identify warblers and sparrows today with the best of bird glasses.[8]

Was it Channing's short legs, or an irregular rhythm, which made Henry walk, by preference, out of step with this frequent companion, or just his incorrigible independence? With Channing and with Emerson, much talk accompanied the walking and rowing; that was why Henry preferred, churlishly sometimes, to go alone. The 'walks and talks' which Channing describes in his book were abnormal, although even in those too artificial dialogues Thoreau has to be stirred into speech by his friends. These daily excursions were business for him, and though he heartily enjoyed them, he was at work every instant.

Extraordinary the details of wind, weather, plant, tree, animal, bird, and comments thereupon which he brought back and set down after a three-hour walk! No other man alive could have seen so much. And all this in a mounting excitement, stirred by his sheer love of wild nature, but also by the constant novelty of familiar places growing daily more complex as he penetrated their infinite variety. When he was able to identify the flowers, there were their habitats and times of opening to be studied. Then suddenly he discovered the lichens, and every weathered rock became a museum. Then the grasses, never really seen before, caught his attention, and proved rich and confusing beyond his guess. After that it was the mosses, the mushrooms, the hawks and owls, the wild ducks, the flora of the swamps, then trees and their succession — and so on and on. One can take this Journal from the fifties on, and label each section as the moss year, the tree year, the muskrat year, the bullfrog year. Of course they overlap.

3

But let him describe some nights and days in his own words I choose first a lengthy record, although here much abbreviated of walks more profitable and various than most, but otherwise typical of this lusty time of his early thirties:

June 11. Wednesday. 1851. Last night a beautiful summer night, not too warm, moon not quite full, after two or three rainy days. Walked to Fair Haven by railroad, returning by Potter's pasture and Sudbury road. I feared at first that there would be too much white light, like the pale remains of daylight, and not a yellow, gloomy, dreamier light; that it would be like a candle-light by day; but when I got away from the town and deeper into the night, it was better. I hear whip-poor-wills, and see a few fireflies in the meadow. . . .
When I rose out of the Deep Cut into the old pigeonplace

field, I rose into a warmer stratum of air, it being lighter. It told of the day, of sunny noontide hours, — an air in which work had been done, which men had breathed. It still remembered the sunny banks, — of the laborer wiping his brow, of the bee humming amid flowers, the hum of insects. Here is a puff of warmer air which has taken its station on the hills; which has come up from the sultry plains of noon. . . .

New beings have usurped the air we breathe, rounding Nature, filling her crevices with sound. To sleep where you may hear the whip-poor-will in your dreams!

I hear from this upland, from which I see Wachusett by day, a wagon crossing one of the bridges. I have no doubt that in some places to-night I should be sure to hear every carriage which crossed a bridge over the river within the limits of Concord, for in such an hour and atmosphere the sense of hearing is wonderfully assisted and asserts a new dignity, and [we] become the Hearalls of the story. The late traveller cannot drive his horse across the distant bridge, but this still and resonant atmosphere tells the tale to my ear. Circumstances are very favorable to the transmission of such a sound. In the first place, planks so placed and struck like a bell swung near the earth emit a very resonant and penetrating sound; add that the bell is, in this instance, hung over water, and that the night air, not only on account of its stillness, but perhaps on account of its density, is more favorable to the transmission of sound. If the whole town were a raised planked floor, what a din there would be! . . .

I now descend round the corner of the grain-field, through the pitch pine wood into a lower field, more inclosed by woods, and find myself in a colder, damp and misty atmosphere, with much dew on the grass. I seem to be nearer to the origin of things. There is something creative and primal in the cool mist. This dewy mist does not fail to suggest music to me, unaccountably; fertility, the origin of things. An atmosphere which has forgotten the sun, where the ancient principle of moisture prevails. It is laden with the condensed fragrance of plants and, as it were, distilled in dews.

The woodland paths are never seen to such advantage as in

a moonlight night, so embowered, still opening before you almost against expectation as you walk; you are so completely in
the woods, and yet your feet meet no obstacles. It is as if it
were not a path, but an open, winding passage through the
bushes, which your feet find. . . .

Ah, that life that I have known! How hard it is to remember
what is most memorable! We remember how we itched, not
how our hearts beat. I can sometimes recall to mind the quality,
the immortality, of my youthful life, but in memory is the only
relation to it. . . .

The wind and water are still awake. At night you are sure
to hear what wind there is stirring. The wind blows, the river
flows, without resting. There lies Fair Haven Lake, undistin-
guishable from fallen sky. The pines seem forever foreign, at
least to the civilized man, — not only their aspect but their
scent, and their turpentine.

So still and moderate is the night! No scream is heard,
whether of fear or joy. No great comedy nor tragedy is being
enacted. The chirping of crickets is the most universal, if not
the loudest, sound. There is no French Revolution in Nature,
no excess. She is warmer or colder by a degree or two.

By night no flowers, at least no variety of colors. The pinks
are no longer pink; they only shine faintly, reflecting more
light. Instead of flowers underfoot, stars overhead. . . .

No one, to my knowledge, has observed the minute differences
in the seasons. Hardly two nights are alike. The rocks do not
feel warm to-night, for the air is warmest; nor does the sand
particularly. A book of the seasons, each page of which should
be written in its own season and out-of-doors, or in its own
locality wherever it may be.

June 13. 1851. Walked to Walden last night (moon not quite
full) by railroad and upland wood-path, returning by Wayland
road. Last full moon the elms had not leaved out, — cast no
heavy shadows, — and their outlines were less striking and
rich in the streets at night. . . .

We do not commonly live our life out and full; we do not
fill all our pores with our blood; we do not inspire and expire

fully and entirely enough, so that the wave, the comber, of each inspiration shall break upon our extremest shores, rolling till it meets the sand which bounds us, and the sound of the surf come back to us.... We live but a fraction of our life. Why do we not let on the flood, raise the gates, and set all our wheels in motion? He that hath ears to hear, let him hear. Employ your senses....

As I climbed the hill again toward my old bean-field, I listened to the ancient, familiar, immortal, dear cricket sound under all others, hearing at first some distinct chirps; but when these ceased I was aware of the general earth-song, which my hearing had not heard, amid which these were only taller flowers in a bed, and I wondered if behind or beneath this there was not some other chant yet more universal. Why do we not hear when this begins in the spring? and when it ceases in the fall? Or is it too gradual?

After I have got into the road I have no thought to record all the way home, — the walk is comparatively barren. The leafy elm sprays seem to droop more by night (??).

Frequently he made the notes, sometimes wrote out the paragraphs, of such passages as these while in the fields, and not infrequently by night light when he could scarcely see his pencil. The rewriting in the Journal is careful, finished, not hurried, usually ready for print as it stands. Thus the Journal is his workshop, as nature was his laboratory.

Constantly, in these first years of his nature period, he is experimenting with varieties of narrative style. In spite of his dislike of fiction, Thoreau is one of the best story-tellers among all our native writers. No one can beat him at the descriptive anecdote, few in his descriptions of persons, or beasts or birds that act like persons. His range of course was limited by his theme, which was nature, not the complexities and personal psychology of man. His art is the art of Aesop at its lowest, of Homer at its highest, vivid, memorable, but dealing with the great simplicities of experience, and among them preferring nature and beasts to men and women. These last he left to others, but could have done much if his essential shyness had not kept him closer to the lower organisms and his reticence had not forbidden him the use of his own intimate experiences. As a story-teller, he recalls the effective simplicity of Defoe. The battle of the ants in 'Walden' is as fine in its way as Moll Flanders' landing in America. Neither Hawthorne nor Melville nor Cooper could have told it so well. Quite as good are the many less formal anecdotes in his Journal:

> I heard a splashing in the shallow and muddy water and stood awhile to observe the cause of it. Again and again I heard and saw the commotion, but could not guess the cause of it, — what kind of life had its residence in that insignificant pool. We sat down on the hillside. Ere long a muskrat came swimming by as if attracted by the same disturbance, and then another and another, till three had passed, and I began to suspect that they were at the bottom of it. Still ever and anon I observed the same commotion in the waters over the same spot, and at length I observed the snout of some creature slyly raised above the surface after each commotion, as if to see if it were observed by foes, and then but a few rods distant I saw another snout above the water and began to divine the cause of the disturbance. Putting off my shoes and stockings, I crept stealthily down the hill and waded out slowly and noiselessly about a rod from the firm land, keeping behind the tussocks, till I stood behind the tussock near which I had observed the splashing. Then, suddenly stooping over it, I saw through the shallow but muddy water that there was a mud turtle there, and thrusting in my hand at once caught him by the claw, and, quicker than I can tell it, heaved him high and dry ashore; and there came out with him a large pout just dead and partly devoured, which he held in his jaws. It was the pout in his flurry and the turtle in his struggles to hold him fast which had created the commotion. There he had lain, probably buried in the mud at the bottom up to his eyes, till the pout came sailing over, and then this musky lagune had put forth in the direction of his

ventral fins, expanding suddenly under the influence of a more
than vernal heat, — there are sermons in stones, aye and mud
turtles at the bottoms of the pools, — in the direction of his
ventral fins, his tender white belly, where he kept no eye; and
the minister squeaked his last. Oh, what an eye was there,
my countrymen! buried in mud up to the lids, meditating on
what? sleepless at the bottom of the pool, at the top of the
bottom, directed heavenward, in no danger from motes. Pouts
expect their foes not from below. Suddenly a mud volcano
swallowed him up, seized his midriff; he fell into those relentless
jaws from which there is no escape, which relax not their hold
even in death. There the pout might calculate on remaining
until nine days after the head was cut off. Sculled through
Heywood's shallow meadow, not thinking of foes, looking
through the water up into the sky. I saw his [the turtle's]
brother sunning and airing his broad back like a ship bottom
up which had been scuttled, — foundered at sea. I had no
idea that there was so much going on in Heywood's meadow.⁹

4

Like many men approaching middle age, Henry idealized
the memories of his youth when 'my life was ecstasy.' It was in
youth, 'before I lost any of my senses,' that he 'inhabited' his
body 'with inexpressible satisfaction; both its weariness and its
refreshment were sweet to me. This earth was the most glorious
musical instrument, and I was audience to its strains . . . I said
to myself, — I said to others, — . . . "I perceive that I am dealt
with by superior powers." . . . The morning and the evening
were sweet to me, and I led a life aloof from society of men. I
wondered if a mortal had ever known what I knew. . . . I was
daily intoxicated, and yet no man could call me intemperate.
With all your science can you tell me how it is, and whence it is,
that light comes into the soul?' ¹⁰ He was idealizing memory.
But the remembered ecstasy had prepared its paths to expression
by 1851, when he wrote these words. Even though such pas-

sionate moods came less often than in his youth, they were stronger when they came, and from them Thoreau's finest nature lyrics are made.

I call them lyrics, although now he seldom wrote metrical poetry. He had given up verse, except for occasional fragments, before distributing his best poems in the 'Week.' Sanborn thought that the reason was Emerson's discouraging criticism when he advised Thoreau to burn most of his early poetry. This is surely not true, nor is his shift to prose explained by any drying up of the sources of poetic inspiration, for in the early fifties he had not yet swung over toward the aridities of science.

Thoreau gave up verse because he found he could write much better prose. He left many of his poems unfinished, assembled others from scattered and not too closely related stanzas, and was capable of lines of excessive crudity and of poems that broke into prose at the end. Yet he spent unceasing pains upon the turning of a prose sentence, and rewrote passages, like the oft-quoted paragraphs on Baker's farm, again and again and again.[11] 'Great prose,' he said in the 'Week,' 'of equal elevation, commands our respect more than great verse, since it implies a more permanent and level height, a life more pervaded with the grandeur of the thought. The poet often only makes an irruption, like a Parthian, and is off again, shooting while he retreats; but the prose writer has conquered like a Roman, and settled colonies.'[12] Whether true or not for others, this was certainly true for Thoreau. In prose he had learned rhythms that carried his imagination far better than the meter of which he was obviously impatient. He could put more poetry into his prose than into his verse — keep it at 'a more permanent and level height.' He was a Parthian at verse, a Roman in prose.

When the cool and humorous observer was in control, one gets such simple yet vivid narrative as the turtle and the pout. When the naturalist took charge later, came pages of monotonous and often futile classification with no distinction of style. When the poet's imagination warmed, the prose warmed with it, lost the sharpness of its epigrammatic edge, took on lyric qualities, and gave us a Thoreau quite as worthy of a high place in literature as the economist of 'Walden.' Here are two prose poems, both records of ecstasy. This is joyful writing, exuberant in its wanton playing with sentences of inordinate length, yet perfect balance. It is the old Marlborough Road:

July 21. 1851... Now I yearn for one of those old, meander-ing, dry, uninhabited roads, which lead away from towns, which lead us away from temptation, which conduct to the outside of earth, over its uppermost crust; where you may forget in what country you are travelling; where no farmer can complain that you are treading down his grass, no gentle-man who has recently constructed a seat in the country that you are trespassing; on which you can go off at half-cock and wave adieu to the village; along which you may travel like a pilgrim, going nowhither; where travellers are not too often to be met; where my spirit is free; where the walls and fences are not cared for; where your head is more in heaven than your feet are on earth; which have long reaches where you can see the approaching traveller half a mile off and be prepared for him; not so luxuriant a soil as to attract men; some root and stump fences which do not need attention; where travellers have no occasion to stop, but pass along and leave you to your thoughts; where it makes no odds which way you face, whether you are going or coming, whether it is morning or evening, mid-noon or midnight; where earth is cheap enough by being public; where you can walk and think with least obstruction, there being nothing to measure progress by; where you can pace when your breast is full, and cherish your moodiness; where you are not in false relations with men, are not dining nor con-versing with them; by which you may go to the uttermost parts of the earth. It is wide enough, wide as the thoughts it allows to visit you. . . . A way which no geese defile, nor hiss along it, but only sometimes their wild brethren fly far overhead; which the kingbird and the swallow twitter over, and the song sparrow sings on its rails; where the small red butterfly is at home on the yarrow, and no boys threaten it with imprisoning hat.   There I can walk and stalk and pace and plod.   Which nobody but Jonas Potter travels beside me; where no cow but his is tempted to linger for the herbage by its side; where the guide-board is fallen, and now the hand points to heaven significantly, — to a Sudbury and Marlborough in the skies.   That's a road I can travel, that the particular Sudbury I am bound for, six miles an hour, or two, as you please; and few there be that enter thereon.   There I can walk, and recover the lost child that I am without any ringing of a bell.

The other, one of his best, has for theme the perfect sublima-tion of human love in nature.   Touched with humor, yet pas-sionate enough, it is an ode to the shrub oak:

> *Dec. 1. 1856* . . . The dear wholesome color of shrub oak leaves, so clean and firm, not decaying, but which have put on a kind of immortality, not wrinkled and thin like the white oak leaves, but full-veined and plump, as nearer earth.   Well-tanned leather on the one side, sun-tanned, color of colors, color of the cow and the deer, silver-downy beneath, turned toward the late bleached and russet fields.   What are acanthus leaves and the rest to this?   Emblem of my winter condition. I love and could embrace the shrub oak with its scanty garment of leaves rising above the snow, lowly whispering to me, akin to winter thoughts, and sunsets, and to all virtue.   Covert which the hare and the partridge seek, and I too seek.   What cousin of mine is the shrub oak?   How can any man suffer long?   For a sense of want is a prayer, and all prayers are answered.   Rigid as iron, clean as the atmosphere, hardy as virtue, innocent and sweet as a maiden is the shrub oak.   In proportion as I know and love it, I am natural and sound as a partridge.   I felt a positive yearning toward one bush this afternoon.   There was a match found for me at last.   I fell in love with a shrub oak.

These ecstasies in prose, those hours of observation, this hard labor with the pen and hard study of science and travel, now, rather than Latin, Greek, and the Hindu classics, this daily filling up of reservoirs, and nightly refining of the waters, all this was Thoreau's real business of living while he was by trade the surveyor of Concord. Surveyor indeed, but not only of lot lines and corners!

20. WHAT HE LIVED FOR

So Concord, with its 'blessed' miles of rivers, lakes, fields, and woods, had become by 1850 and for Henry that friendly universe which Margaret Fuller told Carlyle she was willing to accept. Concord village he was still inclined to deny, but to rural Concord he now gave himself mind and limbs, with only brief withdrawals when 'bleeding Kansas' or the need of love clouded his mind and ruined his day. Wild nature became his obsession.

Obsession is the word for the passion of energy which sent him trudging miles through the wild Easterbrooks country to the northward, climbing trees for hawks' nests, wading rivers till his bare feet had learned their contours, and thrusting and pushing into thickets to give 'the hazel catkins a fillip with my finger under their chins to see if they were in bloom.' He was determined 'to pluck the fruit of each day as it passes, and store it safely' in his bin.

Yet this was not a physical energy like the activities of the Boy Scouts who think they follow his pattern. Nor was he exposing, like the sentimental nature lover, a sensitive soul for the sensation recorded. To call Henry Thoreau in this new phase a nature worshipper or even a student of nature, is to substitute a phrase for a process in a complex character which can be defined only by analyzing a conflict of philosophies. This conflict lies very close to the moving center of change from the nineteenth century to the twentieth.

Thoreau, as I see him, was a man with a foot in each of two worlds, the idealist's and the scientist's, his own as the Concord idealists conceived of it, and ours as every schoolboy now thinks he understands it. And indeed what happened to him when his vision of a spiritual reality behind the visible garment of nature began to be obscured by the intricate pattern of that garment, was typical of the confused philosophy which has given us today new morals and new mores.

While he was still at Walden Pond, he had made collections of fish, turtles, a black snake, and a mouse, all alive or recently so, and sent them through his friend Cabot to Agassiz at Harvard. Agassiz was trying to set in order the vague classifications of American wild life, using his new techniques of research. So absorbing did he find the little-worked American field that Darwin's momentous theory of development, when it arrived, seemed to him an impertinence, likely to interfere with his zoology.

Henry was delighted to find that he had provided several new animal varieties, one of them from the sunfish which he had watched so lovingly in the pond. That they were unnamed stirred in him a naïve enthusiasm for classification. 'How wild it makes the pond and the township to find a new fish in it!' [1] It was unfortunate that the first scientist of real ability who came his way should have been a classificationist. A decade later, when he was reading with mingled interest and unbelief Darwin's 'Origin of Species,' he might have entered the field of professional nature study with a philosophy. As it was, his earliest conception of science as applied to his beloved nature was like Adam's in the Garden of Eden when he was asked to name all living things. Intuitively positive that the outward form of plant, flower, and fish was a translucent pattern hiding an inner significance for universal life, in practice, with Agassiz and Gray to guide him, he became a collector, a namer, a student of behavior as a means of identification. With the familiar woodchuck and muskrat his studies of behavior are touched with genius, but in general, when he tries to be scientific he is a cataloguer imperfectly equipped, a measurer with crude instruments, an observer unwilling to use the means required for absolute accuracy. Doctor Harris, the Harvard librarian and entomologist, said to Alcott that if Emerson had not spoiled him, Thoreau would have made a good naturalist. It may be said with equal truth that if it had not been for the influence of Agassiz and his disciples, Thoreau might have detoured the bog of classificationist detail into which he sank deeper and deeper in the fifties, and attained before his death a working synthesis of science and his Transcendentalism.

As early as 1850 the Boston Society of Natural History elected him a corresponding member, and to it he left his collections. Three years later the secretary of the Association for the Advancement of Science sent him a questionnaire. In what branch of science was he particularly interested? Henry in replying spoke 'to their condition.' As a scientist, as they and he understood science, he was a botanist. But he confided to his Journal that he was really 'a mystic, a transcendentalist, and a natural philosopher to boot.' Though 'as good an observer as most,' he could not, as he knew, put such a statement in his answer without exciting ridicule. Since neither Plato nor Aristotle was president of the Association, he would not have been understood! [2]

His mystic intuition of reality was a reaction against the mechanical deism of the previous period. But with intuitiveness in his heart, the job of identifying and classifying the wild life of Concord led him into a perplexing dilemma. The mystic might feel the secret springs of life in nature, the Transcendentalist might believe in an inner significance, the philosopher might reason from these premises, but none of them knew nature as nature visibly and audibly was in the new world. They had their emotions, like Emerson's in his pine grove, and their theories, like Alcott with his spirals of development, but an observer, who had been in the fields and woods since youth, was aware that to the American idealist his environment was but vaguely known. A Swiss scientist could discover new varieties of fish within twenty miles of Boston. American writers still put the European scene — its weather, its trees, its seasons, even its birds — into their nature poems. No man of letters — unless Audubon and Bartram be so called — had dealt knowingly with the American environment of nature. Apparently, one must classify and understand structure, life processes, and relationships before one could begin to philosophize. And this meant to be a measurer, a classificationist.

Of the dilemma Thoreau was perfectly aware. He knew that he would never identify his seringo until he held one in his hand. 'If you held the bird in your hand ——' said a Boston ornithologist, significantly; 'but I would rather hold it in my affections,' Thoreau replied.[3] He would not kill (birds at least) even for science. Yet when he finds a dead goosander, shot by fast-day sportsmen, he is in rapture, and sets down paragraphs of minute analysis, for which he lacks even an adequate vocabulary. He went so far as to kill a snake and trap a field mouse! But something more powerful than common sense held him back from the next step, which might have made him a professional researcher. The dead bird in his hand might have told him all he wanted to know as a classificationist. Yet once dead, the mystery of life, the secrets of behavior, had escaped forever. Better, so he might have said (one hopes with a blush), to have confused through a lifetime the hermit and the wood thrush, than to have missed the significance of those 'cool bars of melody from the atmosphere of everlasting morning or evening' in the passion for labelling. Of course, a scientist might capture both bird and the beauty of its song. But did they, ever? As for Thoreau, he preferred to know less and guess more, though there was immense labor behind his guessing. He specialized only in botany — where there was no killing of warm-blooded life.

It was in 1855 that his English admirer, Thomas Cholmonde-ley, nephew of Bishop Heber, friend of Clough, and vagrant philosopher, presented him with a library of the Hindu classics. It was too late. He had got what juice he could extract from the Orient years before and read little in his new acquisitions. If he had been really a convert to Orientalism the difficulties which he now faced would not have troubled him. As a mystic it would have been sufficient to dream his way into nature, as a self-searcher it would have been enough to take what he could get from nature into his inner life, and be content with its en-richment. But he was essentially an Occidental, with literature as his profession. He wanted to *do* something with his wood-chucks, his muskrats, his white oak trees, his fertile rivers, and subtly ripening leaves. That curious remark in the midst of a spring rhapsody, 'I am guilty of suckers,' [4] means really no more than that his conscience is not satisfied until he has wrestled with the problem of the seemingly wanton death of suckers in the stream, and perhaps *said something* pertinent about it. He wanted to give the essence of all he saw, felt, and thought to Americans. What were the names of the meadow grasses, what was the moss flower like, how did lichens grow, and what was the relationship between spring and the flowers that made its days a calendar? Only science could answer. So with his left hand he kept firm hold of philosophy and with his right grasped the ruler, the measuring cord, and the spy glass.

No naturalist ever achieved much more in the way of pure observation with such crude instruments. But they were crude because the man himself was half-hearted. Better instruments were procurable, even by him, and far better methodologies than he used. He was far behind even his own day, when research was still in its infancy. The truth was that he would look close enough to learn more, but not too close lest his vision be lost. No scientist is made this way. Even as a classificationist and even in botany, Thoreau was beaten from the start. His laborious experiments, which got him nowhere because they were under no effective control, are pathetic — hundreds of measurements of deep snow with a measuring stick, rough dissections, countings of birds, plumbings of the depths of swamps, even his researches in the newborn science of geography where his intuitions of its importance outran any methods of study which he could devise.

He was well aware of his difficulties, though curiously indifferent, for a handy man, to the crudity of his instruments of research, and ignorant of the rather obvious fact that a methodology, such as he worked out later for studying the flora of the seasons and the succession of forest trees, was indispensable as a first step to any real study of natural phenomenon. He paid now the price of a too great self-reliance.

The conflict is set down again and again:

> *July 23. 1851* ... But this habit of close observation, — in Humboldt, Darwin, and others. Is it to be kept up long, this science? Do not tread on the heels of your experience. Be impressed without making a minute of it. Poetry puts an interval between the impression and the expression, — waits till the seed germinates naturally.

'Do not tread on the heels of your experience.' But this is

just what applied science has done, and transformed the world
by so doing — for good, and more lately for extreme ill. If
planes can fly, let them carry men, and mails, and then — on
the heels of your experience — bombs!

> *Nov. 1. Saturday. 1851*... First of all a man must see, before
> he can say.... See not with the eye of science, which is barren,
> nor of youthful poetry, which is impotent. But taste the world
> and digest it.... At first blush a man is not capable of reporting
> truth; he must be drenched and saturated with it first.

For Thoreau there was no end to the seeing, though he did
say in these years more of the science of behavior than he has
as yet been given credit for. And especially when, as in that
November, he felt blessed, loved his life, warmed toward all
nature. Then truth exhaled from him 'like the odor of the
muskrat from the coat of the trapper.'

> *March 7. 1854*... It is remarkable how true each plant is
> to its season. Why should not the fringed gentian put forth
> early in the spring, instead of holding in till the latter part of
> September? I do not perceive enough difference in the temper-
> ature.

He was in over his neck when he began to ask questions like
that, which neither his temperament nor his training could
solve.

> *May 6. P.M. 1854*.... There is no such thing as pure *objec-*
> *tive* observation. Your observation, to be interesting, *i.e.*, to
> be significant, must be *subjective*. The sum of what the writer
> of whatever class has to report is simply some human experience,
> whether he be poet or philosopher or man of science. The man
> of most science is the man most alive, whose life is the greatest
> event. Senses that take cognizance of outward things merely
> are of no avail. It matters not where or how far you travel, —
> the farther commonly the worse, — but how much alive you are.
> If it is possible to conceive of an event outside to humanity,
> it is not of the slightest significance, though it were the explosion

of a planet. Every important worker will report what life there is in him. It makes no odds into what seeming deserts the poet is born. Though all his neighbors pronounce it a Sahara, it will be a paradise to him; for the desert which we see is the result of the barrenness of our experience. No mere willful activity whatever, whether in writing verses or collecting statistics, will produce true poetry or science. If you are really a sick man, it is indeed to be regretted, for you cannot accomplish so much as if you were well. All that a man has to say or do that can possibly concern mankind, is in some shape or other to tell the story of his love, — to sing; and, if he is fortunate and keeps alive, he will be forever in love. This alone is to be alive to the extremities. It is a pity that this divine creature should ever suffer from cold feet; a still greater pity that the coldness so often reaches to his heart. I look over the report of the doings of a scientific association and am surprised that there is so little life to be reported; I am put off with a parcel of dry technical terms. Anything living is easily and naturally expressed in popular language. I cannot help suspecting that the life of these learned professors has been almost as inhuman and wooden as a rain-gauge or self-registering magnetic machine. They communicate no fact which rises to the temperature of blood-heat. It doesn't all amount to one rhyme.

Here is Thoreau the nature lover in all his strength and in all his weakness. For literature (poetry he would have said) this is a final statement. There is no value in man's report upon life unless he is alive and it *is* life. For science, so far as ultimate ends are concerned, few would dispute that this confession of objectives is true also. It is hard for the least philosophic intellect to conceive of a value in science which is not potentially a human value also. Even the intellectual play of pure mathematics, with no necessary relation to reality as we know it in the physical world, has the double human value of possible usefulness and immediate human pleasure. Yet the researcher knows that the end must never overshadow the means. The goal may be a subjective wish, but the research must be conducted as if it

were an end in itself, otherwise we get not science but the results of wish psychology. This was Thoreau's weakness as a
scientist. Fearing that he would lose his sense of the living
reality behind the appearance, he never gave his whole mind
to the discipline of observation. He wished to know what nature
was like, but never to be deceived into thinking that when he
knew, he knew all.

2

Science lost nothing by this divided allegiance. There were
hundreds, there were to be thousands, of naturalist-observers
better equipped by temperament, as well as with instruments,
than Thoreau for the job of classification. But his studies of the
behavior of bird and beast, his landscapes, waterscapes, and
woodscapes were inimitable by these observers because they
lacked his sympathetic imagination. Yet his own work gained
in truth and force from the specific knowledge happily absorbed into an imaginative whole.

The transforming power of his imagination can be felt in the
single sentence in which he describes the chirp of the cricket in
Concord fields: 'Serenely wise, their song has the security of
prose.' It pervades the most effective of his woodchuck episodes,
where that familiar savage comes alive in words:

> *April 16. 1852.* . . . As I turned round the corner of Hub-
> bard's Grove, saw a woodchuck, the first of the season, in the
> middle of the field, six or seven rods from the fence which bounds
> the wood, and twenty rods distant. I ran along the fence and
> cut him off, or rather overtook him, though he started at the
> same time. When I was only a rod and a half off, he stopped,
> and I did the same; then he ran again, and I ran up within
> three feet of him, when he stopped again, the fence being be-
> tween us. I squatted down and surveyed him at my leisure.
> His eyes were dull black and rather inobvious, with a faint

chestnut (?) iris, with but little expression and that more of resignation than of anger. The general aspect was a coarse grayish brown, a sort of grisel (?). A lighter brown next the skin, then black or very dark brown and tipped with whitish rather loosely. The head between a squirrel and a bear, flat on the top and dark brown, and darker still or black on the tip of the nose. The whiskers black, two inches long. The ears very small and roundish, set far back and nearly buried in the fur. Black feet, with long and slender claws for digging. It appeared to tremble, or perchance shivered with cold. When I moved, it gritted its teeth quite loud, sometimes striking the under jaw against the other chatteringly, sometimes grinding one jaw on the other, yet as if more from instinct than anger. Whichever way I turned, that way it headed. I took a twig a foot long and touched its snout, at which it started forward and bit the stick, lessening the distance between us to two feet, and still it held all the ground it gained. I played with it tenderly awhile with the stick, trying to open its gritting jaws. Ever its long incisors, two above and two below, were presented. But I thought it would go to sleep if I stayed long enough. It did not sit upright as sometimes, but *standing* on its fore feet with its head down, *i.e.* half sitting, half standing. We sat looking at one another about half an hour, till we began to feel mesmeric influences. When I was tired, I moved away, wishing to see him run, but I could not start him. He would not stir as long as I was looking at him or could see him. I walked round him; he turned as fast and fronted me still. I sat down by his side within a foot. I talked to him *quasi* forest lingo, baby-talk, at any rate in a conciliatory tone, and thought that I had some influence on him. He gritted his teeth less. I chewed checkerberry leaves and presented them to his nose at last without a grit; though I saw that by so much gritting of the teeth he had worn them rapidly and they were covered with a fine white powder, which, if you measured it thus, would have made his anger terrible. He did not mind any noise I might make. With a little stick I lifted one of his paws to examine it, and held it up at pleasure. I turned him over to see what color he was beneath (darker or more purely brown), though he turned himself back again sooner than I could have wished. His tail was also all brown, though not very dark, rat-tail like, with loose hairs standing out on all sides like a caterpillar brush. He had a rather mild look. I spoke kindly to him. I reached checkerberry leaves to his mouth. I stretched my hands over him, though he turned up his head and still gritted a little. I laid my hand on him, but immediately took it off again, instinct not being wholly overcome. If I had had a few fresh bean leaves, thus in advance of the season, I am sure I should have tamed him completely. It was a frizzly tail. His is a humble, terrestrial color like the partridge's, well concealed where dead wiry grass rises above darker brown or chestnut dead leaves, — a modest color. If I had had some food, I should have ended with stroking him at my leisure. Could easily have wrapped him in my handkerchief. He was not fat nor particularly lean. I finally had to leave him without seeing him move from the place. A large, clumsy, burrowing squirrel. *Arctomys*, bear-mouse. I respect him as one of the natives. He lies there, by his color and habits so naturalized amid the dry leaves, the withered grass, and the bushes. A sound nap, too, he has enjoyed in his native fields, the past winter. I think I might learn some wisdom of him. His ancestors have lived here longer than mine. He is more thoroughly acclimated and naturalized than I. Bean leaves the red man raised for him, but he can do without them.

3

Yet unquestionably the unity of his achievement suffered. He carved his gallery of studies of the wild, but to use again his curious figure, 'the statues rarely take hold of hands.' There was no time to bring them together. In any volume of his Journal after the early fifties are interminable passages of half-scientific description which satisfy neither science nor the imagination. The habit of observing became too strong to resist. 'I milk the sky and the earth,' he says, even 'at the risk of endless iteration.' It was often skim milk only. 'I feel that I am dissipated by so many observations. . . . I have almost a slight, dry headache as the result of all this observing.' 'I have the habit of attention to such excess that my senses get no rest, but suffer from a constant strain. . . . What I need is not to look at all, but a true sauntering of the eye.' [5] Good self-advice, seldom taken in these later years.

It is probable that the slackening of Thoreau's energy after his prostrating illness of 1855, from which he never fully recovered, is responsible for his frequent descents in his later years into the mere collecting of trivial observations. With the characteristic ups and downs of the tubercular, he was often too listless for imagination, yet still able to carry on his habits of note-taking. Yet he was condemned to do too much of it in any case, once he had taken the school of Agassiz for guide. From that moment his oxen began to pull apart from their yoke.

In all fairness it should be added that his note-taking was his recreation as well as his business. The legend that Thoreau in his last phase was a frustrated and unhappy man has no basis of fact, except in his inevitable grumblings at his failure to reconcile science and the Transcendental. Ecstasies were rare with him in these years, nostalgia for his more impressionable youth frequent, but the joy of free observation was constant. Neither rain, nor snow, nor wind, nor anything but bronchitis could daunt his daily happiness in just being out-of-doors. For a man of his tastes, his temperament, and his philosophy, life had arranged itself ideally. No man was more consistent than Thoreau, and here particularly so, for his resolve made in youth to live his life before he uttered it, was made good in these eager excursions. Failure with his friends, failure to discover the great secret, failure to reach a satisfactory stopping place in his studies of detail, failure to make up his mind how to use his thousands of pages of mixed notebook, essay, and poetic philosophy, troubled him but never disturbed his essential joy in

experience. It did not need fame, or even a certainty of achievement, to make him a very happy man in his relations with
nature — which at this time meant nine-tenths of all his relations. He observed, first of all I should say, because he liked
to do so.

4

If he aspired to any science which was more than classification
and collecting it was to geography, a science scarcely adolescent
in Thoreau's day, although with Humboldt and the young
Darwin it had been brought out of infancy. Geography is the
study of man's environment with reference to its effects upon
man. There could be no better description of hundreds of
pages of Thoreau's later Journal than this. He wished to know
intimately, accurately, every item of the Concord scene because
he loved that scene, but also because he and his fellow townsmen were transplanted Europeans not yet fully adapted to a
new environment, and still ignorant of its differences from the
Old World. And he wanted to know the relations between man
and nature without reference to locality. Read this way the
Journal takes on a wider significance. If it is American weather,
Thoreau records it for New England in descriptions not equalled
elsewhere. If it is the influence of moving water upon a countryside, see not only his remarkable descriptions of the Concord
and Sudbury valleys, but also the specific studies of the beds
the rivers make for themselves.[6] The stream burrowing through
the meadows, the marshy river that determines the economy of
the families on its banks, the climate in its relation to the New
England temperament, the psychological effect and physio-
logical character of mountain zones, all will be found described
in tireless detail in the Journal. Also the wilderness in the
American background that makes its influence felt to the sea,

and the native man, the Indian, conditioned by the geography of that wilderness, and still aware of much the white man has not yet learned. Regarded as geography, Thoreau's Journal is a noble contribution to knowledge, for what it lacks in method and control, it makes up for by an intimacy of observation which few scientists can equal, and a breadth of observation which is a first requisite of geography.

Thoreau was surely a pioneer in American scientific geography, but no more than a pioneer. He was like those other pioneers who crossed the Alleghanies, roughly cleared some fertile valley, and then moved further west to new pioneering. And essentially Thoreau's geography, like his natural history, was intended to make not so much better science as better men. He hoped for a life less cramped and mean than the product of grubbing stony fields and bargaining on the Mill Dam. The New Englanders he was trying to educate were determined money-getters but indifferent to good living. De Tocqueville describes them hacking at the edges of the Western wilderness:

> Race cold and passionate, which traffics in everything, not excepting morality and religion; nation of conquerors who submit themselves to the savage life without ever allowing themselves to be seduced by it, who in civilization and enlightenment love only what is useful to well-being, and who shut themselves in the American solitudes with an axe and some newspapers.[7]

Thoreau's West was of the spirit. His minute and loving study of the geography of his Concord was really an invitation to self-knowledge, for his intuition had already grasped the concept of modern anthropology, that his environment is an inseparable part of the personality of every individual. Let him know it then — not plow it under and go on, like the farmers of Concord.

Thus his objective was literary, philosophic, not really scientific. Even as geography, Thoreau's science is always amateur. It is the science of the self-made student who labors excessively for small returns because he lacks frames of reference and good methods. And in Thoreau's case it remained amateur because he was really more interested in the literature to be made of it than in the facts themselves.

That his aims were often confused is, therefore, not to be disputed. He was snowed under masses of observation, lost in a maze of organized and repetitive research that led nowhere and wasted his time. It was fun for him usually, but death to rapid achievement. And this has led many critics to praise the Excursions and the Travel Books he drew from this later Journal while condemning the tangled mass of geography, botany, essay, reflection, and rhapsody as tragic futility. Formless the Journal is, but not futile, since good books have been drawn from it. And it is probable that there is one book more, and the best of its kind, to be put together by some laborious and self-sacrificing student, from the confusion of its lengthy narrative. For science Thoreau had not advanced, never would have advanced, far enough. But for literature he had more than enough knowledge to depict the relation of the Concord environment to the men of Concord in a record which for scope, intimacy, penetration, and a flexible, pungent, poetic style is not equalled by Gilbert White of Selborne or any other, and incomparably superior to the pious suavities of William Howitt's 'The Book of the Seasons; or, The Calendar of Nature,' which, as Emerson said, was a parody of the real thing. We have parts of this record in his Excursions, but for the whole the reader must now fight his way through swamps of preliminary observation and thickets of iterative detail. Far from throwing out the baby with the bath, which a literary dilettante seeking immediate publication might have done, Thoreau kept bath and baby down to the last soap sud. The result awaits the labors of an editor of genius.

5

One other — and this time a purely literary — influence
had a noticeable effect on Thoreau's eye for nature in these
years. 'I do not the least care where I get my ideas, or what
suggests them,' [8] he once said, and indeed few men could admit
indebtedness so frankly, for few men have subjected all their
borrowings to so strong a drench of personality. Yet even the
most original mind can be given new points of view from which
the familiar world takes on a different aspect. So it was with
Thoreau when he made the not very astonishing discovery
that the beauty of a natural scene depends upon its conformity
to laws of composition as intelligible as the laws of science.
Having learned this, he characteristically asserted that nature,
not marred or thwarted by man, provided her own composition, which was better than the best efforts of art. Nevertheless,
after he had read Gilpin on the picturesque he began to look
at his forest openings and curving valleys with new perception
as to when and why they were beautiful.

Neither Concord nor Boston was sensitive to art. Allston
the painter exhibited and was admired; Margaret Fuller published her notebooks on picture exhibitions in *The Dial*; yet
still the taste of the intellectuals can only be described as
provincial and uninformed. Nowhere was the Victorian idea
of painting and sculpture as a means of inculcating morals or
telling a story more heartily supported. As for the artistic
demands of plain people such as the Wards and the Thoreau
family, let Laura Harris, Prudence Ward's correspondent,
speak of the impression made upon her by Greenough's semi-
nude statue intended to represent Byron's Medora: [9]

Dec. 19, 1833.

. . . Last Friday I summoned courage . . . and went alone
at twelve at noon [when gentlemen were supposed not to be

present].... On a platform covered with green a foot high in the centre of the room was the bier on which lay the beautiful Medora.... I was horrified at the size of what Moore calls woman's loveliness which actually took my eye so that I could not see the face.... The left side of the figure is entirely naked except a sheet drawn up under the arms. It is represented to be of so delicate a texture that the form is distinctly traced. For myself I can say it would have pleased me much better had it been drawn a few inches higher, for I felt for a while completely out of countenance. There was one gentleman present.[10]

Fortunately he was 'old and respectable.' But she did wonder how he and his ladies could examine the figure 'bit by bit and comment on each inch of her, but this objectionable part, I know they felt awkward.... I was in terror lest the ladies should go off before I had gazed enough.'

This delicious Victorianism would certainly have been shared by Sophia or Cynthia Thoreau. It represents the esthetic climate in which Thoreau lived when he was not at Emerson's.

The esthetic taste of the Concord Transcendentalists differed in degree from local opinion, but not in kind. Emerson, who had no ear and could not follow music, had at least studied great masterpieces of painting and sculpture. His intuition told him that there was more than the moral to be got from these works. Yet very seldom does he register an opinion of the arts which is not essentially literary. Thoreau was sensitive to music, lived in a musical family, and was himself an acceptable performer on the flute. Yet he never got beyond the literary view of music. It was the effect upon the thoughts or emotions of the hearer which concerned him in the dozens of paragraphs he devotes to what he evidently regarded as musical criticism. By this criterion the thrumming of the new telegraph wires in the wind might be a nobler music than the best a violin could make. And he thought that it was nobler, because the wire thrumming in the leafy solitudes set his mind vibrating in wonderful patterns. Counterpoint for him was an unnecessary complication, and the simple music of the Greeks would have approached his ideal. When Greeley took him to hear Grisi sing in New York, he was more impressed by Greeley's free tickets than by the music.

It is remarkable, therefore, to find him in 1852 accusing Emerson's friend Greenough, the sculptor, of holding views only a little better than the common dilettantism when he said that architectural ornaments should have a core of truth, a necessity, and hence a beauty. Greenough, said Thoreau, wished to put 'a core of truth within the ornaments' with which they were beginning to stud the new houses, but 'what of architectural beauty I now see, I know has gradually grown from within outward, out of the character and necessities of the indweller and builder, without even a thought for mere ornament' — has been, in short, although of course he did not use the word, functional. 'One of the most beautiful buildings in this country is a logger's hut in the woods. . . . There's a deal of nonsense abroad.' [11]

There was, indeed, since it was precisely in these fifties that the sound tradition of American architecture broke down into a welter of meaningless gimcrack. Yet I quote this just and intuitive criticism of Thoreau's only to show that he could on occasion differ from his neighbors in matters of art as sharply as in questions of economics.

Some months after this conversation he begins to write about the works of William Gilpin (1724–1804), which he handled with complete independence, taking what he needed and nothing more. Gilpin was a clergyman with a taste for the out-of-doors, a strong romantic tendency, and some artistic gifts, who appealed to Thoreau for precisely the same reason that had earlier made Howitt interesting. Gilpin wrote a series of 'Observations' on various parts of England, Wales, and Scotland, but it was his 'Remarks on Forest Scenery,' [12] and his 'Three Essays' on picturesque beauty, picturesque travel, and sketching landscape, which particularly interested Thoreau, because of the parallels between Old and New England. His 'Forest Scenery' is illustrated by scenes of the New Forest done by the author in soft tones, and romantically picturesque to the edge of the sentimental.

The vogue of the picturesque had built ruins in English gardens and put Gothic ornaments on Queen Anne manor houses. It preferred the rough to the smooth, and a taste for the rough, for the wild, Gilpin is constantly recommending. Thoreau was impressed at first. That nature should have her due effect upon the observer, warm the heart, expand the imagination, was good in his philosophy. But this craving for roughness, for artificial wildernesses in place of formal gardens, for blasted trees drenched in greenish moonlight and horrid cliffs such as Gilpin painted, grated on his common sense. There was plenty of honest roughness in New England. Thoreau was romantic about his wild nature, but not sentimental, and sentimentality was the heart of the picturesque. The rough as Gilpin described it seemed as unreal as the smooth. 'The elegant Gilpin. I like his style and manners better than anything he says.'

Unlike Poe, who was also exposed to the picturesque and took it like a disease, Thoreau shook off this cheap romanticism after a few half-hearted experiments. [13] What he took from Gilpin was something much less novel, and far more important for his ill-trained estheticism — a sense of composition and design, which was a very real addition to his pleasure in natural beauty. Thoreau had discussed painting with Rowse, who had drawn him, and visited the studio of F. H. T. Bellew in New York. He had seen galleries, too, though he registered no impression. But Gilpin, who was a saunterer and nature lover like himself, wrote of these artistic principles in relation to Thoreau's own job of nature description. His books were propaganda on how an artist should look at landscapes, and his illustrations in line and color showed how nature should be seen. Thoreau was deeply impressed by these conceptions, new to him, of foreground, background, and the relations of detail to the whole. They gave his imagination something to work upon. He read in Gilpin, 'But whatever beauty these *contrasts* [of foliage and boughs] exhibit, the effect is totally lost, unless the *clump* be *well-balanced*,' [14] then went out into his own woods looking for composition in his favorite views. He sees, for the first time, with the artist's eye:

> In that little pasture of Potter's under the oak, I am struck with the advantage of the fence in landscapes. Here is but a half-acre inclosed, but the fence has the effect of confining the attention to this little undulation of the land and to make you consider it by itself, and the importance of the oak is proportionally increased. This formation of the surface would be lost in an unfenced prairie, but the fence, which nearly enough defines it, frames it and presents it as a picture.[15]

He had never thought of such things in his uncomplicated joy in the stretches of Fair Haven bay or the pools of the Ministerial Swamp. Now he began to analyze his delight in natural beauty, to see why the solitary oak in the pasture drew his steps that way, to follow with a new interest the curves of the hills that lipped Walden Pond. As he was not content until he knew the name of every long-loved flower, so now he rationalized his delight in the mountains that rimmed his West, and the foreground of meadow beneath the slope of Conantum hill.

I have departed from strict biography in this chapter because no biographer who respected his reader would, or could, follow the hundreds of walks and river excursions of these years, with their records purposely repetitive, as Thoreau checks '51 against '54, or follows the history of a wood lot or a clump of azalea through the seasons. This was what he lived for — to study item by item the almost infinite complexity of a New England pasture, to add each season some new interest, while consolidating what was learned before, and to draw off by distillation superb descriptions of a Concord day or night in which each packed sentence has a history of observation and thought behind it. The idealists' interpretation of nature had run ahead of their facts. Thoreau proposed to see the Concord scene, not as Emerson's cloudy veil half hiding an inner reality, but as a patterned garment inseparable from man himself, and to be known as man is known by significant behavior.

This was what he lived for in the fifties, yet by no means all of his life. By preference he was 'self-appointed inspector' of the Concord environment — but by necessity he remained the Thoreau who craved human love, exclaimed against injustice, had his living to make, and was not less difficult for his friends because his road to happiness in the woods was now open five days out of seven.

21. LAST PANGS OF FRIENDSHIP

Day after day Thoreau tramped Jenny Dugan's fields, pushed through the Miles swamp, viewed his beloved western hills from Ponkawtasset or Annursnack, or paddled the rivers studying lilies, pickerel, gulls, hawks, and sandy shallows. By 1853 he was giving names to brooks, glades, and woody stretches, so that they should not remain anonymous in his Concord history.

Meanwhile the routine of village life went on. He walked to the post-office, read *The Tribune*, wrote in his upper chamber, visited George Minott under the hill to hear stories of old hunts with his English gun, swapped muskrat stories with Melvin the trapper. Farmers and fishermen began to please him more than intellectuals. With none did he become intimate, yet he had his own language of everyday life so that for them he was no longer a wandering intellectual, but now the familiar surveyor-naturalist who could tell them more about their own meadows and waters than they knew themselves. Time and again he wrote in his Journal that nature pleased him more than man — by which he usually meant town-dwelling man, or woman.

This was not strictly true. Although he had gone back to

nature he had in no sense deserted the intellectual life. His reading had changed its character, but was as extensive as ever, and broader in scope. On his frequent visits to Cambridge, he talked to the scientists — natural philosophers as they still called themselves — by preference to classicists or literary men; and from the library he drew books on agriculture, in Latin or English, travels where the world was geographically described, and works on primitive peoples, instead of seventeenth-century poetry and the literary classics of Greece and Rome. His interest had definitely shifted from *belles lettres*, yet, as will be seen in a later chapter, was more ardent and earnest than ever before in the problem of how to write. The shift was in emphasis.

Yet the high talk went on in Concord, and was as philosophic and literary as before. Alcott came of an evening for his 'venison,' having been to Emerson's for his 'wine.' And Thoreau himself often settled down for hours at a time in Emerson's parlor, using his privilege as a familiar of the household and a friend of the children.

So John Albee found him one damp day in May of 1852, when he called on the sage. Albee was a student at the orthodox seminary of Andover, who had been stirred to unrest like so many young men of the time by Emerson's radical idealism. He set out 'clandestinely,' and rode and walked to Concord, knowing nothing of the other members of Emerson's circle, 'called sometimes the Transcendentalists.'

> Thoreau was already there.... He had a healthy, out-of-door appearance, and looked like a respectable husbandman. ... When he spoke, it was in either a critical or a witty vein. I did not know who or what he was.... I observed that he was much at home with Emerson; and as he remained through the afternoon and evening, and I left him still at the fireside, he appeared to me to belong in some way to the household. I observed also that Emerson continually deferred to him and seemed to anticipate his view, preparing himself obviously for

a quiet laugh at Thoreau's negative and biting criticisms.... He was clearly fond of Thoreau; but whether in a human way, or as an amusement, I could not then make out.... [As they talked Emerson said] There is no American literature; — Griswold [the editor of Poe] says there is, but it is his merchandise — he keeps its shop.... Thoreau here remarked he had found... [a poet], in the woods, but it had feathers and had not been to Harvard College. Still it had a voice and an aerial inclination, which was pretty much all that was needed. 'Let us cage it,' said Emerson. 'That is just the way the world always spoils its poets,' responded Thoreau. Then... there was a laugh, in which for the first time he joined heartily.[1]

2

Young Albee felt a strain in this friendship at the Emersons', without being able to define it. Surely Emerson did not draw out Thoreau in order to laugh at him, surely he was handling his domesticated woodchuck with gloves. Some strain there had always been between these two who were so much alike in their moral principles, so different in their temperaments and their positions in society. Both men were lonely. 'We stated over again, to sadness almost, the eternal loneliness,' Emerson wrote in his Journal after an October evening's talk in 1851. Yet his loneliness was not the same as Thoreau's. Emerson longed for minds too sympathetic each with the other's spiritual wrestlings to contradict. Noble and fair-minded, he hoped for a plane of intercourse where 'solitaries' like himself could transcend the co-operation of a ship's crew or 'fire-club' and make an intellectual union of good will. As he told the Harvard divinity professors, he had little use for argument.

Thoreau's loneliness was much less intellectual. He wished to be loved by friends who bared their hearts to him, as he (so he thought) bared his heart to the world. They must love him so well that they understood without being told his perverse contradicting to be only a protest against the conventions of politeness and tact. 'I live the life of the cuttle-fish; another appears, and the element in which I move is tinged and I am concealed.' [2]

Emerson irritated the cuttle-fish by retreating into politeness or good humor whenever the waters began to tinge. Thoreau in '51 was yearning toward him, more disappointed in him than in others because he enjoyed him more. By December, Emerson's 'palaver,' so he said, was threatening a friendship which must have a fierce honesty or have nothing of value for the uncompromising Thoreau. 'One of the best men' — and the context shows that he meant Emerson — was 'repeating himself, shampooing himself!' 'It is the misfortune of being a gentleman and famous.' And so the irritation grows. A mannered lecture by Thomas Wentworth Higginson reminds him of Emerson, 'and I could not afford to be reminded of Christ himself.' [3] His friend must like his hate as well as his love, take the depths of him as well as the surfaces.

> Surely, surely, thou wilt trust me
> When I say thou dost disgust me,

he wrote to Blake,[4] defining the kind of truth friends should pass on to each other. But you could not talk to Emerson that way, or to anyone else, including Thoreau himself! Something neurotic was creeping into Thoreau's ideas of friendship. 'Talked, or tried to talk, with R. W. E. Lost my time — nay, almost my identity. He, assuming a false opposition ... told me what I knew — and I lost my time trying to imagine myself somebody else to oppose him.' [5]

Of course, as he told Blake, Thoreau exaggerated whenever he had an opportunity, yet some harm was done. It was a few weeks later, in 1853, that Emerson called him 'stubborn and implacable; always manly and wise, but rarely sweet ....

He ... requires a little sense of victory,' which is a gentle, if somewhat unperceptive, return for so much rancor. Indeed, the so-called quarrel between the Concord geniuses was all on one side. 'Who has it, need never write anything but scraps. Henry Thoreau has it,' Emerson said handsomely that autumn, and then, trying to guess at the trouble, 'Henry Thoreau says he values only the man who goes directly to his needs.' After all, a philosopher who drove away his own calf from his gate could not be expected to notice that Thoreau's familiar cat-scratches had deep feeling behind them!

And this growing irritation was fed by the inevitable resentment against a patron who praised the young man when he did what was expected of him, but who seemed to cool off perceptibly when his protégé discussed his own subject, man's relation to the eternal verities, in terms too hot with scorn, too sharp with sarcasm, for the approval of an apostle of idealism. 'I should value E.'s praise more, which is always so discriminating,' Thoreau wrote in an unusually frank passage, 'if there were not some alloy of patronage and hence of flattery about [it].' [6] And so for a few years there was a coldness between them, of which Emerson seems to have been only a little aware — grievances on Henry's part, some ruffling on Emerson's. Yet as the walks and talks and dinners at Emerson's continued through all, and Emerson more and more took Henry for guide in his botanical studies, their intercourse seems to have found a safe medium in nature, and increased rather than lessened, though the warmth of the friendship never quite returned. There was a little shaking of confidence on either side, which is noticeable even in Emerson's noble funeral speech. But the oft-mentioned alienation between these two high-minded friends was at the most an inevitable misunderstanding.

3

It was not, I feel sure, of Emerson that Thoreau was thinking when he wrote with such deep grief in 1857, 'And now another friendship is ended.'

Bit by bit, a slowly developing crisis in Thoreau's life is recorded in his Journal among the happy nature notes of the years from '51 to '58. His biographers and critics have been misled in their attempts to assign its deep emotion to the cooling friendship with Emerson by a dual reference, in which a 'she' and a 'he' are purposely confused. There are passages like those quoted above in which Ralph Waldo Emerson is mentioned by name with irritation rather than sorrow, and others which sound so much more like the distress of love than the disillusionments of a cooling friendship as to arouse suspicion. Thoreau's friendship with Emerson was never deeply emotional. What specific references we have during these years show an impatience with formality, a dislike of 'shampooing,' scarcely consistent with tenderness and heart pangs. There was another friendship in distress which struck far deeper into Thoreau's sensitive heart.

In February of 1851 some friend of Henry's had begun to deal in confessions, break silence, make a theme of friendship. 'I thought that friendship, that love was still possible between [us]. I thought that we had not withdrawn very far asunder. But now that my friend rashly, thoughtlessly, profanely speaks, *recognizing* the distance between us, that distance seems infinitely increased.'

One remembers the passage already quoted from a letter to Blake on friendship, written the next year: 'I parted from my beloved because there was one thing which I had to tell her. She *questioned* me. She should have known all by sympathy. That I had to tell it her was the difference between us, — the misunderstanding.'

By April of 1851 he is writing, 'I am sure that the design of my maker when he has brought me nearest to woman was not the propagation, but rather the maturation, of the species. Man is capable of a love of woman quite transcending marriage.'

That October, Thoreau awoke one morning feeling an infinite regret after a curious dream in which his body had been a 'channel of melody' — but now he felt like 'a scuttle full of dirt.' Something had gone out of his life which left it poorer — 'a thoroughfare only as the street and the kennel.' [7]

The next morning it was snowing. He stays indoors and sets down this significant passage:

> The obstacles which the heart meets with are like granite blocks which one alone cannot move. She who was as the morning light to me is now neither the morning star nor the evening star. We meet but to find each other further asunder, and the oftener we meet the more rapid our divergence. So a star of the first magnitude pales in the heavens, not from any fault in the observer's eye nor from any fault in itself, perchance, but because its progress in its own system has put a greater distance between.

Who was she who had been the morning and evening star to him, yet now grew more distant at each meeting? It is difficult to avoid the conclusion that she was that Older Sister to whom he wrote from Staten Island, with whom he had lived in close association from 1841 to 1843 and through 1847–48. It would seem to be that Sister recorded in the manuscript lines already quoted, which belong in the year or years just before 1851: 'My sister whom I love I almost have no more to do with. I shall know where to find her . . . . I have annexed a soul to mine. When I love you I feel as if I were annexing another world . . . . O Do not disappoint me . . . . Whose eyes are like the morning stars.' Assuredly it was Lidian Emerson, aging, ill, growing more reserved, more polite, progressing in her 'own system' away from her friend. A love 'quite transcending marriage' was stiffening toward death.

The climax was delayed, as is not unusual in such ethereal relationships, and is recorded some years later in passages which for the expression of personal grief are not equalled elsewhere in Thoreau's Journal or the letters, except at the death of his brother John:

> *Feb. 8. 1857* ... And now another friendship is ended. I do not know what has made my friend doubt me, but I know that in love there is no mistake, and that every estrangement is well founded. But my destiny is not narrowed, but if possible the broader for it. The heavens withdraw and arch themselves higher. I am sensible not only of a moral, but even a grand physical pain, such as gods may feel, about my head and breast, a certain ache and fullness. This rending of a tie, it is not my work nor thine. It is no accident that we mind; it is only the awards of fate that are affecting. I know of no æons, or periods, no life and death, but these meetings and separations. My life is like a stream that is suddenly dammed and has no outlet; but it rises the higher up the hills that shut it in, and will become a deep and silent lake.... I am perfectly sad at parting from you. I could better have the earth taken away from under my feet, than the thought of you from my mind. One while I think that some great injury has been done, with which you are implicated, again that you are no party to it. I fear that there may be incessant tragedies, that one may treat his fellow as a god but receive somewhat less regard from him. I now almost for the first time *fear* this. Yet I believe that in the long run there is no such inequality.

> *Feb. 23. 1857* ... I say in my thought to my neighbor, who was once my friend, 'It is of no use to speak the truth to you, you will not hear it. What, then, shall I say to you?' At the instant that I seem to be saying farewell forever to one who has been my friend, I find myself unexpectedly near to him, and it is our very nearness and dearness to each other that gives depth and significance to that forever. Thus I am a helpless

Lidian Emerson
'*And now another friendship is ended*'
From a crayon picture by Samuel Worcester Rowse

prisoner, and these chains I have no skill to break. While I think I have broken one link, I have been forging another.

I have not yet known a friendship to cease, I think. I fear I have experienced its decaying. Morning, noon, and night, I suffer a physical pain, an aching of the breast which unfits me for my tasks. It is perhaps most intense at evening. With respect to Friendship I feel like a wreck that is driving before the gale, with a crew suffering from hunger and thirst, not knowing what shore, if any, they may reach, so long have I *breasted* the conflicting waves of this sentiment, my seams open, my timbers laid bare. I float on Friendship's sea simply because my specific gravity is less than its, but no longer that stanch and graceful vessel that careered so buoyantly over it. My planks and timbers are scattered. At most I hope to make a sort of raft of Friendship, on which, with a few of our treasures, we may float to some firm land.

That aching of the breast, the grandest pain that man endures, which no ether can assuage.... If the teeth ache they can be pulled. If the heart aches, what then? Shall we pluck it out?

To which should be added one sentence from the Journal of February 19: 'A man cannot be said to succeed in this life who does not satisfy one friend.'

Neither the cooling of Thoreau's friendship with Emerson nor the tragic ending of his intimacy with Lidian account for all these passages and the others associated with them. The Journal in which they were recorded was not a diary of names and circumstances, it was a record of Thoreau's inner life in its relation to the outside world, and his more intimate emotional experiences had always been generalized in writing them into it, and also philosophized, in order to make the description more deeply true. How much of this history of the death of a friendship belongs to Lidian, how much to Waldo, it is impossible to say with entire accuracy. But it is noteworthy that in this tragic year Emerson had been lecturing in the West through January and sending home cheerful letters to his wife, and had not returned to Concord when the poignant February 8th passage was written. And in October of this 1857 he is recording homage to the gods for his 'two gossips, Alcott and Henry T.' [8]

It was Lidian who was lost to Thoreau, and surely Lidian who was causing that 'aching of the breast' which was 'perhaps most intense at evening.' Such pain would be frankly surprising if aroused by the too aloof Emerson, who, by all direct evidence, never stirred those deeper emotional currents in Thoreau which responded so readily to nature and to women. He writes of this 'physical pain' as he wrote only to Lidian, to Lucy Brown, and, probably, to Ellen Sewall. Emerson was his friend, but Henry's friendship with Lidian was mingled with the longing and the agony of love. I suspect that his neurotic irritability in Emerson's society was an offshoot of the more emotional relationship slowly dying in that house.

Of Lidian we know little in these years, except that she was an invalid, so feeble at one time that Emerson thought of giving up his home,[9] deeply pious, a self-effacing person more and more wrapped up in her family as she grew older. She is never mentioned by name in Thoreau's Journal, and never in his published letters after 1848. In Emerson, he was at the most temporarily disappointed. Their meetings were never interrupted and their friendship was close until Henry's death. It was she of the morning and evening star who was leaving Thoreau.

4

Whatever is the exact truth, here is certainly a powerful cause of the sublimation of Thoreau's craving for human love into a passion for nature. A year after that February when his friend confessed the growing distances between them, there is a sudden outburst in his Journal in the midst of routine description of a walk:

> *April 11, 1852....* I hear the sound of the piano below as I write this, and feel as if the winter in me were at length beginning to thaw, for my spring has been even more backward than nature's. For a month past life has been a thing incredible to me. None but the kind gods can make me sane. If only they will let their south winds blow on me! I ask to be melted. You can only ask of the metals that they be tender to the fire that *melts* them. To naught else can they be tender.

The kind gods did make, or rather keep, him sane. 'If I am too cold for human friendship, I trust I shall not soon be too cold for natural influences. It appears to be a law that you cannot have a deep sympathy with both man and nature.' (He knew he was not cold, and often said so.) In November, he had been walking toward Conantum feeling blessed. 'I love my life. I warm toward all nature.' In the long descent into loneliness, which lasted from 1851 to 1857, he found his satisfactions increasingly in nature, in part, certainly, because the human love which meant so much to him was decaying. As a friend and lover he felt like a wreck drifting before the gale; but outdoors, in his new obsession with nature, he was happy. He found compensation there because love of nature was better suited to his intense temperament than any love of man or woman possible for him — at least in Puritan Concord.

22. TOWNSMAN OF CONCORD

Oᴜʀ ᴛʜᴏᴜɢʜᴛs ᴀʀᴇ the epochs of our life: all else is but as a journal of the winds that blew while we were here.'

Those winds blew more to Henry Thoreau than he was willing to admit. His Journal, like most men's lives, steps ahead on experience as often as upon thought. It is his experience as a neighbor, as a townsman of Concord, and as a writer at work in his upper chamber, that I wish to record in this chapter.

At dawn on July 16 of 1850 Margaret Fuller's homecoming ship had struck upon the sands of Fire Island beach, and only some sailors escaped. Thoreau, who was commissioned to visit the scene and recover, if possible, her manuscripts and what might be salvaged of the Ossoli belongings, was surprised that his questioning of the witnesses and the sight of a sailor's dead body on the lonely beach moved him so little. From this most tragic of his Excursions he enriched his Journal with accounts of a drunken Dutchman on the boat from Patchogue and descriptions of the sands after a storm. 'I have never met with anything so truly visionary and accidental as some actual events,' he said. 'They have affected me less than my dreams.' Yet the experience went deeper than he thought. He dreamed of the buttons on dead men's clothes, and remembered in his walks on Cape Cod the relentlessness of the sea, which disregarded his 'snivelling sympathies.' Only a few fragments of clothing and the story of the wreck rewarded his painstaking search. He was not much moved. Margaret herself had never got beyond the frontier of his emotion.

In that year of 1850 he went on a cheap excursion with Channing to Montreal and Quebec, carrying his baggage in a brown-paper parcel, and wearing a palmleaf hat and a duster over his coat. He wanted 'one honest walk' there, and got it.

He was determined in these years not to live a life of prudence, but to 'entertain sublime conjectures.' What conjectures he entertained in 1851 when Lidian was turning cold to him were of love and marriage. He confesses that he is chaste but impure. Purity, which sometimes with him means unworldliness, and sometimes freedom from sexual desire, is an often repeated theme. He is upset by levity in talk of the sexes, yet apparently his thoughts were often warm. These were the speculations on love, marriage, and sensuality which he poured into the several times mentioned letter to Blake the next year — a document extraordinarily discerning for a celibate. Though quite certainly virgin, Thoreau was neither prudish nor pathologically virtuous. 'The intercourse of the sexes, I have dreamed, is incredibly beautiful, too fair to be remembered.' Love for him was inseparably intertwined with idealism.

This year of 1851, he took ether, lost more teeth, and substituted false ones, which may have increased the characteristic pucker of his mouth. Always the scholar, he got a book on dentistry so as to study his own case. This was a Yankee trait, and so was his quiet humor, a silent humor with a grave face, though he could laugh loudly. Wild apples were pleasing him now. He gives Latin names to a series, including the green apple, *Malus viridis*, and the Cholera-morbus apple.

But if Yankee to the core, the germinal seed of the man was still Transcendental and romantic. He awoke on these mornings when all Concord outdoors waited, with a sense of 'sacred and memorable life' and of unremembered dreams that had been divine. His sensitiveness may seem excessive. The music of an organ-grinder thrills the street with harmony, 'loosening the very paving-stones and tearing the routine of life to rags and tatters.... It is after all, perhaps, the best instrumental music that we have.' [1] But this is no more absurd in its way than Clough's description of Walden woods (which he visited with Emerson) as resembling a plantation about a 'prettyish pond.' Thoreau, as Channing said, was fond of maximizing the minimum. No one who heard him lecture would have accused him of too much sensibility; he seemed abstruse and obscure. Yet push his common sense too hard and 'I begin to be transcendental and show where my heart is.' It was a romantic heart joined to a cool and active brain. 'I wonder that I ever get five miles on my way, the walk is so crowded with events and phenomena.'

A few days after his thirty-fourth birthday, July 12, 1851, his life seemed to him still 'almost wholly unexpanded,' which, Transcendentally speaking, may have been true, but not otherwise. That summer he wore his best black pants on a trip to Marston Watson's place at Plymouth, a great gathering spot for Transcendentalists, which he was later to survey. He saw Ellen Sewall at Cohasset, but makes no mention, and wrote up the journey in a plain style very different from the mannered diction recording those excursions which were taken to get materials for lecturing. There was a literary Thoreau, a reporter Thoreau, and just Thoreau who wrote up these notes. The literary Thoreau is evidently the man he describes 'who lives at last by watching his moods. An old poet comes at last to watch his moods as narrowly as a cat does a mouse.' [2]

He caught cold on his Canadian trip, but came home with an edge to his mind. A cold in the head, he reflects, can make a humanitarian of any man. When his bowels are out of order, he finds that he is unduly sympathetic with society and actually cries over a pathetic story. It took illness to make Thoreau read fiction! Emerson's marvellous old Aunt Mary Emerson, the saltiest and youngest woman in Concord in spite of her eighty years, restored him. She was 'singular, among women at least, in being really and perseveringly interested to know what thinkers think,' and could 'entertain a large thought with hospitality' — surely one of the handsomest remarks ever made of a woman's intellect. She liked Thoreau, but not her own sex. 'Be still,' she used to say. 'I want to hear the men talk.'

The next day, in November of 1851, he met two young women at a party. The first was 'loquacious as a chickadee'; the other was 'said to be pretty-looking, but I rarely look people in their faces.' Being pretty might be a reason for look-ing at her, but not for talking to her, so he left. Young women 'are so light and flighty that you can never be sure whether they are there or not there.' Two young women — 'pariahs' — once stole his dipper at Walden. Yet he did talk to young people about Christ and Moses at someone's house, stirring up a ruction with the old people. 'They don't want to have any prophets born into their families, — damn them!' Emerson was still regarded as a dangerous radical in faith and in opinion in the fifties, and Thoreau shared his reputation.

Though so easily moved by the right women, he was no feminist. His sensitive nostrils were outraged by the scent of cologne that lingered after he had carried Elizabeth Oakes Smith's lecture on womanhood in his pocket, while he escorted her to the Lyceum. She was just a woman, after all, in spite of her propaganda for women's rights; and he talked down to her. 'You had to fire small charges.... I had to unshot all

the guns in truth's battery and fire powder and wadding only.' [3]
Now that Margaret Fuller was dead, no one but Aunt Mary
could challenge his intellect successfully. Yet his heart was soft.

He was subscribing to the weekly *Tribune*, the troublous times
having beaten him out of his contempt for newspapers, but he
found reading news once a week distracted him too much from
Concord, which tended to seem dull. With the approaching
crisis in the slavery question, it took discipline, sometimes,
to keep his mind at home.

Channing gave a lecture which was 'a bushel of nuts' and
quite unintelligible to the audience. Henry visited two women,
one of whom (Elizabeth Hoar, I suppose) thought that he was
conceited; the other (Lidian perhaps) believed his actions to
be better than his principles, which grew more not less radical.

His reading now follows close upon his experience, and is
designed to enrich it. For an excursion, like the trip to Canada,
he prepared as for an examination.[4] 'Decayed literature makes
the richest of all soils,' he says, a wise remark, recommended
to young writers. Kossuth makes his triumphal tour (this is
April of 1852) but is snubbed by Thoreau, who does not like
his fondness for publicity. Thoreau lectures in Boston on his
life at Walden, but to a handful only of people; the clerks at
the other end of the reading-room would not put down their
newspapers to listen, even when urged by Alcott. Henry was
really no more pleased by this ill success than Kossuth would
have been, though he pretended to despise the amusement-
seeking multitude. When young Edith Emerson asked whether
he could interest her with his lecture, he was embarrassed.

2

Epigrams now drop frequently into the Journal, for he has
plenty of time to sharpen his sentences: 'Every poet has trembled

on the verge of science,' a profoundly true remark; 'The youth gets together his materials to build a bridge to the moon, or perchance a palace or temple on the earth, and at length the middle-aged man concludes to build a wood-shed with them'; 'A man is wise with the wisdom of his time only, and ignorant with its ignorance.' Such sentences are very different from the labored humor assigned to Thoreau in Channing's 'Walks and Talks' which were supposed to have been about this period. And indeed a little later he turns upon an anonymous friend, quite certainly Channing, who tempts him to 'harsh, extravagant, and cynical expressions concerning mankind and individuals,' not in accord with his 'sober and constant view.' [5] The paradox and the eccentric statement were native to Thoreau, as to all Transcendentalists, but his common sense restrained them, while Channing was always prodding him toward the overemphasis which he knew to be his fault.

These early years of the fifties were not always happy, even in the fields. He was hot-foot after his 'mistress' nature, who, however, was often by no means his mistress but a textbook in which he tried to find a science that was not too scientific. It was hard to find such a science. It was hard to feel 'blessed' while tracing in detail the root system of a tree, absorbing as these amateur researches might prove. He writes to Sophia in Bangor, July 13 of 1852:

> I am... slackened and rusty.... I am not on the trail of any elephants or mastodons, but have succeeded in trapping only a few ridiculous mice, which cannot feed my imagination. ... I would rather come upon the vast valley-like 'spoor' only of some celestial beast which this world's woods can no longer sustain, than spring my net over a bushel of moles.

Concord delighted him not in such moods, nor the United States neither. Frigidity at Emerson's as well as the mice and moles of the countryside may have made his home town seem less of a paradise than formerly, yet he still infinitely preferred its pastoral duties and the high talk of the intellectuals to the great boom on which his countrymen were riding toward the depression of 1857. There is some of the extravagance and cynicism for which he apologized in what he wrote:

> The whole enterprise of this nation, which is not an upward, but a westward one, toward Oregon, California, Japan, etc., is totally devoid of interest to me, whether performed on foot, or by a Pacific railroad. It is not illustrated by a thought; it is not warmed by a sentiment; there is nothing in it which one should lay down his life for, nor even his gloves, — hardly which one should take up a newspaper for. It is perfectly heathenish, — a filibustering *toward* heaven by the great western route. No; they may go their way to their manifest destiny, which I trust is not mine....
>
> As it respects these things, I have not changed an opinion one iota from the first. As the stars looked to me when I was a shepherd in Assyria, they look to me now, a New-Englander.[6]

He was surveying, sometimes for twenty or thirty days at a stretch when weather permitted. In 1853, he laid out house lots in Haverhill, where the young ladies disgusted him by not knowing the way to the nearest woods. In May, he spent a day with Alcott, who was 'forever feeling about vainly in his speech and touching nothing.' Yet Alcott never brought up like other men against an institution. 'Every other man owns stock in this or that one, and will not forget it.' This is the reason Thoreau liked and respected the arch idealist.

It was this spring when the 'beardless woods' had 'downy cheeks as yet' that his marvellous sense of smell detected Melvin's hidden azalea. He could sniff the smoke of a pipe a third of a mile away. And it was this June when three reformers at his mother's house mouthed him all over in their attempt to get his stubborn sympathies. He hated reformers who had not reformed themselves. If possible, he was getting

testier; it was the year that Emerson irritated him. Yet Moncure Conway, on vacation from Harvard Divinity School,
who walked with him in the summer, says his 'every movement
was full of courage and repose.' He speaks of his nose, which
Emerson said was like the prow of a ship, and adds that he was
not talkative, except in spurts of monologue.[7]

In September of '53, he went north for his second trip to
the Maine woods. In October, he was raising funds for a poor
Irishman. Someone should write an essay on Thoreau and the
Irish. They continually exasperated him by living in a wide
margin of the wrong kind of leisure. At Lowell, the voters
were firing off cannon to celebrate a Whig victory, which was
no concern of his. Lecturing he still regards as his profession
and continues to do so, even after 'Walden' made its success.
'A hundred others in New England cannot lecture as well as
I on my themes.' Yet although he has offered himself much
more earnestly as a lecturer than as a surveyor, he was not
wanted at all in the previous winter, and only once, without
pay, in 1853. 'But they who do not make the highest demand
on you shall rue it.... All the while that they use only your
humbler faculties, your higher unemployed faculties, like an
invisible cimetar, are cutting them in twain.'[8] The scimitar
was 'Walden,' still six months from publication.

3

He began 1854 with a journey to Blake at Worcester, and a
new coat, since Cynthia and Sophia would not let him go in
his old one. Having surveyed a disputed water-right, he was
called to court in Cambridge, and is often an expert witness
from now on. All winter, and especially in March, he was
working upon the final draft of 'Walden,' making finally a
little chapter of contents, so that he could recall it page by page

and judge it more impartially than from the manuscript. He
met Concord now on more equal terms, being both surveyor
and author of a second book; yet it seemed stiffer than ever.
'Do they not know that I can laugh?' They might have smiled
at *him*, for in August, with 'Walden' just out, Emerson describes him as 'walking up & down Concord, firm-looking, but
in a tremble of expectation.' ⁹

Sophia and his mother and various naturalist friends often
go boating with him — perhaps because he had to balance his
craft with stones when he sailed alone. He is becoming more
social; drinks tea and coffee and makes himself 'cheap and
vulgar.' 'I have seen more men than usual, lately,' he writes
Blake in August. 'They do a little business commonly each
day ... and then ... paddle in the social slush.' To escape he
went to Fair Haven bay, where he 'got the world, as it were, by
the nape of the neck, and held it under in the tide of its own
events, till it was drowned, and then I let it go down-stream like
a dead dog.' That autumn of '54 he went lecturing to Plymouth, and expected, probably on the strength of 'Walden,' to
be asked like Emerson to the West, but no invitations came.
Thomas Cholmondeley, the English wanderer, who had written
a book on New Zealand, was staying at the house in order to
be near Emerson. Thoreau took him on a walk to Wachusett
and gained his lifelong admiration. In November, Abbé
Adrien Rouquette, of a Creole family in Louisiana, sent him
three books and a letter in French. Rouquette was an admirer
of Chateaubriand, an authority on the history of monastic
solitude, and a friend of the Choctaws, with whom he had
lived.¹⁰ Thoreau's modest fame was spreading. Furness, friend
of Emerson and father of the Shakespearean editor, brings him
to Philadelphia, where he lectures, again unsuccessfully, and is
taken to the American Philosophical Society, 'a company of
old women.' It was en route, in New York, that Greeley took

Crayon portrait of Thoreau by Samuel Worcester Rowse
'His soul was made for the noblest society'

him to the opera, but he was more impressed by Barnum's camelopards. In December, he lectures at Providence and fails again. 'I would rather write books than lectures. That is fine, this coarse.' Unfortunately he continued to write lectures, which had to be rewritten for his books. It is a curious instance of the strength of the New England habit of teaching by word of mouth.

Daniel Ricketson, the well-to-do New Bedford Quaker, bought a copy of 'Walden.' Although he thought much in Thoreau's books was 'namby-pamby' and 'mystical' and wished he would tell men in plain English how to live the simple life, nevertheless he was impressed by the man and learned to like and admire him.[11] When Thoreau went lecturing to New Bedford, he stayed with Ricketson, thus beginning a pleasant habit, for he was much at his ease with this plain, unspiritual Friend, who loved nature but was terribly afraid of thunderstorms and dying. Thoreau arrived the first time carrying a portmanteau in one hand and an umbrella in the other, dressed in a long overcoat of dark color, and wearing a dark soft hat. The drawing Ricketson made of him from memory was 'by no means a bad likeness,' says Sanborn, 'of the plain and upright Thoreau.' It is interesting, for, unlike his other pictures, it shows his receding chin, and his real homeliness from a side view where you could not see his remarkable eyes. Like Furness's caricature, made when Thoreau was in Philadelphia, it does justice to his nose. 'As he came near to me I gave him the usual salutation . . . supposing him to be either a pedler or some way-traveller,' says Ricketson, who was clearing the snow from his front steps when Thoreau arrived. His lecture in New Bedford was 'Getting a Living,' afterward to become famous as 'Life Without Principle'; much of it drawn from the Journal of 1854, and inspired by his outburst over slavery which I am leaving for a later chapter. As for these lectures,

'I do my work clean as I go along, and they will not be likely to want me anywhere again,' — an admirable prescription for any lecturer, but death to a lecture bureau!

4

At the beginning of 1855 he was still the vigorous Henry Thoreau, whose physical activity Emerson admired, capable of tree-climbing, swamp-wading, woods-walking, with swimming in summer and skating (thirty miles of it in one day) in winter. Until this year he never complained of weariness. Something physical pervades his frequent commendation of war as an exercise of the heroic in man, of which there had been a good deal in his youthful 'The Service.' He is a little wiser now. Cholmondeley had left for home, rather expecting to be drawn into the Crimean conflict, already raging in front of Sevastopol. Thoreau doubted the morality of the English cause but doubted also those who were preaching against it: 'It is a pity that we seem to require a war, from time to time,' he wrote to Cholmondeley, 'to assure us that there is any manhood still left in man.' Like all radicals, he was not averse to violence in a good cause, and his faith in the warrior virtues was to make the outbreak of the Civil War welcome, at first!

The vigor of the man, which seemed constantly to thwart itself in inner conflict, was what impressed Cholmondeley, who also was a seeker. Travel and the sensation of Being quieted Cholmondeley's distress, for when he asked God, as Thoreau did so often, 'What, O Lord, will you do with me in particular?' God's answer was, 'Enjoy yourself, and leave the rest to itself.' He was a dilettante in life as Channing was in literature, and, like Channing, tried to penetrate Thoreau's reserve of discontent beneath the joy of simple living. 'You are not living altogether as I could wish,' he wrote to him from Rome in 1856. 'You

A pencil sketch by Daniel Ricketson. It carried the inscription:
H. D. Thoreau as he presented himself at the door of
Brooklawn, Dec. 25th, 1854
'*By no means a bad likeness . . . of the plain and upright Thoreau*'

ought to have society. A college, a conventual life is for you. You should be the member of some society not yet formed.... Your love for ... Nature is ancillary to some affection which you have not yet discovered.... What you are engaged in I suspect to be Meditations on the Higher Laws as they show themselves in Common Things. This ... may become too desultory. Try a history. How if you could write the sweet, beautiful history of Massachusetts? ... Or take Concord.... Take the spirit of Walton and a spice of White!' [12] But this wise letter was as unlikely now to change Thoreau's mode of life as the Hindu books which Cholmondeley had sent to him the year before.

It was in this March of 1855 that his biographer Sanborn took a small school in Concord, on invitation from Emerson and his friends, and began to dine at Mrs. Thoreau's, where he saw Henry almost daily for three years.

The winter of 1855, with its suggestion of spring, was to be his last with full assurance of health and outdoor happiness. The warm airs that blew made him forget his chagrins in society, and love nature again. 'Here is my Italy, my heaven, my New England. I understand why the Indians hereabouts placed heaven in the southwest, — the soft south.... It would not be worth the while to die and leave all this life behind one. ... The sky ... seems like the inside of a shell deserted of its tenant, into which I have crawled.' 'Ah, bless the Lord, O my soul! bless him for wildness, for crows that will not alight within gunshot! and bless him for hens, too, that croak and cackle in the yard!'

In March, he was flapping his sides with his elbows, as with wings, and 'uttering something like the syllables *mow-ack* with a nasal twang and twist in my head,' to see whether he could draw down the flocks of geese that flew over. It was in this month that he caught and tried vainly to tame a flying squirrel.

The Journal for this spring is entirely objective, packed with scientific detail, the dissection of a dead duck, for example, so that it is with surprise that one comes upon a note of his old morbidity on June 11:

> I knock on the earth for my friend. I expect to meet him at every turn; but no friend appears, and perhaps none is dreaming of me.... One complains that I do not take his jokes [Channing surely]. I took them before he had done uttering them, and went my way. One talks to me of his apples and pears [Emerson presumably], and I depart with my secret untold. His are not the apples that tempt me.

This time the melancholy may have been due to his health. Sometime in April he began to decline, but now it was not bronchitis. His legs began to fail him; what the trouble was he did not know, and the Journal shows that in the spring when, so he told Blake, he was good for nothing but to be on his back, he was still pushing himself relentlessly to walk, and climb. In June he gave up, went to Cape Cod in July, where he sat in the sun, tried to cheer himself by reflecting on men who outlived their companions, and was still wondering at the end of September how strength was to be got into his legs again. 'God *does* delight in the strength of a man's legs.' It was Christmas before Henry had any confidence in his, nor were they ever quite the same again.

Sanborn, who was eating at the Thoreau house this spring, says he was much occupied with his home duties. There is no mention of graphite, but unpublished letters indicate that the orders for electrotype graphite dust were coming in abundantly this year. It is possible, even probable, that Thoreau helped, at least with the packing, and may have suffered from inhaling the dust. This illness was the most serious since his breakdown in his junior year in college, and this time it was presumably an onset upon the tissue of the lungs, with resulting weakness, which was slowed down by his healthy life outdoors, but never stopped. For Thoreau, of course, weakness would be most resented in those sturdy pistons that had to propel him over so many miles of wood and pasture walking. If he could not count on his legs, he was a sad man indeed.

Still, by October, he could survey again, split wood, carry on in general, but when he visited Ricketson he drove out to the ponds instead of walking. His outdoor life this autumn is chiefly on the river, where he sees more people, for the farmers work in the meadows and Goodwin and Melvin are hunting and fishing. Once again the Journal expands into set-pieces for lectures and a possible book. 'Autumnal Tints' begins to accumulate paragraphs, as 'Wild Apples' had done earlier. Yet among these abundant nature notes is that curious list of the many houses in which he had lived, set down with the aid of his mother's memory. The first step of a biographer, he notes, and presumably means his own, if he ever should have one, 'will be to establish these facts.' 'No doubt,' he wrote earlier, 'the healthiest man in the world is prevented from doing what he would like by sickness.' Yet he still regarded himself as the healthy member of a frail family, and still admitted illness only as an alternate to health, from which profit could be drawn by a stout mind. Fortunately, he was to have a respite, a renewal of vigor, and a chance for the final maturing of his talents.

23. TRAVELS AND EXCURSIONS

Although, with his love of paradox, Henry Thoreau said that he had travelled much in the town of Concord, his excursions were, of course, not always limited by the rivers and the boundaries of the town. Regularly, when July and August came, he set off for a trip, sometimes alone, more often with a companion, the first of which was the week on the Concord and the Merrimack rivers, the last his melancholy pilgrimage West in search of health. These were his vacations, his recreation as distinguished from his business of observation. While he studied and read in preparation for these summer trips, and wrote up most of them from careful notes, still he did not feel responsible for America and even for New England, outside of Concord: these regions were extra-curricular, not related with the same intensity of emotion to himself. His travels abroad are usually cooler, much less intimate than his Concord books. They have the air, and rightly, of having been done for a change from work at home. Yet those who find 'Walden' too much of a tract read 'Cape Cod' with more pleasure than his more thoughtful books.

Excursions he called all his walks or rows or paddles, when

he used them for lectures or magazine articles. But there are three kinds of excursions, with significant differences among them. That week on the rivers with John was originally such a narrative as his story of his trip to the Maine woods, but became something very different — a record, indeed, of his inner life with a narrative thread. 'Walden,' too, was originally an excursion into the woods, with an idea behind it which spread filaments of hard thinking and brilliant satire through the narrative.

His travel books on Maine, Canada, and Cape Cod and his mountain essays have their own character also. They are really guide books to the forest wilderness, to the ocean and its sands, and to France in America. Motion by canoe or by sturdy legs is the thread which holds them together. They are a reporter's journals, useful and suggestive rather than provocative and stimulating.

His excursions within the bounds of Concord were quite different, although, of course, the genres overlap. These dealt with aspects of that Concord environment about which some day he proposed to make a book. Here are his observations of wild animals and birds, of wild apples, of the tints of autumn leaves, of night and moonlight. Although 'Wild Apples,' particularly, is one of the most successful of his writings, these travels in Concord are experimental, not finished. As good examples exist unassembled within his Journal as the lectures which were hastily polished off in his last months and published in the posthumous book called 'Excursions.'

The guide books are complete in themselves, though not finished. I think Thoreau fell into the way of writing them, and his briefer accounts of trips to the mountain summits, because he liked to travel, and wanted to publish as well as to lecture. American magazines have always been hospitable to travel narratives. They would print, and the readers would read, a story of sights by the road, when a thoughtful essay would go begging. Thoreau's first break into print, outside the friendly *Dial* (which itself printed reluctantly his 'Winter Walk'), was with 'A Walk to Wachusett' in *The Boston Miscellany*. Except for the essay on Carlyle, which Greeley railroaded into *Graham's*, and the review of Etzler in *The Democratic Review*, no important piece of his, except travel narrative, was published in his lifetime in a magazine for the general public.

What was true of the magazines was still more true of the lecture platform. If Thoreau was ever successful as a lecturer, it was with stories of excursions, including the adventure at Walden Pond.

2

His three guide books, 'A Yankee in Canada,' 'The Maine Woods,' and 'Cape Cod,' are all propaganda for the art of sauntering with an open eye, and for the proper use of leisure. Except for this they carry little of his philosophy, and are relatively simple in their writing, factual, and direct. His personality is dominant, but not egocentric; only the reporter and the observer are active in these stories. The tone is light, events and people abundant. It is a good kind of writing, a flow of narrative unchecked by much introspection, yet carrying history, natural science, character study, and interesting aspects of novel scenes on its easy current. Much more could be said of them by way of literary criticism. Biographically, however, they are less interesting than the Journal because they represent Thoreau as a man on vacation, free of his personal problems and his duties in Concord.

The 'Yankee in Canada' is the most casual of these books. Thoreau and Channing had only twelve and a half days on their round trip in 1853, so that in spite of Henry's study of

Canadian background books, the description is thin, and the narrative that of any intelligent tourist. The paragraphs on the Catholic cathedral in Montreal, with their recognition, surprising in this arch Protestant, of the beauty and importance of a religious environment, are worth all the rest.

To Cape Cod, however, that 'bared and bended arm of Massachusetts,' he went four times — in 1849 with Channing, in 1850 alone, in 1855 with Channing, and in 1852 alone again, taking a week or more on each trip. The first trip he used as the outline for his book, stuffing in incidents from the two later ones. He was still working at the whole story in 1859, and probably later, yet the book, as we have it, is only revised, not finished. The records of his fourth trip remain in his Journal.

This was an expedition more sympathetic to his own genius than the excursion among the alien French. The explorer of lakes and rivers wished to know the sea, and the botanist of the inland hoped to study the effect of sea wind and sand upon the New England flora. To these natural phenomena he added sea folk and their ways, thus humanizing a narrative which has always been a favorite. Off on vacation, he escapes from the tensity of his home books — writes less passionately, less richly, but with an ease and fluency that is engaging. He needed this expansion of experience in order to make his view of nature more complete. The tropics and the West were next on his agenda, but health kept him from the West Indies and made his Western journey a mockery.

'The Maine Woods' is not so much one book as three essays recording trips to the wilderness in 1846, in 1853, and in 1857. It lacks a fourth and summary chapter, which might well have been such an essay on wilderness as 'Wild Apples' is a study of pastures on their way back to nature. When he left his Walden hut in the summer of 1846, it was to see such a wilderness as

Concord had been when the first settlers came. He had to go
far to find it, for the loggers had already stripped the pine from
the lakes and rivers, and only on Katahdin, the highest mountain of the region, did he find primeval conditions. His second
journey was a study of fluvial transportation by canoe, and was
inspired chiefly by his desire to learn more of the great moose,
that most primeval of all dwellers in the wilderness, and most
mythologically representative of the environment. He had an
Indian guide this time; and for the third trip made the Indian
his theme and study, fortunately getting a better specimen of
the race. Joe Polis taught him (after much questioning) the
science and instinct of the forest man. He learned from him,
as he learned from the muskrat and the snapping-turtle in
Concord, how wild life adapts itself to its environment. To
say that this interest was anthropological is to say too much.
In spite of the mass of notes he accumulated for a book on
Indian history, his real interests stopped with behavior, and a
contrast with European civilization. He wanted to see an
instinctive woodsman in action. He himself was only a villager
gone partly wild.

'The Maine Woods' is still as good a book as can be read in
preparation for a north woods journey. It is full of practicable
description, and will stir in advance the imagination of the
wilderness tramper. That is what he wrote it for. The other
virtues of admirable description, of shrewd and humorous comment, and an unsurpassable atmosphere of forest and of lake,
were added naturally because the writer was Thoreau. Less
mannered, less picturesque, and less adventurous than George
Borrow's almost contemporary 'Lavengro' and 'The Bible in
Spain,' this book and 'Cape Cod' are not less excellent in
imaginative description.

They are good Yankee books, curious, factual, intelligent,
books of Thoreau the inquiring reporter, lacking, except here

and there, the Transcendental depths and also the tortuousness of Thoreau the man of letters. This was the kind of book he set out to write when he was, as he said, a reporter of the wild life about Walden Pond; but that famous narrative was enriched into wider significance because it had an idea.

Readers who take too literally Thoreau's attacks upon society and his praise of nature, beasts, and solitude have found 'Cape Cod' the most human of his books, and 'The Maine Woods' the most normal. 'Normal' is not always an adjective of praise when applied to a genius; but 'human' is — and there is a good deal of warrant for it in both of these narratives. Outside of Concord, with its intellectuals, and its stiff shirts who condemned him, Thoreau reveals himself as his family knew him at home. He is a good traveller in the Maine woods, considerate of his companions, helpful in camp, careful to treat his Indians like friends, and so get the best of them. And on Cape Cod, his talent for friendship with eccentric personalities is very evident. The lighthouse keeper became his companion; the old man badgered by women opened out to him; he could get the right word from children and fishermen's wives. With simple people he was kindly, humorous, and interested. His prickles subsided, because there was no arrogance, no manner, and no triviality to raise them. At a symposium, Henry was a little frightening, but anyone would have liked to walk the beach with him, or take the bow paddle in his canoe.

3

Innocuous as these books seem to be in comparison with the radicalism of 'Walden,' the publication of the original essays from which they were assembled made more trouble for Thoreau and his editors than his more famous books. The rows in which he was involved over the attempts to make him palatable to the narrow-minded shed light on the ill success with the public of 'A Week' and the long deferring of 'Walden.'

'Our tough Yankee must have his tough verse,' Emerson had written to Margaret Fuller when Thoreau insisted upon his own version of a line in *The Dial*.[1] He was always tough with editors. George William Curtis, who edited *Putnam's Monthly*, objected to his 'defiant Pantheism'[2] and cut from the Canadian articles such passages as: 'I am not sure but this Catholic religion would be an admirable one if the priest were quite omitted.'

'The editor requires the liberty to omit the heresies without consulting me,' Thoreau wrote to Blake, 'a privilege California is not rich enough to bid for,' and got back the unpublished remainder of the series. There was another row over 'Cape Cod,' the first instalments of which were severely, indeed abominably, cut, and the rest withdrawn.[3] But the tough Yankee's most violent explosion came later.

Curtis was his friend. But James Russell Lowell, the first editor of *The Atlantic Monthly*, belonged to the gilded world which Thoreau distrusted in Harvard and afterward. When he asked Thoreau for an account of his last trip to the Maine woods, he got 'Chesuncook,' since the third essay contained too much personal to Joe Polis to permit of immediate publication. But when he published 'Chesuncook' in June and July of 1858, and cut without permission, as Curtis had done, omitting a 'pantheistic' sentence about a pine tree, Thoreau boiled over. The letter he wrote when he discovered that his heresy had disappeared between proof and magazine has, I believe, never been printed. It should be framed in every editorial office, as a reminder of what angry authors (too angry to be elegant) think of editors who meddle with their text.

Concord June 22^d 1858.

Dear Sir,

When I received the proof of that portion of my story printed in the May number of your magazine, I was surprised to find that the sentence — 'It is as immortal as I am, and perchance will go to as high a heaven, there to tower above me still.' — (which comes directly after the words 'heal my cuts,' page 230, tenth line from the top,) had been crossed out, and it occurred to me that, after all, it was of some consequence that I should see the proofs; supposing, of course, that my 'Stet' &c in the margin would be respected, as I perceive that it was in other cases of comparatively little importance to me. However, I have just noticed that that sentence was, in a very mean and cowardly manner, omitted. I hardly need to say that this is a liberty which I will not permit to be taken with my Ms. The editor has, in this case, no more right to omit a sentiment than to insert one, or put words into my mouth. I do not ask anybody to adopt my opinions, but I do expect that when they ask for them to print, they will print them, or obtain my consent to their alteration, or omission. I should not read many books if I thought that they had been thus expurgated. I feel this treatment to be an insult, though not intended as such, for it is to presume that I can be hired to suppress my opinions.

I do not mean to charge you with this omission, for I cannot believe that you knew anything about it, but there must be a responsible editor somewhere, and you to whom I entrusted my Ms. are the only party that I know in this matter. I therefore write to ask if you sanction this omission, and if there are any other sentiments to be omitted in the remainder of my article. If you do not sanction it — or whether you do or not — will you do me the justice to print that sentence, as an omitted one, indicating its place, in the August number?

I am not writing to be associated in any way, unnecessarily, with parties who will confess themselves so bigoted & timid as this implies. I could excuse a man who was afraid of an up-lifted fist, but if one habitually manifests fear at the utterance of a sincere thought, I must think that his life is a kind of night-mare continued into broad day-light. It is hard to conceive of

one so completely *derivative*. Is this the avowed character of the
Atlantic Monthly? I should like an early reply.

Yrs truly,

HENRY D. THOREAU [4]

Lowell never made the acknowledgment — perhaps it was
too late. He had taken a beating from Parke Godwin on
March 26 for a much more outrageous example of editorial
interference, and was probably not in a mood for apologies.[5]
Thoreau wrote him stiffly in October asking for a settlement.
The Atlantic owed him $198 for thirty-three pages at six dollars
a page, which was more than he got from *Putnam's*, more than
he ever got from any magazine, but not enough for an insult.[6]
It was not till *The Atlantic* had a new editor in the publisher
Fields that Thoreau consented to prepare some of his Excursions
for the magazine, and he was dead before they were published.

4

The hypothetical book, which was to be the synthesis and
summary of these years of close observation in Concord, has
been mentioned many times in this biography. I have called
it for convenience, and because Thoreau used the term, the
natural history of Concord. Yet its scope was clearly to be
broader than this title implies. It was certainly not to become
a scientific volume classifying all natural phenomena. Nothing
is more evident to the reader of the Journal than the preliminary
character of Thoreau's classifying work. He made his repeated
observations of the seasons year by year, his great sheets of
flower-bloomings, now in the Morgan library, and his elaborate
analyses of the appearance, behavior, and structure of every
variety of natural object, as a means of knowing, not as an end
in themselves. When he has studied the lichens, the andromedas,
the owls, and the muskrat, they begin to appear with more

specific mention in those purely literary descriptions which are the distillations of his studies. And those descriptions are themselves submitted to a refining, condensing, and truing process until each sentence faces the elements with its feet squarely on the ground. His nature essays were, indeed, broader in purpose than any mere natural history, and so would have been his book. They imply, and often contain, a philosophy; they aim at beauty, and often reach it; they are humanized, not factual; and they have the quality inherent in all good art of suggesting more than the reason alone can apprehend. Nature in them is an aspect of the 'sweet mystery of life.'

Alcott urged him on when he took tea with him in February of 1861, after his fatal illness had begun. Thoreau had been 'classifying and arranging his papers by subjects, as if he had a new book in mind. I wish him to compile his Atlas of Concord, for which he has rich material, and the genius; but he must work in his own ways and times.' [7] All that was salvaged was the 'Excursions,' revised from old lectures and printed in *The Atlantic Monthly* and later in book form after his death. Yet these show what he might have done, even with what was at hand in his Journal, if he had begun, say, in 1857 or 1858, to bring together a book of representative nature studies, instead of working at science until there was only time to polish up what had already been quarried from his diaries.

Such a book might well have advertised one aspect of Thoreau's writing for which he has never received due credit. As he grew older, his travels in Concord became more and more fluvial. No river, not even the Thames, has been more lovingly, more accurately, observed and interpreted than were the Concord and the Sudbury by him. A volume of Fluvial Excursions needs only to be lifted and assembled from his Journal pages. There are the quaint and charming paragraphs on the watery search for driftwood, which, trailed home behind his boat, reveals its varying nature in the flame. There are midsummer idylls, when, naked, he takes the river bottom for his path and walks through the underworld of turtles and fish. 'In one somewhat muddier place, close to the shore, I came upon an old pout cruising with her young. She dashed away at my approach, but the fry remained. . . . They came round my legs and felt them with their feelers, and the old pouts nibbled my toes.' There are sagas of giant snapping turtles, antediluvians, under green, shaggy shells, tougher than the rocks they are mistaken for. There is the frequent tragedy of the innocent muskrat:

> *Nov. 25, 1850.* . . . I saw a muskrat come out of a hole in the ice. He is a man wilder than Ray or Melvin. While I am look-ing at him, I am thinking what he is thinking of me. He is a different sort of a man, that is all. He would dive when I went nearer, then reappear again, and had kept open a place five or six feet square so that it had not frozen, by swimming about in it. Then he would sit on the edge of the ice and busy himself about something, I could not see whether it was a clam or not. What a cold-blooded fellow! thoughts at a low temperature, sitting perfectly still so long on ice covered with water, mum-bling a cold, wet clam in its shell. What safe, low, moderate thoughts it must have! It does not get on to stilts. The genera-tions of muskrats do not fail. They are not preserved by the legislature of Massachusetts.

There are floral curvings down banks in bloom, the 'dump-ing' chorus of awakened bullfrogs, and toads that sing in the water, lilies which open and close with the sun, and the excite-ment of elusive wild ducks. There are careful studies of the waters themselves: 'Thus in the course of ages the rivers wriggle in their beds, till it feels comfortable under them. Time is cheap and rather insignificant.' [8] It is doubtful whether any possible aspect of swamp and water life lacks its paragraph of observation distilled into description and tightened into admirable prose.

5

Why was all this richness, much of it accumulated before his breakdown in 1855, left inchoate and unused for reputation? Did the man think he had another four decades ahead to work in? I have given one reason already: his Puritan conscience that demanded he should know all there was to be known before he said his say. Yet there must have been a more cogent reason in the conflict between his ideals of science and his steady faith in a significance beyond science. The tensity of that struggle for understanding cannot be exaggerated. Obsessed by it, he felt that the solution of the problem was more important than his literary achievements. It was insoluble, of course, yet he could not deny the possibility of a solution by the new science until he had exhausted its resources. He was writing, had written, descriptions of the Concord scene which would be more memorable, more suggestive, more truly valuable than any research; yet, determined to push still further into the secrets of nature, he let them wait in his Journal, hoping that they might be synthesized by some final philosophy. Like many a man of letters before him, he took his philosophy too seriously. The middle-aged man of his epigram used the materials of his dreams to build a woodshed. Thoreau, hoping still to construct a temple of Transcendental knowledge, let them lie. If he had applied his own principles of architecture, he might have seen that the simple edifice he was ready to put together would have been as much of a masterpiece in its way as the loggers' huts he so much admired in the Maine woods.

And, indeed, most of these extensive and numerous descriptions scattered through the Journal were, it seems, waiting for use. He had experimented with nature study in his *Dial* days, he had swept some notes together for lectures and completed the 'Succession of Forest Trees,' which was a specialized piece of research, but made no attempt, as far as is known, to publish the ripest of his nature descriptions in the magazines which, in the fifties, were printing his travel narratives, until at last he knew it was too late ever to lift them into a unity. Then he rushed them hurriedly into printable form.

Their popularity, fragmentary as they are, is well deserved. The Excursions, revised and unrevised, are the most pleasing if not the most powerful of his writings. In them he is positive and constructive, not critical or reforming, even of himself. He is no longer the scholar discharging his erudition, nor the philosopher exaggerating in order to drive his moral home, but rather a man of letters full to the brim of his subject, and transmitting its essences into an easy and expressive style. No reader will ever forget the charm of that essay on the stubborn apple tree gone wild in pastures on their way back to wilderness.

24. SLAVERY IN MASSACHUSETTS

In spite of bursts of eloquent satire, 'Walden' was a good-natured book. It was an *apologia* for a life, intended to convert Henry's townsmen to a more sympathetic view of his ideas on how to live. As in all great studies of values in living, the imagination went beyond Thoreau's personal quarrel with human nature, and gave his book broad significance.

'Walden' told how he earned the right to live as he pleased. But no sooner was it finally revised and out of his system than a backwash of indignation reminded him of the contempt of Concord for an Apollo without a job. Back in Concord and established there, he began to brood on what bourgeois society, as we would call it now, had done to him. By summer or autumn of 1854, he was searching his Journal for relevant paragraphs that could be used in a blow straight from the shoulder. When they were assembled, he wrote a lecture called 'Getting a Living,' which became, when published in *The Atlantic Monthly* after his death, the famous essay, 'Life Without Principle.' [1] As a lecture it was given at New Bedford in 1854 and also at Nantucket, and probably to the unenthusiastic audience which Furness records in Philadelphia.

'Life Without Principle' is the finest of Thoreau's negatives. Here is the woodchuck Thoreau, gritting his teeth until they are powdered. A money-making fellow has asked him to spend three weeks digging the foundations of a wall. 'I prefer to finish my education at a different school.' 'It is remarkable that there is little or nothing to be remembered written on the subject of getting a living; how to make getting a living not merely honest and honorable, but altogether inviting and glorious; for if *getting* a living is not so, then living is not.' On this theme he prepared to write, and did so, while his indignation ran away with him. Men would rather gamble for gold in California than earn a good life. If we do try to live a good life, it is likely to be corrupted by the sewers that flow through the newspaper columns, which we read in default of any inner satisfaction. Americans may be free politically, but economically and morally they are still slaves. As for our morals: 'We quarter our gross bodies on our poor souls, till the former eat up all the latter's substance.' As for government, it spends its time regulating the breeding of Negro slaves or furthering a commerce that makes wage slaves of the sailors that work for it. 'The chief want, in every State that I have been into, was a high and earnest purpose in its inhabitants.' 'What is called politics is comparatively something so superficial and inhuman, that practically I have never fairly recognized that it concerns me at all.' And so he snaps, snarls, and grumbles throughout the essay.

What was the irritant that set off this explosive mixture of truth and exaggeration? The dates tell the story. Thoreau, the recluse-individualist, had been drawn into the great anti-slavery agitation, and was returning to his *res privata* with a headache and a rage.

2

Henry Thoreau was never an Abolitionist, although at last, and somewhat reluctantly, he associated himself with the Abolitionist organizations. His home, however, from a very early period was a nest of Abolitionists, one of those household centers of agitation of which the South complained. Mrs. Colonel Ward, Aunt Maria, and Helen were all active members of one of the earliest of the societies. All of them, including Henry, read *The Liberator*, Garrison's paper, fought successfully to open the Lyceum to such radical orators as Wendell Phillips, and (the women at least) talked Abolition incessantly. Sanborn, who was nearly kidnapped by United States marshals in the John Brown agitation, found a congenial atmosphere at Mrs. Thoreau's table.

Henry held aloof. He told the Temperance Society that he was too Transcendental to join societies for reforming other men. When he does mention Abolition, his tone is skeptical. 'I was glad to hear the other day that Higginson and —— were gone to Ktaadn; it must be so much better to go to than a Woman's Rights or Abolition Convention.' [2] Indeed, he made no sharp distinction between African slavery and other kinds less frequently condemned by his neighbors. 'It is hard to have a Southern overseer; it is worse to have a Northern one; but worst of all when you are yourself the slave-driver.' 'I wonder men can be so frivolous almost as to attend to the gross form of negro slavery, there are so many keen and subtle masters who subject us both. Self-emancipation ... of a man's thinking and imagining provinces ... one emancipated heart and intellect! It would knock off the fetters from a million slaves.' [3]

As so often when the thief was not in his wood lot, he was philosophic, not condemning wage slavery the less because he hated the very thought of involuntary servitude. Yet a continued detachment was impossible. The results of the Fugitive Slave Law of 1850 soon laid the question of slave ownership on his own doorstep.

It was a situation very different from the moral conflict which had sent him to jail in support of his principles. The Mexican War and its extension of slavery into the Southwest had been far away geographically. He proposed then no violence against a state, which, though quite capable of crushing him, was a cowardly organization that could be defied. Instead, he quietly declared war 'after my fashion,' which was passive resistance against its attempt to collect a tax of $1.50. What he did belonged, as he said, to himself and to the hour.

It was a very different hour in the early fifties when the slave power forced the state governments of the North to return its lost slaves. To most Americans, the Federal Government at Washington still seemed remote and impersonal. A man was a South Carolinian, a Massachusetts man, first of all, a citizen of the United States afterward, sometimes a long way afterward. Thirteen years later than the Mexican War, Lee, who believed in union and hated slavery, was to secede with his state because he was a Virginian. For Thoreau, Massachusetts was not only home, it was what he lived by and what represented him. It was one thing for South Carolina to threaten, another for Washington to make compromises, but when in Massachusetts, and with the consent of her officials, a slave was to be seized and sent back into slavery, the moral problem for men like Thoreau was transferred from the South to the North, and responsibility settled squarely upon the state which was their own creation. Massachusetts was acting for him and he was responsible for Massachusetts. Its officials had become agents for the slave trade; he himself was personally concerned, since the law required his assistance in the capture of a thief. The commissioners of the court had the right to 'summon and call to their aid

the bystanders or a *posse comitatus* of the proper county' to prevent a rescue of the captured slave, who had no right of jury
trial, and could not testify in his own defense. 'Every freeman
of the North was thereby,' as McMaster says, 'made a slave-
catcher.' Refusal might (and in one instance did) lead to a
trial for treason. That the law was *ex post facto*, and might be
applied to a Negro long resident in the North, increased the
sense of injustice.⁴ That Thoreau himself had tenderly aided
more than one escaped slave on his way to Canada made his
own reaction more personal and more violent.

Like most men, Thoreau could be detached and philosophic
until someone trod on his toes. Then and then only did he
react with truly human fervor. It had been so in the Walden
days; it was so now. On April 12, 1851, the authorities of
Boston, 'having the sympathy of many of the inhabitants of
Concord,' sent back the Negro Sims, 'a perfectly innocent man,'
into slavery. Thoreau steamed for a week, then exploded into
his Journal, setting down what was designed to be an address,
but which apparently was never given as such. The courts
had assumed jurisdiction over human values (it sounds like the
Supreme Court controversies of 1937), and his townsmen have
let him down, involving him in a crime of conscience. Has
Concord no other bridge to defend in a new Revolution!

When in 1854, after an attempt at rescue, the Negro Burns
was returned to slavery in a cutter provided by the government,
and in opposition this time to the sentiment of the best of Boston,
the recluse came back to the world with a still more vehement
protest. He had been listening for the voice of his Governor and
had heard only the crickets. His serenity, his walks are spoiled.
The state, his own state, has implemented injustice. 'My
thoughts are murder to the State.' And indeed something more
vital than the course of anti-slavery was threatened by this
subservience to a power denying human rights to slaves. A

philosophic individualism can subsist only in a community where moral principles are recognized as having a validity beyond political expediency. Thoreau's own freedom was threatened, and he knew it. The slave-holder who stood up for his rights was 'in some respects a better man than we.' Not to resist was to connive with his own elected officials in the betrayal of the principle of freedom.

3

This time he was heard. The address which he gave on the fourth of July, 1854, to an Abolitionist audience at Framingham was significantly entitled 'Slavery in Massachusetts.' Moncure Conway, who was there, says that he was 'clamoured for,' [5] apparently as a spokesman for many hitherto aloof intellectuals. 'You have my sympathy,' he began; 'it is all I have to give you, but you may find it important to you'; and then continued with a speech which *The Tribune* on August 2 summarized at length, accompanying it with an editorial in which the editor said that Thoreau, and not Sumner, Seward, and Haines, should be called the real champion of a 'Higher-Law.'

The description was correct. This address is not on slavery, of which Thoreau knew little or nothing in its historical and economical aspects, nor on the South and Southerners, of which he knew less. He was, in fact, not competent to speak upon the immediate problems of slavery. Indeed, he seems to have been unaware that thousands of the best Southerners wished to abolish slavery, and he had never thought of the social problems involved in immediate abolition, or reflected, as he certainly would have reflected if slavery had existed in Concord, on the conditioning of the Negro by his environment. For him, the slave was a symbol of servitude, as the woodchuck was a symbol of the courage of the wild.

It was the North, not the South, that he attacked in this speech at Framingham. And, specifically, he spoke to a Massachusetts that had denied to its citizens the legal right to preserve their own moral integrity. The minority he defended became, in the North, a majority, the war was precipitated by extremists on both sides, ruined the South, demoralized the North for a generation, and left the Negro a national problem. Yet Thoreau's arguments still have point and force because they deal with questions of principle on a plane above expediency. If he was wrong in estimating the effect of war upon the country, he was right in his attack upon Massachusetts. She had slid down-hill from her principles. That was the moral weakness which the agitation over slavery exposed in the character of his townsmen and his friends.

> I wish my countrymen to consider that whatever the human law may be, neither an individual nor a nation can ever commit the least act of injustice against the obscurest individual without having to pay the penalty for it.

> Recent events will be valuable... as showing what are the true resources of justice in any community.

> The majority of... men... are not men of principle.... It is the mismanagement of wood and iron and stone and gold which concerns them.

> Rather than do thus, I need not say what match I would touch, what system endeavor to blow up; but as I love my life, I would side with the light, and let the dark earth roll from under me....

> I have lived for the last month — and I think every man in Massachusetts capable of the sentiment of patriotism must have had a similar experience — with the sense of having suffered a vast and indefinite loss. I did not know at first what ailed me. At last it occurred to me that what I had lost was a country.

> We have used up all our inherited freedom. If we would save our lives, we must fight for them.

His words echo ominously in the trying days of the twentieth century.

Thoreau's statesmanship was what you would expect from an uncompromising idealist, legislating for eternity. He urged Massachusetts to cut the bonds which tied her to the slave-holding states, with little consideration of what secession would mean. He urged his fellow citizens to fight for their rights, not reflecting that rights, principles, and a culture might be sacrificed in the course of violence. His doctrine was that of the 'Bhagavad-Gita,' let the slayer slay if it is his genius to do so, and his motives are just. But statesmanship was not his concern. His concern was precisely what it had been in 'Life Without Principle,' which he had been writing the same year: the proper attitude of the man of principle, and most of all himself. He could have taken no other position than of resistance *à outrance* to any attempts to coerce his fixed beliefs. If the lover of freedom did not act according to principle, no statesmanship could defend him. If he did, there was something for statesmanship to work with. This is no hater of the South, no professional reformer speaking, but Thoreau the upright man, taking his stand, and challenging the like-minded to resist injustice at all costs.

4

This was his position in 1854, and not a merely theoretical one. One can be sure that if he had been in Boston on the day when the rescue was attempted of Anthony Burns, he would have risked assault with Higginson and Alcott. But there was, as yet, no other action to take. His sympathies were worth more than potential deeds.

Yet it was not his final position. The cause, which, it must be repeated, was not for him slavery *per se*, but the integrity of men of principle, lacked a man. 'It is for want of a man that there are so many men,' he had written in 'Life Without Principle,' and by a man, he meant a man of principle. 'Men have been hung in the South before,' he wrote in 'The Last Days of John Brown,' 'for attempting to rescue slaves, and the North was not much stirred by it. Whence, then, this wonderful difference? We were not so sure of *their* devotion to principle.'

He found his man in John Brown of Osawatomie. The old hero, murderer according to some, had come East from bleeding Kansas to get support. He and his sons had adventured their lives almost daily against the Border Ruffians in the attempt to keep Kansas free soil. He had been hunted for his life, was known to be brave, honest, and indomitable, was supposed to be a fanatic in the cause of freedom. The twenty-five that were slaughtered by his band 'had a perfect right to be hung,' he said. Thoreau met him twice: once at his own house, to which Sanborn had brought him in 1857, and again the next evening at Emerson's, where they had congenial talk.[6] At first Thoreau held off. 'I subscribed a trifle when he was here three years ago,' he wrote later in his Journal, 'I had so much confidence in the man, — that he would do right, — but it would seem that he had not confidence enough in me, nor in anybody else that I know, to communicate his plans to us.'[7] It was the personality that impressed him, a rock of an old man, evidently sincere, not believing in expediency.

Two years later in the Concord Town Hall he heard Brown speak for the last time before he left for Virginia. No hint of his plans was let slip, so that the raid on Harper's Ferry was as great a surprise to the Concord group as to the rest of the country. That raid, the last stand of a courageous man of principle, and his arrest on October 16, 1859, was the match that touched off the smouldering fire in Thoreau. Sanborn says very justly that he and a very few others saw what became apparent to the country only later — the momentous importance of the assault at Harper's Ferry. Almost single-handed, a man had attacked an institution which governments were afraid to touch. The timing was perfect. If there was to be resistance, a heroic example was the best way to organize it. Two years later they were singing 'John Brown's Body' in the camps at Boston.

It was a situation calculated to arouse Thoreau's imagination. Here was that minority of one which he had always contended might overturn a government. Even the Republicans condemned John Brown, even the Abolitionists gave him no hearty approbation. 'He died as the fool dieth,' said the Concord postmaster. He was a madman, said the Republican editors. Here was a cardinal example of that philosophy of individual action which Thoreau had supported, here was an appeal to his prejudice against the useful expediences by which a society not made up of Thoreaus and Emersons has to be conducted. On the nineteenth of October, he wrote some two thousand words in his Journal, only stopping his reflections on Brown's deed to record the falling of the autumn berries. On the twenty-first, some two thousand more; on the twenty-second, impassioned paragraphs stretching for another six thousand. And then, on October 30, while Brown was in captivity before his execution, he summoned his fellow townsmen to hear him make a plea on Brown's behalf.

Concord was against him. A story recorded in *The Independent* by an admirer of Thoreau is garbled in its reference, which evidently confuses the 'Plea' with the memorial ceremony on December 2, the day of Brown's execution, in which many distinguished citizens joined. Yet this anecdote represents accurately Thoreau's independent spirit when he held his own meeting and raised the first voice in the country in defense of old Brown:

On the day when John Brown was hanged he sent a boy about to notify people that he would speak in the vestry of the church. The boy returned, and said that Mr. Sanborn thought it a bad thing to do, that the time was dangerous, and it would be better to wait until there was a better feeling among the people. Thoreau sent the boy back with this message: 'Tell Mr. Sanborn that he has misunderstood the announcement, that there is to be a meeting in the vestry, and that Mr. Thoreau will speak.'[8]

And it is true that there was much violence threatened for the later memorial meeting. Doctor Bartlett had heard five hundred damn Thoreau for proposing it. The selectmen refused to ring the bell of the Town Hall, which, so tradition says, Thoreau rang himself. 'A considerable part of Concord,' including Doctor Bartlett, who had the minister under his wing, were 'afraid of their own shadows.' And John Brown was burned in effigy that night; which indicates that Thoreau's speech a month earlier had struck home.[9]

5

The 'Plea' was not a vain attempt to save the life of Captain John Brown. It was not an attack on the South and slavery. Essentially it is an argument for the occasional necessity of civil disobedience, a defense of violence in a good cause, and a eulogy of courage, uprightness, and the will to achieve in a man of principle.

Subtly, slowly, as is happening with so many idealists in the twentieth century, the belief in justified violence had been capturing Thoreau's mind. Passive resistance was not enough in a state that had ceased to recognize human rights and was overriding personal integrity. He had outgrown his youthful, romantic faith in war as an antidote to selfish commercialism, but his new creed reflected, as creeds usually do, the increasing

violence of the conflict. In Kansas, private men had been wag-
ing war against each other. Sumner had been beaten to in-
sensibility in the Capitol, and the act approved by hot-heads
in the South. Blows and shots on both sides were taking the
place of argument. Henry Ward Beecher had sent rifles with
his Bibles to the Kansas immigrants. If Thoreau's new conception of force to meet force was philosophic at all, it was the
philosophy of the 'Bhagavad-Gita' — in the eyes of God the
blow of a sword and the impact of an idea might reach the
same end, and, with a man of principle, have the same justification.

But it was not really philosophic. Thoreau was a peaceful
person angered by brute violence, who sees a man of action,
with principles like his, rise and smite. Shall John Brown be
disparaged for resorting to violence when Massachusetts, which
defends the hen-roosts of Concord by violence if necessary,
maintains slavery? This is not philosophic arguing, but human
enough. Let the man be high principled and we shall approve
of his deeds, and if necessary share them. 'I do not wish to kill
or to be killed,' Henry wrote in his Journal while Brown was on
trial, 'but I can foresee circumstances in which both of these
things would be by me unavoidable. In extremities I could
even be killed.' But in order to die effectively you must have
been really alive first. Most men — and here he returned to a
pet idea — had never effectively lived. John Brown, in action,
as he himself in thought and in occupation, had been a man
alive.

And so in his 'Plea,' which is surely one of the great public
addresses in American history, he proposed to describe and
defend his man. John Brown was 'one of that class of whom we
hear a great deal, but, for the most part, see nothing at all, —
the Puritans.' And Thoreau also was a Puritan, a Puritan in
the root sense of a word used to describe perfectionists 'not

making many compromises.' A Puritan in thought, he was defending a Puritan in deed (as Milton defended Cromwell), a little envious perhaps because Captain Brown, whose genius was for action, had taken the quick, short way of force to put his mark upon injustice.

There is no apology in Thoreau's words. He believed that violence, if justified, must be justified by moral necessity, and so argued the essential morality of an attack which seemed madness, and certainly led toward war. 'Truth,' he had said in 'Civil Disobedience,' 'is always in harmony with herself, and is not concerned chiefly to reveal the justice that may consist with wrong-doing,' which means in plain English that there is a quality in the acts of a man of principle which must be separated from the immediate results of those acts, and praised by all right-thinking men. This is a dangerous thesis which may be used to justify the wildest fanaticism, but Thoreau makes it credible for John Brown. If the Civil War was an irrepressible conflict, he was historically right in his praise, since John Brown gave the North a moral hero. If it was not (as many now think), he was still right in his praise of a man not afraid to die for his beliefs.

There is a simplicity and forthrightness in this 'Plea' very different from the sputter of fireworks with which Thoreau usually proceeds; it contains few epigrams and few quotable sentences. Indeed, it is taken almost verbatim from his Journal and thus is fresh from his mind, still colloquial in parts, and impressive, not from any effect of rhetoric but from the weight and passion of the unpolished sentences. 'I put a piece of paper and a pencil under my pillow, and when I could not sleep I wrote in the dark.'

> The momentary charge at Balaklava, in obedience to a blundering command, proving what a perfect machine the soldier is, has, properly enough, been celebrated by a poet

laureate; but the steady, and for the most part successful, charge of this man, for some years, against the legions of Slavery, in obedience to an infinitely higher command, is as much more memorable than that as an intelligent and conscientious man is superior to a machine. Do you think that that will go unsung? . . .

Is it not possible that an individual may be right and a government wrong? Are laws to be enforced simply because they were made? or declared by any number of men to be good, if they are *not* good? Is there any necessity for a man's being a tool to perform a deed of which his better nature disapproves? Is it the intention of law-makers that *good* men shall be hung ever? Are judges to interpret the law according to the letter, and not the spirit? What right have *you* to enter into a compact with yourself that you *will* do thus or so, against the light within you? Is it for *you* to *make up* your mind, — to form any resolution whatever, — and not accept the convictions that are forced upon you, and which ever pass your understanding? I do not believe in lawyers, in that mode of attacking or defending a man, because you descend to meet the judge on his own ground, and, in cases of the highest importance, it is of no consequence whether a man breaks a human law or not. Let lawyers decide trivial cases. Business men may arrange that among themselves. If they were the interpreters of the everlasting laws which rightfully bind man, that would be another thing. A counterfeiting law-factory, standing half in a slave land and half in a free! What kind of laws for free men can you expect from that?

I am here to plead his cause with you. I plead not for his life, but for his character, — his immortal life; and so it becomes your cause wholly, and is not his in the least. Some eighteen hundred years ago Christ was crucified; this morning, perchance, Captain Brown was hung. These are the two ends of a chain which is not without its links. He is not Old Brown any longer; he is an angel of light. . . .

Well, no, I don't suppose he could get four-and-sixpence a day for being hung, take the year round; but then he stands a chance to save a considerable part of his soul, — and *such* a soul! — when *you* do not. No doubt you can get more in your market for a quart of milk than for a quart of blood, but that is not the market that heroes carry their blood to.

Emerson was there to hear him speak, and records that the 'Plea' was delivered by this unsuccessful lecturer with such eloquence and passion that it 'was heard by all respectfully, by many with a sympathy that surprised themselves.' Afterward Thoreau read it again in Worcester, and finally to a great audience in Theodore Parker's Boston Temple. No Boston publisher would print it. But his minority of one soon increased to the million of which he spoke.

6

It is quite unnecessary to use this outburst from the 'hermit of Concord' as a justification of Thoreau's character and a proof that he was not indifferent to the affairs of his country. Such an apology for Thoreau has been made by various biographers, following Sanborn, and is absurd. No act in the man's life was more consistent with both his philosophy and his instincts. If he took to the woods to escape Concord, it was because the emotions by which he lived were not satisfied by the cool contacts of that respectable town and were too warm and too demanding for the Emersons. If he kept out of politics, it was because politics had seemed to him devoid of principle or meaning. 'Naked truth,' he wrote to Charles Sumner in an unpublished letter of July 16, 1860, has been employed in our Congress only 'to perfume the wheel-grease of party in national politics.' [10] If he kept away from the politics of reform, it was because reform seemed to him only to harrow over the still unplowed human heart. Having made his own economics and provided his own happiness, he asked that the state should let him alone. But when it would not let him alone, when it asked him to become a slave catcher, and invaded his own province of a man of principle, the state became his deep concern. And when John Brown put his head in the noose and carried on his private war from that uncompromising position, there was a cause for which it was worth his while to leave nature and the woods.

He left nature reluctantly, 'forced' to go. 'There was a remarkable sunset, I think the 25th of October.... But it was hard for me to see its beauty then, when my mind was filled with Captain Brown.' 'It appeared strange to me that the little dipper should be still diving in the river as of yore.' When it was all over he went back, yet it was mid-December before his mind was free again for relative serenity. The outbreak of the Civil War, unnoted in his Journal, restored his faith in the willingness of Massachusetts men to fight for a cause, but stirred up no such volcano of emotion as did old Brown's private challenge to injustice. By this time he was ill and guessed that he was dying. Yet if he had been well and younger I doubt whether he would have enlisted. These were not the circumstances he foresaw in 1857 in which he would be willing to kill or even (an honest confession) be killed. War was fought by institutions. The defense of John Brown seemed to him, so I guess, more important than the conquest of the South, as important as the abolition of slavery. That would do away with only 'the present form of slavery,' as he said. A true revenge for the death of John Brown would be to make his fight for principles memorable in national history.[11]

25. SENTENCE MAKER

Thoreau's writing was to an unusual extent a by-product of his experience. His profession was living, yet, as with all those born to be men of letters, his life seemed incomplete until he had got it described satisfactorily in words. 'You ... have the best of me in my books,' he wrote to an admirer in Michigan, Calvin H. Greene, and of course he was right. Therefore, as was natural, he took his writing seriously, and was rich in self-criticism as all writers should be, but are not.

It took him most of the 1840's to get rid of Carlyle's religio-mystical view of literature, which made preachers of the young men of Thoreau's generation. When, in the fifties, his reading swung from literature toward science, he shrugged off this stale generalizing, for there was neither time nor inclination for it. It is only rarely that, after 1850, he writes about a literary masterpiece, for he was no longer studying in that school. Yet it is precisely in this last decade of his life that he makes the shrewdest comments on the art of writing — which is natural, for he had then matured his own. And here he is worth listening to, as is any first-rate writer who tries to analyze his own processes. Not the most philosophic perhaps, but certainly the most valuable, criticism we have is the occasional comment of a good writer on how to write — which means almost invariably how he writes himself.

It was a decade, as we have already seen, of crowded experiences for him with men, women, nature, and the state. There was plenty to write about, so that his Journal sometimes has sudden expansions for a day's thought and adventure which must have taken hours to set in order and express. The whole into which he hoped to fit his parts eluded his grasp, but his faith was firm that if he could reduce his observations to perfect sentences, somehow they would see the light, reach their mark, accomplish their destiny. This optimism has been justified, but only by the labor of many editors, and the enthusiasm of readers searching the trackless Journal for his best.

It was the sentence — a *sententia* — that most occupied his thought. The sentence was his medium — whatever he does and writes about, however often he rewrites or enriches, the fruit of it can be found ripened in a sentence. In the revision of 'Walden' for the press, it was doubtful sentences that he threw out, then looked them over, and took back the good ones. They smelled right, as he says, using quaintly his keenest sense as if it could extend itself to words.[1] Naturally he writes best about writing when he is writing about sentences, and these remarks have a biographical value, for they describe as no one else can do the man's mind at work. Only in those deeply impassioned pages about his Sister, so strongly felt as to be scarcely articulate, does he fail to get sentences equal to the emotional intensity or the intellectual insight of his experience. And these, of course, were not meant for publication. With Bacon, Shakespeare, Pope, Doctor Johnson, the makers of the English Bible, and Benjamin Franklin, he belongs among the great makers of the English sentence. Therefore his account of his own practice is interesting.

2

Two principles, especially, guided him in his writing as, sitting under a pasture oak, he set down his things seen or thought about, or, upstairs in the house on Main Street, worked his notes into his Journal. The first principle might be called intuition made articulate, a favorite idea with all the romantic Transcendentalists:

> *April 1. Sunday. 1860* . . . The fruit a thinker bears is *sentences,* — statements or opinions. He seeks to affirm something as true. I am surprised that my affirmations or utterances come to me ready-made, — not fore-thought, — so that I occasionally awake in the night simply to let fall ripe a statement which I had never consciously considered before, and as surprising and novel and agreeable to me as anything can be. As if we only thought by sympathy with the universal mind, which thought while we were asleep. There is such a necessity [to] make a definite statement that our minds at length do it without our consciousness, just as we carry our food to our mouths. This occurred to me last night, but I was so surprised by the fact which I have just endeavored to report that I have entirely forgotten what the particular observation was.

That is the difficulty, of course, with these flashes from a mind in which the heat of long brooding turns to light — if they are not recorded on some sensitive film they are lost and gone, often irrevocably. It was Thoreau's practice to wait for the flash and then anxiously develop the impression until a sentence was made that was true to the original inspiration, yet communicable to the reader. 'There is no more Herculean task than to think a thought about this life and then get it expressed.' [2] To write that way is dangerous, since the flow of thought is checked while expression is made perfect; yet it is hard not to believe that here is the secret of Thoreau's durability. The rifle is more penetrating than the shotgun; the line is remembered when the poem is forgot.

But these sudden luminosities of thought or irradiations of experience were seldom made articulate at the first trial:

> *Jan. 26. 1852.* . . . Whatever wit has been produced on the spur of the moment will bear to be reconsidered and reformed with phlegm. The arrow had best not be loosely shot. The most transient and passing remark must be . . . made sure and warranted, as if the earth had rested on its axle to back it, and all the natural forces lay behind it. The writer must direct his sentences as carefully and leisurely as the marksman his rifle. . . . If you foresee that a part of your essay will topple down after the lapse of time, throw it down now yourself.

Inspiration pricking him on, he writes several such sentences as these lines describe: 'I feel the spur of the moment thrust deep into my side. The present is an inexorable rider.' Then, with a shift of theme: 'The truest account of heaven is the fairest, and I will accept none which disappoints expectation.' ³ Here are other comments:

> *Nov. 12. 1851.* . . . Those sentences are good and well discharged which are like so many little resiliencies from the spring floor of our life . . . . Sentences uttered with your back to the wall . . . . Sentences in which there is no strain.

> *Aug. 22. 1851.* . . . It is the fault of some excellent writers — DeQuincey's first impressions on seeing London suggest it to me — that they express themselves with too great fullness and detail. They . . . lack moderation and sententiousness. They . . . say all they mean. Their sentences are not concentrated and nutty. Sentences which suggest far more than they say, which have an atmosphere about them, which do not merely report an old, but make a new, impression . . . to frame these, that is the *art* of writing. Sentences which are expensive, towards which so many volumes, so much life, went; which lie like boulders on the page, up and down or across; which contain

the seed of other sentences, not mere repetition, but creation; which a man might sell his grounds and castles to build. If DeQuincey had suggested each of his pages in a sentence and passed on, it would have been far more excellent writing. His style is nowhere kinked and knotted up into something hard and significant, which you could swallow like a diamond, without digesting.

That last sentence describes the way Thoreau wrote, and the reason for reading him deliberately. To skim his pages, except in parts of 'Cape Cod' or in 'The Maine Woods' or in some of the 'Excursions,' is like walking rapidly down a gallery of fine paintings. Even with every assistance from theme and narrative, as in 'Walden,' Thoreau's work reads slowly — which is not always a virtue, but often a fault, like the faults of paradox and exaggeration, of which he accused himself. He favored his best sentences at the expense of his chapters and paragraphs. They contained the most of him.

3

His second principle of writing was native to a man who put the art of life ahead of the art of literature. It was, to be vital:

Sept. 2. 1851. . . . We cannot write well or truly but what we write with gusto. The body, the senses, must conspire with the mind. Expression is the act of the whole man, that our speech may be vascular. The intellect is powerless to express thought without the aid of the heart and liver and of every member.

Jan. 30. Friday. 1852. . . . It is in vain to write on chosen themes. We must wait till they have kindled a flame in our minds. There must be the copulating and generating force of love behind every effort destined to be successful. The cold resolve gives birth to, begets, nothing. , , , Obey, report.

July 14. 1852. A writer who does not speak out of a full experience uses torpid words, wooden or lifeless words, such words as 'humanitary,' which have a paralysis in their tails.

And finally, by way of warning, the original of Barrett Wendell's often quoted phrase, 'a diarrhoea of words and constipation of thought':

> *Dec. 31. 1851.* .... The ... creative moment ... in the case of some too easy poets ... becomes mere diarrhoea, mud and clay relaxed. The poet must not have something pass his bowels merely; that is women's poetry. He must have something pass his brain and heart and bowels, too .... So he gets delivered.

4

The rhetorical quality that many feel, even in Thoreau's best writing, is sometimes only a tone and attitude which he sustains, like a good lecturer, through all of such a book as the 'Week' or 'Walden.' Yet I think that the difficulty which the modern reader finds in what seems to him the stylized writing of 'Walden,' or even of the 'Excursions,' has a more important source in this habit of the packed and intensely expressive sentence. Our education in science, or its derivatives, has made us more inductive in our mental processes than were our immediate ancestors. We are accustomed to the kind of writing — especially in newspapers and magazines — that assembles facts, which we call news. The packed statement, which is a deduction handed over for our thinking, is unfamiliar and inspires distrust. Our writing escapes the dogmatic by being dilute and often inconclusive. It is easy to abbreviate, as the success of such magazines as *The Reader's Digest* has shown. We write, not by sentences, not even by paragraphs, but in a stream directed at one outlet. The reading of poetry has decreased in proportion to the increase of this homeopathic way of writing, for the effectiveness of poetry is an effectiveness of charged words and lines. If it is not to have high specific gravity, it would be better to write it in prose. Thoreau suffers from this changed habit of reading, since his sentences, with their backs to the wall, and their feet on Mother Earth, differ from poetry in this respect only in a freer rhythm.

Yet there is no intentional obscurity. 'I am thinking,' he wrote one day, 'by what long discipline and at what cost a man learns to speak simply at last.' [4] Nor was there any literary affectation in his creed, although it cannot be denied that, like his contemporaries, he let his words strut and crow now and then with the 'Walden' cock. 'Why, the roots of *letters*,' he says aptly, 'are *things*. Natural objects and phenomena are the original symbols or types which express our thoughts and feelings, and yet American scholars, having little or no root in the soil, commonly strive with all their might to confine themselves to the imported symbols alone. All the true growth and experience, the living speech, they would fain reject as "Americanisms."' 'It is a great art in the writer to improve from day to day just that soil and fertility which he has. . . .' 'Your mind must not perspire,' — which last, if said of walking out-of-doors, was surely meant for writing indoors also.[5]

The art of writing is much broader and more complex than Thoreau's remarks on sentence-making imply. There is no doubt, however, that his particular art has a survival value much greater than any novelty in his ideas. But, inevitably, it became a perfectionist art, and so a curb upon free writing. Whoever writes by sentences writes slowly, and will often follow his own nose instead of his theme. And being perfectionist, this art made the completion of any whole exceedingly difficult, because each sentence had to be a finished production. He used the spot light instead of the flood. No wonder, then, that, as a student of nature trying to put between the covers of a book an account of that age-old Concord scene in which man had found a new home, Thoreau's work was left half done. Nevertheless, he mopped up his trenches as he crossed them, and left a noble sentence for each significant experience.

26. AFTERNOON OF A LIFE

WITH A WALT WHITMAN EPISODE

AFTER HENRY THOREAU's long illness in 1855 it was late afternoon with him, a New England afternoon in winter, of cold, clear light, flaming up once before sunset. There were five years of renewed energy, then dusk, decline, and death.

The year 1856 was 'the long snowy winter,' a delight to Henry, for, although by spring his strength had not all returned, he could once again be the greatest walker in Concord, 'to its disgrace be it said.' In his Journal are fine set-pieces of description, notably one of the elm tree, pride of New England. Nevertheless, his notes seem more than usually concerned with dry detail, as if there was some lack of vitality. Even his self-contained father protested against his experiments with maple sugar, saying that they took him from his studies. He argues too much this year that Concord is better for him than the intellectual luxuries of great capitals. 'I wish ... to derive my satisfactions and inspirations from the commonest events ... so that ... I may dream of no heaven but that which lies about me.' For the first time since early youth he is not driving himself, either physically or mentally. Yet there was more than the weakness of convalescence to account for his slackening. It was in 1856 that his relations with the Emersons seemed to him 'one long tragedy'; and from that sister, whom I take to be Lidian, he believed that he was about to be held apart forever.

Ricketson in New Bedford and Blake in Worcester were comforting. In his relaxed mood he writes to them with the pleasant confidence of a man who can count on sympathy and admiration. Channing, a tragic figure of unsuccess to everyone but himself, was working at journalism in New Bedford, though he insisted he could not remember the name of the place where he was living. Thoreau tried to help him. 'He will accept sympathy and aid,' he wrote to Ricketson, 'but will not bear questioning.' Not always had he been so kind. In Concord that year his friend was left on the river bank because, while there was room for a companion in Thoreau's boat, there was none in his mind.

Spring, as usual, warmed Thoreau's temperament. With his legs going again, he takes on many surveying jobs, finding some advantage in seeing nature with the side of the eye, while he manipulates his instruments. 'Precision and authority' is what he thinks he is acquiring by his continued study of natural science, and this was true. Yet he confesses to Blake that philosophy and sentiment are buried under a multitude of details. Some were of his own invention, as, for example, time-consuming attempts to make wine from the sap of birch trees. He drank it, but apparently no one else would.

In January, he went to Worcester, and while there had a daguerreotype taken by B. D. Maxham, in three sittings, with some slight variation. By this time he had grown a throat beard, perhaps to protect his delicate chest; although if it were not the fashionless Thoreau, a simpler explanation would be that beards were coming back, to reach their peak of fashion in the Civil War period. No picture of Thoreau is as revealing as this daguerreotype, for Rowse's drawing has not done him justice, and when Dunshee made an ambrotype of him in New Bedford just before his death, the beard had spread over his face, hiding its strong lines and remarkable contours. He wrote Greene that his friends thought the daguerreotype 'pretty good, though better-looking than I.' [1]

That spring Greeley invited him to come to live in his 'country cot' as a tutor for his children. Thoreau agreed to come by the first of July. Mrs. Greeley, then abroad, expressed herself as heartily gratified, and it was hoped he would stay for a year or two at least. His books and belongings were to come along.[2] What interfered with this second proposal to establish himself in the New York area I do not know — surely not the amount of compensation which Thoreau was to get, for Greeley insisted that money would not divide them. Probably his father's failing health — he had been seriously ill before this and recovered — kept Thoreau nearer home, as it kept him from joining Cholmondeley on a trip to the West Indies in 1858.

As his strength came back, his activity increased. Helping to catch his father's pig after it had escaped into the Hoars' garden, he shows no lack of wind in the long chase which he wrote up for his Journal, in an amusing narrative that might have persuaded even Lowell of his sense of humor. In the autumn, he tramped about Walpole, New Hampshire, where Alcott was living, his idea being to compare the Connecticut and the Concord valleys at the same time of year. They discussed Frémont, Garrison, Emerson, and politics all morning in Alcott's study, and Thoreau took to bed with him all available books on Walpole, getting ready for a possible excursion.[3]

The days were not long enough to do the work he had set for himself before bedtime, for he was a 'learner' still, not a teacher. Alcott describes him as having 'doors opening on all sides of him, slides in slides, to admit her [nature] to his intelli-

gence.' ⁴ Indeed, the Savannah sparrow alone kept him busy
for days. Was it or was it not his seringo? Birds' nests, too,
had become a study, and they took hours of searching. Also
new plants — 'I spent my afternoon among the desmodiums
and lespedezas, sociably.' It was better than 'to go consul to
Liverpool [he was thinking of Hawthorne] and get I don't
know how many thousand dollars for it, with no such flavor.'
For he had discovered in these social and studious rambles that
'the wisely conscious life springs out of an unconscious suggestion.' There was a conscious purpose, as he told Calvin H.
Greene, answering his question as to whether a new book was
in prospect. 'I am drawing a rather long bow, though it may
be a feeble one, but I pray that the archer may receive new
strength before the arrow is shot.' He was still, as he told
Ricketson, 'far, far short of my best estate.' Yet by September
he was climbing Fall Mountain near Brattleboro with a heavy
valise on his back.

                                    2

In the fall of 1856, his money seems to have run short — or
was it a reaction from all this self-preaching about the advantages of staying at home? Marcus Spring, the philanthropist
interested in 'newness,' who with his wife had taken Margaret
Fuller abroad, was the patron of Eagleswood, an educational
colony on land which he owned near Perth Amboy in New
Jersey, and which once had been the seat of a community
paralleling Brook Farm. It was to be a society of 'radical
opinions and old fashioned culture' gathered about a school
for the young. Alcott, who buzzed toward communities as
a bee to a clover bed, was there holding Conversations, and
suggested Thoreau for the job of surveying the two hundred
acres, laying out streets, and giving lectures in his spare time.

Actually, though the idea of the colony was to provide the right educational environment for children, its purpose seems to have been to provide a home and centre of activity among sympathetic friends for a group of prominent expatriated Abolitionists.

The school was run by Theodore Weld, 'one of the greatest figures of his day,' says his biographer, an anti-slavery orator, the director of seventy Abolitionist agents, and largely responsible for the organization of anti-slavery sentiment throughout the West. In the community also was J. G. Birney, who had freed his slaves in Alabama, and as an anti-slavery candidate for the presidency in 1844 had split the New York State vote, and thrown the election to Polk, who favored the Mexican War. He had married one of the Grimké sisters, famous South Carolina Abolitionists, and she with her sister were among the émigrés at Eagleswood. With them were gathered a miscellaneous collection of Quakers and near-Quakers, including Arnold Buffum, Mrs. Spring's father. Horace Greeley was friendly and a visitor, Caroline M. Kirkland, author of highly successful Western stories, was a recent recruit. It was an interesting, indeed, a distinguished community.

Thoreau was not impressed — except by the prevalence of long white beards. Co-operative action looking toward reform always set his skeptical teeth on edge. Though he spent nearly a month there, not getting back to Concord until November 25 of 1856, and lectured with unusual success, especially among the young people, the New Jersey flora made more impression upon him than these advocates of a brave new world. I know of no more Thoreauvian letter than the one he wrote to Sophia from Eagleswood. Emerson would not print it in the collection he published in 1865, the reason being obvious:

Eagleswood, Perth Amboy, N. J.
Saturday eve, November 1, 1856.

Dear Sophia, — . . . This is a queer place. There is one large
long stone building, which cost some forty thousand dollars,
in which I do not know exactly who or how many work (one or
two familiar faces and more familiar names have turned up),
a few shops and offices, an old farm-house, and Mr. Spring's
perfectly private residence, within twenty rods of the main
building. The city of Perth Amboy is about as big as Concord,
and Eagleswood is one and a quarter miles southwest of it, on
the Bay side. The central fact here is evidently Mr. [Theodore]
Weld's school, recently established, around which various
other things revolve. Saturday evening I went to the schoolroom, hall, or what not, to see the children and their teachers
and patrons dance. Mr. Weld, a kind-looking man with a
long white beard, danced with them, and Mr. [E. J.] Cutler,
his assistant (lately from Cambridge, who is acquainted with
Sanborn), Mr. Spring, and others. This Saturday evening
dance is a regular thing, and it is thought something strange
if you don't attend. They take it for granted that you want
society!

Sunday forenoon I attended a sort of Quaker meeting at
the same place (the Quaker aspect and spirit prevail here, —
Mrs. Spring says, 'Does thee not?'), where it was expected that
the Spirit would move me (I having been previously spoken
to about it); and it, or something else, did, — an inch or so.
I said just enough to set them a little by the ears and make it
lively. I had excused myself by saying that I could not adapt
myself to a particular audience; for all the speaking and lecturing here have reference to the children, who are far the greater
part of the audience, and they are not so bright as New England
children. Imagine them sitting close to the wall, all around a
hall, with old Quaker-looking men and women here and there.
There sat Mrs. Weld [Grimké] and her sister, two elderly gray-
headed ladies, the former in extreme Bloomer costume, which
was what you may call remarkable; Mr. Arnold Buffum, with
broad face and a great white beard, looking like a pier-head
made of the cork-tree with the bark on, as if he could buffet a

considerable wave; James G. Birney, formerly candidate for the presidency, with another particularly white head and beard; Edward Palmer, the anti-money man (for whom communities were made), with his ample beard somewhat grayish. Some of them, I suspect, are very worthy people. Of course you are wondering to what extent all these make one family, and to what extent twenty. Mrs. Kirkland (and this a name only to me) I saw. She has just bought a lot here. They all know more about your neighbors and acquaintances than you suspected.

On Monday evening I read the moose story to the children, to their satisfaction. Ever since I have been constantly engaged in surveying Eagleswood, — through woods, salt marshes, and along the shore, dodging the tide, through bushes, mud, and beggar-ticks, having no time to look up or think where I am. (It takes ten or fifteen minutes before each meal to pick the beggar-ticks out of my clothes; burs and the rest are left, and rents mended at the first convenient opportunity.) . . .

It seems a twelvemonth since I was not here, but I hope to get settled deep into my den again ere long. The hardest thing to find here is solitude — and Concord. I am at Mr. Spring's house. Both he and she and their family are quite agreeable.

I want you to write to me immediately (just left off to talk French with the servant man), and let father and mother put in a word. To them and to Aunts, love from

HENRY

There is reverence neither for institutions nor for reformers in this letter. Weld actually had as much, if not more, to do with bringing on the Civil War than John Brown, but he was a negotiator, an orator, an executive, not a hero. John Brown also had a beard, but behind it there was, Thoreau would have said, a man, not a statesman.

3

It was on this trip, by way of curious contrast, that Thoreau met an individual then far less conspicuous than the Eagleswood Abolitionists, and much further removed from Concord and, indeed, Thoreau's own philosophy than these semi-Transcendentalists of New Jersey, yet far more impressive according to his way of estimating men. Henry came back to Concord eager to talk of a new personality, Walt Whitman.

Alcott, who could sniff idealism even further than communities, and was never put off by an ego, brought the men together. Two diverse minds, both fertilized by Emerson, two sets of sympathies a thousand miles apart, the prophet of *en masse* and the lover of solitude, the passionate lover of men and the passionate lover of nature, the sensual Quaker and the sensuous Puritan, the romantic democrat and the intellectual aristocrat! Each in his way posed in life and seems to have posed a little at this meeting, though beside Whitman's bluffing Thoreau's cockcrowing seems naïvely sincere. Both were rebels against the American convention that dollars measure success, both had visions of an individualism which set the emotions free from use and wont and respectability. Whitman was visibly and audibly expansive, Thoreau practised restraint and concealment as naturally as breathing. One embraced the world without much discrimination, the other lifted his prickles even at Emerson. Whitman often faked his scholarship, Thoreau was sometimes buried beneath the mass of his erudition. Yet for both the chief issue was how to live, not how to get a living, in which they were to become spiritual leaders of two wings of an American minority.

Thoreau had surely read Emerson's copy of 'Leaves of Grass' when it was sent to Concord in 1855, but he does not mention the book until December of 1856, after he had met Whitman.[5] 'I do not so much wish,' he wrote in his Journal, and afterward inserted in a letter to Blake, 'that it was not written, as that men and women were so pure that they could read it without harm,' which may represent his end of an argument with

Emerson. He was not a prude in any sense, yet the author of 'Friendship' evidently felt that there was too much pleasure per pound of uplift in Whitman's passion. Only the pure, thought Thoreau, could afford to be passionate. The fault was not with Whitman's honesty, which he approved, but with the low ideals of love as currently practised.

Alcott picked up Thoreau at Eagleswood and took him to New York, and then off with Alice Cary, the poetess, for a day at Greeley's farm, where the great journalist was compensating for an unhappy married life by agricultural efficiency. On the way back, they heard Henry Ward Beecher preach a sermon on justice to a vast audience in Brooklyn, which Thoreau thought 'pagan,' perhaps because it was intended to raise up reformers. In New York, Alcott frequented many houses where good talk was to be had (he once said to Thoreau that his idea of heaven was a place where you could have pleasant conversation). He got Henry to one of them, the Mannings', but Thoreau balked when Mrs. Botta, described as a 'hostess and poet,' invited him to what seems to have been a party. At the Mannings' they found Mrs. Tyndall, 'a solid walrus of a woman [this is Alcott speaking in his Journal] spread full many a rood abroad,' who argued both noon and evening for humanitarianism, Thoreau opposing. After dinner they called on Whitman, but got only a mother's tribute to her son from Mrs. Whitman, Walt being out, and some hot cakes, which Thoreau, rather surprisingly, went into the kitchen and asked for. Perhaps the Manning dinner had been Transcendental in its fare. The next day, taking the walrus with them, they went again, and found Whitman in his attic study, presumably dressed as Alcott had seen him there in October, red-flannel undershirt open-throated, striped calico jacket, and overalls. 'Has never been sick, he says [Alcott speaking], nor taken medicine, nor sinned; and so is quite innocent of repentance,' which last, if Whitman repeated it in November, must have pleased Thoreau, who did not believe in repentance.

'I hoped,' says Alcott, 'to put him into communication direct with Thoreau, and tried my hand a little after we came down stairs and sat in the parlour below; but each seemed planted fast in reserves, surveying the other curiously, — like two beasts, each wondering what the other would do, whether to snap or run; and it came to no more than cold compliments between them.' And so they said good-bye, leaving 'the voluminous Mrs. Tyndall ... with the savage sovereign of the flesh.' Whitman promised to call at the hotel the next day and 'deliver himself further' — but he did not come.[6]

It was Whitman who snapped and ran, not Thoreau. As so often at Emerson's, Henry was hiding an intense interest behind his reserve. Writing to Blake only nine days later, he speaks with unexpected enthusiasm of this encounter:

> He is apparently the greatest democrat the world has seen.
> Kings and aristocracy go by the board at once, as they have
> long deserved to. A remarkably strong though coarse nature,
> of a sweet disposition, and much prized by his friends. Though
> peculiar and rough in his exterior, his skin (all over (?)) red,
> he is essentially a gentleman. I am still somewhat in a quandary
> about him, — feel that he is essentially strange to me, at any
> rate; but I am surprised by the sight of him. He is very broad,
> but, as I have said, not fine. He said that I misapprehended
> him. I am not quite sure that I do. He told us that he loved
> to ride up and down Broadway all day on an omnibus, sitting
> beside the driver, listening to the roar of the carts, and some-
> times gesticulating and declaiming Homer at the top of his
> voice. He has long been an editor and writer for the news-
> papers, — was editor of the *New Orleans Crescent* once; but now
> has no employment but to read and write in the forenoon, and
> walk in the afternoon, like all the rest of the scribbling gentry.

Even then he could not get Whitman out of his mind. He wrote to Blake in another letter of December 7:

That Walt Whitman, of whom I wrote to you, is the most interesting fact to me at present. I have just read his second edition (which he gave me), and it has done me more good than any reading for a long time. Perhaps I remember best the poem of Walt Whitman, an American, and the Sun-Down Poem. There are two or three pieces in the book which are disagreeable, to say the least; simply sensual. He does not celebrate love at all. It is as if the beasts spoke. I think that men have not been ashamed of themselves without reason. No doubt there have always been dens where such deeds were unblushingly recited, and it is no merit to compete with their inhabitants. But even on this side he has spoken more truth than any American or modern that I know. I have found his poem exhilarating, encouraging. As for its sensuality, — and it may turn out to be less sensual than it appears, — I do not so much wish that those parts were not written, as that men and women were so pure that they could read them without harm, that is, without understanding them. One woman told me that no woman could read it, — as if a man could read what a woman could not. Of course Walt Whitman can communicate to us no experience, and if we are shocked, whose experience is it that we are reminded of?

On the whole, it sounds to me very brave and American, after whatever deductions. I do not believe that all the sermons, so called, that have been preached in this land put together are equal to it for preaching.

We ought to rejoice greatly in him. He occasionally suggests something a little more than human. You can't confound him with the other inhabitants of Brooklyn or New York. How they must shudder when they read him! He is awfully good.

To be sure I sometimes feel a little imposed on. By his heartiness and broad generalities he puts me into a liberal frame of mind prepared to see wonders, — as it were, sets me upon a hill or in the midst of a plain, — stirs me well up, and then — throws in a thousand of brick. Though rude, and sometimes ineffectual, it is a great primitive poem, — an alarum or trumpet-note ringing through the American camp. Wonderfully like the Orientals, too, considering that when I asked him if he had read them, he answered, 'No: tell me about them.'

I did not get far in conversation with him, — two more being present, — and among the few things which I chanced to say, I remember that one was, in answer to him as representing America, that I did not think much of America or of politics, and so on, which may have been somewhat of a damper to him.

Since I have seen him, I find that I am not disturbed by any brag or egoism in his book. He may turn out the least of a braggart of all, having a better right to be confident.

He is a great fellow.[7]

It is interesting to compare this sympathetic and tolerant estimate of Whitman, at a moment when the respectable were being outraged by his poems, with Lowell's contemptuous dismissal of Thoreau as an egotist lacking familiarity with ordinary men and so ignorant of qualities common to the race; also as an ascetic condemning 'a world, the hollowness of whose satisfactions he had never had the means of testing.' True enough, Henry had to see a man before he warmed to his acts or his principles, but after only two hours of restricted conversation he could praise, as the greatest democrat of them all, the Whitman in whom Lowell could see only brag, egoism, and sensuality. When the muskrat hunter Melvin approached his end, 'I trust the Lord will provide us,' Thoreau wrote, 'with another Melvin when he is gone. . . . He is one tribe, I am another, and we are not at war.' [8] This was how he felt about Whitman.

The Brooklyn Quaker found the New England Puritan a harder nut to crack. Thoreau was right in guessing that he had damped him with his attacks on America. Here was evidently no easy convert to the ideals of a sweaty brotherhood of man, nor even one who could sympathize with Whitman's society of lovers. It was the uninhibited emotion enriching Whitman himself that moved Thoreau, who seemed, and rightly, to be too fastidious for social democracy. Traubel, in his 'With Walt Whitman in Camden,' records Whitman's memory of the meeting:

'Thoreau had his own odd ways. Once he got to the house while I was out — went straight to the kitchen where my dear mother was baking some cakes — took the cakes hot from the oven. He was always doing things of the plain sort — without fuss. I liked all that about him. But Thoreau's great fault was disdain — disdain for men (for Tom, Dick, and Harry): inability to appreciate the average life — even the exceptional life: it seemed to me a want of imagination. He couldn't put his life into any other life — realize why one man was so and another man was not so: was impatient with other people on the street and so forth. We had a hot discussion about it — it was a bitter difference: it was rather a surprise to me to meet in Thoreau such a very aggravated case of superciliousness. It was egotistic — not taking that word in its worst sense.' Corning broke out: 'He was simply selfish, that's the long and short of it.' W. replied: 'That may be the short of it but it's not the long. Selfish? No — not selfish in the way you mean, though selfish, sure enough, in a higher interpretation of that term. We could not agree at all in our estimate of men — of the men we meet here, there, everywhere — the concrete man. Thoreau had an abstraction about man — a right abstraction: there we agreed. We had our quarrel only on this ground. Yet he was a man you would have to like — an interesting man, simple, conclusive.' [9]

They may have met again, for Walt in 1876 told his English friend, Ann Gilchrist, that he liked Thoreau even though he was morbid in his dislike of humanity. He said that walking with him in Brooklyn Thoreau asked what he saw in the people, in '"all this cheating political corruption?" I did not like my Brooklyn spoken of in this way.' [10] This other meeting, when they walked together, may have been in May of 1858, when Thoreau was in New York, en route to Staten Island.

4

And so Thoreau came back to Concord in 1856 with a Man in his imagination, soon to be contrasted with another Man, John Brown — one a booster and the other a fanatic, but each in his way a prophet of freedom.

He came back enthusiastic as usual for Concord, remembering happily his youth there when he ranged the woods 'like a gray moose,' and warming with a riper affection to 'the simple, reserved countrymen, my neighbors, who mind their own business, and let me alone. . . . I am grateful for Minott, and Rice, and Melvin, and Goodwin, and Puffer even. . . . He [Melvin] takes up as much room in nature as the most famous.' And he gets to work again, recording 'homely every-day phenomena and adventures.' Concord was his allotment of heaven. 'God could not be unkind to me if he should try. . . . I have never got over my surprise that I should have been born into the most estimable place in all the world, and in the very nick of time, too.' If his heart was sick from the alienation of the Emersons, there was plenty of his kind of cakes and ale to be found in the life out-of-doors.

Surveying and lecturing punctuated his walks and boating excursions. In December, he sleighed into Amherst, New Hampshire, lectured in the basement of the orthodox church, 'and I trust helped to undermine it.' This lecture was his later essay, 'Walking.' He wrote Blake that he could make a lecture on dry oak leaves but no one would hear him, and, later, in 'Autumnal Tints' did so. His social contacts are obviously expanding, though he still maintains that there is better company in Brown's shrub oak lot than in England. At Emerson's he dines with Agassiz, discussing the copulation of turtles, and in April goes with Alcott for a real visit at Ricketson's. Conservation of natural resources is more and more in his thoughts.

The wild pigeons are nearly gone now, the fish are being shut off from the rivers by so-called improvements, the forest trees are falling everywhere in Concord. 'No doubt there is *some* compensation for this loss, but I do not at this moment see clearly what it is.' He is still weak, in spite of his deceptive activity. Now he is talking of a two-year invalidism. Perhaps for this reason, 1857 is a boating year. His legs are not always the levers they used to be, and so the fluvial and the prairial excursions on the rivers and their margins fill his Journal. But if the decline had begun it was slow and intermittent. At Ricketson's shanty he had danced solo and sung 'Tom Bowling.' He told Sophia that he had stepped on Alcott's toes.[11] In an unpublished letter to Ricketson of May 13, 1857, he wrote that he was suddenly 'much stouter,' meaning stronger.[12] By June he was on Cape Cod, in July planning another trip to the Maine woods.

To the Galway whiskers, as they called a throat beard then, Thoreau now added a pair of corduroy trousers at the other end, costing $1.60 and some disturbance among his friends, who did not approve of his becoming a complete Irishman. 'Anything but black clothes,' he said, for black clothes were symbolic of the respectability he had hated from his Harvard days. The birds and the beasts were not disturbed by these clay-colored pants. A mink came within twenty feet of him, and might have come closer if he had put his 'gray sack' on also.

Ricketson brought his fear of death and thunderstorms on a return visit to Concord this May of 1857, and went to the cliffs near Fair Haven with Thoreau and Emerson. He talked of the suffering in life, to which Thoreau responded that 'no ecstasy was ever interrupted, nor its fruit blasted. . . . We want no completeness but intensity of life,' a motto he might have written above his desk. Emerson was pleased with the remark about ecstasy, as with every confirmation of his optimism in

things of the spirit. All through this May and June, Thoreau
and Emerson walked and botanized together, nor is there any
comment in Emerson's Journal that would explain the despairing outcry of February when 'another friendship ... ended.'
Certainly it was not with Waldo, who speaks of his generosity
in sharing his woods, his birds, his flowers, that his relations
were ending.

Those readers, and they are many, who find a salty quality
in Thoreau's 'Cape Cod,' should read in the June Journal of
this year the account of his fourth trip, alone this time, to the
Cape, which never got into the book. There they will see
Henry beach-walking with a dead Mother Carey's chicken
tied to the top of his umbrella, and share his night with the
cats and the bedbugs at Provincetown. It was after his return,
his imagination refreshed by the sea, that he succeeded at last
in lifting his dreams of friendship into an ideal region far above
the 'ordinary courtesy and intercourse of men,' and stilled
perhaps finally that aching in his breast. 'The universe gives
me three cheers.'

By October of that year the great panic was under way, with
banks and merchants suspending throughout the country —
a disease of the pocketbook which was to be cured only by the
antitoxin of war profits in the sixties. But the sandbanks with
their blackberry vines stood firm. 'Let your capital be simplicity
and contentment,' said Henry, a little smugly. This year he
was reading Ruskin's 'Modern Painters' — too much an indoor
book for his taste. Glow-worms came into his range of interest.
He writes as if he saw them for the first time, and indeed he
knows now that he has never really seen anything in nature
until he has studied it. Others were now writing about nature,
a Wilson Flagg, for example, who described rural scenery.
Thoreau in a letter to Ricketson wiped him out as he would
have wiped out many of his later imitators. He was too mild.

'New ideas come into this world . . . with a flash and an explosion,' like meteorites. This man 'wants stirring up with a pole.'

Mrs. Thoreau's house was full of boarders, and this increased Henry's appetite for solitude, which was like an 'infant's for sleep.' Was it to protect his shyness that by the end of this year he had let his beard cover his face, as in his last portrait, which is a perfect picture of a shy man? Channing said the beard was terrible to behold. Some solitude was more than ever necessary to him, for he seems to have resolved now that the poet was bound to write his own biography, and that biography would be found in his Journal. 'The seasons and all their changes are in me. . . . Almost I believe the Concord would not rise and overflow its banks again, were I not here.' He wished to record the 'perfect correspondence of Nature to man, so that he is at home in her!' [13] Here at last in this phrase is the purpose, happily expressed, in all this labor. 'Correspondence,' I think, is not used in any technical Swedenborgian sense. He meant that man was incomplete until his mind's responses to the nature which was his environment were as familiar as his contacts with other men. It was the Hindu idea of the assimilation of the human mind in the other manifestations of God, transferred to Concord where so few looked beyond the pavement, the furrow, or their noses.

The resolve, whether it was to make a book from, or to enrich, his Journal, set him hard at work again. 'Here I have been these forty years learning the language of these fields that I may the better express myself,' he wrote in this year of 1857, and soon was striking off some of his liveliest and most memorable phrases. One reads of the rusty grackles, whose 'melody flew off in splinters,' a perfect replica of the blackbirds' stridency; of the ferns, 'the cool, slowly retreating rearguard of the swamp army'; of the skunk cabbages which 'see over the brow of winter's hill'; — and 'I do not know exactly what that sweet word is which the chickadee says when it hops near to me now in those ravines.'

It was in 1857 also that he day-dreamed 'for the twentieth time at least' of the grand mountain-top up which he ascended through dark woods, only to see sunny pastures running to its base. The allegory was of his life, in which spiritual exaltation could be reached by a dark tensity of mental struggle, or through the healthy pursuits of a cheerful life in nature. It was like his other frequent dream of the rough and the smooth. This year, in spite of his defeats of friendship, was sunny in its endeavors.

Emerson records in his Journal some of Thoreau's best sayings in 1858, as for example: 'He thought nothing to be hoped from you, if this bit of mould under your feet was not sweeter for you to eat than any other in this world, or in any world.' He quotes him again on the Indians, whose fingers were 'the sons of hands'; to which may be added a sentence from Thoreau's own Journal of April, 1858: 'Men are the inveterate foes of all improvement. Generally speaking, they think more of their hen-houses than of any desirable heaven.' This was one of those thoughts of which he wrote a little later: 'If you think the fatal thought of men and institutions, you need never pull the trigger.'

5

The year 1858 was a frog and toad and turtle-egg year; a restless one also, for he is much away from Concord, to Worcester to see his friends there, and to New York, where a muskrat in a pool on Manhattan Island gets as much attention as the Egyptian relics in the museum. In June, he climbed Monadnock with Channing, spending two nights on top. In July, with Edward Hoar, who had helped start the forest fire that made so much trouble, he drove to the White Mountains, climbing and camping on Mount Washington. He was vigorous now, outstripping the rest in the climb, pitying Blake and Brown who, 'wet, ragged, and bloody with black flies,' joined them. They got no more sympathy than did Channing with a head-ache. There were people sick that way every morning who went about their business, he said, meaning probably himself, for, in spite of his strenuosity, it is clear that he was now fighting for health.

Five slept in one tent that night. Next day Henry fell in Tuckerman's Ravine, spraining his ankle. But he had noticed *Arnica mollis* growing the day before, and soon had his plaster ready. Both of these excursions are described at length in the Journal, but the style and subjects chosen are matter-of-fact. His imagination did not lift with the heights, possibly because he was not alone. He could not do as in Concord: 'If I am visited by a thought, I chew that cud each successive morning, as long as there is any flavor in it. Until my keepers shake down some fresh fodder.'

His local fame is now established, but not as a man of letters. Irishmen come to the kitchen in the morning to ask what the weather will be.

In spite of the slavery issue, he was still thinking as little as possible of politics. 'As for the Presidency,' he wrote this year in an unpublished letter to George William Curtis, now in the Middlebury College library, 'I cannot speak for my neighbors, but for my own part, I am politically so benighted that I do not know what Seward's qualifications are. I know, however, that no one in whom I could feel much interest would stand any chance of being elected. But the nail which is hard to drive is hard to draw' — a cryptic remark which seems to recognize his own obstinacy when his principles had fixed upon a cause and a man.

In September, he is off again with Channing to Cape Ann

and the Russells'. At home, he has a new sail for his boat, some five feet by six, which pulls like an ox — a homely, square sail, all for use, not show, and, like many of Thoreau's self-inventions, not very efficient. Never was life in Concord more revealing and more sweet. He studies the familiar pastures now like an old spellingbook. Even his friends cease to worry him in the mellow ripeness of his affection for home. 'Why, I never had any quarrel with a friend but it was just as sweet as unanimity could be. I do not think we budge an inch forward or backward in relation to our friends.' This mood was as near the sentimental as he could get, but surely this was a happy man. It was a gorgeous autumn — with from any hill a hundred tinted oaks looking like great roses on the slopes. Goodwin guessed his age this year as forty. Emerson was young-looking for his years, but 'he has not been out o' nights as much as you have.'

While he walked he meditated. What revived his lifelong animosity against the church — 'a baby-house made of blocks' he calls it — I do not know; but another outburst of indignation may have been inspired by a smarting memory of Lowell's mishandling of his *Atlantic* article. 'Look at your editors of popular magazines.... They are afraid to print a whole sentence, a *round* sentence, a free-spoken sentence. They want to get thirty thousand subscribers, and they will do anything to get them. They consult the D.D.'s and all the letters of the alphabet before printing a sentence.' 14 As for the Lyceums — and he still thought of himself as by profession a lecturer — 'They want all of a man but his truth and independence and manhood.' And, of course, these were bad times for free speakers. Intolerance was preparing for war.

Yet there was still high talk at Concord. In November of 1858, Alcott held a Conversation at Mrs. Emerson's, Thoreau, as often before, taking the place of Emerson, who was absent on a lecture tour. This time the indomitable Aunt Mary Emerson was present, with a black band over her left temple, and Henry James the elder, a hearty man, said Thoreau, with whom you could differ very satisfactorily. When James began on witty paradoxes, Alcott fell into polite silence — it was supposed to be *his* evening. But James this time spoke scornfully of the Moral Law, which called forth lightning from the old lady, whose wit, said Emerson, was the wild horse of the desert. She did not shake him, as was reported, though she did rise to her four feet, three, of height to emphasize her words. What she thought of his doctrines of Satan was not left in doubt! James had proposed, said Thoreau, to give criminals sympathy instead of turkeys on Thanksgiving. Neither the stoic Thoreau nor the Calvinist Aunt Mary had much use for such a metaphysical philanthropy.[15] Yet Henry must have said something sharper, for James remembered him in 1881 as 'literally the most childlike, unconscious and unblushing egotist it has ever been my fortune to encounter.' [16] These two, though they had liked each other at first meeting, did not belong to the same tribe.

Cholmondeley, with his Oxford culture, was back again and went to New Bedford with him. His father was ill and dying. For this, and other reasons, he refused to accompany his English friend to the West Indies. So ended the year of 1858.

6

Winter of 1859 brought out the musquash hunters, and, from Thoreau, reflections on animal death that would shock the S.P.C.A. In some guise, he thought, the aboriginal Indian in us is always seeking God's nourishment. The hunters in search of wild food keep a savage hold on life while they kill, which is better than to be weak and despairing.

His quiet father, grown more talkative of late years as Henry's
interests increased in old Concord and its traditions, died on
February 3. 'I have touched,' Thoreau wrote, 'a body which
was flexible and warm, yet tenantless.' John senior had belonged to the village street as Henry to the woods and his study.
He loved to sit in the shops and 'remembered more about the
worthies (and unworthies) of Concord village forty years ago . . .
than any one else. . . . I perceive that we partially die ourselves
through sympathy at the death of each of our friends or near
relatives. Each such experience is an assault on our vital force.'
For a while the notes of the winter birds cease to stir Thoreau,
but soon he is writing contentedly that a river begins where a
drop strikes and runs down the ravine on the slope of his
nose.

In February, 'Autumnal Tints,' long accumulating, was read
in Worcester. Someone in the audience asked, did the lecturer
think his audience had never seen them? He replied that
they never had. And of course they never had seen what he
put into his prose, which shows no decline in power in these
years. Soil erosion, arrowheads, forest care are his obsessions
now, which his Journal records in lengthy notes for each day.
There is a quarry here of nature-writing — ripples of water,
hounds' voices, grasses, birdsongs — which was full of promise
for the book that was never completed. Temper interrupts occasionally, as when he slams at the English fur traders for using
British America for their mousing. The cruelties of the musquash
hunters had not offended him, but theirs was a small business,
and in Concord! At night he thinks with inexpressible satisfaction of the arrowheadiferous sands of Concord, exulting in
his life with a clinging quality of emotion as if he were unsure:
'Nothing must be postponed. . . . There is no other land; there
is no other life but this, or the like of this.'

7

In 1859, the river-meadow proprietors were suffering from the flooding of their haying land by water backed from various obstructions, and so Thoreau got what, in the eyes of Concord, must have been his first important job. Both mill dams and bridges were involved. He was employed to study depths of water, and at the same time investigate the history of bridges and their abutments.[17] No task could have been more congenial. It took him for sixteen miles up and eleven down the Concord and Sudbury, and for five or six up the Assabet. Until mid-August his Journal records measurings, researches, and the hydraulic speculations of a fertile mind. He and his companion drank the muddy water when thirsty, bathed, and made long days out-of-doors, and he brought home a fresh crop of observations of his prairial regions of more value than his wages. It was about this time that he inscribed a map now in Concord, 'Henry D. Thoreau, Civil Engineer.' Even his recurrent ill health (he felt 'heavy-headed'), which may have been the result of too much hard exercise, yielded its dividends. 'It occurs to me that probably in different states of what we call health, even in morbid states,' he wrote, 'we are peculiarly fitted for certain investigations.'

Since his father's death, the responsibility for the now profitable graphite business had fallen on him. That September he might have been met searching the woods near Acton for a stone suitable for 'my lead-mill.' In spite of his dispraise of property, Thoreau had become, in his small way, a capitalist, which, contrary to the Marxian theory, had no effect on his sets of values, except perhaps to increase his intolerance of 'beggars and parasites.' 'I have many affairs to attend to,' — this in September — 'and feel hurried these days. Great works of art have endless leisure for a background, as the universe has space. . . . The artist cannot be in [a] hurry.' 'How many enemies there are to sane thinking,' he wrote to Blake this month. 'It is easy enough to maintain a family, or a state, but it is hard to maintain these children of your brain.' Then, as if to test his creative powers, he chants in the Journal his prose paean on the old Carlisle road, humorous, vivid, and never exceeded in gusto.

Now he begins to see dimly what the twentieth-century scientist has come to know, that the conclusions of science may be based on false premises without necessarily invalidating their practical usefulness. 'If you would make acquaintance with the ferns you must forget your botany. . . . You must be aware that *no thing* is what you have taken it to be. . . . Your greatest success will be simply to perceive that such things are. . . . If it were required to know the position of the fruit-dots or the character of the indusium, nothing could be easier than to ascertain it; but if it is required that you be affected by ferns, that they amount to anything, signify anything, to you . . . this end is not so surely accomplished. . . . So far science goes, and it punctually leaves off there, — tells you finally where it [the meaning] is to be found and its synonyms, and rests from its labors.'

But since the new skepticism of science as a substitute for reason is still in its infancy, a more convincing illustration of Thoreau's prophetic foresight will be found in his October paragraph on public forests:

> *Oct. 15. 1859.* . . . Each town should have a park, or rather a primitive forest, of five hundred or a thousand acres, where a stick should never be cut for fuel, a common possession forever, for instruction and recreation. We hear of cow-commons and ministerial lots, but we want *men*-commons and lay lots, inalienable forever. Let us keep the New World *new*, preserve all the advantages of living in the country. There is meadow

and pasture and wood-lot for the town's poor. Why not a forest and huckleberry-field for the town's rich? All Walden Wood might have been preserved for our park forever, with Walden in its midst, and the Easterbrooks Country, an unoccupied area of some four square miles, might have been our huckle-berry-field. If any owners of these tracts are about to leave the world without natural heirs who need or deserve to be specially remembered, they will do wisely to abandon their possession to all, and not will them to some individual who perhaps has enough already. As some give to Harvard College or another institution, why might not another give a forest or huckleberry-field to Concord? A town is an institution which deserves to be remembered. We boast of our system of education, but why stop at schoolmasters and schoolhouses? We are all school-masters, and our schoolhouse is the universe. To attend chiefly to the desk or schoolhouse while we neglect the scenery in which it is placed is absurd. If we do not look out we shall find our fine schoolhouse standing in a cow-yard at last.

Thoreau, that hater of institutions, had become by this time something of an institution in his own village. And he had established himself without compromise. Even now he refused to black his shoes, although the argument for economy was destroyed by the current practice of giving away a box of blacking with each pair. The boxes accumulated while the shoes stayed raw and red.

8

He had lectured in Theodore Parker's Temple in October, probably with success, or he would hardly have been invited to repeat the 'Plea for John Brown' there later to the usual great audience. The year 1860 begins for him as if there had been no execution of Brown, and no irreconcilable conflict impending. He is absorbed in his walks, out sometimes at sunrise, and keeping a copious Journal, with constant concern lest all the phenomena of Concord be not included. Little surveying is to be noted now, and less lecturing — the family business was probably all that he wished to carry on beside his real work, and brought in what cash was needed. The Thoreaus owned their home and the Texas house also; Henry, as executor for his father's estate, had given bond for ten thousand dollars, and the family, with its growing business, could now be reckoned among the comfortably well-to-do of Concord. But he was still economical. When, in the previous year, Emerson raised a fund to keep Alcott out of trouble, Henry set down one dollar unblushingly with Longfellow's and Lowell's fifty dollars apiece, and Emerson's one hundred dollars! [18]

In the winter he reads of fabulous beasts in Conrad Gesner's seventeenth-century volume, reflecting that the ancients took their animals into the imagination, which is what modern scientists fail to do. They drew them, even with four strokes, more beastlike than Mr. Ruskin's artist could make a tiger. 'A man has not seen a thing who has not felt it.' Yet his prejudice against classification does not blind him to the progress of science. This year he is reading and taking notes from Darwin's 'Origin of Species,' published in 1859. Emerson had earlier than this reported him as saying that Agassiz would make separate species out of two thrushes, but insists that two utterly diverse types of men have a common ancestor, which shows that the origin of species was being argued. Evolution as a theory was interesting him, but he was not converted.[19]

This year, too, he begins work on his notes of the characteristic qualities of the various months, more preparation for what he calls his Kalendar of Concord. In December, he had helped F. J. Merriam, one of Brown's followers, toward Canada, handling him tactfully, for the man was out of his mind. In the summer, he goes again to Monadnock for a still more strenuous excursion, builds a cabin, and stays for five nights, while Channing lies awake expecting some beast to nibble his toes. Hawthorne was in Concord after his consulship, 'as simple and childlike as ever,' says Thoreau, but there was not to be time for either to develop their friendship. In September, his long-continued studies of the propagation of forest trees was put into form for the Middlesex Agricultural Society, and printed afterward in *The Tribune* of October 8. In this paper and the further notes succeeding it in the Journal, Thoreau showed that he could accept, when he wished, both the discipline and the limited objectives of science. In the course of these notes is recorded the use of the rings of trees for dating natural phenomena,[20] although not until the twentieth century was this put into brilliant practice in the study of climate and archeology. Yet when Charles C. Morse asked him if he was open for lecture engagements, he still could answer: 'I *am* in the lecture field — but my subjects are not *scientific* — rather transcendental & aesthetic.' [21]

For the critics who have described these last years of Thoreau as decline and disintegration, the vigorous writing of 1860 is a sufficient rebuttal. His interest, to be sure, is more than ever obsessed by nature. But, interspersed with brief records which may indicate bad health, are brilliant passages of description and speculation. Page after page carries a headlong series of sentences recording evidence, set down with the confidence of one who expects results. His wrestlings with nature were producing concrete results, and this made him happy, even though the philosopher in him might have smiled at his excitement over his discovery that squirrels and birds had planted his oak trees.

It was his last enthusiasm. On the third of December at Smith's Hill, near the Cambridge turnpike, he was counting rings on a cut hickory and measuring the three white oaks on the southeast side. As it snowed the next day, it was probably

damp and cold; if so, dangerous for a man subject to bronchitis
who was prostrate counting rings on a length of hickory. He
came home to argue with Walcott and Sam Staples, who said
John Brown 'threw his life away,' and 'as good as said that, if
Christ *had* foreseen that he would be crucified, he would have
"backed out." Such are the principles and the logic of the
mass of men.' It sounds like a heated discussion, probably on a
street corner. Whatever the cause, Thoreau took a severe
cold, and this, as he wrote to Ricketson the next March, developed into 'a kind of bronchitis' which, except for experimental walks as far as the post-office on fine noons, kept him
in the house for the winter. His health, otherwise, he said, was
not affected, nor his spirits, yet 'if I knew how it began, I
should know better how it would end.' The answer came
quickly.

27. NEW ENGLAND SUNSET

THERE CAN HAVE been few deaths more enviable — if death is ever envied by happy people — than the decline and death of Henry Thoreau. For examples of such quiet adaptation to the new experience of dying, one must go back to the accounts of those Northumbrian saints and holy men — nature lovers, some of them, like Thoreau — in the Venerable Bede's 'Ecclesiastical History.' The certain knowledge of his irretrievable decay, which, by December, or January of 1862, was apparent to his friends, distressed but did not depress him. He had expected, said Channing, who was with him constantly, to live for forty years more. 'It was hoped that he would write a natural history of Concord, like White's Natural History of Selborne,' wrote Edward Jones.[1] 'His researches ... promised important acquisitions to science,' said Doctor C. T. Jackson, addressing the Boston Society of Natural History just after his death. 'If I were to live, I should have much to report on Natural History generally,' he wrote himself to a new admirer, Myron B. Benton, a few weeks before the end. In that still unorganized frontier where the interpretive spirit transforms science into literature, he had half a lifetime's work yet to do.

Still, as Channing said in his biography, 'No man had a better unfinished life.'

But he was amply prepared for disappointment. Thoreau had always lived in the present; if he left no wake, he had no discontented reachings toward the future. Immortality, he said, had not been his study, and therefore, in illness as in health, it was how to use his immediate life which was his concern. The anti-slavery orator Parker Pillsbury, an old friend of the Abolitionist Thoreaus, visiting him in the last weeks, wished to talk to him of the next world. Thoreau whispered, 'One world at a time.' [2]

2

In the winter of 1861, the Journal begins bravely with fragments of a lecture on wild berries, probably additions to his unpublished manuscript called 'Fruit Notes,' gathered mostly from the Journal of 1859, and now in the Morgan library. 'The berries which I celebrate,' he begins, preparing, I suppose, for the next lecture engagement, which may have been the fatal one in Waterbury, Connecticut, his last, which renewed his illness. The entries are intermittent, grow briefer, consist soon chiefly of memories and notes on reading. When earliest spring arrives, he describes the response of the willows, and then breaks into a rare note of defeat: 'Ah, willow! willow! Would that I always possessed thy good spirits.' Had increasing feebleness of limb and lungs spread to his inquiring spirit? In April and May his records become infrequent and drop to a sentence or two. After the May to July trip to Minnesota there is no date noted until October, then a few scattered notes, a storm described on November 3, and with it the end of his long Journal.

The spring of 1861 was a time of crisis for the country as well as for Thoreau. Lincoln, in whom, like most of the New Englanders, Thoreau seems to have had little confidence, had been inaugurated.[3] On April 12–14, Fort Sumter was bombarded and taken by South Carolinians. Two days earlier Thoreau had expressed the hope in a letter to Pillsbury that an unnamed friend would ignore 'Fort Sumter, and "Old Abe," and all that; for that is just the most fatal, and, indeed, the only fatal weapon you can direct against evil, ever; for, as long as you *know of it*, you are *particeps criminis*. What business have you, if you are an "angel of light," to be pondering over the deeds of darkness, reading the *New York Herald*, and the like? I do not so much regret the present condition of things in this country (provided I regret it at all), as I do that I ever heard of it.... Blessed were the days before you read a President's Message.... Blessed are they who never read a newspaper, for they shall see Nature, and through her, God.'

This is the mood of 'Civil Disobedience,' natural and justifiable in one who detested a compromising government, and who presumably despaired (as Sophia said later for herself) 'of ever living under the reign of Sumner or Phillips,' Sumner who was against all compromise, Wendell Phillips who was willing to let the Southern states depart, taking their curse of slavery with them.[4] To concern oneself with the vacillating leadership of the North before Sumter was a waste of valuable time. Such an attitude was good morals, if bad statesmanship, for it was not the Union Thoreau wanted to save, but his own personal integrity. A weak and muddling government was best ignored for issues more eternal than a squabble over states' rights. That was how he felt.

But if he was not reading *The New York Herald*, he was poring over the Abolitionist *Tribune*, and when the North rallied to an unreconcilable conflict and Lincoln took his stand, he forgot about nature. When the first reverses came in battle, he told his sister that he would never get well until the war was ended. And yet Moncure Conway says that after the battle of Bull Run he was the only cheerful man in Concord; he was in a state of exaltation about the moral regeneration of the nation.[5] War seemed the noblest way, and his support of it was un- questioned. Cholmondeley, who had experience in the realities of war, wrote him that he believed the human race would some day get rid of its stupidity altogether. War would become too frightful. If Thoreau had answered his letter, he would not have agreed; like Ortega y Gasset in his 'Invertebrate Spain,' he deprecated soldiering while praising war. As with many another idealist, his attitude toward the disastrous conflict just beginning was more honest than wise.

3

In May of this year, he was persuaded to seek a dryer climate. Channing and Blake both failing him, he set out with the young naturalist, Horace Mann, for Niagara Falls, en route for Chicago and the upper Mississippi at St. Paul and Minneapolis, and home by way of Mackinaw. Some benefit was hoped from inland air, but as a journey and as a cure, the trip was inevitably disappointing. The old Northwest had been a favorite place of emigration for Massachusetts folk, and was much talked about in Concord. Emerson, in 1850, had planned to go to the Council of the Indians at the Falls of St. Anthony.[6] It was safely distant from the seat of war, and there was the great Mississippi for a river-lover, and, on reservations on the near-by plains, the Sioux for a student of Indian history who had never seen a savage in his primitive state. Two years earlier, the marvellous river and the wild men of the plains might have been the subject for the richest of his Excursions. It was too late. The man was dead-alive, and the letters he wrote and the notes he kept [7] are perfunctory, uninspired, dull. Not even the Indian council at the Redwood agency, with its oratory and half-naked dances, which 'Henry D. Thoreau, Esq. the celebrated abolitionist,' [8] as the Minneapolis paper called him, journeyed to see on a river steamer, could stir him to more than a faint interest. It was too late for new experiences.

And yet, knowing Thoreau, it is easy to guess another reason for his indifference to a sight which Easterners far less concerned with primitive life would have found thrilling. The Indians were genuine. Thoreau met Little Crow, their chief, who later, as a government scout in charge of a war band which would obey only him, took part in wild Indian battles in which Arapahoes and Winnebagoes stripped themselves naked before fighting to the death. But the 'Payment,' as they called the expedition to carry subsidy to the natives, was a commercialized affair, a river party with a German band aboard, 'a bevy of beautiful ladies,' gamblers to bring the Indians' money home again, and a circus atmosphere at the agency, which must have put off this lover of sincerity.[9] It was not the Western Indians, but the show-off at the agency which failed to impress Thoreau.

Only one incident of the two months' trip moved him to show any strong interest, and that was linked with his past. Still able to get about, hunt birds' nests, study the Minnesota gopher and the wild pigeon, he found at last the wild crab apple which he had seen in bloom from the window of his train. For the last time the romance of nature pursued in her difficult secrets appears in his pages. Whether the West would ever have stirred him as he was daily stirred to love and excitement in his New England woods and pastures, is uncertain, for this experiment of travelling far away from Concord came too late.

Though writing was difficult for him, he could still talk with pleasure, so in August he paid a last visit to Ricketson in New Bedford, of which nothing is recorded except the ambrotype taken with full beard — a sick man's face, from which and from memory Walton Ricketson, son to Daniel, made the idealized medallion in profile, with magnificent nose and waving beard. In November or December, he began to sink.

4

It was a strange last illness, in a household drawn together as never before, with friends and acquaintances dropping in constantly, and boys and neighbors bringing game and flowers to the invalid. He had his narrow rattan day-bed, made by himself, brought down to the parlor for sociability, and as long as he could do so insisted upon eating with the family at table. His voice sank to a whisper, he had an incessant cough, but his serenity was never disturbed. Sam Staples, once his jailer, later his rodman on surveying jobs, came to see him. 'Never spent an hour with more satisfaction,' he told Emerson. 'Never saw a man dying with so much pleasure and peace.' Theophilus Brown, Blake's Worcester associate, heard him talk with 'the same depth of earnestness and the same infinite depth of fun going on at the same time.' [10] Aunt Louisa, still a Calvinist, asked if he had made his peace with God. But he had never quarrelled with Him, he replied. And to Channing, who spoke of the approaching solitude, he murmured, 'It is better some things should end.'

Until the very end he worked whenever his strength would permit, for often in his feebleness he could not rouse himself to labor. Fields, the new editor of *The Atlantic Monthly*, had commissioned a series of articles, and paid him a hundred dollars down, probably for the first. [11] They were to be his old nature lectures converted into essays, and these he was editing while

Henry David Thoreau
'A sick man's face'
From an ambrotype taken by E. S. Dunshee in 1861

he could. 'Walking,' 'Autumnal Tints,' 'Wild Apples' were published just after his death. 'Night and Moonlight,' printed in 1863, was also being revised. 'You know it is the fashion to leave an estate behind you,' Mary Hosmer Brown reports him as saying, and it was a desire to leave literary assets for his family rather than any lingering hope of designing his Concord history which kept him at work under such hardships.

Fragments of correspondence show that he was at the same time trying to arrange through Ticknor and Fields for a new edition of the 'Week.' [12] Channing notes on the margin of his copy of this book that he was working also upon his Allegash narrative of the Maine woods, which may account for his last murmured words of 'moose' and 'Indian.' It would seem that his concern at the very end was not, as his biographers have assumed from these mutterings, with his life in the forest, but with some question of editing or of style. Nor was it the humor, as Sanborn reports, that he was editing out of these manuscripts as too trivial for high purposes, but rather, as Channing who was with him authentically states, the 'innuendoes, sallies, or puns, that formerly luxuriated amid the serious pages,' [13] stylistic vices to which he knew himself subject and which at the brink of death he tried to reform.

And so, quietly, at nine in the morning of May 6, 1862, having been lifted upright on his couch, he died imperceptibly with neither apparent struggle nor pain.

5

They gave him a public funeral in the parish church — an irony for this man who loved neither church nor publicity. Alcott read his 'Sic Vita,' that poem on youth's indecisions, all now decided. Emerson, 'with broken, tender voice,' read a eulogy which, somewhat expanded, was published in the

Atlantic for August, and included later in his Works. It was a tribute of one friend with genius to another younger, whose genius was different, but not less.

That day they buried him in Sleepy Hollow Cemetery on those woody knolls which were his pleasure in Concord. He lies near Emerson and Lidian, and Cynthia and Sophia, and John the father and his beloved brother, John.

28. THOREAU IN HISTORY

THOREAU'S REPUTATION AFTER his death became the property of a cult, for although so doubtful of the success of human relationship, and in his own opinion so unsuccessful in love, he left behind him friends sensitive to every slight upon their Henry, and determined to make his name prevail. Unfortunately their love for him was greater than their love for each other, and they venerated in their hero their own favorite beliefs.

Sophia, who was his literary executor, lived in his memory and often wept over it. She had to be handled carefully by friends and publishers, for even when they escaped from the volubility of her mother, they found her fanatical in her desire to carry out what she thought would have been her brother's wishes. She quarrelled with Sanborn — 'I never associate him with my brother,' she said to Mrs. Fields, wife of the publisher [1] — and wished to put the manuscripts of the Journal in the Concord library so that Channing could not get at them, after which he would not speak to her on the street. A vast mass of manuscript was left to her. 'Make Helen feel [Alcott is speaking to Mrs. Fields, and must have said 'Sophia,' for Helen was long dead] that Henry will receive as much for his books as if he had made his own bargain, for he was good at a bargain and ... they do not understand all the bearings of many subjects,' which was Alcott's way of urging the publishers to be tactful. But Sophia, though in control of the unpublished work, did not try to write herself.

Channing was different. Sanborn and he both felt that the attacks of Thoreau's contemporaries after his death — Lowell in *The North American Review*, James Freeman Clarke, Transcendentalist and friend of Margaret Fuller, in an unspecified article, and W. R. Alger — had all given a false impression of Thoreau as an egoist, a poseur, and a crank, which must be corrected. Alger, Unitarian minister and anti-slavery man, had included in his curious book, 'The Solitudes of Nature and of Man; or, The Loneliness of Human Life,' some sketches of lonely characters, among them Thoreau. His thoughtful criticism is a sympathetic and more penetrating statement of Lowell's point of view. It was Thoreau's marked egoism that troubled him: 'The key of his life is the fact that it was devoted to the art of an interior aggrandizement of himself.' Every trifle had to be associated with self, which is always a mark of spiritual disturbance. 'There was uncommon love in him, but it felt itself repulsed,' and so put on a mask of stoicism.

All this was true, but Alger and Lowell both overestimated the society from which Thoreau withdrew. 'Many a humble and loving author,' Alger thought, had braced and enriched his readers, while Thoreau taught them to be unsatisfied. These men, and other critics, could not believe that radical dissatisfaction with the nineteenth century was anything but an egoistic pose. They could not see, like the wise Howells, that while the reformers were concentrating on the evils of slavery, Thoreau was prophetically criticizing the 'infinitely crueler and stupider vanity and luxury bred of' industrial slavery, and the 'unworthiness' of our civilization. 'If there was then any prevision of the struggle now at hand, the seers averted their eyes, and strove only to cope with the less evil.' [2] They did not foresee the twentieth century and the collapse of Victorian complacency, and so Thoreau's flank attack on their optimism seemed merely neurotic, although they did not use the word. Of course it was neurotic, but only a neurotic egotist could, in the Concord of that day, have been irritated into a truth-seeing discontent.

This was not Channing's view or Sanborn's. They objected to these criticisms because the strictures on Thoreau's character threatened his reputation. There seems to have been little reason for their fears. The articles published in quick series in *The Atlantic Monthly*, the books edited by Sophia and her friends and printed by Ticknor and Fields — first the 'Excursions' in 1863, then 'The Maine Woods' in 1864, then, in 1865, Emerson's edition of Thoreau's letters, with the most human left out, and 'Cape Cod' in the same year — gave Thoreau to a wider reading public than he reached in his lifetime. 'Walden' was reprinted in 1863, 1864, and 1866, the 'Week' was reissued in 1862, and reprinted in 1868. And these publications were well received, though it would be too much to say that they were widely popular. Before he had been dead three years, the best of Thoreau, except his Journal, was readily accessible in print.

2

Yet his reputation did not grow in proportion, and for reasons much more significant than any damning review or personal attack. His Transcendental intensities were already out of date, his nature love was still prophetically in advance of a craze which was to sweep the country in another generation, and his criticism of society had to wait for due appreciation until nineteenth-century optimism and American manifest destiny had crashed in the twentieth century.

The Civil War gave the death blow to American Transcendentalism. It lingered, or was transformed into other varieties of idealism, often debased, yet its high hopes, its splendid intensity, its beautiful confidence were gone. Pressing upon utterance everywhere in Thoreau except in his factual nature notes and the Travel Books, its high idealisms became less and less congenial after the early sixties, and soon were almost unintelligible. Even Emerson, who knew how to write a sermon, began then to lose his eminence as a leader of thought.

Nor was the humorous skepticism of the author of 'Walden,' who was so doubtful of what his fellow townsmen called progress, and so scornful of expansion Westward and dollarward, any more congenial to the readers of this gilded age after the Civil War. His skepticism must have seemed incomprehensible, or impertinent, to the Northern or Western reader who saw manifest destiny building the greatest of plutocracies under his eyes. The South, if it had read in the days of its ruin, might have understood Thoreau better, for some of its best citizens had known how to live.[3] Yet his sarcasm heaped upon gold-diggers and promoters buried under their own wealth was more understandable by the tough new times of get-rich-quick than were the spiritual exaltations of Transcendentalism.

Ellery Channing's fervid biography, 'Thoreau, the Poet-Naturalist,' served only to emphasize that an age as well as a man was dead. Written in 1863, although not published until 1873, and, in complete form, not until 1902, it is on the defensive. Without plan and without restraint, it is not so much a biography as a series of essays in praise of the spiritual insight of a beloved friend who has been accused of egoism and eccentricity. Thoreau, for Channing, is a master of the secrets of nature who sees with a poet's eye truths too ethereal for science to grasp, and a moralist unwilling to live in corrupted air. All that was Transcendental, romantic, and moralistic in Thoreau is defiantly celebrated in this book, which was not likely to make Thoreau popular in the go-getting seventies, or indeed in any age, except among those already converted who could appreciate the passionate friendship throbbing in this partisan estimate. In Channing's book, for the first time, extensive quotations, well chosen, from the Journal appeared, but the over-literary style of the context made them seem tense and extravagant. Thoreau in this book is a superman of nature, a seer and hero no more viable than Channing himself, and quite alien to contemporary America. Unfortunately, Emerson's selections of the less personal and more exalted letters of Thoreau for publication in 1865 must also have contributed to the impression that the dead man belonged to another era.

Nor did Thoreau's younger friend, Frank Sanborn, help when in 1882 he published a biography of his acquaintance who was scarcely his friend. Sanborn himself had the inconsecutive mind which seemed to be one of the by-products of the Transcendental movement. His first book, and his larger volume of 1917, were quite as much eulogies of Concord as of Thoreau, and were stuffed and warped with ideals of reform and mistaken views of Thoreau's scientific importance. Yet his carefully collected reminiscences made Thoreau seem at least human.

It was not until 1890 that a coherent and intelligible life of Thoreau was written, and then by an Englishman, H. S. Salt, whose task was to set in order the discursive narratives of Thoreau's friends, with some additions, and a more judicial view. But Annie Russell Marble's 'Thoreau. His Home, Friends and Books' of 1902 is again on the defensive; and it was left to the Frenchman Léon Bazalgette, in 'Henry Thoreau. Sauvage,' [4] written in what was then a new style of dramatized biography, to recognize that Thoreau was one of the significant personalities of the modern age.

Yet in spite of the attempts of his friends to make him a philosopher of science when science was not yet ready to be philosophized, and a hero of stoicism in an age when stoicism was out of date, Thoreau's reputation slowly spread. 'Walden' persisted. There were numerous editions in the nineteenth century here and in England, some of them, of course, only reprints, and two translations into German, though only one American edition in the go-getting seventies. Nevertheless, not only the comments of Lowell and his other contemporaries, but also the strictures of Oliver Wendell Holmes in his 'Ralph Waldo Emerson' of 1885, and Robert Louis Stevenson's essay on Thoreau of 1880, show how antipathetic to both the gilded and the genteel age were the social radicalism and the ruthless analysis of values in that book. To those who did not understand the significance of its ideology, 'Walden' seemed exaggerated, impertinent, conceited. As an editorial writer on *The New York Commercial Advertiser* said on July 12, 1888, 'His "thoughts" are of no use to anybody nowadays, but his pictures of hill and valley, forest and field and stream, have an enduring and great value.'

That was the precise truth for the eighties. The series of Excursions published as one volume after Thoreau's death, the Travel Books, and the nature scenes from 'Walden' gave him a vogue, richly deserved of course, as a nature writer, and kept him in moderate popularity until the writers of the romantic back-to-nature movement of the eighties, nineties, and early 1900's picked him up. They found in his writings a point of departure, and in him a progenitor whose passion for nature they understood far better than the deep spiritual convictions which gave his style an eloquence and an edge which they could never attain. With better instruments and with libraries of scientific classification, they corrected his errors in observation. Yet already Burroughs and Muir fade, while the best of Thoreau's nature studies outlast the sentimentality which was the disease of the movement that called him father.

In his native country, and in spite of occasional appreciation by shrewder minds than the editor of *The New York Advertiser*, his reputation remained that of a nature writer until the second decade of the twentieth century. In my own youth he was known to us as a man who wrote about birds and animals for children! When the study of English literature began to be a mainstay of the curriculum in American colleges, Thoreau had no fixed place there. The gusty Carlyle and the 'indoors' Ruskin were firmly established as meat for young Americans, while 'Walden' was neither mentioned nor read. His terse, pungent style was, in fact, too staccato, too American, and his subjects too homely, for the taste of professors of English — with exceptions that could be counted on the fingers of one hand.

It seems probable that the first recognition of his modest but certain place in world literature came abroad, and in England, where the nascent British Labor Party, offspring of William Morris and Marx, used 'Walden' as a pocket-piece and travelling Bible of their faith.⁵ And rightly, for this movement, truly Fabian in character, was social rather than narrowly economic, its purpose being to restore and create and distribute true values in everyday living. Robert Blatchford's 'Merrie England' of 1895, one of the background books of English socialism, and much influenced by Thoreau, sold two million copies.

In the twentieth century, there has been no lack of appreciation of all aspects of Thoreau's genius. The studies of Edward Carpenter, of Paul Elmer More, of Mark Van Doren, of Lewis Mumford, of Brooks Atkinson, of Van Wyck Brooks, of Vernon L. Parrington, and many others have shown a lively awareness of his social significance and literary merit beyond the arts of narrative and description. The sixties and seventies were no more certain to deprecate his 'message,' the eighties and nineties and 1900's were no more sure to celebrate nature writing, than the tens, twenties, and thirties were bound to recognize his prophetic insights. For by then, and particularly by the 1930's, the smug complacence of the Victorian age had crumbled into disillusion. Daily living in America was no longer invigorated by the speculative excitement of a moving frontier; it had been mechanized into comfort, and was threatened by a dull discontent, except when menaced by social disturbances or by war. An economic system which had offered an illusory freedom to the individual who worked for its ends, no longer promised even the illusion. A political system which had been ignored by the self-reliant began to set limits upon the rights and customs of personal desire. For the first time in the history of our republic, the individual had to take his stand, determining what he proposed to yield to the state, and what he proposed to fight for as essential to his spiritual and physical well-being. And, thanks to a wide shift in moral standards, with a resulting breakdown of the old controls, and the failure of material success to produce happiness, there was a doubt of the values we had sought in living not equalled in the memory of living man.

3

Nevertheless, these general statements hardly account for the increase in vitality of Thoreau's best books in recent years. His influence had been felt earlier by first-class minds like Tolstoy [6] and Gandhi,[7] and by many writers throughout the world otherwise ignorant of the golden age of New England. It is characteristic of his curious influence that William Butler Yeats, felt by many to be the greatest poet in English of this day, should have been inspired to seek his island paradise of Innisfree, where he could live alone and search for wisdom, by 'Walden,' read to him in his early youth by his father.[8] Today, there is a curious working upward in his own country from some unrecognized substratum of interest, and his sentences begin to appear with increasing frequency as quotations and themes for editorials, articles, and chapters in native books. The man may or may not be extensively read, but he seems to be better read now than any other writer, including Emerson, among the so-called classic writers of our tradition. What has given Thoreau so enviable a place in our literature?

Thoreau, unlike Emerson, was not one of the wise men of the earth whose serenity transfuses their style. He was too maladjusted psychologically to be a preacher, a healer, or even a humorist. That *anima* of his, as Jung would call it, created by unsatisfied desires and unexpanded elements in his being, was constantly plaguing him in one guise or another, and sometimes driving him to extremes of contradiction or attack which were symptoms of a mind in distress. In spite of all his efforts at self-knowledge, he learned to understand only his conscious desires, never the ultimate causes of his temperamental disorders. And this was most true of his sexual impulses, which were distorted, transformed, sublimated, or suppressed, in the attempt to make them conform to his moral ideas and economic necessities. The effect of this tension upon his body he seems to note, even in its physical details,[9] but did not know that his softness toward women was the feminine in his nature, constantly thwarted or repressed either by himself or by circumstance. There is a straining tensity in Thoreau, and a frequent distortion of human relations, which make him seem, in comparison with other great writers, emotionally immature, and is reflected in the unevenness of his style.

But he was and is, without qualification, a great critic of

values in living; perhaps, considering the radical and realistic application of his criticism to the trend of a century, the greatest critic of values among modern writers in English. This is because of the homeliness of his own experience, and because of his habit of referring every speculation to himself and to Concord. Like Socrates in this respect if in no other, he talked always of his townsmen and of himself, who were real people in a real environment. I am aware, of course, that his times were fruitful in criticism of the values men set upon their ways of living. Carlyle's career was built upon such criticism. Ruskin carried it into a war against the debasements of industrialism. Emerson set new values for souls starved by formalized religion. Yet it was only Thoreau who went into the desert like the Egyptian eremites to live his belief. And it was Thoreau who spoke direct to the condition of everyday men caught in the quiet desperation of difficult careers — men who were not speculative, not even religious, yet unable to do what they wanted, even to know what they wanted. His account of the pressure of subsistence upon freedom, upon happiness, upon content, came closest to the general problem of a rapidly industrializing society.

It was to preserve what for him were essential values in living that he took his stand for civil disobedience, and for a life based on principle. Carlyle's loud cries for heroes to set new ideals for society reverberate through marginal regions where dictators wait their opportunity. Emerson appealed to spiritual impulses already confused by the revelations of science. Ruskin, rich man and aristocrat, would have driven out mass production, without which the masses could never be prepared for civilized life. In contrast to these preachers and orators was Thoreau's simple test of the makers of programs and pronunciamentos — I shall see how they treat me first. In a century of growing collectivism, where the balance between the rights of

the individual and the needs of the state was to swing precari-
ously toward the loss of personal freedom, his is the most manly,
most common-sense voice. 'Here is coloring for half a dozen
Socialisms,' said Alcott, writing of Thoreau.[10] If an individual
is to remain a person, be himself and not a belt-driven wheel in a
machine, what does he need and how can he keep it? That was
his theme.

4

But theme alone is no preservative of reputation. The final
and most important cause of Thoreau's lasting success is his
power over words. At his best he is a superb writer, one of
those shapers of language who give age-old ideas their final
form. Thanks to this, his sentences and paragraphs escape
from the dead hands of time.

Of course, he was by no means always or often at his best.
His writing is like some of those old Concord houses he liked to
clamber over, impressive in spite of many faults in design and
execution. He is too mannered, too inconsecutive, too unre-
strained, to be numbered among the impeccable talents who
can be safely imitated. But we quickly forget makeshifts and
experiments if a masterpiece comes out of the disorder. Thoreau's best nature studies are good not on account of their
science but because of the flowing garment of words. They are
good because they are interesting, they are interesting because
of the 'perfect correspondence' between nature and the scene
as felt and as described by the observer.[11] His chapters on
values, his declarations of private independence, are not so
much philosophy as a creation in words of the man himself.
He understood very well that intuition, thought, and imagination are not enough. Therefore he learned how to make sentences ring in the memory.

Without this power of style, Thoreau would still be a good subject for a Stracheyan study of a noble eccentric, and a theme for social historians. As a writer who could transform imagination into words themselves creative of thinking, he has a more significant place in biography. If his style is himself, it is equally true that all that he had gets into his style.

5

Thoreau has earned his high place in modern literature, but there are many moderns ranking with him in eminence who do not have the peculiar timeliness which readers today are finding in his books. He has become timely in a way which would have surprised his friends, who prophesied that some day the world would recognize its greatest poet-naturalist. That has not happened — there was too much poetry in Thoreau's natural history for such a reputation. But if we are better naturalists than he could have been, we have also learned that some of his favorite topics, such as the correspondence between man and nature, are far more important than his scientist-contemporaries realized. The strain of living in a high-pressure society, whose tempo increases year by year, has but recently begun to make us understand that the dependence of man upon his natural environment is many aeons older than our need of the gadgets which we have invented for our comfort, and is far more necessary for physical and mental health. Also, we have learned from our psychiatrists the psychological importance of an outgoing of love, whether for a woodchuck, a bird, or a woman. Thanks to psychological studies, we are now well aware that the suppression of instinctive desires by conformity to a conventional pattern of worldly success may be disastrous to the personality. And, on a more material level, in America, we see clearly at last the results of the destruction of our heritage of woods, water, and wild life by the commercialism which, even in Thoreau's day, was felling all the noblest trees in Concord. All this is in Thoreau, with the freshness and vigor of prophecy.

His doctrine of simplicity seems to be more appropriate to the economy of scarcity from which it sprang than to the economy of abundance which is now at least possible for civilized man. This is not true. Thoreau's idea of simplicity was to sacrifice the inessential for the essential. He would have heartily enjoyed a bathtub if he could have bought one without paying too much for it in unprofitable labor and valuable time. But worship of technical skill while wisdom remained adolescent seemed to him a tragedy of unregulated energy. World history since 1914 has proved that he was right. The doctrine of simplicity, as he outlined it, supplies a standard of values, without which an economy of abundance can be a mere fattening yard for Thanksgiving turkeys.

In this also Thoreau is timely. As one of the modern advocates of this economy of abundance has said:

> The burden of our civilization is not merely, as many suppose, that the product of industry is ill-distributed, or its conduct tyrannical, or its operation interrupted by embittered disagreements. It is that industry itself has come to hold a position of exclusive predominance among human interests, which no single interest, and least of all the provision of the material means of existence, is fit to occupy. Like a hypochondriac who is so absorbed in the processes of his own digestion that he goes to the grave before he has begun to live, industrialized communities neglect the very objects for which it is worth while to acquire riches in their feverish preoccupation with the means by which riches can be acquired.[12]

Most timely of all, perhaps, are Thoreau's ideas of personal independence. It is personal independence which is being threatened on every hand today. In a society like ours, built upon an intricate technology which must be kept working. abstract principles of individualism may be abstractly true, and yet have little relevance to the business of living unless they can be applied without turning off the current, breaking the water pipes, halting the trains, and stopping the milk. Thoreau was able to live without the utilities in a hut in the woods; but that recourse solves none of our problems. His more important contribution to our thinking is a ringing definition of the values which the individual must, and can, preserve, even against the pressure of a mechanized society or a totalitarian state. Thoreau's stand was for himself, on his own Concord soil. It may seem to the pessimist to have been merely the obstinacy of a man fortunate enough to be born in a century when human rights were still respected. But the obstinacy itself is his message to the future. If human rights are to be preserved for the citizen, someone has to be obstinate, and particularly today. Although no political party will ever adopt his program of self-searching individualism, no private man, determined to keep the essentials of freedom, can afford to be ignorant of this armor against the tyranny of the state.

6

It has been my attempt in this book, with what means were in my power, to make the man as well as his work live on in American consciousness. Let the last word go, therefore, to Emerson, who knew him best, and loved him. His address at Thoreau's funeral closed with words of eloquent poignancy:

> The country knows not yet, or in the least part, how great a
> son it has lost. It seems an injury that he should leave in the
> midst his broken task, which none else can finish.... But he,
> at least, is content. His soul was made for the noblest society;
> he had in a short life exhausted the capabilities of this world;

wherever there is knowledge, wherever there is virtue, wherever there is beauty, he will find a home.

But more personal and even more touching were the simple phrases of his obituary notice, written for a Boston newspaper: 'When we now look back at the solitude of his erect and spotless person, we lament that he did not live long enough for all men to know him.' [13]

And it was not Thoreau of the haughty independence, nor the Thoreau who 'sometimes felt like a hound or a panther,' but the Henry whose friendship had the strength of love, that Emerson remembered in the twilight of his age. The wise man of Concord was serene and cheerful when Mrs. Gilchrist, Walt Whitman's English friend, visited him in the fall of 1878. His mind dwelt happily in the past but already dimness was spreading backward from a present which was no longer greatly his concern. '"What was the name of my best friend?" he will inquire of his wife. "Henry Thoreau," she will answer. "Oh, yes, Henry Thoreau." ' [14]

THE END

NOTES

THESE NOTES, with a few exceptions, have been prepared for students of Thoreau, and are not intended for the general reader unconcerned with sources and verification.

All references to the writings of Thoreau are to the Walden Edition. ('The Writings of Henry David Thoreau.' Boston and New York, Houghton Mifflin Company, cop. 1906. 20 vols.) Citations are made by the volume and page numbers only, the Roman numerals designating the volumes (I–XX) of the entire edition.

Where the date of a quotation from either the Journal of Thoreau or the Journal of Emerson has been sufficiently indicated in the text, no further reference has been deemed necessary. The author of this biography has, of course, drawn much biographical data from the two books on Thoreau by Frank B. Sanborn, and, to a less extent, from William Ellery Channing's biography of his friend, though he has checked, wherever possible, statements which, with Sanborn particularly, are not always accurate. Specific page references to these three volumes have been made only when such reference seemed useful or necessary.

The following sources of information are signified by corresponding short titles or abbreviations:

Rusk: 'The Letters of Ralph Waldo Emerson,' ed. R. L. Rusk. New York, Columbia University Press, 1939.

Emerson, Journal: 'Journals of Ralph Waldo Emerson. With Annotations,' ed. E. W. Emerson and W. E. Forbes. Boston and New York, Houghton Mifflin Company, 1909–1914.

Alcott, Journal: 'The Journals of Bronson Alcott,' ed. Odell Shepard. Boston, Little, Brown and Company, 1938.

Howe Collection: The collection of manuscripts and printed books in the possession of Mr. W. T. H. Howe at Freelands, Mentor, Kentucky.

Ward Correspondence: The correspondence, extending from 1770 to 1876, of the Ward family, preserved in Evanston, Illinois, as part of the Ward Trust.

H. M.: Manuscripts preserved in the Huntington Library.

Fi: Part of the correspondence of James T. Fields, preserved in the Huntington Library.

PREVIEW

1. The 'Biographical Sketch' was first published in 'Excursions' (Boston, 1863), 7–34.
2. VI, 171.
3. 'Shall I tell them [in New York] that I live in Concord, and in Concord we never drink tea sociably?' (Emerson to Lidian Emerson, Feb. 10, 1842; Rusk.)

CHAPTER I

1. So Alcott spelled it in his Journal for 1839. Hawthorne, when he first heard the name, spelled it 'Thorow.'
2. Class Book of the class of 1837; Harvard library. The entry is in Thoreau's hand.
3. There was cordiality, however, if not social familiarity, between the Thoreau family and the Emersons. Mrs. Thoreau spent the night with Lidian before the birth of her first daughter. (Emerson to Lucy Jackson Brown, Feb. 24, 1839; Rusk.)

CHAPTER II

1. IX, 304.
2. Morgan Library.
3. XV, 132.
4. The mortgage was for $1000, as Sanborn says. ('The Life of Henry David Thoreau. Including Many Essays Hitherto Un-

published and Some Account of His Family and Friends.'
Boston, 1917, 31.) The house looks small and humble as de-
picted in Edward G. Porter's 'Rambles in Old Boston, New
England' (Boston, 1887, 118.) Porter says that the sisters sold
it for $1000 in 1825, but this is an error. It was mortgaged then
for $1000 and again in 1832.

5. In a letter to his mother from Staten Island, July 7, 1843,
   Thoreau says: 'The demon which is said to haunt the Jones
   family, hovering over their eyelids with wings steeped in juice
   of poppies, has commenced another campaign against me. I am
   "clear Jones" in this respect at least.' This was the demon which
   led Uncle Charles Dunbar to sprout potatoes on Sunday mornings in order to keep awake.

6. Annie Russell Marble, 'Thoreau. His Home, Friends and Books'
   (New York, 1902), 43.

7. Mary Hosmer Brown, 'Memories of Concord' (Boston, cop.
   1926), 101.

8. Walter Elliott, 'The Life of Father Hecker' (New York, 1894),
   140. As, however, according to Channing's annotation on his
   gift copy of 'Walden,' he was the youth who tried to live on dry
   corn, coddling him would have been easy.

9. Edward Waldo Emerson, 'Henry Thoreau as Remembered by
   a Young Friend' (Boston, 1917), 124, 125; XV, 381; Marble,
   op. cit.; 'Reminiscences of Thoreau,' by an anonymous friend of
   Sophia's, *The Outlook*, LXIII, 14 (Dec. 2, 1898), 818.

10. E. W. Emerson, *op. cit.*, 60.

11. Fragment of a letter, Sept. 7, 1848; Ward Correspondence.

12. X, 440.

13. (Boston, 1885), 86.

14. (London, 1794), 5, 6.

15. J. A. C. Chaptal, comte de Chanteloup, 1756–1832.

16. VI, 12, 13.

17. E. W. Emerson, *op. cit.*, 125.

CHAPTER III

1. From an unpublished manuscript of Thoreau's; quoted by
   Sanborn, 'Henry D. Thoreau' (Boston, 1883), 152, 153.

2. *The Outlook, op. cit.*, 820.

3. XV, 210, 211.
4. VIII, 306.
5. 222–224.
6. From an early manuscript draft of 'A Week on the Concord and Merrimack Rivers'; quoted in 'The First and Last Journeys of Thoreau,' ed. Sanborn (Boston, 1905), I, xviii.
7. From an unpublished draft for the Journal, Oct. 6, 1851; Middlebury College Library.
8. H. M. 13182.
9. Class Book of the class of 1837; entry made for Thoreau in 1847.
10. 232.
11. 365.

CHAPTER IV

1. John Albee, 'Remembrances of Emerson' (New York, 1901), 22.
2. 'A New England Boyhood' (New York, cop. 1893), 217, 218, 228.
3. While at Harvard Thoreau lived, sometimes alone, sometimes with a roommate, at 20, 31, 31, 32, and 23 Hollis in that order. So states Henry Waterman, *The Boston Home Journal*, Jan. 17, 1903.
4. Sanborn, 'Recollections of Seventy Years' (Boston, 1909), II, 319.
5. Herbert S. Gorman, 'A Victorian American. Henry Wadsworth Longfellow' (New York, cop. 1926), 217.
6. Report of the President, 1836–1837.
7. Sanborn, 'Henry D. Thoreau,' 55, 56.
8. 'Life of Henry Wadsworth Longfellow. With Extracts from his Journals and Correspondence,' ed. Samuel Longfellow (Boston, 1886), I, 251. This evidence is also drawn from Longfellow's mark books, in the possession of Henry W. L. Dana.
9. David Greene Haskins, 'Ralph Waldo Emerson. His Maternal Ancestors. With Some Reminiscences of Him' (Boston, 1887), 119.
10. He was capable of this atrocity for his Class Book:

> 'Friends! that parting tear reserve it,
> Tho' 'tis doubly dear to me!
> Could I think I did deserve it,
> How much happier would I be.'

11. *Op. cit.*
12. 150.
13. E. W. Emerson, *op. cit.*, 17.
14. 55–57.
15. (Boston, 1898), 52, 53.
16. In their senior year Thoreau had 190 points, Morison, 310.
17. 72.
18. Moncure Daniel Conway, 'Emerson at Home and Abroad' (Boston, 1882), 281.
19. VI, 138.

CHAPTER V

1. William Ellery Channing, 'Thoreau. The Poet-Naturalist. With Memorial Verses' (Boston, 1902), 32.
2. III (July, 1840).
3. See Arthur M. Schlesinger, Jr., 'Orestes A. Brownson: A Pilgrim's Progress,' Boston, 1939. The statement as to the influence upon Thoreau is made upon my own responsibility.
4. Brownson, 'The Convert: or, Leaves from My Experience' (New York, 1857), 96.
5. Henry F. Brownson, 'Orestes A. Brownson's Early Life: From 1803 to 1844' (Detroit, 1898), 204–206.

CHAPTER VI

1. VI, 12.
2. See page 165.
3. The date of the Journal entry was October 22d. On October 23d Emerson notes in an unpublished paragraph of his own Journal that he could think of but three, aside from himself, Alcott, M. M. E. (his Aunt Mary), and Montaigne [!] as keeping journals. It seems evident that he had been urging a like practice on Thoreau.
4. Channing, *op. cit.*, 18.
5. VI, 39.
6. Channing, *op. cit.*, 32.
7. E. W. Emerson, *op. cit.*, 21.

8. Odell Shepard, 'Pedlar's Progress. The Life of Bronson Alcott' (Boston, 1937), 121.

9. Prudence Ward to Mrs. Ward, April 13, 1838; Ward Correspondence.

10. John Thoreau to George Sewall, Dec. 31, 1839; Ward Correspondence.

11. VII, 211.

12. VI, 33, 34.

13. George F. Hoar, who was in school with Henry, though younger, says that Thoreau walked eighteen miles to Boston and eighteen back at night in order to hear Emerson lecture. ('Autobiography of Seventy Years.' New York, 1903, I, 72.)

14. Sanborn, 'The Life of Henry David Thoreau,' 128, 129. See Emerson to James Bradley Thayer, August 25, 1865; Rusk.

15. Sanborn, *op. cit.*

16. Emerson to William Emerson, Nov. 16, 1838; Emerson to Margaret Fuller, Sept. 28, 1838; Rusk.

17. *Op. cit.*, 73.

CHAPTER VII

1. I, iv, 535.

2. See Lowell, 'A Fable for Critics.' I believe that the 'brother bard' of this well-known quotation was undoubtedly Channing. It was Channing who puffed and blew after Thoreau in the bushes. It was Thoreau who knew Emerson first and had 'picked up all the windfalls before.'

3. 'The Memoirs of Julian Hawthorne,' ed. Edith Garrigues Hawthorne (New York, 1938), 94.

4. Emerson to Margaret Fuller, May 8, 1840; Rusk.

5. 'The Complete Works of Ralph Waldo Emerson,' ed. E. W. Emerson (Boston, 1903–1904; Centenary Edition), X, 342 ('Historic Notes of Life and Letters in New England').

6. *Ibid.*

7. I owe this suggestion to Professor Filmer S. C. Northrop, of Yale University.

8. Haskins, *op. cit.*, 121, 122.

9. Henry S. Salt, 'The Life of Henry David Thoreau' (London, 1890), 57.

10. Emerson to Margaret Fuller, Feb. 7, 1839; Emerson to Mary Moody Emerson, Dec. 22, 1839; Rusk.
11. Conway, *op. cit.*, 282.
12. Emerson, Journal, III, 460, 461.
13. VI, 84.
14. The context suggests that Thoreau was meant.
15. Emerson to Thoreau, Feb. [?] 15 [?] 1839 [?]; Rusk.

CHAPTER VIII

1. Emerson, Journal, VI, 469.
2. *The Dial*, ii, iv (April, 1842), 426.
3. VII, 26, 27.
4. *Idem*, 18.
5. *Idem*, 28.
6. *Idem*, 62–64.
7. *Idem*, 13.

CHAPTER IX

1. Most of the pleasures which Esther Alice Peck describes in 'A Conservative Generation's Amusements' (University of Maine Studies, 2d ser., no. 44, April, 1938) are mentioned in Thoreau's Journal.
2. Sanborn, 'Henry D. Thoreau,' 144–146.
3. VI, 32.
4. This story was first told with some of its more intimate details by T. M. Raysor. ('The Love Story of Henry Thoreau,' *Studies in Philology*, xxiii, 4 [Oct., 1926], 457–463.) I have relied, however, not upon his paper, but upon the complete correspondence of the Ward family, upon which he drew; upon sections of a largely unpublished Journal of Thoreau's for 1840–1841; and upon my own deductions from the Journal, the poems, and passages in the 'Week' which can be shown to have a direct relationship.
5. In March of 1840.
6. Thoreau's first published poem; *The Dial*, i, i (July, 1840), 71, 72.
7. Edmund in later years was both piqued and puzzled when he was called by the family the 'gentle boy.'

8. Mrs. Louise Osgood Koopman, of Cambridge, Mass.

9. These and other quotations from Ellen's letters are from the Ward Correspondence.

10. His words 'after many months' in describing the dream of January, 1841, soon to be recounted, indicate some such time as July of the previous year. The voyage, when confidences might have been exchanged and the sacrifice could have been made, was a year and a half in the past.

11. As his letters to her have been destroyed and all references deleted from her Journal, we can only infer what happened.

12. When, after John's death, Prudence or Sophia spoke of his love for Ellen, Henry is said to have exclaimed, 'What! did John love her too?' But if he did say this, it was camouflage.

13. 311.

14. VI, 201.

15. Comparison of these intense statements with the cool and deferential references to Emerson at the same period, show that he could not have been intended.

16. The complete poem is in an unpublished section of Thoreau's Journal, in the possession of a private collector. It was published, with a few lines omitted, in 'Autumn. From the Journal of Henry David Thoreau,' ed. H. G. O. Blake (Boston, 1892), 223, 224.

17. From the unpublished Journal. A slightly different version appears in 'Winter. From the Journal of Henry David Thoreau,' ed. Blake (Boston, 1888), 202.

18. Yet she had justice done her. Prudence Ward, so says family tradition, told Henry later that Ellen had cared for him deeply. If so, she must have said also, what she well knew, that it was devotion to her father and his principles that made Ellen explicit in her refusal. She was a girl of character. Thoreau records in his Journal of [December] 12, Sunday, 1841:

'Now that lately I have heard of some traits in the character of a fair and earnest maiden whom I had known only superficially, but who has gone hence to make herself more known by distance, they sound like strains of a wild harp music.... Every maiden conceals a fairer flower and more luscious fruit than any calyx in the field.... There is apology enough for all the deficiency and shortcoming in the world in the patient waiting of any bud of character to unfold itself. . . .

> 'I've felt within my inmost soul
> Such cheerful morning news,
> In the horizon of my mind
> I've seen such morning hues. . . .'

Which, by combining with a poem on friendship which he had written the previous April, became the famous

> 'Packed in my mind lie all the clothes
> Which outward nature wears. . . .'

That the 'calyx' passage is copied into his letter on love to Blake and appears with so much else that has reference to Ellen in the 'Week' (p. 293), makes the supposition that Thoreau is commenting on Prudence's statement very probable. The growth of this poem has been confused by the tentative dating of this section of the Journal in December, which should be in some warm month, as the reference to the season (p. 295) and the general sequence show.

19. The idea for the poem is in the Journal for March 20, 1840. There is an interesting stanza in the Harvard version:

> 'What I can raise
> I will plant thick,
> What I can lose
> I will lose quick.'

20. Sanborn, *op. cit.,* 172.

21. The manuscript of the 'Week' was already in the works. There is a version of the early chapters in the Huntington Library (H. M. 956) in the characteristic handwriting of Thoreau's earliest period, and Margaret may very well have seen some draft of the later chapters, which do contain various references needing explanation by the author if he had submitted, as apparently he did, something about the *'good week'* to his friends. It is tempting to guess that, whatever the paper contained, it was sent as a background of explanation for the poem 'Friends, Romans, Countrymen, and Lovers,' which Margaret Fuller was publishing in *The Dial* that month, and which afterward appeared in the essay on Friendship in the 'Week.' He had given

it in a new version to Emerson in August, as is recorded in Emerson's letter of August 19 to Margaret Fuller (Rusk). But the passage may have been the account of the dreams discussed in the next paragraphs.

22. Emerson to William Emerson, Jan. 24, 1842; Rusk.
23. 292–294.
24. 305.
25. The Reverend Joseph Osgood, who for over fifty years was minister in Cohasset.
26. Channing, 'Poems of Sixty-Five Years,' ed. Sanborn (Philadelphia, 1902), xxxviii.

CHAPTER X

1. VII, 114.
2. His idea was to retire from the meanness of life. By the time of 'Walden' he had, like the Supreme Court, reversed himself. See VII, 133, 146.
3. Emerson, Journal, VI, 74.
4. This is the version in the 'Week' (p. 365). In the Journal, quoted above, the second line appears, 'But I could not both live and live to utter it.'
5. Emerson reported to the secretary of the South Danvers Lyceum that people laughed till they cried when they heard Thoreau's lecture on Cape Cod. He must have been inspired that night, for there is no other such success recorded. (Emerson to Thoreau, Feb. 6, 1850; Rusk.)
6. George Wilson Pierson, 'Tocqueville and Beaumont in America' (New York, 1938), 422, 423.
7. Theodore Parker's Ms. Journal, August 10, 1840. See Rusk, II, 323, 324.
8. *The Dial*, II, iv (April, 1842), 409.
9. *Idem*, I, i (July, 1840), 3.
10. 'The Correspondence of Thomas Carlyle and Ralph Waldo Emerson. 1834–1872' (Boston, 1883), II, 14, 15.
11. *Idem*, II, 285.
12. Margaret Fuller to Thoreau, Oct. 18, 1841; quoted by Sanborn, *op. cit.*, 169–172.
13. It was 'alleged' to have five or six hundred subscribers, but on

March 26, 1842, Emerson writes his brother William that he can find only three hundred paying ones. (Rusk.)

14. *The Dial*, IV, i-iv (July, 1843–April, 1844). It contains a hitherto unnoticed characterization of Thoreau.

15. 'Memoirs of Margaret Fuller Ossoli' (Boston, 1852), II, 322, 323.

16. Emerson to Margaret Fuller, March 30, 1840; Rusk.

17. Emerson to William Emerson, June 1, 1841; Rusk.

18. VI, 38.

19. Emerson to Margaret Fuller, Sept. 13, 1841; Rusk.

20. 'Henry has found no work such as he has sought for.' (Emerson to Margaret Fuller, Oct. 11, 1842; Rusk.)

21. He was to exercise his 'influence' on Haven as well as teach him, and was to have board, a room to himself, and $100 a year. He was not strong enough for manual labor, but hoped for some clerical work until such time as he could get 'literary labor from some quarter in New York.' (Emerson to William Emerson, March 12, 1843; Rusk.)

22. VI, 51.

23. Sanborn, 'The Emerson-Thoreau Correspondence,' *The Atlantic Monthly*, LXIX, 415 (May, 1892), 586.

24. VI, 94. This is his comment on Margaret Fuller's article on the rights of women in *The Dial*, I, i (July, 1840).

25. VI, 83.

26. Sanborn, *op. cit.*, 137–140.

27. H. M. 13182.

CHAPTER XI

1. From the unpublished Journal already noted. A slightly different version appears in 'Winter. From the Journal of Henry David Thoreau,' 111.

2. VII, 207.

3. Sanborn, 'The Life of Henry David Thoreau,' 128.

4. VI, 40, 36.

5. Emerson, Journal, IV, 430.

6. Emerson to Lidian Emerson, March 8, 10, 1848; Rusk.

7. Brown, *op. cit.*, 35, 36.

8. Mary Howland Russell, friend of Lidian's, was resident in the house through the summers of 1840 and 1841, teaching little

Waldo. See note on Emerson's letter to William Emerson, June 1, 1841; Rusk.

9. Afterward Caroline Sturgis Tappan, a poet and woman of great charm, whose relation to Emerson, who called her always his Sister, may have suggested the like term to Thoreau when his intimacy with Lidian became emotional. See Emerson's letter to Margaret Fuller, July 21, 1840; Rusk.

10. This was his room in his second stay; presumably in his first.

11. Emerson, Journal, VI, 237.

12. VII, 350.

13. H. M. 13182.

14. *Ibid.*

CHAPTER XII

1. Howe Collection.

2. Howells, *op. cit.*

3. From a lecture of George Parsons Lathrop at the Brooklyn Institute, reported in *The Brooklyn Citizen*, Dec. 12, 1894.

4. Unpublished paragraph in Emerson's Journal for June, 1839; Harvard Library.

5. Wakeman Catalogue, no. 997.

6. Emerson, Journal, VI, 46, 47.

7. 'The American Notebooks by Nathaniel Hawthorne. Based Upon the Original Manuscripts in the Pierpont Morgan Library,' ed. Randall Stewart (New Haven, 1932), 166, 167.

8. (Boston, 1897), 53.

9. Emerson thought Hawthorne was a better critic than a writer, which is a commentary on the Transcendentalists' taste, or lack of it, in fiction. (Emerson to Benjamin Peter Hunt, August 8, 1843; Rusk.)

10. Emerson recommended Mrs. Thoreau's as a 'boarding place' to Ellery Sedgwick in 1842. Margaret Fuller wonders why it is preferred to Mrs. Pritchard's, since the latter was 'the pleasantest family.' (Margaret Fuller to Emerson, August 10, 1842; Rusk.)

11. Alcott, Journal, 127.

12. The word is illegible.

13. These quotations are from the Ward Correspondence.

14. Joseph Hosmer, in the 'Thoreau Annex,' *The Concord Freeman*, IV, 24 (May 6, 1880).

15. The date in the Vital Statistics of Concord is wrong, and both the day of his death and a relevant letter are misdated by Sanborn. (*Op. cit.*, 213, 214.) *The Concord Freeman* for January 14 gives the correct date.

16. These quotations are from the Ward Correspondence.

17. 'Nor is it ['Moods'] the less attractive to us for the personal and family history, but slightly shaded, scattered along its pages.' (Alcott, Journal, 336.)

18. VI, 80, 81.

19. *Idem*, 81.

20. *Ibid.*

21. *Idem*, 96, 97.

22. *Idem*, 97.

23. 'He is a bold and profound thinker though he may easily chance to pester you with some accidental crotchets and perhaps a village exaggeration of the value of facts.' (Emerson to William Emerson, May 6, 1843; Rusk.)

24. VI, 92, 93, 82.

CHAPTER XIII

1. In a commonplace book, the Index Rerum, in the Huntington Library (H. M. 945), are five closely written pages of adjectives, metaphors, and figurative language in general selected from his reading, as if this attribute of style interested him particularly.

2. VII, 210, 212, 257, 266, 282, 288, 294, 300, 312, 315, 330, 345, 350, 352, 356, 357.

3. Letter in the possession of a private collector.

4. In one sense the influence of Howitt's 'Calendar' was considerable, in that it gave Thoreau a model for a series of observations of the seasons, the purpose being frankly literary, instead of scientific as in Gilbert White's 'Natural History of Selborne.' But neither Emerson, who must have introduced Thoreau to him, nor Thoreau himself, thought highly of the mild Howitt. His book was a 'parody' of what Emerson wished to write. Thoreau criticized his own 'Winter Walk' as being 'Howittish.'

5. He wrote critical essays on Chaucer, Ossian (a supposed 'genuine' Ossian), Raleigh, the Bible, Hindu literature, Carlyle, Anacreon, the Greek dramatists, Homer, Persius, Confucius, Persian poetry, Goethe, Shakespeare, Quarles, etc., etc. And his lists of books read or to be read, including a long list of English dramatists, Anglo-Saxon writers, etc., etc., are extensive. In Confucius he found a fellow spirit who regarded the relationship of men to each other and the arts with essential seriousness, was not averse to jollity, yet disliked light, predatory, or sensual behavior.

6. Channing, *op. cit.*, 149–151.

7. For a full discussion of the Hindu influences upon Transcendentalism, see Harold Clarke Goddard, 'Studies in New England Transcendentalism,' New York, 1908; and Arthur Christy, 'The Orient in American Transcendentalism. A Study of Emerson, Thoreau, and Alcott,' New York, 1932.

8. 'The Ten Principal Upanishads,' tr. Shree Purohit Swāmi and W. B. Yeats (London, 1937), 16, 17.

9. VII, 266–268, 277, 278.

10. 'The Ten Principal Upanishads,' 29.

11. Emerson had known before 1845 only the sketch of the book in '*Introduction à l'histoire de la philosophie*,' volume I of Victor Cousin's '*Cours de l'Histoire de la Philosophie*' (presumably in the English translation by H. G. Linberg, 'Introduction to the History of Philosophy,' Boston, 1832, 71–73). (Emerson to Max Müller, August 4, 1873; Rusk.)

12. Moncure Conway had much the same experience when, in 1853, Emerson lent him the book. Whittier, who was also lent it, did not react!

13. I, 145, 146.

CHAPTER XIV

1. Elliott, *op. cit.*, 82.

2. 'Henry David Thoreau: His Character and Opinions' in 'Familiar Studies of Men and Books' (London, 1882), 129–171. First printed in *The Cornhill Magazine*, XLI, 246 (June, 1880), 665–682.

3. '*Ueber die Einsamkeit*,' by J. G. Zimmermann, was translated into

English as 'Solitude' in various selections, of which Thoreau
owned an Albany edition of 1796, containing the author's arguments for the advantages of solitude. It was, however, far from
being a romantic book. With characteristic eighteenth-century
common sense, Zimmermann advises a limited dose of solitude
as a specific cure for certain ills of the mind, the heart, and the
moral nature. 'The retirement which is not the result of cool
and deliberate reason ... generally renders men less able to
discharge the duties and endure the burdens of life,' the author
says in Chapter III of his section on the Disadvantages of Solitude. It was such cool and deliberate reason as a reading of
Zimmermann may have encouraged, but certainly did not
suggest, which sent Thoreau to Walden pond.

4. VII, 211, 227, 471.
5. 'Recollections of Seventy Years,' 392.
6. *Op. cit.*, 33, 134, 135. Who invented the air-blast process is
   uncertain, but Henry worked out the details, and, judging from
   Emerson's remarks quoted below, probably did the inventing
   also.
7. E. Harlow Russell, 'A Bit of Unpublished Correspondence
   Between Henry D. Thoreau and Isaac T. Hecker' in 'Proceed-
   ings of the American Antiquarian Society at the Semi-Annual
   Meeting Held in Boston, April 30, 1902,' n.s. xv, pt. 1 (Worcester, Mass., 1902), 58–69.
8. A fire in 1938 destroyed much of the roof and upper story of the
   house.
9. VIII, 21–25.
10. VII, 413.
11. Rusk.
12. *The Concord Freeman, op. cit.*
13. Sanborn, 'Henry D. Thoreau,' 209, 210.
14. Nov. 16, 1842; Rusk.
15. 'Homes of American Authors' (New York, 1853), 250–252.
    This account has been wrongly used as a description of a meet-
    ing of the Symposium of the Transcendentalists.
16. Maria Thoreau, in the letter quoted on page 243, says he sold
    the cabin to Emerson.
17. In the collection at the Alcott-Lane house at Fruitlands.
18. Ward Correspondence.

19. Annotation in Channing's copy of 'Walden.' The garage is on the estate of Mrs. Willieta Dodge at Concord.
20. Channing, *op. cit.*, 7, 8.
21. Howe Collection; VII, 409.
22. Mrs. James Fields is recorded as saying that Thoreau was an excellent son and came home every day while he was at Walden. (M. A. De Wolfe Howe, 'Memories of a Hostess. A Chronicle of Eminent Friendships Drawn Chiefly from the Diaries of Mrs. James T. Fields.' Boston, cop. 1922, 62.) I doubt the latter statement.
23. Two hundred and seventy-five pages of the Journal, the first leaf of which is dated 'Walden, April 17, 1846,' is in the possession of a private collector. These contained much material afterward used in 'The Maine Woods.'

CHAPTER XV

1. II, 108, 109.
2. VI, 102, 107; IV, 280–305.
3. 'The New World: or, Mechanical system to perform the labours of man and beast by inanimate powers, that cost nothing, for producing and preparing the substances of life . . .,' Philadelphia, 1841.
4. See also Bernard De Voto, 'Forays and Rebuttals' (Boston, 1936), 204–212.
5. Charles Lane had also been arrested and put into jail for failure to pay taxes. Rockwood Hoar paid the debt. This arrest was presumably also for principle. (Emerson to Margaret Fuller, Dec. 17, 1843; Rusk.)
6. Thoreau in 'Walden' (p. 190) says definitely that his arrest occurred toward the end of his first summer at Walden, which was in 1845, and that the next summer, which was 1846, he went to the Maine woods. Yet Alcott speaks in his Journal for July 26, 1846, of Thoreau's 'late' imprisonment; and Emerson notes in July of that year that his friend has gone to jail, and writes to Elizabeth Hoar on July 27, 1846, 'Mr. Thoreau has spent a night in Concord jail on his refusal to pay taxes.' (Rusk.) The date, according to Thoreau's statement, was late summer —

August or the first weeks of September — for men were sitting in their shirt sleeves and when he left jail he joined a huckleberry party. But July of 1846 is an incredible time for the first and seemingly immediate notices in his two friends' journals for an 1845 incident. As Henry himself said in 'Walden' that he had compressed for convenience the experience of two years into one, it seems probable that he changed '46 to '45. Alcott's conversation with Emerson was on July 25, 1846. On the 26th Thoreau tells him of his late experience. Huckleberries are not pickable in July, but blueberries, which Thoreau sometimes calls huckleberries, are ripe, but not in quantities to justify a picking party till the end of the month. We may assign, I think, about the 23d or 24th of July, 1846, to Thoreau's night in jail. There is no record of his stay there, since his tax was paid before the case could be recorded.

7. IV, 376.
8. S. A. J. [Samuel Arthur Jones], 'Thoreau's Incarceration,' *The Inlander*, ix (Dec., 1898), 96–103.
9. Thoreau's only recorded visitor in the brief time before Sam, having taken off his boots, locked him up for the night, was a veiled woman, and he was released immediately after breakfast. (Jones, *op. cit.*)
10. Sanborn to Charles Goodspeed, Sept. 9, 1910; H. M. 945. According to Sam, the 'veiled lady' paid the fine. Emerson in his funeral address (x, 458), says that the annoyance was threatened the next year, but 'as his friends paid the tax notwithstanding his protest, I believe he ceased to resist.' It seems probable that by 1849 he had decided that 'Civil Disobedience' was protest enough.
11. Emerson, Journal, VII, 186, 187.
12. 'The Correspondence of Thomas Carlyle and Ralph Waldo Emerson. 1834–1872,' II, 130.
13. The Huntington and Howe Collections contain fragments dating from about 1839 to 1847. Sanborn prints from two of these drafts. ('The First and Last Journies of Thoreau,' I, 7–61.) There are also several experimental beginnings in the Journal.
14. Emerson to Charles King Newcomb, July 16, 1846; Rusk.

CHAPTER XVI

1. Word illegible.
2. Ward Correspondence.
3. IX, 214; II, 355, 356.
4. Emerson to William Emerson, August 30, 1847; March 12, 1843; Rusk.
5. Emerson to Lidian Emerson, Nov. [?] 4 [?] 1847 [?]; Rusk.
6. VI, 137, 146.
7. H. M. 957.
8. 'Records of a Lifelong Friendship. 1807:1882. Ralph Waldo Emerson and William Henry Furness,' ed. H. H. F. (Boston, 1910), 61.
9. 'Greeley has sent me $100.00.' (Thoreau to Emerson, May 21, 1848; Rusk.)
10. Munroe offered to print and bind one thousand copies of Margaret Fuller's 'Summer on the Lakes' for $359.90. Thoreau's edition of the 'Week' was also one thousand copies, but not all were bound. (Emerson to Margaret Fuller, April 26, 1844; Rusk.)
11. H. M. 924.
12. Quoted by Emerson, Journal, VIII, 75.
13. Rose Hawthorne Lathrop, *op. cit.*, 420.
14. *Idem*, 92, 93.
15. Letter to Longfellow, Nov. 21, 1848; in the possession of H. W. L. Dana.
16. The quotations are from Longfellow's Journal, Nov. 16, 23, 1848. 'Meek philosophers' is wrongly printed as 'meet his philosophers' in Samuel Longfellow's edition, and the phrase 'and Sam; — all the philosophers' is omitted.
17. Sanborn, 'Recollections of Seventy Years,' II, 469.
18. From a letter of Mrs. Mather, wife of the Congregational minister, who lived across the street from the Thoreaus; in the possession of Mr. Van Wyck Brooks.
19. Sanborn, 'Henry D. Thoreau,' 228.
20. Alcott, Journal, 204, 205.
21. Howe, *op. cit.*, 89.
22. VI, 158, 159.
23. Howe, *op. cit.*, 89, 90.

24. Ward Correspondence.
25. The Mortuary Records of Dorchester, Mass.
26. 'Louisa May Alcott. Her Life, Letters, and Journals,' ed. Ednah Dow Cheney (Boston, 1889), 42.
27. *Idem*, 26; Caroline Ticknor, 'May Alcott. A Memoir' (Boston, 1928), 21–23; Alcott, Journal, 178; Emerson to Lidian Emerson, August 18, Sept. 11, 1846; Emerson to William Emerson, Oct. 26, 1846, April 1, 1847; Sophia Foord to Emerson, July 27, 1847 (Rusk).
28. Except in passing by Annie Marble, who says that Thoreau's friends reported two women as 'quite willing, even anxious' to marry him. (*Op. cit.*, 218.)
29. So Emerson implies in a letter to her, Nov. 5, 1843; Rusk.
30. Emerson to Margaret Fuller, Oct. 24, 1840; Rusk.
31. 'Memoirs of Margaret Fuller Ossoli,' II, 229, 224, 239.
32. This letter is in the possession of the Ralph Waldo Emerson Memorial Association.
33. I have been unable, in the short time after the discovery of Sophia Foord and before the publication of this book, to learn how and when she died. Her death is not recorded in the mortuary records of her home town of Milton, Mass.

CHAPTER XVII

 1. And of course written in its first diary form in 1839. See I, 354.
 2. Alcott, Journal, 213, 214.
 3. II, 274.
 4. I, 181.
 5. Ward Correspondence.
 6. There is no record of a trip to New York after 1850 and before 1853.
 7. XI, 459, 460, 512, 521.
 8. H. M. 13182.
 9. Emerson to Margaret Fuller, Feb. 28, 1847; Rusk.
10. 'Nearly all this volume . . . was written eight or nine years ago,' Thoreau says in the Huntington manuscript of 'Walden,' which probably belongs in 1850 to 1853, just before the lost final draft for the printers, 'and a considerable part was read at that

time as lectures.' (H. M. 924.) As very much was added from his Journal after the Walden Pond period, this can only mean that the theme of his book was complete in the lectures he then read.

11. II, 17, 18.
12. *Idem*, 79.
13. 'The Rise of American Civilization' (New York, 1928), *passim.*
14. II, 16, 17.
15. XI, 1 (July, 1852), 66–68 ('The Iron Horse'); 2 (August, 1852), 127 ('A Poet Buying a Farm').
16. Untitled review, *The North American Review*, CI, 209 (Oct., 1865), 597–608. Reprinted as 'Thoreau' in 'My Study Windows' (Boston, 1871), 193–209.
17. I have taken Channing's version of the Watson story, noted in his copy of 'Walden.' See also VI, 310, 410. For a possible source for the Oriental imagery, see Edith Peairs, 'The Hound, The Bay Horse, and The Turtle-Dove: A Study of Thoreau and Voltaire,' *Publications of the Modern Language Association*, LII, 3 (Sept., 1937), 863–869.

CHAPTER XVIII

1. Thoreau 'reads less in books lately, & more in nature.' (Emerson to James Elliot Cabot, Nov. 18, 1856; Rusk.) This might have been written with equal truth in 1850.
2. Unpublished letter to A. H. Jocelyn and Company, Dec. 22, 1854; Middlebury College Library.
3. Emerson, Journal, VIII, 178, 119.
4. VIII, 306, 77, 101, 285; IX, 66.
5. Emerson, Journal, VIII, 131.
6. Emerson to George Partridge Bradford, August 28, 1854; Rusk.
7. XII, 21.

CHAPTER XIX

1. The fragments preserved, both published and unpublished, of earlier date, have only an occasional daily note of what he did or what he saw.

2. Morgan Library.
3. VIII, 150, 151.
4. XV, 156–158.
5. Many of these have been preserved.
6. XII, 115.
7. X, 133.
8. The author has experimented with this spy-glass, which is now in the Antiquarian Society museum at Concord. He found it hard enough to focus upon robins on Emerson's lawn, nearly impossible to catch the shyer birds in the trees and hedges.
9. VIII, 13–15.
10. *Idem*, 306, 307.
11. See the various versions in his Journal, in the work-sheets of 'Walden,' and in 'Walden' itself. Odell Shepard, before the Modern Language Association in December, 1937, assembled a group of these passages.
12. 365.

CHAPTER XX

1. XVII, 358.
2. XI, 4.
3. XII, 253.
4. *Idem*, 294.
5. XI, 478, 45; X, 351.
6. For example, XI, 400–402.
7. Pierson, *op. cit.*, 244.
8. XIV, 135.
9. That the bride of the Corsair was Greenough's model is indicated by a letter from Alfred Greenough to his brother Henry: 'I am more impatient to see the Medora than I was to see the Cherubs. You have never mentioned from what part of the "Corsair" the statue is taken.' ('Letters of Horatio Greenough to his Brother, Henry Greenough,' ed. Frances Boott Greenough. Boston, 1887, 74.)
10. Ward Correspondence.
11. IX, 182, 183.
12. 'Remarks on Forest Scenery, and other Woodland Views,

(Relative chiefly to Picturesque Beauty) Illustrated by the Scenes of New-Forest in Hampshire,' London, 1791. (2 vols.)

13. In this he resembled Edward in Jane Austen's 'Sense and Sensibility,' who preferred tall, straight, and flourishing trees to crooked, blasted, and twisted ones.

14. 'Remarks on Forest Scenery,' I, 176.

15. IX, 428.

CHAPTER XXI

1. Albee, *op. cit.*, 18, 19, 31, 32.
2. X, 315.
3. IX, 141, 213.
4. Sept., 1852; VI, 202.
5. XI, 188.
6. IX, 256.
7. *Idem*, 81, 82.
8. Emerson to Lidian, Jan. 29, 1857, and note; Rusk. Emerson to Caroline Sturgis Tappan, Oct. 13, 1857; Rusk.
9. Emerson to Abel Adams, August 7, 1854; Rusk.

CHAPTER XXII

1. VIII, 218.
2. *Idem*, 428.
3. IX, 168.
4. In this instance his reading was continued in preparation for his 'Yankee in Canada.' There is a mass of disorderly notes on the discovery and later history of Canada in the Morgan Library, far more ambitious in scope than his informal narrative could justify.
5. XII, 165.
6. VI, 210.
7. 'Autobiography. Memories and Experiences of Moncure Daniel Conway' (Boston, 1904), I, 141–143.
8. XII, 21.
9. Letter to George Partridge Bradford, August 28, 1854; Rusk.
10. I derive this information from Professor Odell Shepard. One of

the books sent Thoreau (who spelled the donor's name 'Rou-
gette') was presumably Rouquette's *'La Thébaïde en Amérique,
ou Apologie de la Vie solitaire et contemplative'* (1852).

11. VI, 259.

12. Sanborn, 'Thoreau and his English Friend Thomas Cholmondeley,' *The Atlantic Monthly*, LXXII, 434 (Dec., 1893), 746,
749, 750.

CHAPTER XXIII

1. August 4, 1840; Rusk.
2. So Greeley reported; Sanborn, 'Henry D. Thoreau,' 237.
3. See an unpublished letter in the possession of Mr. George Hellman; and Sanborn, *op. cit.*
4. Harvard Library.
5. Bliss Perry, 'Park Street Papers' (Boston, 1908), 259–264.
6. The first project for *The Atlantic Monthly* was under Francis H.
Underwood in 1853. Thoreau replied to his request for a contribution: 'If you will inform me in season at what rate per page
(describing the page) you will pay for accepted articles, —
returning rejected within a reasonable time, — and your terms
are satisfactory, I will forward something.' He knew what he
wanted. In a later letter, he says that Putnam's pays him four
dollars a page. (Perry, *op. cit.*, 216, 217.)
7. Alcott, Journal, 334.
8. XIII, 268.

CHAPTER XXIV

1. This essay as posthumously printed is addressed to 'my readers.'
It may have been sent to Greeley or Curtis, in which case it was
one of the manuscripts mentioned as rejected.
2. VI, 260.
3. VII, 427, 362, 363.
4. John Bach McMaster, 'A History of the People of the United
States, From the Revolution to the Civil War' (New York,
1883–1913), VIII, 44.
5. *Op. cit.*, I, 184.
6. Sanborn, 'Recollections of Seventy Years,' I, 102–104. The
date of the visit is erroneously given as 1856.

7. XVIII, 437.
8. XLVIII, 2506 (Dec. 10, 1896), 1672.
9. XVIII, 457. But Alcott says no bells were rung, by desire of Brown's friends, who did not wish their sorrow to be signified by the clamor of steeples awakening angry feelings. (Journal, 323.)
10. Harvard Library.
11. IV, 440.

CHAPTER XXV

1. X, 40.
2. XVI, 405.
3. IX, 231, 232.
4. *Idem*, 134.
5. XVIII, 389, 390; XVII, 304; VIII, 338.

CHAPTER XXVI

1. There are three authentic portraits of Thoreau in existence. Samuel Worcester Rowse, painter, illustrator, lithographer, whose crayon drawings earned for him an international reputation, did a crayon portrait of Thoreau while staying at the Thoreau house in Concord in 1854. (See XIII, 11, 12.) Mary Hosmer Brown tells of Rowse's difficulty in getting a satisfactory likeness. (*Op. cit.*) In 1858, Rowse did a portrait of Emerson. The undated portrait by him of Lidian Emerson was perhaps done in 1853.

In June of 1856, while on a visit to Blake in Worcester, Thoreau sat for three daguerreotypes, which differ only in some slight detail. These were taken by Benjamin D. Maxham. These pictures show his 'Galway' whiskers. One copy is now in the possession of Mr. W. T. H. Howe. A copy was sent to Calvin H. Greene by Thoreau in 1856, who charged him $.50. The other two seem to have belonged to his Worcester friends, Blake and Brown. The Greene copy is regarded as the best.

In August of 1861, while on his last visit to New Bedford, an ambrotype was taken of him with full beard, by E. S. Dunshee of that city. A copy is in the Antiquarian Society of Concord.

The only other authentic portraits known to me are the caricatures by Daniel Ricketson and William Furness, reproduced in this volume.

The painting of December of 1837 or 1839 — the date recorded on the stretcher is hard to read — now in the possession of the Concord Antiquarian Society, is of doubtful authenticity. It was bought by Mr. George S. Hellman from a Dr. Miller of Bangor, with certain Thoreau manuscripts, all said to have come from Mr. Beebe Thatcher of Bangor, who inherited them from Miss Thatcher, Sophia's niece. No picture is, however, mentioned in Sophia's will, and Mr. Beebe Thatcher's son, George T. Thatcher, of Bangor, has no memory of ever seeing this picture in his father's house, and believes that it was not in the lot sold to Dr. Miller. The portrait, which has been much retouched, has dark eyes, dark hair, and a mouth unlike Henry's as shown in later portraits. It is by a good artist, and the unlikeliness of Henry's sitting for such a picture, without record, either in 1837 or 1839, is obvious. Furthermore, this is certainly not the portrait of Thoreau painted by his sister Sophia, and traditionally left to someone in Concord with instructions that it should never be reproduced. Sophia's portrait of her brother John is in the Concord Antiquarian Society, and is crude and utterly unlike the alleged portrait of Henry in style and execution. It may be suggested, as a possibility, that after Thoreau's death and his established fame, some artist repainted her picture, leaving the lettering Henry D. Thoreau, 1839 (or 1837), on the stretcher, but this is only a wild guess. No description of Thoreau in the late '30's and early '40's fits the dark face and eyes and regular features of this painting.

Professor Odell Shepard states that Henry Kirk Brown, the sculptor, is reported by Alcott in his Journal for October 30, 1854 to have made a sketch of Thoreau and his Canadian woodchopper Therien, at Walden.

The portrait reproduced in *The Century Magazine* for July, 1882 (XXIV, 3, 368), is obviously a woodcut based upon the Maxham daguerreotype.

2. Unpublished letters of Horace Greeley; in the possession of the Morgan Library and of Mr. Van Wyck Brooks.
3. Alcott, Journal, 284, 285.

4. *Idem*, 309.

5. Both the first edition of 1855 and the second edition of 1858 were in Thoreau's library, entered in pencil as accessions of 1858.

6. Alcott, Journal, 287–290.

7. VI, 291, 295, 296.

8. XV, 148.

9. (New York, 1906), I, 212, 213.

10. 'Ann Gilchrist. Her Life and Writings,' ed. H. H. Gilchrist (London, 1887), 237.

11. 'Daniel Ricketson and his Friends. Letters, Poems, Sketches, Etc.,' ed. Anna and Walton Ricketson (Boston, 1902), 149. For a good account of Ricketson and the shanty, see Alcott, Journal, 297, 298.

12. H. M. 7018.

13. XVI, 127.

14. XVII, 325.

15. Sanborn, *op. cit.*, 383–385; VI, 346, 347; Alcott, Journal, 310.

16. Austin Warren, 'The Elder Henry James' (New York, 1934), 182.

17. See an unpublished letter of July 8, 1839, in Charles Goodspeed's catalogue for January, 1938; and Thoreau's water survey papers in the Concord Library.

18. Emerson to Lowell, July 13, 1859; Rusk.

19. In a commonplace book in the Howe Collection are scattered notes from 'Origin of Species,' taken in 1860. Emerson's remark, quoted above, indicates that Darwin's famous letter of 1857, stating his case to Gray, the botanist, had set them all talking of the new ideas. On October 18, 1860, Thoreau wrote in his Journal: 'The development theory implies a greater vital force in nature, because it is more flexible and accommodating, and equivalent to a sort of constant *new* creation.' But he seems to have written to Cholmondeley that the theory was in his opinion doubtful, for Cholmondeley writes him on April 23, 1861: 'Darwin's "Origin of Species" may be fanciful, but it is a move in the right direction.' And, indeed, on March 22d of this year he speculates on how many plants of a given kind were created in a given place, which indicates either that he did not understand the development theory, or had discarded it, like Agassiz.

20. XIV, 147.
21. H. M. 20592. For an excellent description of Thoreau's philosophic attitude, see Alcott, Journal, 317, 318.

CHAPTER XXVII

1. 'Houses and People of Concord, 1810 to 1820,' 252; ms. in Concord Library.
2. Sanborn, 'The Personality of Thoreau' (Boston, 1901), 69.
3. Alcott, Journal, 337, 343.
4. VI, 397.
5. Conway, *op. cit.*, I, 335. See also VI, 378, 379.
6. Emerson to William Emerson, July 1, 1850; Rusk.
7. H. M. 13192.
8. The Minneapolis *State Atlas*, July 3, 1861.
9. John T. Flanagan, 'Thoreau in Minnesota,' *Minnesota History*, XVI, 1 (March, 1935), 35–46.
10. 'Daniel Ricketson and His Friends,' 214.
11. Fi 4246.
12. H. M. 209; Fi 4241–4248.
13. *Op. cit.*, 232.

CHAPTER XXVIII

1. Howe, *op. cit.*, 68.
2. Howells, *op. cit.*, 58.
3. If he had been able to disregard the ugly fact of slavery, Thoreau would have found the plantation life of the old South in closer accord with his philosophy than Concord ways of living. See his reluctant fascination by a book of hunting episodes in South Carolina, read on the eve of war. (XX, 315–319.)
4. Translated in 1924 by Van Wyck Brooks as 'Henry Thoreau. Bachelor of Nature,' New York.
5. This is the testimony of H. M. Tomlinson, who joined the movement early in the century.
6. Leo Tolstoy, 'A Message to the American People,' *The North American Review*, CLXXII, 533 (April, 1901), 503. See also 'The Complete Works of Count Tolstoy,' tr. and ed. Leo Wiener (Boston, 1905), XXI, 445, XXII, 525, 526, XXIII, 208, 293.

7. Henry S. Salt, 'Gandhi and Thoreau,' *The Nation and Athenaeum*, XLVI, 22 (March 1, 1930), 728.

8. 'The Autobiography of William Butler Yeats. Consisting of Reveries Over Childhood and Youth, The Trembling of the Veil, and Dramatis Personae' (New York, 1938), 64.

9. XII, 483.

10. Alcott, Journal, 238.

11. This seems to be the quality felt by Lin Yutang, the Chinese man of letters, who has asserted in public statements, and in a letter to the author of this biography, that among all writers in English Thoreau translates with least loss of value and most easily into Chinese. The Chinese, like Thoreau, as their paintings show, can inspire a realistic treatment of nature with a deep significance.

12. R. H. Tawney, 'The Sickness of an Acquisitive Society' (London, 1920), 86.

13. *The Boston Daily Advertiser*, XCIX, 109 (May 8, 1862).

14. Clara Barrus, 'The Life and Letters of John Burroughs' (Boston, 1925), I, 207.

A SELECTED BIBLIOGRAPHY

BIBLIOGRAPHIES

Adams, Raymond William, 'A Thoreau Checklist. 1908–1930' in 'A Selection of American and English First Editions and Other Desirable Books.' Catalogue no. 1, iss. Richard Malcolm Sills. Chappaqua, N.Y., 1930, 35–40.

Adams, Raymond William, 'The Thoreau Library of Raymond Adams. A Catalogue.' Chapel Hill, N.C., 1936. (Mimeographed.)

Adams, Raymond William, 'The Thoreau Library of Raymond Adams. A Catalogue. Supplement.' Chapel Hill, N.C., 1937. (Mimeographed.)

Allen, Francis H., 'A Bibliography of Henry David Thoreau.' Boston, Houghton Mifflin Company, 1908.

Crawford, Bartholow V., 'Selected Bibliography' in 'Henry David Thoreau. Representative Selections, with Introduction, Bibliography, and Notes,' ed. B. V. Crawford. New York, American Book Company, cop. 1934. (American Writers Series, ed. H. H. Clark), LIX–LXIX.

Hartwick, Harry, 'Henry David Thoreau' in Walter Fuller Taylor, 'A History of American Letters.' New York, American Book Company, cop. 1936, 513–515.

'Henry David Thoreau' in 'A Check List of Books in the Julian Willis Abernethy Library of American Literature,' comp. Harriet Smith Potter, Curator. Middlebury College Bulletin, xxv, 2 (Oct., 1930), 200–211.

'Henry David Thoreau' in 'The Stephen H. Wakeman Collectiön of Books of Nineteenth Century American Writers. The Property of Mrs. Alice L. Wakeman. First Editions, Inscribed Presentation and Personal Copies, Original Manuscripts and Letters of Nine American Authors. Bryant, Emerson, Hawthorne, Holmes, Longfellow, Lowell, Poe, Thoreau, Whittier.' New York, American Art Association [1924], nos. 972–1075.

Van Doren, Mark, 'Henry Thoreau' in 'The Cambridge History of American Literature.' New York, G. P. Putnam's Sons; Cambridge, England, University Press, 1917–1921, II, 411–415.

White, William, 'A Henry David Thoreau Bibliography, 1908–1937,' *Bulletin of Bibliography and Dramatic Index*, xvi, 5 (Jan.–April, 1938), 90–92; 6 (May–August, 1938), 111–113; 7 (Sept.–Dec., 1938), 131, 132; [to be continued].

COLLECTED WORKS

'The Writings of Henry David Thoreau. With Bibliographical Introductions and Full Indexes.' Boston and New York, Houghton, Mifflin and Company, 1894 [1893]. 11 vols. (Riverside Edition) Introductory notes by H. E. Scudder; V–VIII, 'Early Spring in Massachusetts,' 'Summer,' 'Autumn,' 'Winter,' ed. H. G. O. Blake; XI, 'Familiar Letters,' 1894, ed. F. B. Sanborn.

'The Writings of Henry David Thoreau.' Boston and New York, Houghton, Mifflin and Company, cop. 1906. 20 vols. (Walden Edition) VI, 'Familiar Letters,' ed. F. B. Sanborn; VII–XX, 'Journal,' ed. Bradford Torrey. From the same plates, Manuscript Edition, cop. 1906. (600 numbered copies.)

'The Works of Henry D. Thoreau.' New York, Thomas Y. Crowell and Company, 1914. 5 vols.

'The Works of Henry D. Thoreau.' Boston, Houghton Mifflin Company, 1929. 5 vols. (Concord Edition.)

SELECTIONS

'The Heart of Thoreau's Journals,' ed. Odell Shepard. Boston and New York, Houghton Mifflin Company, 1927.

'Henry David Thoreau. Representative Selections, with Introduction, Bibliography, and Notes,' ed. B. V. Crawford. New

York, American Book Company, cop. 1934. (American Writers Series, ed. H. H. Clark.)

'The Living Thoughts of Thoreau,' ed. Theodore Dreiser. New York and Toronto, Longmans, Green and Company, 1939. (The Living Thoughts Library, ed. Alfred O. Mendel.)

'Men of Concord and some others as Portrayed in the Journal of Henry David Thoreau,' ed. F. H. Allen, illus. N. C. Wyeth. Boston, Houghton Mifflin Company; Toronto, Thomas Allen, 1936.

'Walden and Other Writings of Henry David Thoreau,' ed. Brooks Atkinson. New York, cop. 1937. (The Modern Library Series.)

'The Works of Thoreau,' sele. and ed. Henry Seidel Canby. Boston, Houghton Mifflin Company, 1937.

Various manuscripts of Thoreau's, including the work-sheets of 'Walden,' have been printed, with some unjustifiable editing, by F. B. Sanborn and H. H. Harper, for the Bibliophile Society.

BIOGRAPHY

Adams, Raymond William, and Canby, Henry Seidel, 'Henry David Thoreau' in 'The Dictionary of American Biography,' ed. Dumas Malone. New York, Charles Scribner's Sons, 1936, XVIII, 491–497.

'The American Notebooks by Nathaniel Hawthorne. Based Upon the Original Manuscripts in the Pierpont Morgan Library,' ed. Randall Stewart. New Haven, Yale University Press; London, Humphrey Milford, Oxford University Press, 1932, *passim*.

Atkinson, Justin Brooks, 'Henry Thoreau. The Cosmic Yankee.' New York and London, Alfred A. Knopf, 1927.

Bazalgette, Léon, 'Henry Thoreau. Sauvage.' Paris, F. Rieder et Cie, 1914. Tr. Van Wyck Brooks, 'Henry Thoreau. Bachelor of Nature.' New York, Harcourt, Brace and Company; London, Jonathan Cape, 1924.

Channing, William Ellery, 'Thoreau. The Poet-Naturalist. With Memorial Verses.' Boston, Roberts Brothers, 1873. Rev. ed., ed. F. B. Sanborn. Boston, Charles E. Goodspeed, 1902.

Emerson, Edward Waldo, 'Henry Thoreau as Remembered by a

Young Friend.' Boston and New York, Houghton Mifflin Company, 1917.

Emerson, Ralph Waldo, 'Biographical Sketch' in 'The Writings of Henry David Thoreau.' Boston and New York, Houghton, Mifflin and Company, cop. 1906 (Walden Edition), I, [xiii]–xxxviii. First printed as 'Thoreau,' *The Atlantic Monthly*, x, 58 (August, 1862), 239–249.

Flanagan, John T., 'Thoreau in Minnesota,' *Minnesota History*, xvi, 1 (March, 1935), 35–46.

[Japp, Alexander Hay], Page, H. A., 'Thoreau. His Life and Aims. A Study.' Boston, James R. Osgood and Company, 1877; London, Chatto and Windus, 1878.

'The Journals of Bronson Alcott,' ed. Odell Shepard. Boston, Little, Brown and Company, 1938, *passim*.

'Journals of Ralph Waldo Emerson. With Annotations,' ed. E. W. Emerson and W. E. Forbes. Boston and New York, Houghton Mifflin Company, 1909–1914, *passim*.

'The Letters of Ralph Waldo Emerson,' ed. R. L. Rusk. New York, Columbia University Press, 1939, *passim*.

Marble, Annie Russell, 'Thoreau. His Home, Friends and Books.' New York, Thomas Y. Crowell and Company, 1902.

Moore, John Brooks, 'Thoreau Rejects Emerson,' *American Literature*, iv, 3 (Nov., 1932), [241]–256.

Raysor, T. M., 'The Love Story of Thoreau,' *Studies in Philology*, xxiii, 4 (Oct., 1926), 457–463.

Salt, Henry S., 'The Life of Henry David Thoreau.' London, Richard Bentley and Son, 1890. Rev. ed., 'Life of Henry David Thoreau.' London, Walter Scott, Limited, 1896. (Great Writers Series.)

Sanborn, Franklin Benjamin, 'Henry D. Thoreau.' Boston, Houghton, Mifflin and Company. (American Men of Letters Series, ed. C. D. Warner); London, Sampson Low, Marston, Searle and Rivington, 1882. Rev. ed. Boston, Houghton Mifflin Company, 1910. (Riverside Popular Biographies.)

Sanborn, Franklin Benjamin, 'The Life of Henry David Thoreau. Including Many Essays Hitherto Unpublished and Some Account of His Family and Friends.' Boston and New York, Houghton Mifflin Company, 1917.

Sanborn, Franklin Benjamin, 'The Personality of Thoreau.' Boston, Charles E. Goodspeed, 1901. (515 numbered copies.)

Van Doren, Mark, 'Henry David Thoreau. A Critical Study.' Boston and New York, Houghton Mifflin Company, 1916.

CRITICISM

Adams, Raymond William, 'Henry Thoreau's Literary Theory and Criticism.' Chapel Hill, N.C., 1928. (University of North Carolina Dissertation, unpublished.)

Adams, Raymond William, 'Thoreau's Literary Apprenticeship,' *Studies in Philology*, xxix, 4 (Oct. 1932), 617–629.

Boynton, Percy H., 'Henry David Thoreau' in 'A History of American Literature.' Boston, Ginn and Company, cop. 1919, ch. XV, 221–235.

Bruel, Andrée, 'Emerson et Thoreau.' Paris, Les Presses Modernes, 1929. (University of Paris Dissertation.)

Burroughs, John, 'Another Word on Thoreau' in 'The Last Harvest.' Boston and New York, Houghton Mifflin Company, 1922, sect. III, 103–171.

Canby, Henry Seidel, 'Henry David Thoreau' in 'Classic Americans. A Study of Eminent American Writers from Irving to Whitman with an Introductory Survey of the Colonial Background of Our National Literature.' New York, Harcourt, Brace and Company, 1931, ch. 5, 184–225.

Canby, Henry Seidel, 'Introduction' in 'The Works of Thoreau,' sele. and ed. Boston, Houghton Mifflin Company, 1937, [xi]–xviii. First printed as 'The Man Who Did What He Wanted. A Proposed Definition of Thoreau,' *The Saturday Review of Literature*, xv, 9 (Dec. 26, 1936), 3, 4, 15.

Christy, Arthur, 'The Orient in American Transcendentalism. A Study of Emerson, Thoreau, and Alcott.' New York, Columbia University Press, 1932, 187–233.

Cournos, John, 'The Comparison of Gauguin with Thoreau' in 'A Modern Plutarch.' Indianapolis, The Bobbs-Merrill Company, 1928, 70–77. First printed as 'Gauguin and Thoreau: A Comparison,' *The Bookman*, lxvii, 5 (July, 1928), 548–551.

Crawford, Bartholow V., 'Introduction' in 'Henry David Thoreau. Representative Selections, with Introduction, Bibliography, and

Notes,' ed. B. V. Crawford. New York, American Book Company, cop. 1934 (American Writers Series, ed. H. H. Clark), xi–lvii.

De Armond, Fred, 'Thoreau and Schopenhauer: An Imaginary Conversation,' *The New England Quarterly*, v, 1 (Jan., 1932), 55–64.

Dreiser, Theodore, 'Presenting Thoreau' in 'The Living Thoughts of Thoreau,' ed. Theodore Dreiser. New York, Longmans, Green and Company, 1939 (The Living Thoughts Library, ed. Alfred O. Mendel), 1–32.

Foerster, Norman, 'Thoreau' in 'Nature in American Literature. Studies in the Modern View of Nature.' New York, The Macmillan Company, 1923, ch. IV, 69–142.

Foerster, Norman, 'Thoreau as Artist,' *The Sewanee Review*, xxix, 1 (Jan., 1921), 2–13.

Goddard, Harold Clarke, 'Studies in New England Transcendentalism.' New York, Columbia University Press, 1908, *passim*.

Gohdes, Clarence L. F., 'Henry Thoreau, Bachelor of Arts,' *The Classical Journal*, xxiii, 5 (Feb., 1928), 323–336.

Hicks, Granville, 'The Great Tradition. An Interpretation of American Literature since the Civil War.' New York, The Macmillan Company, 1933, 9, 10, *passim*.

Hicks, Philip Marshall, 'Thoreau' in 'The Development of the Natural History Essay in American Literature.' Philadelphia, 1924 (University of Pennsylvania Dissertation), 69–99.

Hurd, Harry Elmore, 'Henry David Thoreau — A Pioneer in the Field of Education,' *Education*, xlix (Feb., 1929), 372–376.

Jones, Samuel Arthur, 'Pertaining to Thoreau.' Detroit, Edwin B. Hill, 1901.

Keiser, Albert, 'Thoreau — Friend of the Native' in 'The Indian in American Literature.' New York, Oxford University Press, 1933, ch. XV, [207]–232.

Keiser, Albert, 'Thoreau's Manuscripts on the Indians,' *The Journal of English and Germanic Philology*, xxvii, 2 (April, 1928), 183–193.

Lorch, Fred W., 'Thoreau and the Organic Principle in Poetry,' *Publications of the Modern Language Association*, liii, 286–302 (March, 1938).

Lowell, James Russell, 'Thoreau,' in 'My Study Windows.' Boston, James R. Osgood and Company, 1871, 193–209. First printed as untitled rev. of 'Letters to Various Persons,' *The North American Review*, ci, 209 (Oct., 1865), 597–608.

MacMechan, Archibald, 'Thoreau,' in 'The Cambridge History of American Literature,' New York, G. P. Putnam's Sons; Cambridge, England, University Press, 1917–1921, II, bk. II, ch. X, 1–15.

Moore, John Brooks, 'Crèvecœur and Thoreau' in 'Papers of the Michigan Academy of Science, Arts, and Letters,' vol. V, Containing Papers Submitted at the Annual Meeting in 1925. New York, The Macmillan Company, 1926, 309–333.

More, Paul Elmer, 'Thoreau's Journal' in 'Shelburne Essays. Fifth Series.' New York and London, G. P. Putnam's Sons, 1908, 106–131.

Peairs, Edith, 'The Hound, The Bay Horse, and The Turtle-Dove: A Study of Thoreau and Voltaire,' *Publications of the Modern Language Association*, LII, 3 (Sept., 1937), 863–869.

Powys, Llewellyn, 'Thoreau: A Disparagement,' *The Bookman*, LXIX, 2 (April, 1929), 163–165.

Rickett, Arthur, 'Henry D. Thoreau' in 'The Vagabond in Literature.' London, J. M. Dent and Company; New York, E. P. Dutton and Company, 1906, sect. IV, 89–114.

Salt, Henry S., 'Gandhi and Thoreau,' *The Nation and Athenaeum*, XLVI, 22 (March 1, 1930), 728.

Snyder, Helena Adell, 'Thoreau's Philosophy of Life. With Special Consideration of the Influence of Hindoo Philosophy.' Heidelberg [1902]. (University of Heidelberg Dissertation.)

Stevenson, Robert Louis, 'Henry David Thoreau: His Character and Opinions' in 'Familiar Studies of Men and Books.' London, Chatto and Windus, 1882, 129–171. First printed in *The Cornhill Magazine*, XLI, 246 (June, 1880), 665–682.

Templeman, William D., 'Thoreau, Moralist of the Picturesque,' *Publications of the Modern Language Association*, XLVII, 3 (Sept., 1932), 864–889.

Warren, Austin, 'Lowell on Thoreau,' *Studies in Philology*, XXVII, 3 (July, 1930), 442–461.

Wood, James Playsted, 'English and American Criticism of Thoreau,' *The New England Quarterly*, VI, 4 (Dec., 1933), 733–746.

INDEX

21333   (card 2)   921

Canby, Henry S.   T39c

Thoreau.

3-91

DATE	ISSUED TO